Apple Training Series

iLife '11

Dion Scoppettuolo / Mary Plummer

Apple Training Series: iLife '11
Dion Scoppettuolo, Mary Plummer

Published by Peachpit Press. For information on Peachpit Press books, contact:

Peachpit Press
1249 Eighth Street
Berkeley, CA 94710
(510) 524-2178
www.peachpit.com
To report errors, please send a note to errata@peachpit.com. Peachpit Press is a division of Pearson Education.

Apple Series Editor: Lisa McClain
Project Editor: Nancy Peterson
Development Editor: Bob Lindstrom
Production Coordinator: Kim Wimpsett, Happenstance Type-O-Rama
Contributing Writers: Michael E. Cohen, Michael Wohl, Richard Harrington
Technical Editors: Klark Perez and Brendan Boykin
Copy Editors: Darren Meiss and Liz Merfeld
Media Reviewer: Jay Payne
Media Producer: Eric Geoffroy
Compositor: Chris Gillespie, Happenstance Type-O-Rama
Indexer: Jack Lewis
Cover Illustrator: Kent Oberheu
Cover Producer: Happenstance Type-O-Rama

ISBN 13: 978-0-321-70097-1
ISBN 10: 0-321-70097-X
9 8 7 6 5 4 3 2 1
Printed and bound in the United States of America

Contents at a Glance

Table of Contents

iDVD and iWeb: Sharing and Publishing with iLife

Getting Started

Welcome to the official Apple training course for the iLife '11 suite of products: iPhoto, iMovie, GarageBand, iWeb, and iDVD. You don't need to have any special background to get started, other than having a Mac (and perhaps a healthy curiosity about what you can do with it).

Learning iLife will teach you how to integrate your Mac comfortably into your home, school, and work by weaving digital audio, photos, and videos into your daily life.

In this book, we concentrate on how real people use the applications in iLife. We may even skip some of the more advanced functionality with an eye toward having fun, achieving quick success, and forming a foundation of confidence on which you can build.

What iLife Does for You

There was a time when your photographs were in a shoebox in the closet; your music equipment was in the garage; and VHS videotapes were scattered around the television. Each medium was tricky to keep organized.

But when all your media is digital—in the form of digital snapshots, digital audio (CDs, MP3s, and so on), and digital video (movie files and DVDs)—keeping it organized is streamlined, sharing content is easy, and using the material interchangeably between formats is both simple and kind of fun.

A Mac is designed to sit at the heart of your digital life. It's a computer designed for creativity and for combining all this content effortlessly. Better than that, Apple provides software—free on all Macs—that orchestrates the commingling of all this content. iLife is a family of applications designed to stand alone but also tuned to work together in remarkable ways.

What iLife teaches you is *media literacy:* the ability to communicate in a variety of powerful ways that are different from speaking or writing. Making professional-quality videos, podcasts, and slideshows, and being able to combine picture and sound effectively, are skills that can be applied throughout your life. Once you develop these skills, you'll be stunned by how often you use them, whether for personal pleasure or to commercial advantage.

It's too simplistic to say that iPhoto is the picture software and iMovie is the video software. iPhoto handles the organization of your pictures, true, but once your images are there, using them in slideshows, in print, and on the web is very easy. You can't build a box around each component of iLife. So rather than focus on each product in turn, this book helps you create real-world projects, which sometimes involves dipping into other iLife applications in a single lesson. Learning software is seldom fun. But making movies or podcasts, promoting your business, or building a creative report for school can be. You'll end up learning the software along the way.

The Methodology

This book moves through lessons by progressively increasing the complexity of the media you're using. You start by managing still images alone, and then move to publishing still images, turning still images into moving (dynamic) images, and exploring the possibilities of video and sound. With digital content and the three core iLife applications—iPhoto, iMovie, and GarageBand (along with iWeb and iDVD)—you can create photo books, DVDs, podcasts, dynamic websites, professional-sounding songs, and high-quality movies.

Above all, these lessons are meant to be practical—not esoteric projects to show off the software, but real-life projects for real-life people with time constraints and well-worn equipment. The lessons cover four general areas: still images, movies, music, and sharing.

iPhoto: Rediscover Your Photos

In Lessons 1 through 7, you'll work with photos. You'll learn how to import pictures from your digital camera; how to organize, fix, enhance, and back up your library of photos; and how to share your pictures in slideshows, in printed books, and on popular photo-sharing websites.

iMovie: A Little Slice of Hollywood at Home

In Lessons 8 through 14, you'll work primarily with video—though you'll also combine still photos, music, special effects, graphics, and titles in iMovie. You'll learn to use themes and trailers; edit to maximum effect; add narration to your videos; mix sound; and share your movie on the web or on your iPad, iPhone, or iPod.

GarageBand: Making Great-Sounding Music

In Lessons 15 through 19, you'll learn your way around GarageBand, from taking a music lesson to sharing a finished song with iTunes. You'll connect your instruments, and explore the Learn to Play piano and guitar lessons within GarageBand, and then you'll jam with a virtual band and create and arrange music. Finally, you will check out some advanced project finishing techniques as you complete and share a song, podcast, and movie score.

iDVD and iWeb: Sharing and Publishing with iLife

In Lessons 20 and 21, you'll put it all together, using iWeb and iDVD to build a dynamic, small business website, and create a DVD with a full interactive menu to share your movie and photo projects.

A Word About the Lesson Content

Often, training materials are professionally created—using actors and complicated productions with multiple cameras and a crew. The resulting material is of high quality but probably bears little similarity to the kind of photos and videos most families have.

To make this training as real-world and practical as possible, virtually all the media used in this book was made in precisely the way you would make your own videos and photos. The quality of the pictures (for better or worse) is comparable to what you can get with home video and photo equipment, and the sophistication of the projects is precisely what you can achieve using the iLife tools, with settings (and challenges) you will commonly encounter yourself.

We tried to make sure the events depicted here were recorded in the way you are being taught to work. Ideally, this will give you clear and realistic expectations about what you can do with your newfound skills.

System Requirements

This book is written for iLife '11, which comes free with any new Macintosh computer. If you have an older version of iLife, you will need to upgrade to the current iLife '11 version to follow along with every lesson. The upgrade can be purchased online at www.apple.com and is available from any store that sells Apple software.

Before you begin the lessons in this book, you should have a working knowledge of your Mac and its Mac OS X operating system. You don't need to be an expert, but you do need to know how to use the mouse and standard menus and commands, and how to open, save, and close files. You should have a working understanding of how OS X helps organize files on your computer, and you should also be comfortable opening applications (from the Dock or at least the Applications folder). If you need to review any of these techniques, see the printed or online documentation that came with your computer.

For a list of the minimum system requirements for iLife, please refer to the Apple website at www.apple.com/ilife/systemrequirements.html.

Copying the iLife Lesson Files

The *Apple Training Series: iLife '11* DVD-ROM includes all the project files and media you'll need to complete the lessons in this book. You must install the iLife '11 software before you install the lesson files.

To install the iLife lesson files:

1. Insert the *ATS iLife11* DVD into your DVD drive.

2. Double-click the installer on the DVD to run it. When the installation is complete, a dialog will appear indicating "Installation completed successfully." Click OK and eject the disc.

   This will copy the ATS_iLife11_Book_Files folder to your desktop, and will install certain iMovie, iPhoto, and GarageBand files in the locations where they need to be on your hard drive.

   The ATS_iLife11_Book_Files folder contains the lesson files used in this course. Each lesson has its own folder. Note that several lessons use files from a previous lesson; in those cases, the start of the lesson will list the Event or existing content used in that lesson.

   If you have previously imported photos into iPhoto, you will already have an iPhoto library in your Pictures folder. The ATS iLife11 DVD installs an ATS iPhoto library in your Pictures folder. Before starting any iPhoto, iMovie, iWeb, or iDVD lesson, you must first open the ATS iPhoto library to ensure that you have all the correct photos.

3. In your Pictures folder, double-click the ATS iPhoto library.

   iPhoto opens, but you will not see your personal photos in the library. You will see the photos and Events used in the ATS iLife '11 book.

4. Choose File > Quit.

   Every time you open iPhoto from the Dock or the Applications folder, you will now be opening the ATS iPhoto library. When you complete the lessons in the book, you can return to your personal library by double-clicking the iPhoto library in your Pictures folder.

   If you have imported video clips into iMovie, you will see your personal Events along with the Events and video content from this book. In this case, the example pictures in the book may not exactly match the Event Library you have in iMovie.

Resources

Apple Training Series: iLife '11 is not intended to be a comprehensive reference manual, nor does it replace the documentation that comes with the applications. Rather, the book is designed to be used in conjunction with other comprehensive reference guides. These resources include:

- Companion Peachpit website: As iLife '11 is updated, Peachpit may choose to update lessons as necessary. Please check www.peachpit.com/ats.ilife11.
- The Apple website: www.apple.com.
- Apple Training Series books: *Apple Training Series: iWork '09*, by Richard Harrington, is an excellent companion to this book. Learn how to use iLife applications with iWork to create first-class presentations, slideshows, newsletters, publications, and spreadsheets. *Apple Training Series: GarageBand '09*, by Mary Plummer, is an in-depth look at GarageBand, in which you build songs, podcasts, and movie scores from scratch, and explore some of the advanced mixing and arranging features of GarageBand.
- Other books: *The Macintosh iLife*, by Jim Heid (Peachpit Press), an accessible and popular reference guide for the iLife products. *The Little Digital Video Book*, by Michael Rubin (Peachpit Press), a concise resource on how to make your videos have more impact and look professional. Although the book is not about the iLife software specifically, it expands on many of the concepts touched on in the video lessons.

Acknowledgements

We would like to thank the following individuals for their contributions of media used throughout the book. Paula Duley for photos of Cameron's soccer matches. Leo Bechtold for glass blowing photos. Guido Hucking, Theo Bialek, and Pam Fernandez for photographs of Greg and Caren's wedding. Brian O'Maille for playing all of the guitar recording examples as well as photos of the recording session. Roger Kruppa for the Krupps family photos. Raymond Melcher for Marlins spring softball video and Krupps family photos. Alexander Blakley for the Max and Louisa in NYC video. Ken Koontz for the old holiday movies. Jonathan Amayo for the Sara goes sky diving photos and video. Mary Plummer for her original song "Space Bass" used as the podcast theme song and her performance of the Major Scales, as well as orchestration for the Scales song used in Lesson 18. Dion Scoppettoulo for photos of the Taj Mahal, San Francisco, and Kauai, as well as glass blowing video. TouchPets Dogs game trailer, courtesy of NGMOCO:) for use in Lesson 19. Klark Perez for hosting the Visual and Media Arts Showcase podcast Caren Sarmiento episode. To Caren Sarmiento for the podcast interview, as well as the use of photos of her artwork for the book.

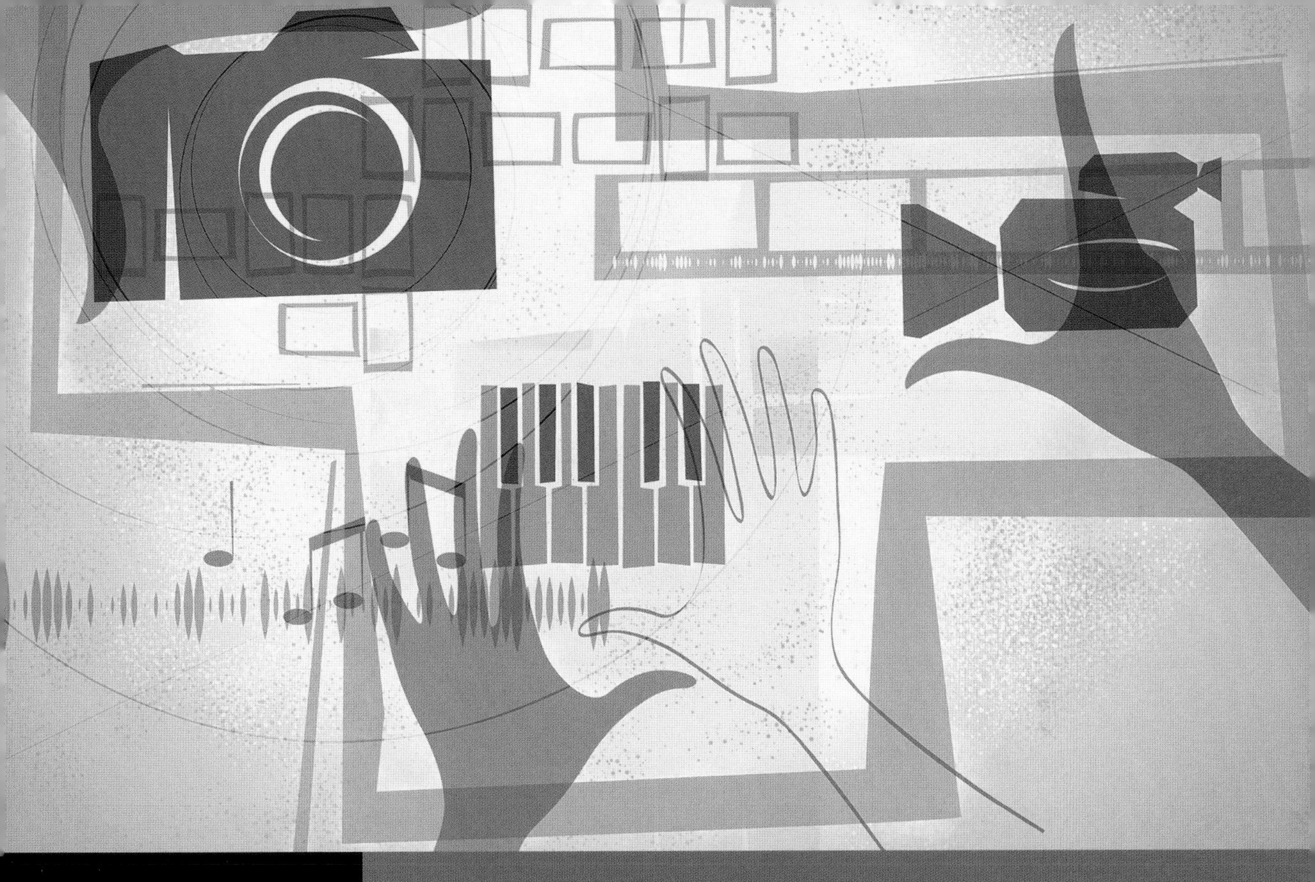

iPhoto: Rediscover Your Photos

1

Lesson Files	Pictures > ATS iLIfe11 Book Files > Lesson 01 > Memory Card.dmg
Time	This lesson takes approximately 45 minutes to complete.
Goals	Import images from a camera Navigate the viewing area Delete images Send images via email

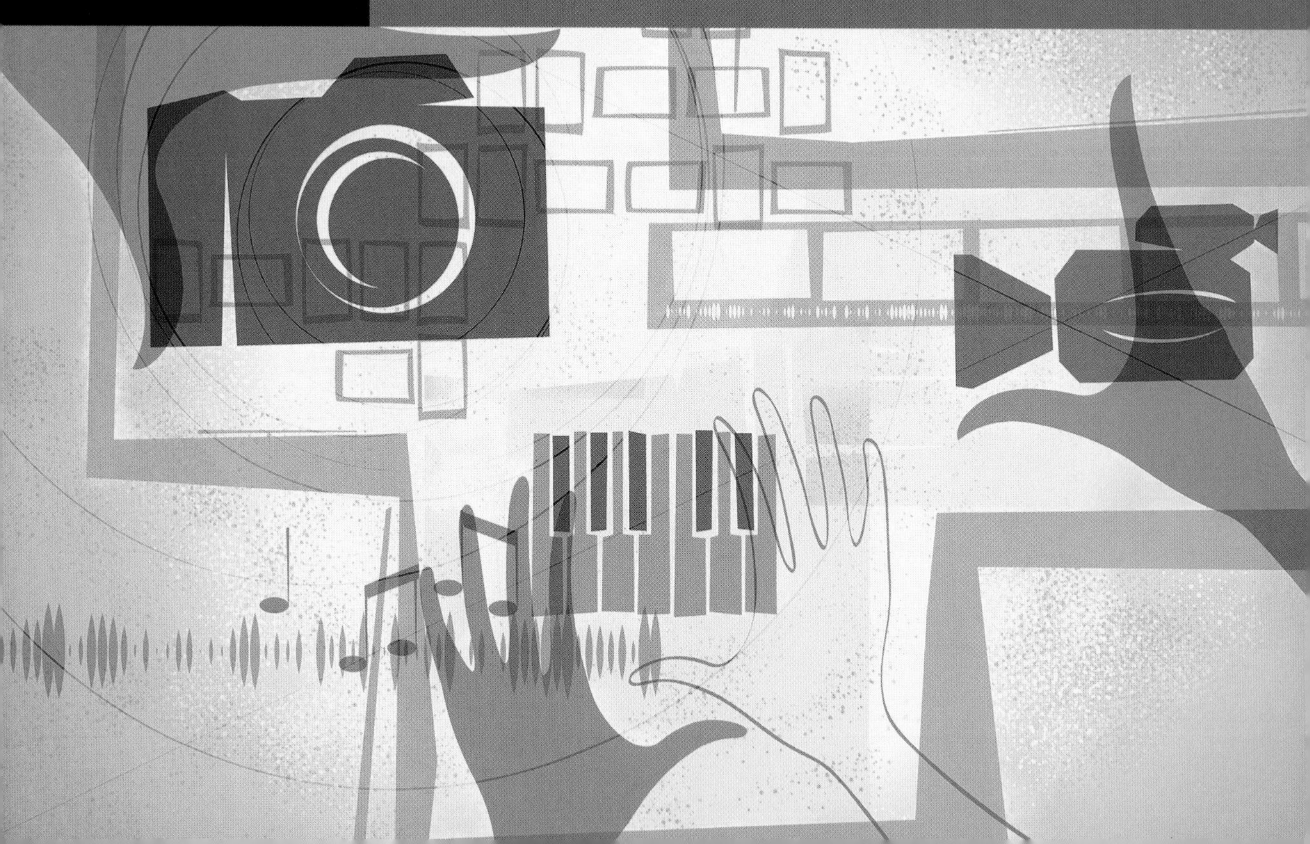

Lesson 1

Viewing and Emailing Photos

Our photos are so important. They are lasting memories from the best times in our lives, with a few embarrassing teenage moments tossed in to keep us humble. Making these memories easy to find, effortlessly organized, and shared with friends and family are the basics of iPhoto. It's not difficult to learn those basics—in fact you'll learn them in this one lesson.

Opening iPhoto

You open iPhoto in one of two primary ways:

- In the Dock, click the iPhoto icon.
- Insert a memory card or attach a camera to your Mac.

Let's start by opening iPhoto from the Dock.

NOTE ▸ Before opening iPhoto, be sure to read "Getting Started" in this book in order to use the correct ATS iPhoto Library. Also, verify that you've installed the DVD content for this book by running the ATS iLife '11 Installer.

1 In the Dock, click the iPhoto icon.

When you open iPhoto for the first time, you'll see a dialog in which you can configure iPhoto to open automatically whenever you connect a digital camera to your Mac.

2 Click Yes.

Next, iPhoto asks if you want to display your photos on a map. If your photos were taken with an iPhone or a camera with GPS, iPhoto can use that information to display a map that identifies where the photos were taken. You'll learn more about GPS-tagged images in Lesson 3.

3 Click Yes to display the welcome screen. The welcome screen contains links to online tutorials and provides information about iPhoto training available in Apple Stores.

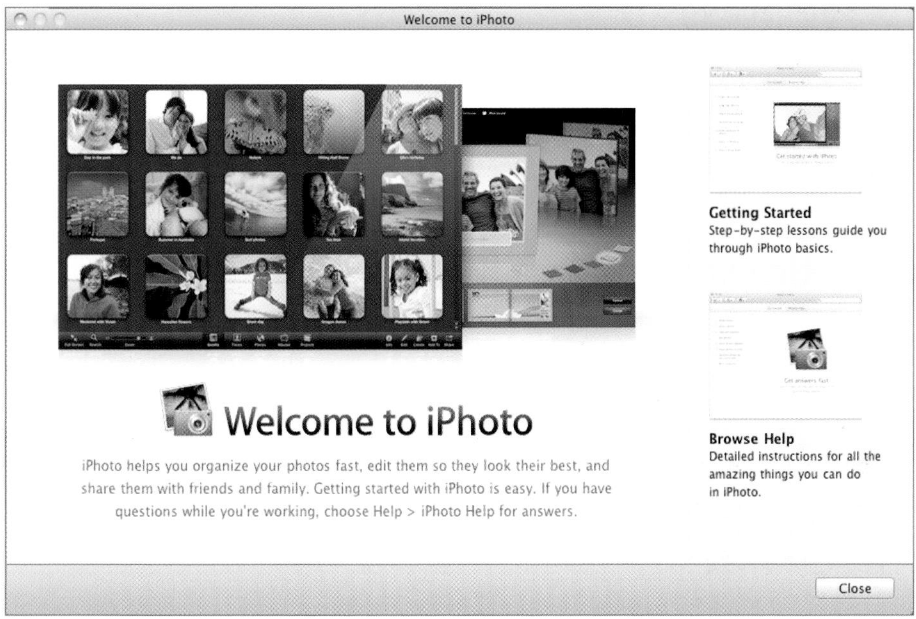

NOTE ▸ If you've previously opened iPhoto, the welcome screen may not appear. You can access it from the Help menu.

4 Take some time to read the information and then click Close. The window closes, and the main iPhoto window appears.

NOTE ▸ If you've previously opened iPhoto and aren't sure if it is set as your default image capture application, when iPhoto opens choose iPhoto > Preferences. In the Preferences window, click Import, and from the "When a camera is connected, open" pop-up menu, choose iPhoto. Then close the Preferences window.

Understanding the iPhoto Window

The iPhoto window has three main sections, which are described in the following figure:

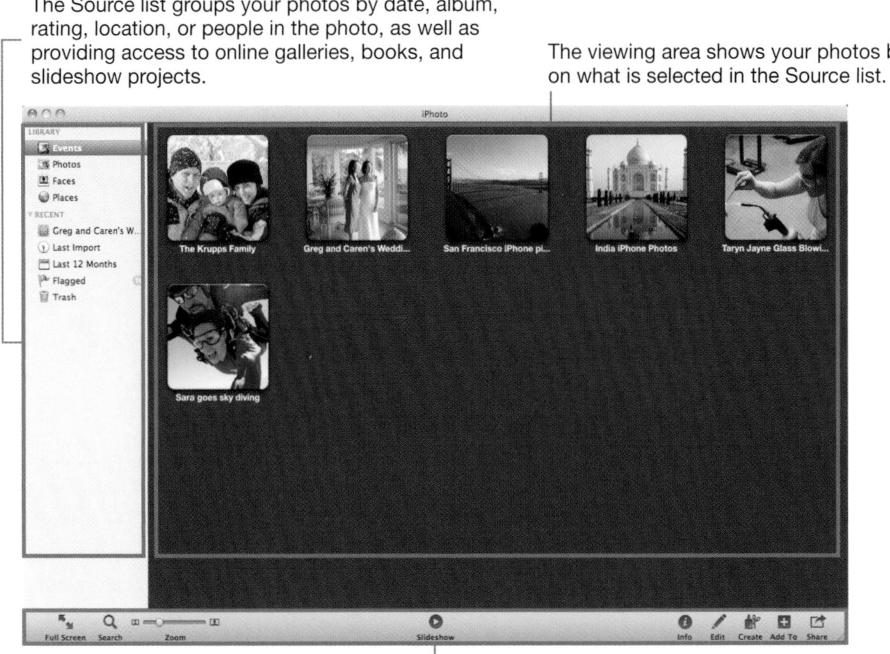

In the toolbar you can access commonly used features and viewing area controls.

Importing Photos from a Camera

You'll most often transfer photos into the iPhoto library by connecting your camera or a memory card reader directly to your Mac.

> **TIP** When transferring photos, using a card reader is almost always faster than connecting your camera directly to the Mac.

For this exercise, you'll open a disk image that will simulate connecting a camera or memory card to your Mac.

1 In the Dock, click the Finder icon to open a Finder window.

2 In the Finder window, navigate Desktop > ATS iLife11 Book Files > Lesson 01, and double-click the disk image **Memory Card.dmg** to open it on your desktop.

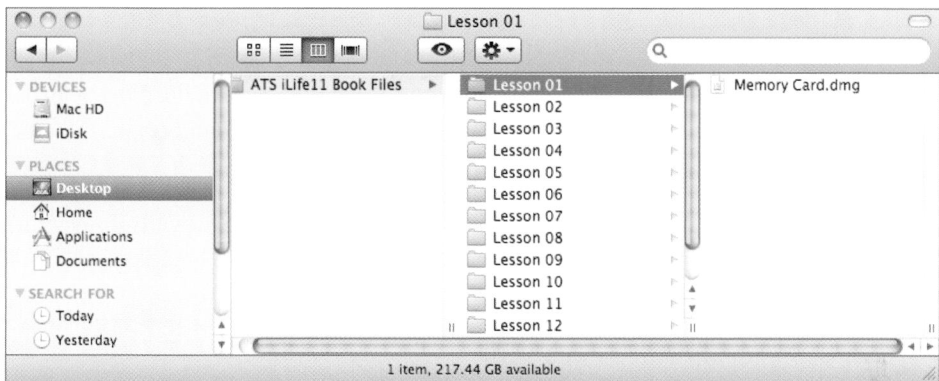

When the **Memory Card.dmg** is mounted, iPhoto automatically comes to the front, displaying the import view with your camera (called No_Name by default) selected in the Source list on the left.

All the photos on the camera's memory card are displayed so you can select which photos to transfer to your iPhoto library. When you import photos, iPhoto organizes them as *Events* in the iPhoto library. Events initially combine photos based on the dates they were created. An Event can contain thousands of photos or just one.

TIP If you have photos contained in a Mac folder, you can import them by choosing File > Import to Library, or by dragging the folder into the iPhoto Source list.

3 At the top of the import view in the Event Name field, type *Cameron's Matches*.

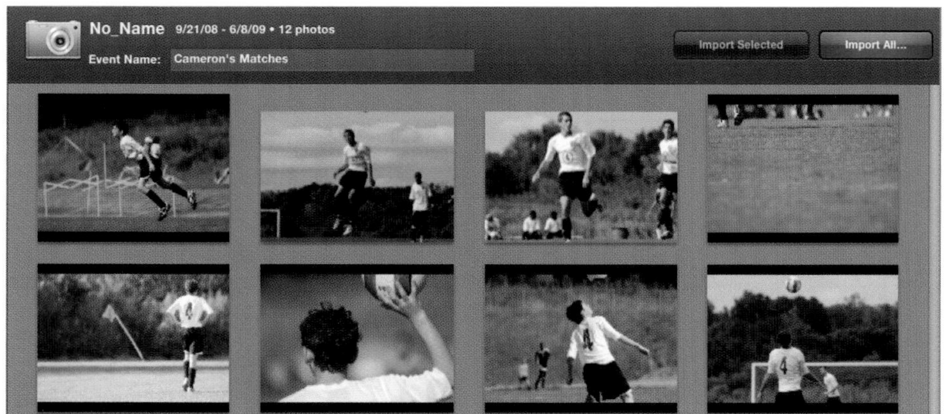

When you installed iPhoto, it automatically created a library in your Pictures folder. The iPhoto Library is a container in which every Event, album, and photo is stored. Photos are imported into the library by copying them from your camera.

Now it's time to import your photos. At the upper right of the import view, you'll find two buttons: Import Selected and Import All. When you click the Import Selected button, you import only those photos you select. When you click Import All, you import all the photos on your camera. For this lesson, you'll import all the photos.

4 Click Import All. A status bar appears at the top of the import view to show your progress.

When the import process is complete, a dialog appears with the options to delete the photos on your camera or retain them.

5 Click Keep Photos.

6 From the Source list, click the eject button next to the No_Name disk.

TIP Erase media cards by using the format function on your camera rather than the Delete button in iPhoto or any other application. Media cards are formatted for specific camera models, and a camera-specific format will more reliably erase a memory card than a generic erase function in an application.

You've just imported your first group of pictures and created your first Event in the iPhoto Library. Breathe in proudly, with a sense of accomplishment.

Viewing Photos in an Event

The iPhoto viewing area changes depending on the view you are using. The default view is organize view, where you select and view your photos either as an entire group or a single picture.

1 In the Source list, click Events. All the Events in the library are displayed, starting with the earliest Event in the upper left to the most recent Event in the lower right.

2 Double-click the Cameron's Matches Event to open it. All of that Event's photos are now displayed in the viewing area.

3 In the lower left of the viewing area, drag the Zoom slider to fit four photos across, if necessary.

4 Double-click the first photo in the viewing area. The photo fills the viewing area, and the other Event photos are displayed below it as thumbnails.

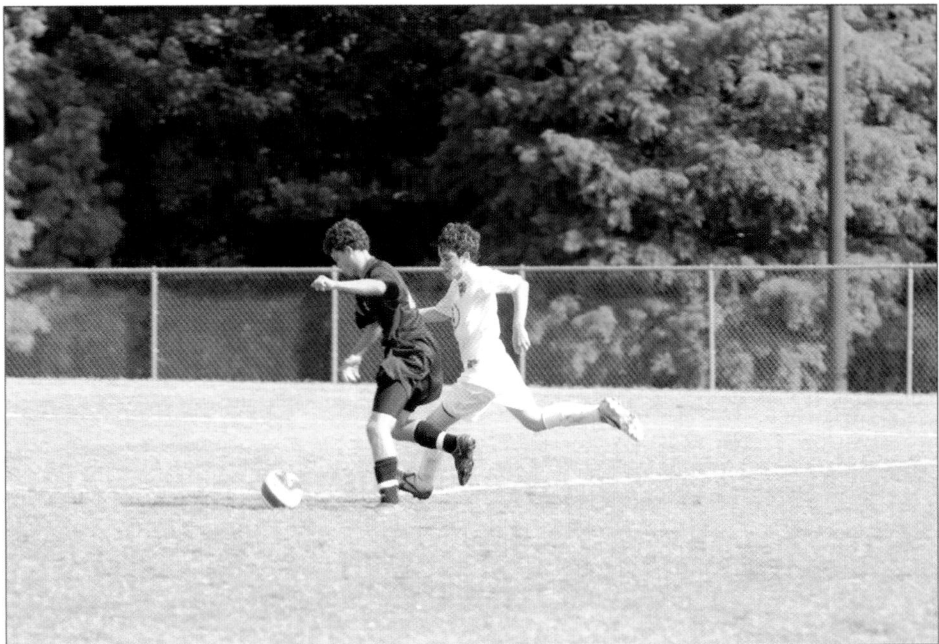

5 Double-click the photo again. The photo scales down, and the Organize view returns.

6 To see all the Events in your library, click the All Events button in the upper-left corner of the viewing area.

You just completed the iPhoto steps that you'll probably use the most! Although importing and viewing your photos may be the most common activities with iPhoto, you can do even more to further enjoy organizing and browsing your photos.

Viewing All Your Photos

If you take just a few pictures occasionally, you may not want to take the time to organize your photos using Events. If so, you can directly view all your photos in the library.

1 In the Source list, select Photos to see all your photos.

2 To the right of the viewing area, drag down on the scroll bar to view more photos in your library.

As you drag the scroll bar, the Scroll Guide appears in the middle of the viewing area, showing the date of each Event, making it easier for you to locate the photos you want.

Viewing Photos and Events Full Screen

You can also view your photos in full-screen view, displaying them larger, clearer, and with no surrounding visuals.

1 In the Source list, select Events.

2 In the lower-left corner of the toolbar, click the Full Screen button. The viewing area fills your computer's screen with Events, and the toolbar now includes icons to change the view.

3 In the toolbar, click Albums. The top row of albums include many of the albums from the Source list.

4 Double-click the Last Import album. The viewing area now fills with all the photos included in the most recent Event you imported.

5 Double-click the first photo in the viewing area. The photo now scales up to completely fill your screen.

6 To return to the organize view in the viewing area, click the Last Import button, and then click the All Albums button in the upper-left corner. Finally, click the Full Screen button to exit full-screen view.

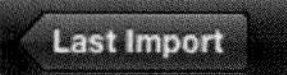

Viewing your photos full screen enhances their impact, especially when you are sharing them with others. But keep in mind that full-screen view is not only for viewing photos. You'll use it in future lessons to show more detail when you are modifying photos.

Deleting a Photo

After you import photos, you may find yourself looking at dozens or even hundreds of pictures in a single Event. One way to quickly reduce their numbers is to delete the images you don't want to save.

1 Double-click the Cameron's Matches Event, and then click the photo of grass.

Oops. We all take a few bad photos. Our camera wasn't set correctly, someone jumped in front of us, or we just pressed a button accidently. Whatever the reason, you don't need photos like this taking up space in your library. You can delete them.

2 Press the Delete key to delete the picture. A warning dialog asks you to confirm your choice.

3 Click Delete Photo.

Despite the warning dialog, your photo isn't actually deleted. Photos deleted in iPhoto are placed in the iPhoto Trash, which protects you from deleting a picture you may later decide you want to keep. To retrieve it, you can drag it from the Trash and into an Event.

4 In the Source list, select Trash to see all the images you have deleted from your Events.

Now you'll take the next step in deleting these photos by placing them into the Mac Trash.

5 Choose iPhoto > Empty iPhoto Trash.

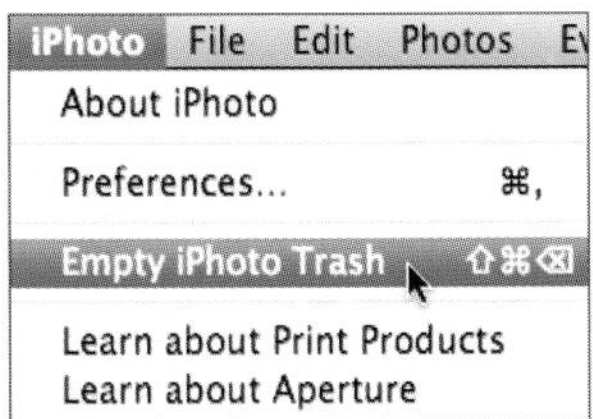

A dialog once again asks you to confirm your decision.

6 Click OK.

Even at this point the photo is not totally gone. It's now located in the Mac Trash. This is your last chance to save it before you permanently remove it from your hard disk. Going once…going twice…!

7 In the Dock, click the Trash icon, then choose Finder > Empty Trash.

8 In the warning dialog, click Empty Trash.

Now, and only now, have you completely deleted the photo from your hard disk and freed up a tiny bit of storage space in doing so.

9 In the Dock, click the iPhoto icon to return to iPhoto.

Emailing Your Photos

It's inevitable that at some point you'll want to share photos with family and friends. iPhoto has a number of ways to do so, but the most common way is via email. Everyone is familiar with emailing photos, but iPhoto lets you do it in style using email templates. Before you email photos though, let's make sure your email is properly configured.

Setting Up Email Preferences

iPhoto can directly transfer images to your email application. By default, it will use the Mail application, but you can change this and many other properties in iPhoto preferences.

To set up your Sharing accounts:

1 Choose iPhoto > Preferences.

2 Click Accounts to view the accounts available to share photos. If you are a MobileMe member, iPhoto automatically configures to email your photos from your MobileMe account, but you can add other accounts, such as Facebook, Flickr, and email.

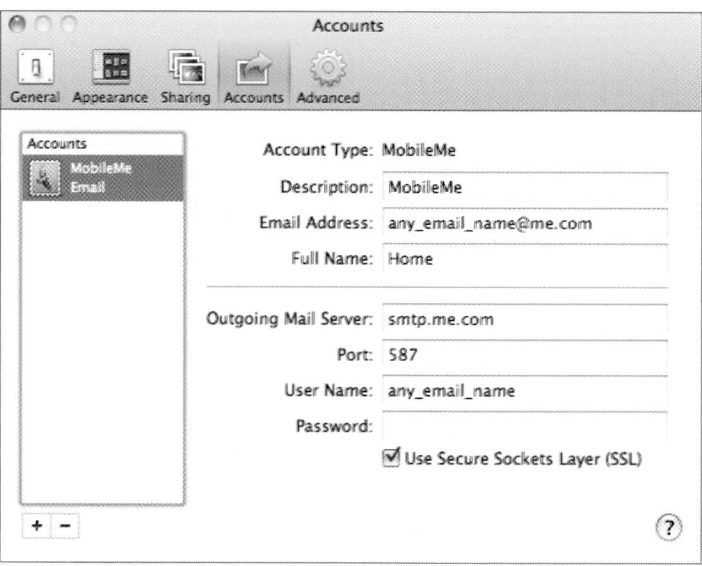

3 In the lower-left corner of the Accounts window, click the New Account (+) button.

4 Select Email and then click the Add button to view the email options.

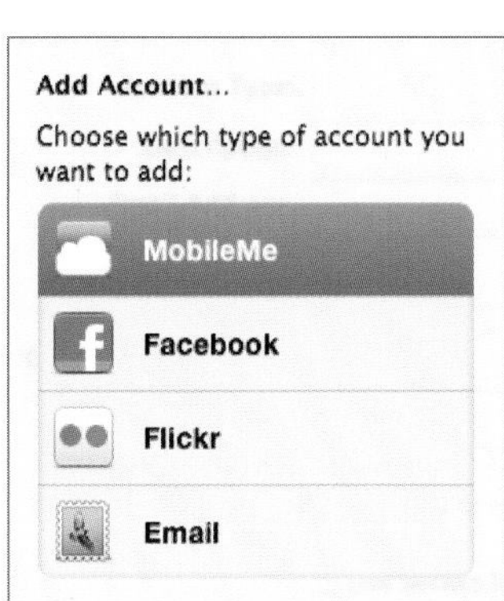

5 Click the button for your email provider.

A dialog appears in which you fill in your full name, email address, password, and an account description.

NOTE ▶ If you have an email provider that is not listed, select Other. During configuration, however, you will be required to know the address of your provider's outgoing mail server.

6 Fill in the Full Name, Email address, and Password fields, and then click OK.

7 Close Preferences.

TIP You can add email accounts for every person that uses this iPhoto Library and allow them to email photos under their own accounts.

For any email provider in the email dialog, iPhoto can automatically configure the email settings.

Placing Photos into an Email Theme

When your email preferences are entered, sending photos is very easy. In fact, the whole process takes only a few moments.

NOTE ▶ If you did not add an email account, you will not be able to complete the email exercises.

1 From the Source list, select the Events icon, and then double-click the Cameron's Matches Event.

2 In the viewing area, Command-click the first three photos to select them.

3 In the lower-right corner of the iPhoto window, click the Share icon. A pop-up menu appears with your sharing accounts.

NOTE ▶ You can also access the sharing options in the Share menu.

4 Click Email. An email window opens, and the photos you selected are now embedded into the default email theme called Snapshots.

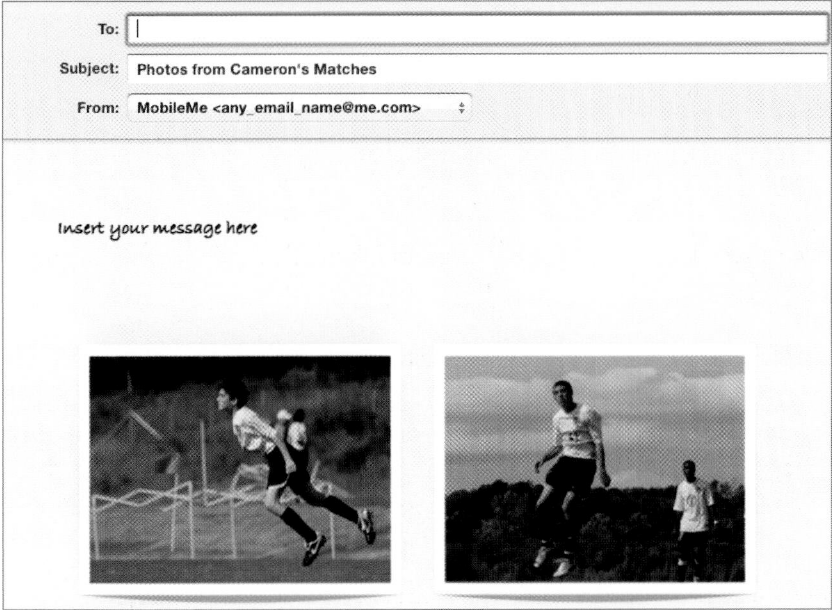

A theme is a visually embellished email design complete with background graphics, placeholder text for a message, and stylized typefaces.

5 To the right of the email window, select the Postcard theme. The email changes to the Postcard theme.

NOTE ▶ Each theme layout changes to accommodate the number of photos you've attached.

The Postcard theme has room for a message on the background postcard and, unlike some of the other themes, includes a larger main photo with a title under it.

Moving and Framing Photos in a Theme

The position where a photo ends up in a theme can be changed, allowing you to select which one gets the primo spot.

1 Drag the photo of running kids on top of the larger center photo to have the photos change places, if necessary.

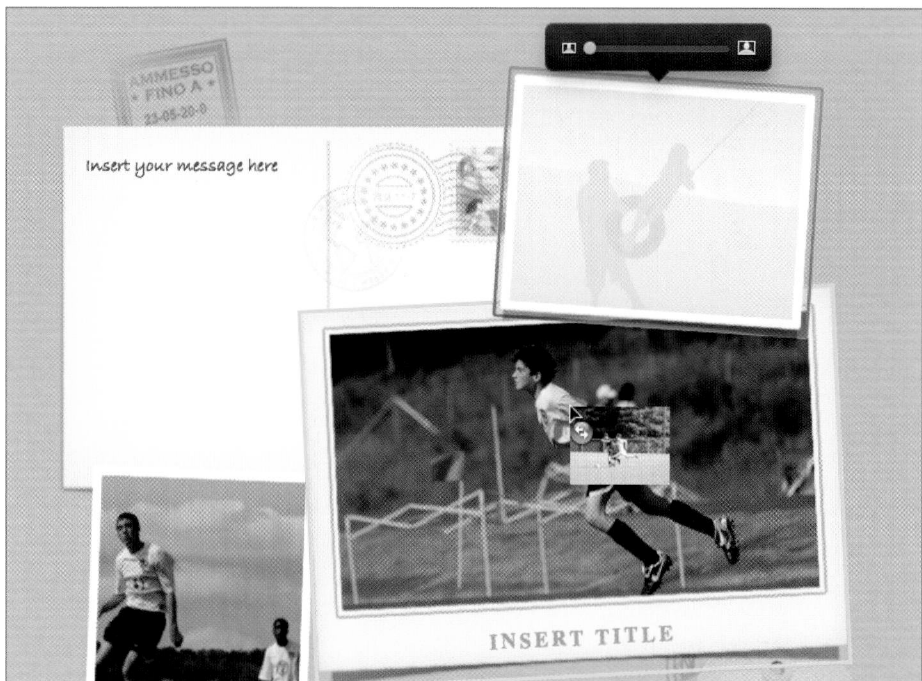

Once you have the photos in the general locations you like, you can move and scale them to better fit the frame.

2 Click the center photo to open the Size slider.

TIP The Size slider appears when you click any photo in an email.

3 Drag the Size slider to the right to increase the photo's size within the frame.

Scaling a photo sometimes causes an important part of a photo—such as a person's face or a specific detail—to get cut off, or *cropped*. When this happens, you can reposition the scaled photo to improve the framing.

4 Place the mouse pointer over the scaled photo and drag it to center the two kids in the frame.

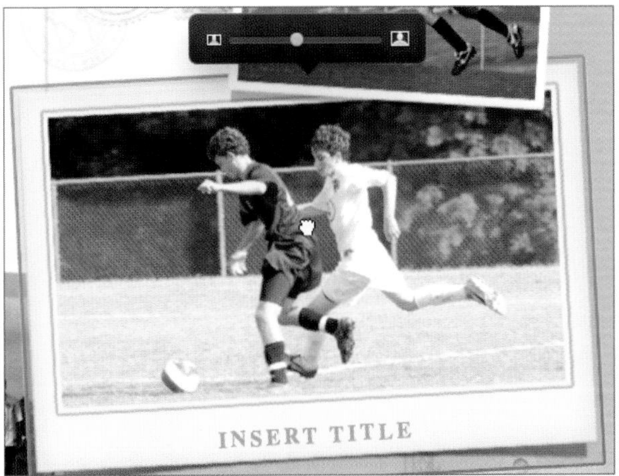

5 Click the email background to deselect the photo and close the Size slider.

Attaching a Photo to an Email

By default, iPhoto attaches the photos so people who receive the email not only get the images in a beautiful theme, but also can download the photos. If you decide to allow your photos to be downloaded, you can set the quality level of the downloaded photos.

1 Below the themes, make sure the "Attach photos to message" is selected.

2 From the Photo Size pop-up menu, choose Actual Size.

> **TIP** iPhoto displays the size of the email in the lower-left corner of the email window. This number changes based on the settings of the "Attach photos to message" checkbox and the Photo Size pop-up menu.

With these settings, your friends will be able to download your high-quality photos from your email and add them to their own iPhoto libraries.

> **TIP** If you don't want email recipients to download your photos, deselect the "Attach photos to message" checkbox. This has the added benefit of making the email much smaller in size and faster to send.

Adding Text to Your Email

The last steps before you actually send your email involve adding a message and most importantly filling in the To, Subject, and From fields at the top of the email.

1 At the top of the email, enter the email addresses and add a subject line. If you have multiple email accounts, choose the correct email account in the From pop-up menu.

TIP If you want to confirm the appearance of your iPhoto theme email, you can include yourself as an email recipient by selecting "Automatically Bcc myself" in the Advanced tab of iPhoto Preferences.

With the addresses set correctly for the email, add a message, and a title in the email itself.

2 Click the placeholder message text *insert your message here.*

When the placeholder text is selected, it highlights in blue and a text format display allows you to reformat your text.

3 Type *Today was our first game. I hope you can make it to our next game on Saturday.*

4 Click the Insert Title field under the main photo to select that text.

5 Type *WE WON!*

6 Click the email background to deselect the text and close the text format display.

All you have left to do is click Send, or for the purpose of this exercise, click Cancel. (Unless you want to send this email to all your friends and make them wonder who these soccer kids are.)

In this lesson, you learned most of the everyday activities you're likely to perform in iPhoto. But let's not stop there! If you do, you'll be missing more than half the fun of using iPhoto and fully enjoying your photos.

Lesson Review

1. How do you import just one photo from your camera?
2. How do you view all the photos in a single Event?
3. How do you completely remove an image from the iPhoto library and the Mac hard disk?
4. How do you view one photo in full-screen view?
5. True or false: iPhoto email recipients cannot save the original, full-quality photos to their own iPhoto libraries.

Answers

1. In the import view, click one photo to select it, and then click the Import Selected button to import only that photo.
2. In the Source list, select Events, and then double-click the Event you want to view.
3. Select a photo, press Delete, and choose iPhoto > Empty iPhoto Trash. Then, from the Finder, choose Finder > Empty Trash.
4. Click the Full Screen button, and then double-click the photo you want to view full screen.
5. False. By default iPhoto attaches photos to emails so they can be saved from the email. You must deselect the "Attach photos to message" checkbox to prevent recipients from saving the original, full quality photos attached to your email.

2

Lesson File	Pictures > ATS iPhoto Library: The Krupps Family Event
Time	This lesson takes approximately 75 minutes to complete.
Goals	Rate and flag photos Understand non-destructive editing Rotate and straighten pictures Remove red-eye problems Enhance photos with one click Cut out unwanted parts of a photo Remove dust and skin blemishes Make albums and Smart Albums Transfer photos to your iPad, iPhone, and iPod

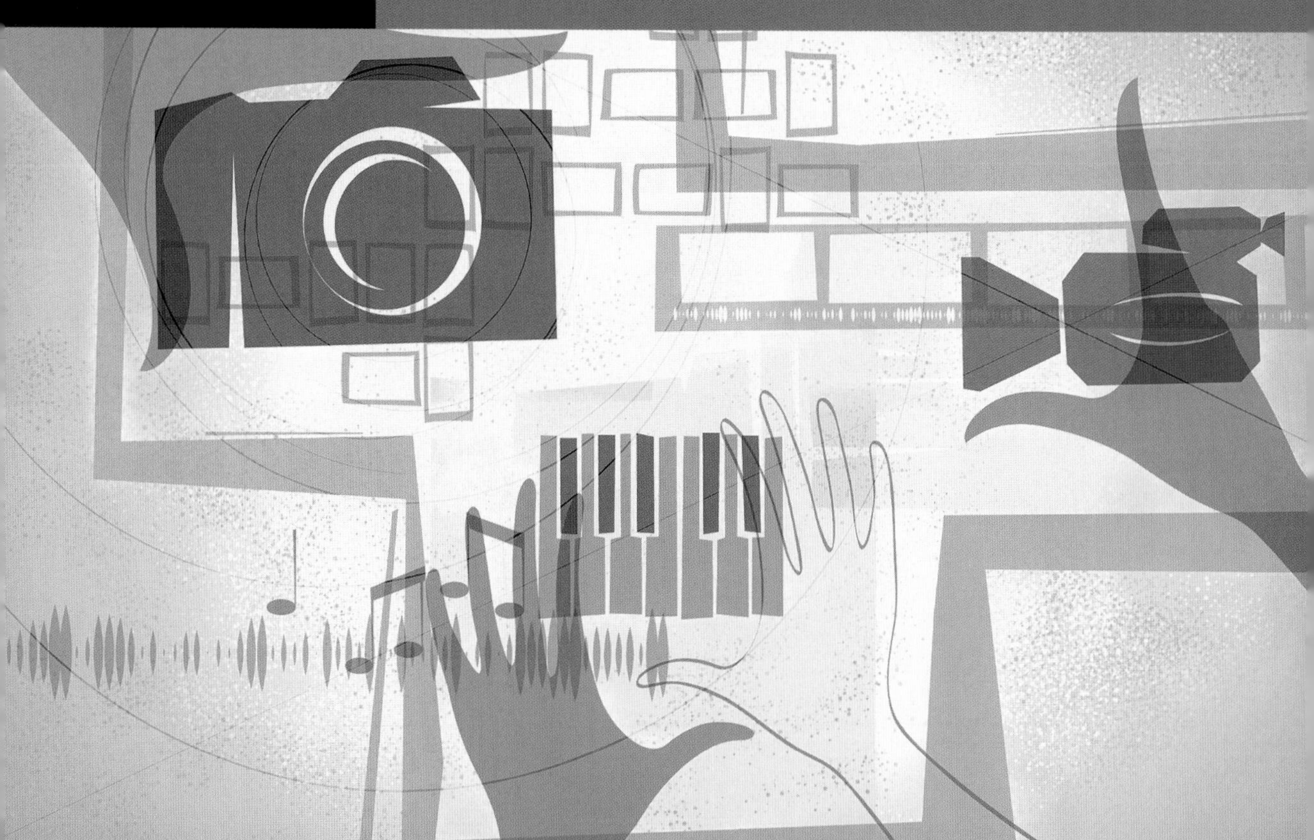

Lesson **2**

Rating and Fixing Photos

Between the photos you take and those that people send you, your library usually grows to a point where finding the standout photos takes time. The cream of the crop photos in your library are more than likely the ones you want to keep on your iPad, iPhone, or iPod, so sorting them out and sending them to your Apple mobile device becomes more important. In this lesson, you'll learn how to rate your photos, make them look their best, and transfer them to your Apple device.

Rating Photos

Assigning ratings to photos helps you quickly find your best photos when you want to post them to the web, sync them to your Apple mobile device, make a keepsake book, or just view them full screen on your Mac.

iPhoto uses a five-star rating scale to help you identify the worst pictures (one star), the best pictures (five stars), and all the pictures in between.

1 In the Source list, select Events, and then double-click "The Krupps Family" Event to view all its photos.

2 If you do not see four photos across in the viewing area, drag the Zoom slider to display four columns.

3 Position the mouse pointer over the first picture in the Event.

4 In the lower-right corner of the photo, click the down arrow to display the Photo pop-up menu. In this menu, you have access to several commonly used features, including ratings.

TIP You can get the same Photo pop-up menu by Control-clicking (or right-clicking) the photo.

The current photo is a very nice family shot, so give it the highest rating.

5 Click the fifth star.

The Photo pop-up menu disappears, but rest assured, you've just rated this photo as an excellent, five-star photo.

6 Click the Photo pop-up menu again to verify that you assigned a five-star rating, and then click the photo to hide the menu.

Using the Photo pop-up menu is convenient, but it's not necessarily the most efficient way to apply and view photo ratings.

7 Choose View > Ratings.

The ratings are now displayed under each photo. If no rating has been assigned, you'll see a blank space under the photo. It's now easier to browse photo ratings, but you can also speed up the process of applying ratings.

8 Select the second photo in the Event, a pleasant shot of mother and child, marred by a little red-eye effect.

9 Press Command-3 to apply a three-star rating.

10 Press the Right Arrow key to move to the next image, a rosy-cheeked outdoor portrait with no red-eye.

11 Press Command-4 to apply a four-star rating.

> **NOTE ▶** To see all the ratings and their keyboard shortcuts, choose Photos > My Rating. You can also apply ratings here.

Your ratings appear under each photo. If you later want to change a rating, you can reselect a photo and assign a new rating using the methods you just learned. Ratings can be modified and updated as often as you like.

Flagging Photos

Now you have an Event in which your best photos are easy to find. Browsing through the Event, you'll see that some photos are perfect (ahem), and some of them are close to perfect but might need a little enhancement. If you have a photographic memory (sorry), you might be able to recall which photos need attention. If not, it would be handy to mark those images in some way. To help out, iPhoto gives you a *flag*.

A flag is a visual indicator attached to a photo that marks it for further scrutiny. You can use flags to mark photos that you want to sync to your iPad, photos that you want to post to Facebook, or in this case, photos that need a little editing.

1 In the viewing area, position your mouse pointer in the upper left of the second photo, the baby and his mother. A small, ghosted flag icon appears.

2 Click the flag icon to indicate that this photo needs editing.

That was easy enough, but instead of flagging photos one-by-one, you can use a shortcut to flag multiple photos at once.

3 Click the third photo and then Shift-click the fifth photo in the Event.

4 Choose Photos > Flag Photos, or press Command-. (period) to flag all three photos.

Once your photos are flagged, iPhoto can show you just those flagged photos.

5 In the Source list, select Flagged to show the album of flagged photos in your library.

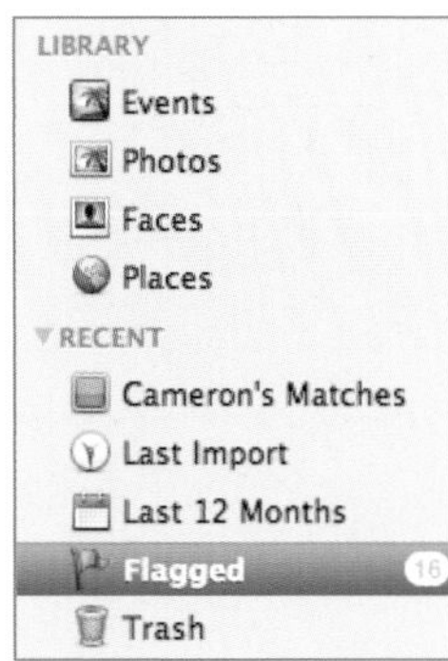

TIP You can remove a flag by clicking a photo's flag icon, or by selecting the photo and choosing Photos > Unflag Photo.

You've added flags to identify a few photos with problems, but don't be surprised if you find you have more flagged photos than you selected. In fact, your album includes flagged photos from other Events because the Flagged album shows all flagged photos across your entire library, not just one Event.

Applying Quick Fixes

Now that you're looking at your flagged photos, give them the attention they deserve. Although iPhoto has several methods to make photos look better, you'll start by using a few Quick Fixes.

Rotating Photos

Most digital cameras now sense if they are held horizontally (landscape) or vertically (portrait). They embed that information into the photo so that iPhoto can automatically correct the image orientation. However, if you've scanned photos in a scanner or you use a camera without an orientation sensor, the iPhoto Rotate tool allows you to rotate a photo in 90-degree increments.

1 In the Flagged album, find the first incorrectly oriented photo (the last photo in the fourth row). Click the down arrow in the lower-right corner of the photo to open the shortcut menu.

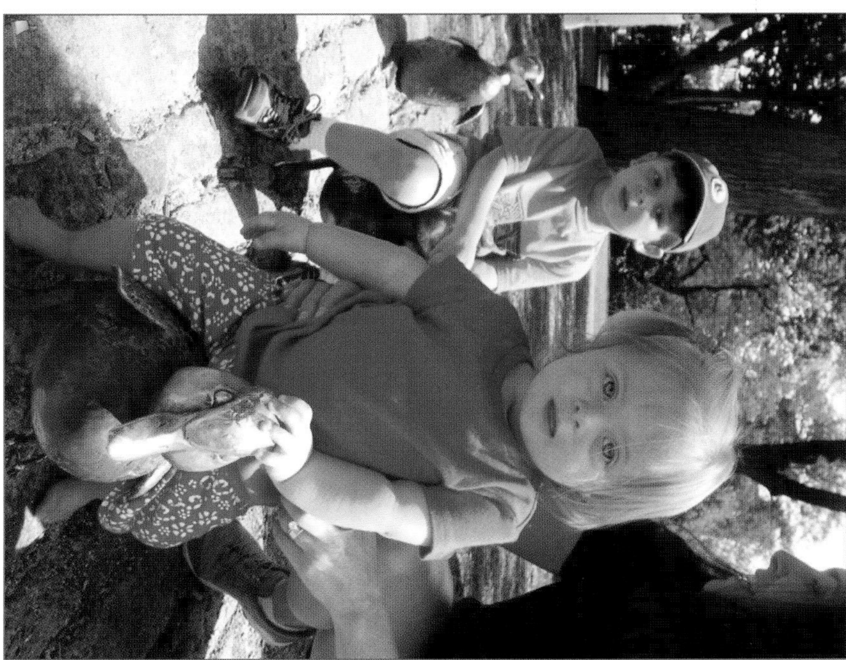

2 In the Photo pop-up menu, choose Rotate. The image rotates 90 degrees clockwise, in the direction the rotate arrow was pointing.

TIP Option-click Rotate in the shortcut menu to rotate the image counter-clockwise, or select multiple photos and choose Photos > Rotate Clockwise/Counter Clockwise to rotate them all at once.

That photo is now fixed and looks great, so you can rate it five stars and remove the flag.

3 Select the photo you just rotated, and press Command-5 to rate this picture.

4 With the photo still selected, choose Photos > Unflag Photo to remove the flag.

   If you have a photo that needs to be rotated but still requires other edits, you can use the edit view.

5 Select the next incorrectly rotated photo of the two kids yawning and leaning on each other.

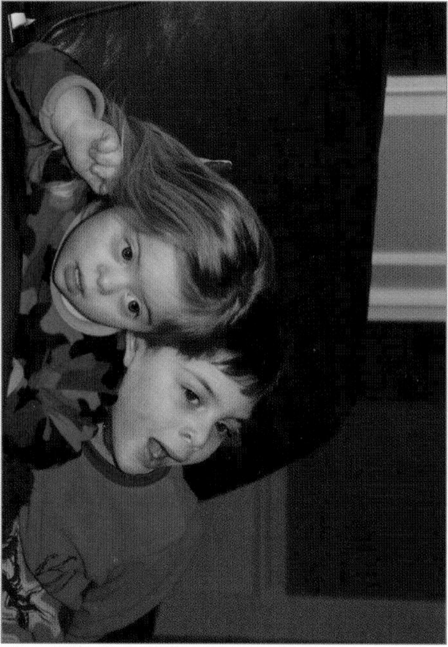

   This photo needs to be rotated, but it is also dark so it could use some other edits as well. When you want to perform multiple fixes to a photo, as you do with this one, you can use the edit view.

6 At the lower right of the iPhoto window, click the Edit button.

This viewing area changes to edit view. In edit view the selected photo fills the viewing area, and the other photos from the Event or album are shown below as small thumbnails.

At the top of the edit pane on the right side of the viewing area are three tabs; the first tab for Quick Fixes provides easy-to-use adjustments for fixing common problems with photos.

7 At the top of the Quick Fixes list, click the Rotate button.

The photo is rotated correctly. It ultimately doesn't matter where you rotate photos. You can rotate a photo as many times and whenever you want using any method you choose. But the benefit of rotating it in the edit view is that you can perform more adjustments if need be.

Fixing Photos in Edit View

In the edit view, you can use simple quick fixes to adjust visual qualities such as brightness, and color tint and saturation.

Understanding Nondestructive Editing

When you alter a photo by changing its brightness or intensifying its color, iPhoto does not permanently change your original photo. Although the original photo appears changed in your Library, behind the scenes iPhoto has actually modified a copy of your photo. As a result, you can easily revert to the original photo at any time.

More importantly, you can later add or remove any individual change at any time because iPhoto remembers all your changes as an *edit list*. This ability to constantly rethink edits is called *nondestructive editing* since the edits you make in iPhoto are never permanently "destructive" to your photo. Using nondestructive editing, you can try out various edits and effects with no worries that successive edits will degrade your photo's quality.

Editing Photos with Quick Fix Enhancement

The photo of the yawning kids is somewhat dark and could use some brightening. The Quick Fix Enhance button offers a magical one-click way to improve many photos. Without knowing anything about photo correction, you can automatically repair exposure, saturation, shadows, white balance, and much more. Just click the button.

1 With the yawning children picture selected, in the Quick Fixes pane, click the Enhance button.

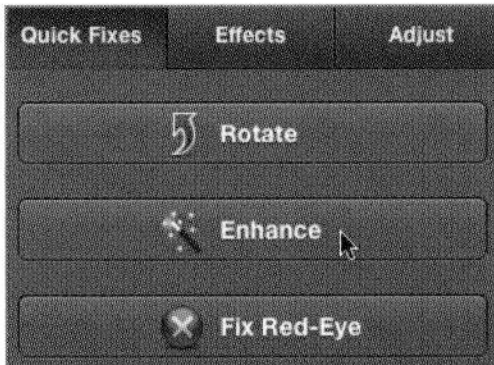

Original

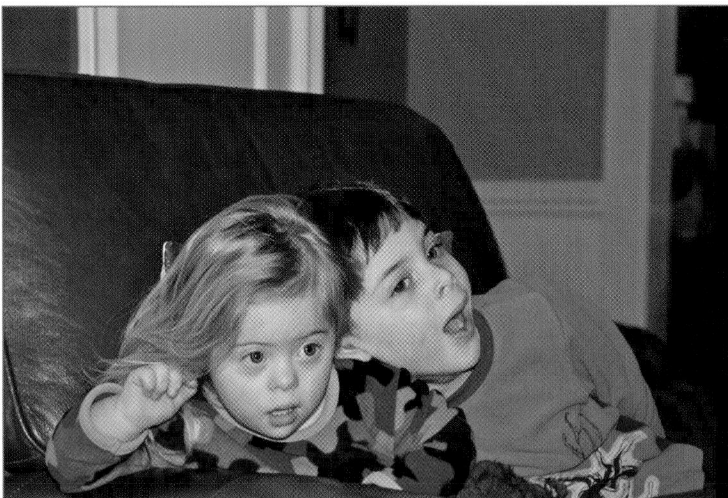

Enhanced

Much better. Instead of being completely flat, the picture pops with brighter and more vibrant colors. Now you can rate it and remove the flag to indicate that it needs no additional edits.

2 Press Command-4 to rate this as a four-star photo. Click the Info button to view the rating, then click the Edit button to return to editing your pictures.

3 Choose Photos > Unflag Photo to remove the flag from the photo. The photo is removed from the Flagged album when you unflag it.

Clicking the Enhance button improves almost every image. Next you'll try it on a picture that looks pretty good to begin with and see what happens.

4 In edit view you can select a photo using the thumbnails. Scroll to the left, if necessary, and click the first thumbnail from the left to select the picture of mother and child.

5 Click the Enhance button.

Once again, the image is improved. You'll see more detail in the mother's hair and a boost in the overall brightness of the photo. However, that pesky red-eye effect remains. For that you'll need to use another Quick Fix button.

Removing Red-Eye

You've probably seen red-eye more than a few times in your photos. When a camera's flash directly reflects from the back of the eye, it causes a red color to fill the pupil. Fortunately, red-eye is very easy to remove in iPhoto.

1 With the mother and child photo selected, click Fix Red-Eye in the Quick Fixes pane to reveal the red-eye controls.

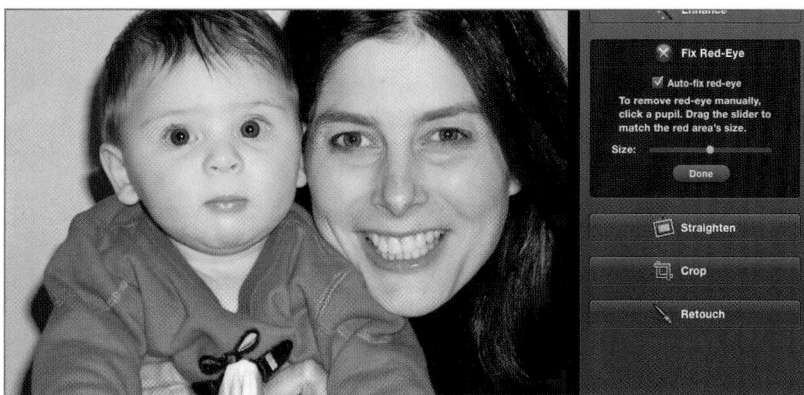

Fix Red-Eye works automatically by detecting the red eyes in the photo and removing the red. In rare situations, the automatic detection is unable to correct automatically and you must manually select the red pupils.

In this exercise, the automatic detection worked flawlessly, but for practice, you'll try the manual method.

2 Deselect the "Auto-fix red-eye" checkbox to return the child's red-eye to the photo.

The first step to manually apply the red-eye correction is adjusting the pointer's size to match the pupil size.

3 Drag the Size slider in the red-eye controls until the circular pointer is approximately the same size as the red pupils.

4 In the lower-left corner of the iPhoto window, drag the Zoom slider to the right to zoom in to the photo.

5 Hold down the Spacebar as you drag the photo to center the child's face.

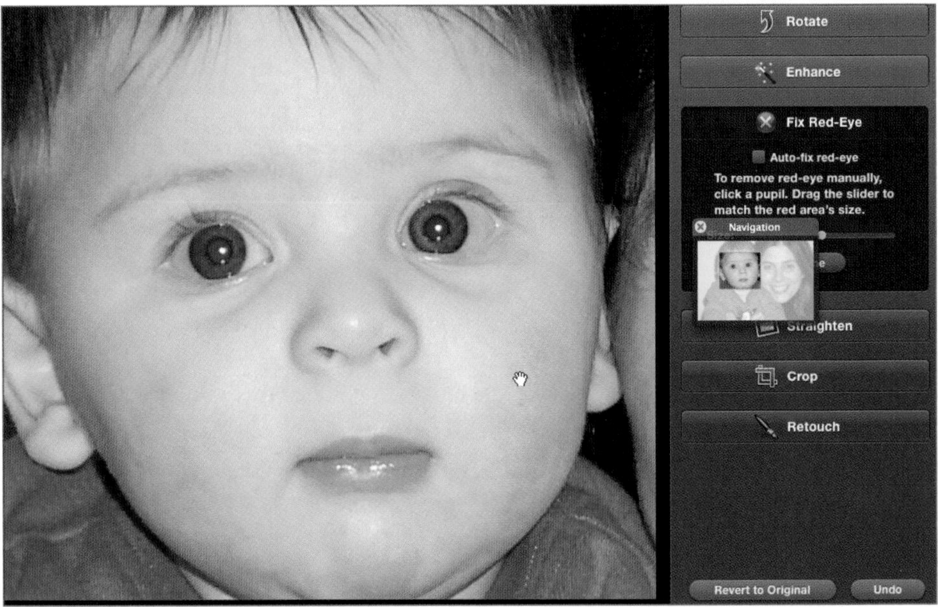

6 Click directly over each pupil to remove the red-eye.

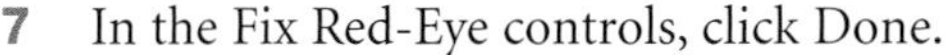

7 In the Fix Red-Eye controls, click Done.

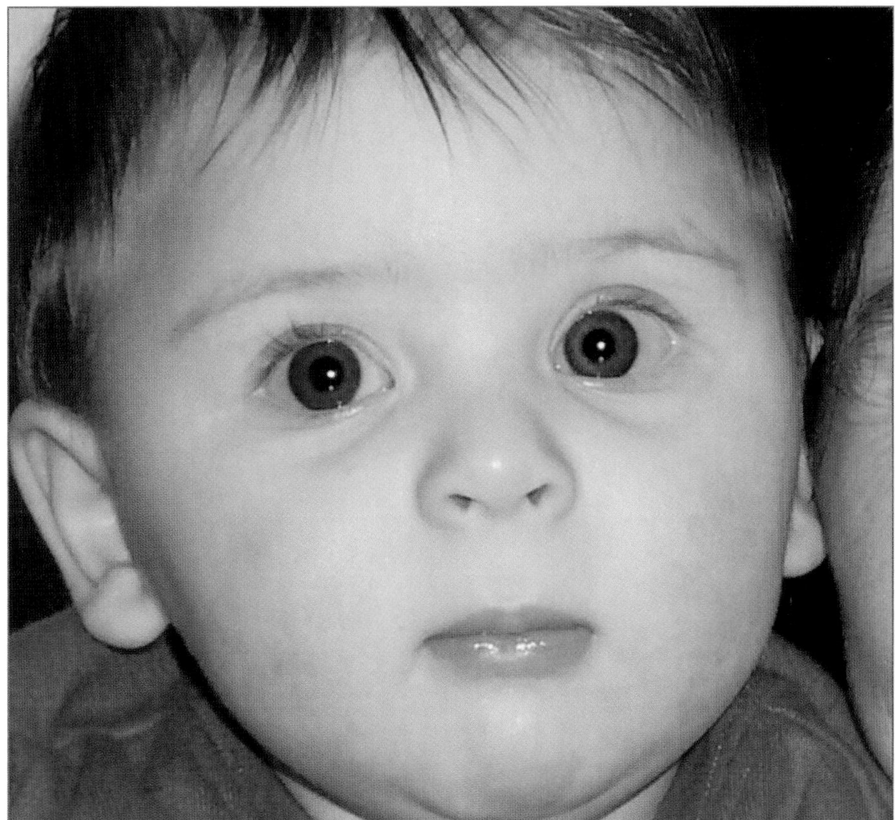

8 Drag the Zoom slider all the way to the left to see the entire photo in the viewing area.

9 Press Command-5 to rate this as a five-star photo. Click the Info button to view the rating, then click the Edit button to return to editing your pictures.

10 Choose Photos > Unflag Photo to remove the flag for the photo and remove the photo from the Flagged album.

The red-eye is removed without a trace. If it's not, undo your work and try again, increasing the zoom level of the photo to make sure the pointer exactly matches the pupil size and your placement is accurate. More often than not, the auto-fix setting will work; but it's good to know that if it doesn't you have the manual skills to resolve the problem.

Straightening Photos

Most cameras do not come with built-in controls to ensure that you're holding it level. So, it's up to you to either shoot straight, or fix tilted photos after the fact using the iPhoto Straighten tool.

Unlike the Rotate button, which you would use for serious alignment problems, the Straighten slider subtly rotates the photo in one-degree or smaller increments.

1 In the thumbnails, select the third photo from the right (the photo of the siblings embracing).

TIP You may have to scroll to the far right of the Thumbnail browser to find the photo.

It's a wonderful photo of an endearing moment when neither child is crying or fighting. But if you look at the background, it's pretty obvious that the camera wasn't held level. The tree isn't straight and the house looks like it's about to fall over.

2 In the Quick Fixes pane, click Straighten. A grid appears over the photo that you can use as an alignment guide.

3 Drag the Straighten slider to the right until the tree and house are more properly vertical, around 6.0 on the slider.

4 Click Done.

5 Press Command-4 to rate this picture with four stars. Click the Info button to view the rating, then click the Edit button to return to editing your pictures.

6 Choose Photos > Unflag Photo to remove the flag.

When straightening photos, try looking for the horizon or a vertical pole in the photo. That way you can use the guidelines to create a photo that is perfectly level horizontally and vertically.

Cropping Photos

When a photo has objects along the sides, top, or bottom that detract from the main subject, you can use Crop to cut them out.

1 In the thumbnails, select the second photo from the right (the children cheering).

2 In the Quick Fixes pane, click Crop. The Crop controls appear, and a crop rectangle is placed around the edge of the photo.

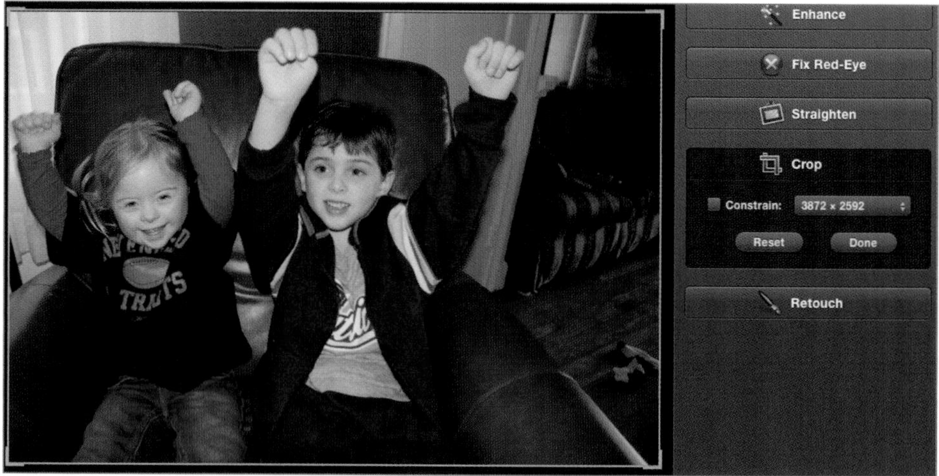

This photo shows socks on the floor to the right. Do you really need to betray this lapse in housekeeping? The best choice for this photo (and the family reputation) is to crop out the socks and improve the overall framing.

3 Hover the pointer in the lower-right corner of the picture until it changes to a crosshair.

4 Drag the corner of the rectangle up and to the left until all the socks and the couch on the right are outside the crop rectangle.

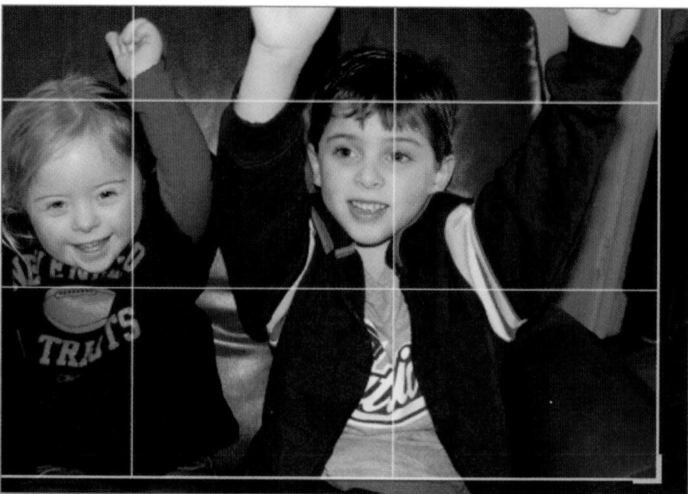

5 Click Done to close the crop tool. The newly cropped photo is displayed for your viewing pleasure.

TIP In the Constrain pop-up menu in the Crop controls, you can force the crop to conform to the common dimensions of printed picture frames, postcards, and iPhone screens.

6 Press Command-3 to rate this picture with three stars. Click the Info button to view the rating, then click the edit button to return to editing your pictures.

7 Choose Photos > Unflag Photo to remove the flag.

Cropping can improve a photo by removing unwanted areas, and also by reframing it to create a more interesting composition. Just remember the *rule of thirds*, which started as a theory in painting and has since been extended to photography. It suggests that you visualize a photo with two evenly spaced horizontal lines and two evenly spaced vertical lines (similar to a tic-tac-toe grid). Then try to place important elements at the grid intersections or along the grid lines. By doing so, you will produce a more visually balanced picture.

Conveniently enough, iPhoto provides a rule of thirds grid to help you reposition the crop rectangle.

8 In the Thumbnail browser, select the third photo from the left (the child in the snow).

The top of this picture has the snow edges that take away from the pure white surrounding the child. You'll crop this photo to remove the unwanted areas at the top and improve the overall framing.

9 Click the Crop button.

10 Hover the pointer in the upper-right corner of the picture until it changes to a crosshair.

11 Drag the corner of the crop rectangle down and to the left until the edges of the snow banks and the small object in the upper-right corner are outside the rectangle.

12 Position the pointer in the center of the crop rectangle, and drag the crop rectangle to place the upper-left grid intersection over the child's face.

13 Drag the resize handles on the crop rectangle to resize the crop, if necessary.

14 Click Done to close the crop tool.

This is a very special picture and your cropping has enhanced it. The boy is sitting perfectly and he stands out against the pure, surrounding white.

15 Rate this picture with five stars, and choose Photos > Unflag Photo to remove the flag.

Cropping can come in really handy when you first start taking pictures. It can transform an average photo into a great one just by following the rule of thirds. But the more photos you take, the more skillfully you'll frame your shots while taking the photo, bypassing the need to crop in iPhoto. Try taking pictures according to the rule of thirds. Cropping isn't necessarily bad, but if you can get the pictures near-perfect at the time you take them, you can spend less time correcting them in iPhoto.

Retouching Photos

You can use the iPhoto Retouch tool to cover small problem areas in a photo such as skin blemishes, dust spots, and other extraneous marks. It works by copying an area or a *source* from one part of the photo and allowing you to "paint" it over a *destination*. The Retouch tool then blends the source colors to match the destination colors.

1 In the Thumbnail browser, select the first photo on the left (the boy in the white shirt).

2 In the Quick Fixes pane, click Retouch.

The boy's chin has a slight rash on it. It's an adorable picture as it is, but it would be a really sweet picture if you could correct his chin.

3 To see the skin blemishes in greater detail, drag the Zoom slider all the way to the right.

4 In the Navigation window, position the small rectangle over the boy's face to center his face on the screen.

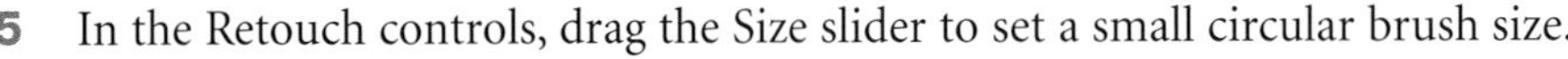

5 In the Retouch controls, drag the Size slider to set a small circular brush size.

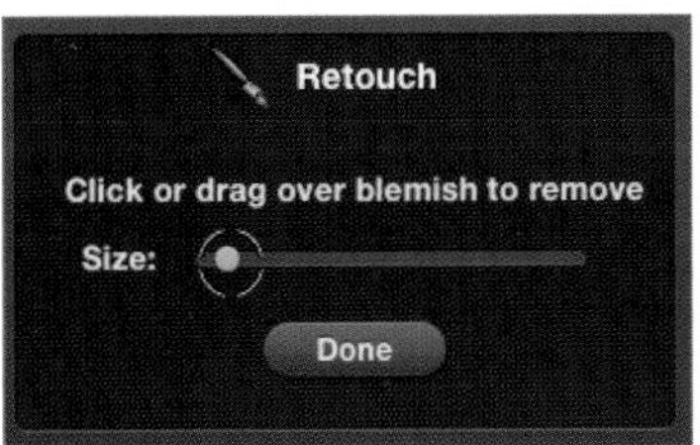

TIP You can also place the circular pointer over the area of the photo you want to retouch and press the Left Bracket ([) and Right Bracket (]) keys to set the size of the circle.

Set the circular brush size to the size of one of the small blemish areas. You want to set the brush size just large enough to cover the area but no larger.

6 Position the brush over one of the chin blemishes, and then drag across the blemish to remove it.

Short drags over small areas work better than longer drags across the entire area. Ideally, try to cover a blemish with a single click and without dragging.

7 Continue selectively dragging over the boy's chin until all the blemishes are removed.

iPhoto automatically selects the source area that works best for matching the area you want to retouch. To clearly see your progress, remember to compare the photo to the original.

TIP If you want to override source selection in iPhoto, Option-click a source area on the photo. When you next drag over a blemish you want to remove, iPhoto will use that selected source area.

8 To compare the original photo to your edited version, press the Shift key repeatedly to toggle between the two versions of the photo.

As you hold down the Shift key, you are viewing the original photo without any fixes applied. Release the Shift key and you are viewing the edited picture.

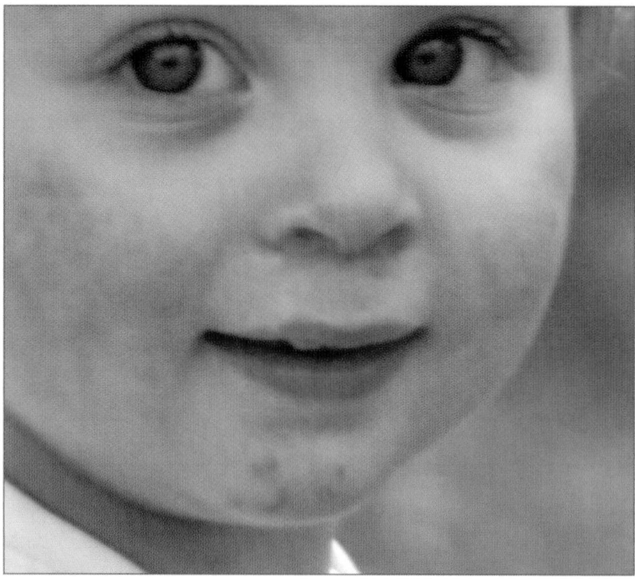

Before retouching chin blemishes

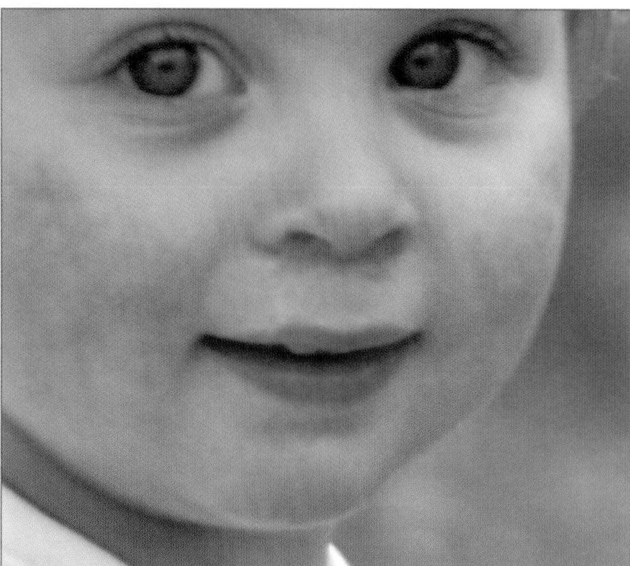

After retouching chin blemishes

This before-and-after comparison method is a good sanity check to ensure that you really are improving the photo and not just making it different. In this exercise, however, you've clearly improved this photo, removing the distracting element from the child's face.

9 Rate this photo with five stars, and choose Photos > Unflag Photo.

TIP You can remove all the Quick Fixes and return to your original photo by clicking the Revert to Original button.

10 Click Done in the Retouch pane to close it.

The Retouch tool is very reliable on small areas that can be removed with a single click or short drags. Attempting to remove an entire person from a photo, no matter how much you want that person to go away, is not really possible with this tool.

Using Effects

Quick Fixes address many common problems you'll come across, and improve the quality of your photos. Effects are used for a different reason. They target more artistic endeavors, such as setting a mood and enhancing the emotional impact.

1 In edit view, click the Effects tab.

2 In the Thumbnail browser at the bottom of the screen, select the photo of the young boy in the cowboy hat.

This is a classic picture that many kids can relate to. Using the effects in iPhoto, you can improve the mood by giving this image the look of an old photograph.

The Effects pane includes two areas of circular and square effect buttons.

The six circular buttons at the top act more like Quick Fixes than effects because they alter brightness, contrast, and color.

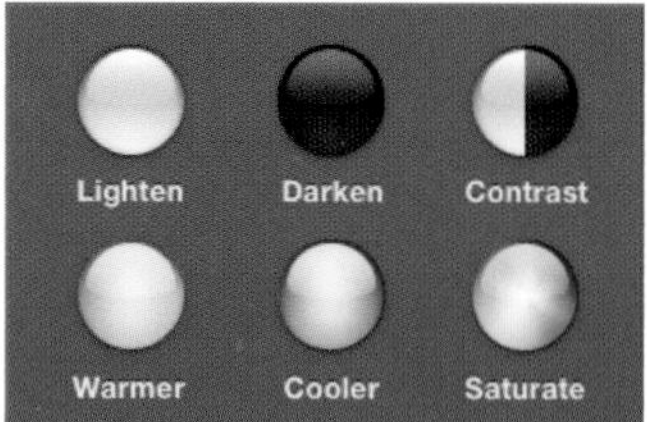

The nine square buttons, which display your selected photo with the effect applied, are creative effects.

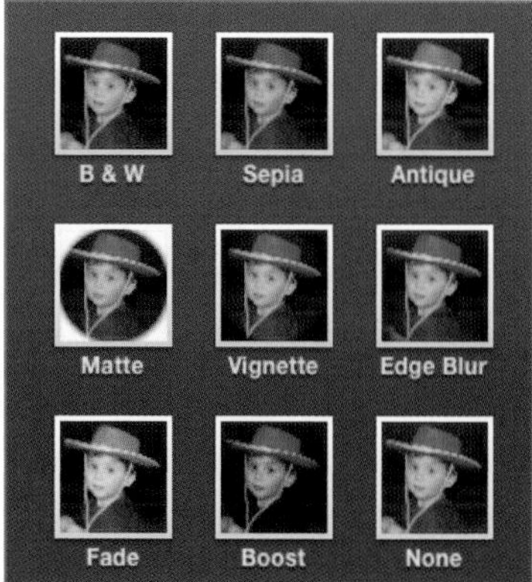

3 In the Effects pane, click the Antique button to apply that effect to your photo. It now has an older, faded look with a subtle sepia tint.

Each time you click the button it increases the intensity of the effect. A number at the bottom of the effect button displays the number of times you have intensified the effect. You can also click other effects buttons to apply multiple effects to a photo.

TIP Option-click the thumbnail to reduce the effect level. You can reduce it until the number at the bottom of the thumbnail disappears, indicating that the effect has been removed completely.

4 Click the Antique button three more times to increase the effect amount.

5 Click the Vignette button to add a vignette effect.

6 Click the Edge Blur button five times to blur the edges of the vignette.

You've now added three effects to this photo to give it an old-time appearance. To remove all your effects, you could click the None button in the lower-right corner. You can also compare your results with the original photo.

7 Press the Shift key to view the original photo and then release the Shift key to view the edited photo.

Original

With Antique effect applied

8 Rate this photo with five stars, and choose Photos > Unflag Photo to remove the flag.

The top six circular effect buttons operate in a similar way. The results are generally more creative adjustments than Quick Fixes. Let's look at one to help you understand how they work.

9 At the bottom of the viewing area, select the last photo to the right in the Thumbnail browser (the boy in the blue cap).

This photo was taken outside during winter, and while the boy looks cold, the entire photo shouldn't have a blue tint. You can use the Warmer effect to add more orange to this photo until the boy's skin tone looks more lively.

10 Click the Warmer button three times.

11 Press and release the Shift key to compare the original photo and the edited photo. The skin tones look more realistic and the snow looks less blue, as it should.

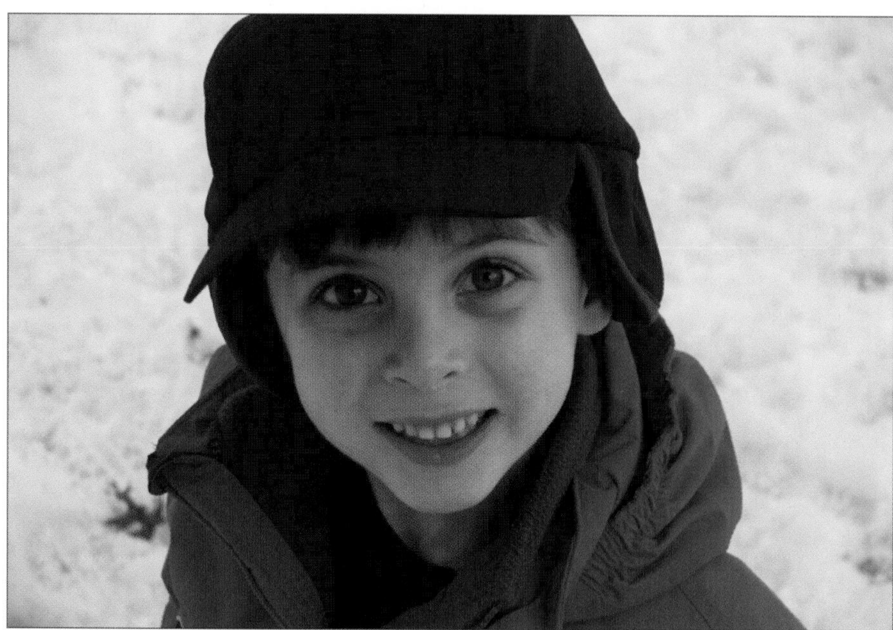

Original

Warmer tone applied

12 Rate this photo with three stars, and choose Photos > Unflag Photo to remove the flag.

13 Click the Edit button to close the edit pane.

14 Click the Flagged button at the top left of the window to return to the Flagged album.

Effects are useful not only when you want to explore some creative options, but also when you need more repairing prowess than the Enhance button provides. It's easiest to start your photo fixing with the Enhance button and, if that isn't sufficient, move over to Effects and try your hand there. You'll gain a bit more control in fixing the color and brightness of your photos, as well as a chance to explore your artistic side.

Working with Albums

Albums allow you to group selected photos from one or more Events. It's a way to organize and locate specific groups of photos more quickly. The photos in an album are not moved out of their Events; they are just referenced into an album and displayed in both places.

1 In the Source list, select Events and double-click The Krupps Family Event.

2 Select the first photo in the viewing area of mom, dad, and the baby.

3 Shift-click the last photo in the second row to select all eight photos in the viewing area.

4 Choose File > New > Album, or press Command-N.

The new album appears in the Source list, and the eight selected photos are displayed in the album viewing area.

5 With the Untitled album highlighted blue in the Source list, type *Krupps: The early years* and press Return.

To add photos to an album at any time, you can drag them from an Event onto the album's name in the Source list. You can also remove photos from an album by selecting them and pressing Delete. Deleting a photo in an album doesn't delete it from your Event; it just removes it from the album.

Working with Smart Albums

In the previous exercise, you manually added photos to an album by selecting the photos.

Smart Albums use information contained in the photos to automatically create an album. For instance, you could create a Smart Album based on photos taken by a specific camera and within a specified date rage. Any time you import photos taken by that camera model within that date range, they would automatically be added to the Smart Album.

Creating Smart Albums

To become familiar with Smart Albums, you'll create a Smart Album that contains only the five-star photos you rated earlier.

1 Choose File > New > Smart Album, or press Command-Option-N.

The Smart Album conditions dialog appears. Like creating rules in an email application, you select conditions that photos must match to be included in the album.

2 In the "Smart Album name" field, type *Best of the Krupps Family*.

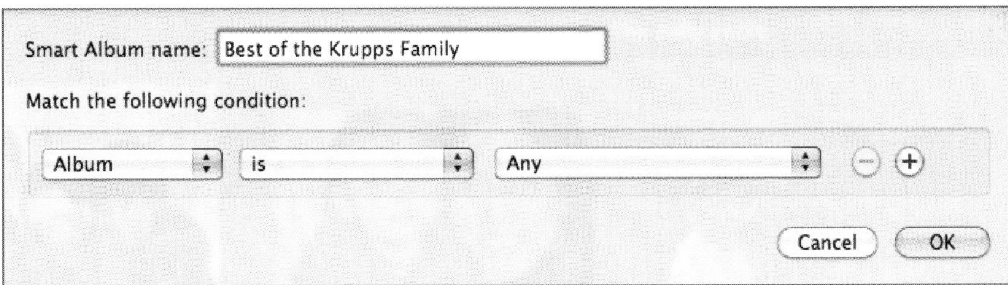

3 In the "Match the following condition" area, from the three pop-up menus choose "My Rating," "is greater than," "★★★" These conditions will place all four- and five-star-rated photos in the "Best of Krupps Family" album.

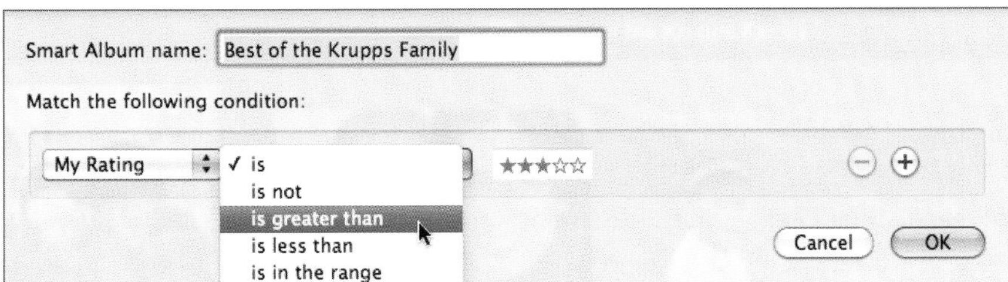

4 Click OK to create the Smart Album and add it to the Source list.

In the viewing area, you'll see a lot more photos than you rated. It's showing the four- and five-star photos from your entire iPhoto library when you want it limited to just the Krupps family Event.

5 Choose File > Edit Smart Album.

The Smart Album conditions window reappears. You can add as many conditions as you want, and these conditions will update the existing Smart Album.

6 Click the Add Condition button.

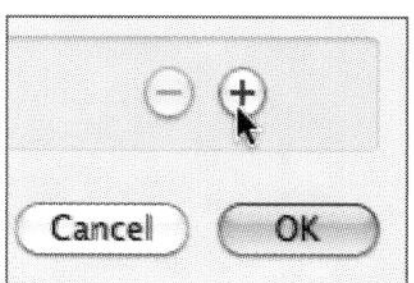

A new condition is added under the Rating condition, and a new Match pop-up menu, set to All, appears. You could change the Match conditions menu to Any if you wanted to add photos that match *any* of these conditions. In this exercise, however, you want to match *all* your conditions.

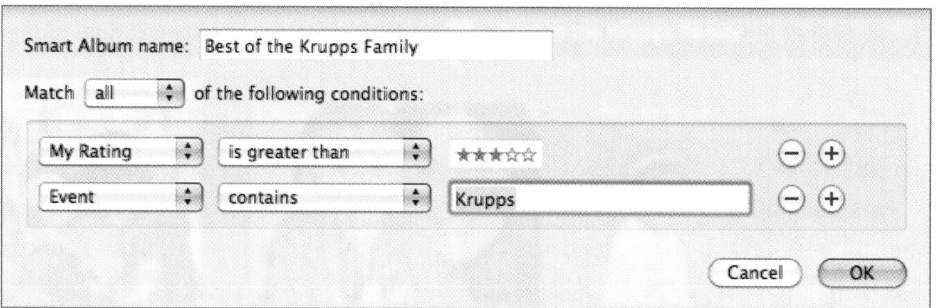

7 To create the new condition, set the second set of pop-up menus to "Event," "contains," "Krupps."

8 Click OK.

The photos matching all the conditions appear in the viewing area. If you change the conditions or import new photos that match the existing conditions, iPhoto will update the Smart Album automatically.

Transferring Photos to Mobile Devices

You can transfer photos directly to an iPad, iPhone, or iPod by selecting the albums and Events in iTunes when the mobile device is connected to your Mac. That way you'll have all your favorite photos to show family members and friends no matter where you are.

NOTE ► To perform the following steps, you'll need an iPod, iPad, or iPhone.

1 Connect your iPad, iPhone, or iPod to your Mac. iTunes opens automatically.

2 To the left of the iTunes window, select your connected device.

3 At the top of the iTunes window, click the Photos button.

The settings window for syncing photos appears in the main iTunes window. iTunes can examine your iPhoto library and see all the photos, albums, and Events without the need to export or share anything.

4 Select the "Sync Photos from iPhoto" checkbox.

You have the choice to sync all your photos, albums, and Events onto your mobile device. If you intend to transfer your entire iPhoto Library, make sure you have enough free space on your device. Otherwise, you can sync just selected albums and Events, which is why you rated the photos in the first place, isn't it?

5 Select the "Selected albums, events and faces, and automatically include" option.

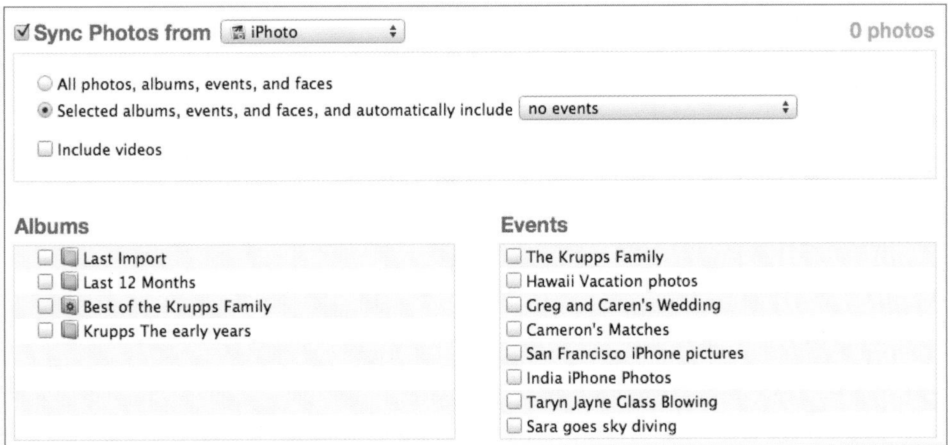

Because your Events contain many photos that may not be rated highly, you may not want to devote precious mobile storage space to your lesser-quality photos. That's where albums and Smart Albums come in handy. You can sync only those albums that contain your favorite, highly rated photos.

By default, the associated pop-up menu is set to "no events" to exclude Events from syncing to your device. You'll use that setting.

6 From the Albums list, select the "Best of the Krupps Family" checkbox.

7 At the lower right of the window, click Apply.

NOTE ▸ A warning dialog may appear if you already have photos on your device and are syncing it with a new library. It's your choice to replace the photos on your device or cancel the sync operation.

iTunes automatically syncs and transfers the photos to your connected device. When it's done, you can disconnect your mobile device and use its Photos app to view the album.

Lesson Review

1. When using the organize view, how do you view ratings on photos?
2. Describe two of the three ways to rotate a photo.
3. What is the rule of thirds?
4. True or false: You must export albums and photos into iTunes to sync them to your Apple mobile device.
5. What is the difference between albums and Smart Albums?

Answers

1. Choose View > Ratings.
2. To rotate a photo, do one of the following:
   - From the Photo pop-up menu, choose Rotate in the lower-right corner of each photo.
   - Choose Photos > Rotate Clockwise, or Photos > Rotate Counter Clockwise.

- Press Command-R to rotate clockwise, or pressing Command-Option-R to rotate counter-clockwise.
- Click the Rotate button in the Quick Fixes pane.

3. The rule of thirds suggests that you visualize a photo divided by two evenly spaced horizontal lines and two evenly spaced vertical lines. Then try to place important elements at the grid intersections or along the grid lines to create a more balanced picture.
4. False. You do not need to export. iTunes knows what is in your iPhoto library and transfers the albums and photos directly from iPhoto onto your mobile device.
5. Albums are static groupings of photos that you create manually. Smart Albums are dynamically updated based on conditions that you choose.

3

Lesson Files

Pictures > ATS iPhoto Library: The Krupps Family

Pictures > ATS iPhoto Library: Greg and Caren's wedding

Time

This lesson takes approximately 60 minutes to complete.

Goals

Name faces in your library

Confirm and reject images in Faces

Add names to missing faces

Use GPS photos in Places

Place photos on a map

Add your own locations

Create Smart Albums of specific people and places

Post photos to Facebook, Flickr, and MobileMe

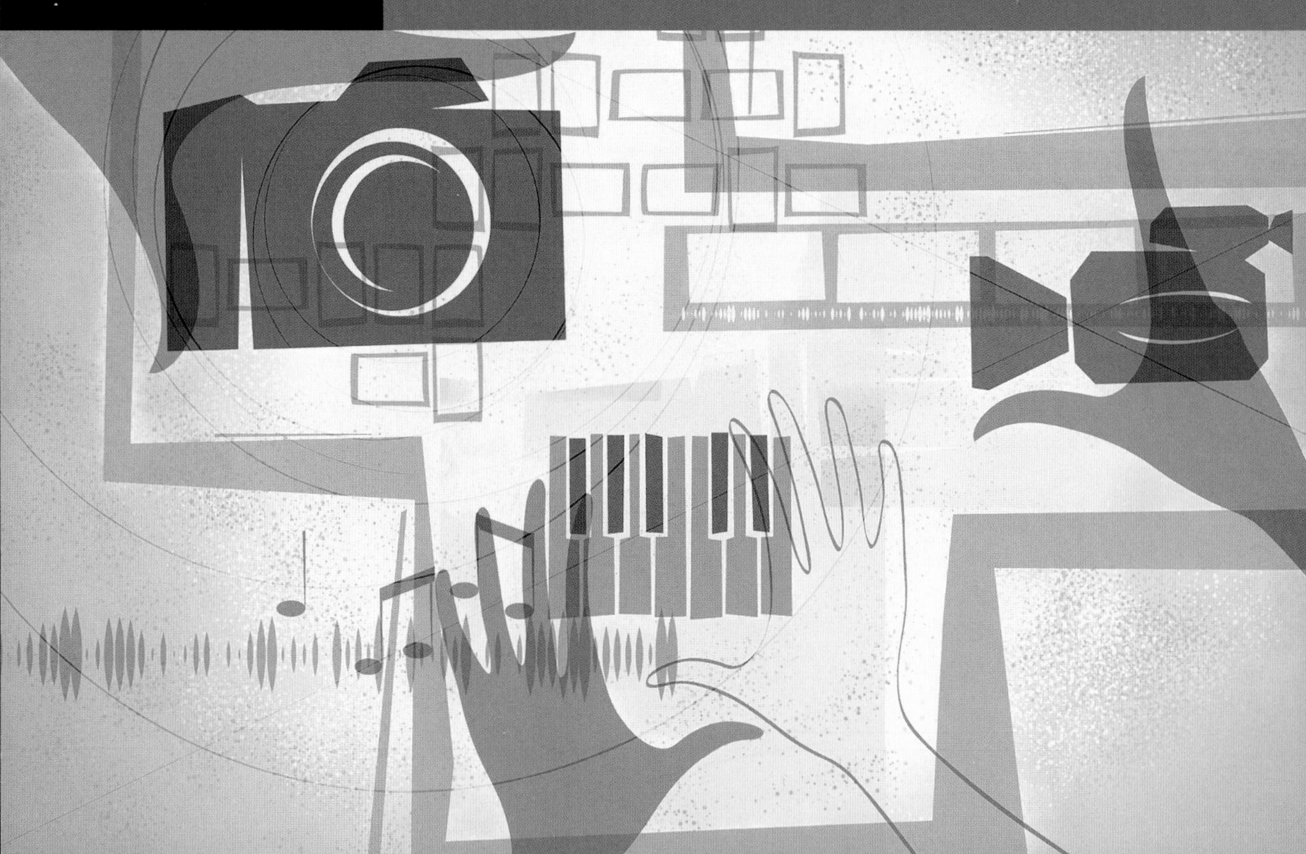

Lesson **3**

Arranging Photos by Faces and Places

In Lesson 2, you learned that rating and flagging photos can make it easier to locate the photos you want to share. But what do you do when you want to share photos of specific people in your life or email photos taken at the cabin that you rent every winter? Star ratings and flags don't help much in those cases. Thankfully, you can put iPhoto to work finding all the people and all the places depicted in your photos.

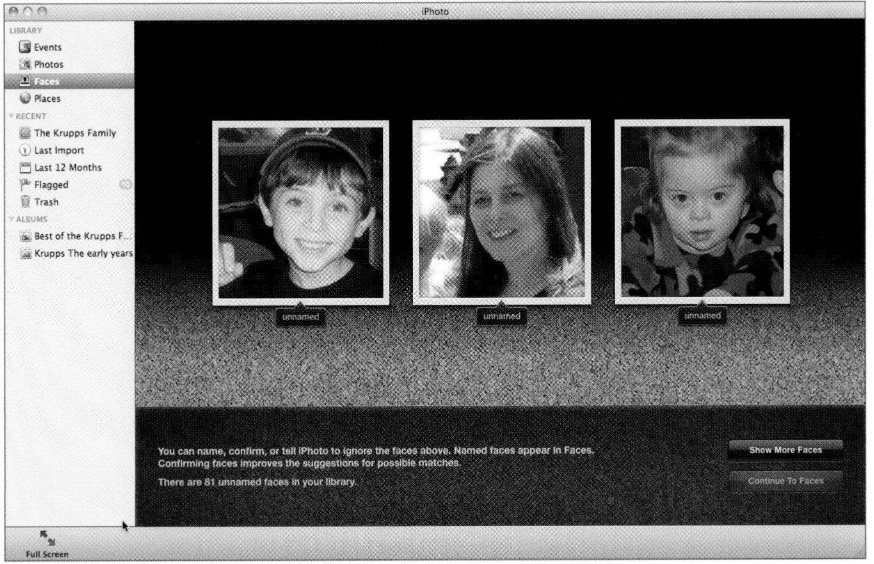

Finding People in Your Photos

When you are trying to find photos in your library, the most useful information is knowing who is in them. iPhoto can help immensely in providing an answer because it not only *detects* people's faces in your pictures (sorry Bowser and Fluffy, pets not included), it can also *recognize* the same face throughout your library.

Using Faces View

You start using Faces by putting names to faces that iPhoto detects. Once iPhoto has names to associate with faces, it then can suggest other photos those people might be in.

1 In the Source list, select Faces.

The first time you select Faces, the Find Faces view is shown with a few people from your library displayed as starting points. iPhoto found these faces in your library but has no idea who they are. It's up to you to add their names.

NOTE ▸ You should see three faces in the Find Faces view. If you see more than three, shrink the window size by dragging the lower-right corner. This will make it easier to follow the examples shown in this lesson.

2 Click the "unnamed" label below the first picture.

3 Type *Damian*, and then press Tab to move to the next picture.

4 Under the second photo, type *Joy*, then press Tab.

5 Under the third photo, type *Maria*, then press Tab to confirm the final name.

iPhoto could continue finding faces for you if you clicked the Show More Faces button, but it can take some time to find every face in your library.

Confirming and Rejecting Suggestions

When you have put a name to a face, iPhoto can then continue to search your library and suggest other photos that may include that person.

1 Click the Continue To Faces button.

The Faces view shows a snapshot for each person you've named on a corkboard background. The snapshot is a Faces group that represents all the confirmed photos of that person in your library.

TIP If you add an email address in the Faces view info panel, when photos of that person are posted to Facebook, the subject will be notified via a Facebook message.

2 On the corkboard, double-click the Faces group of Damian to view all the photos that have been confirmed to include Damian.

iPhoto has found only one photo so far, but at the lower left of the window, a message indicates that other Damian photos may exist.

3 In the lower right of the window, click Confirm Additional Faces to show pictures that may include Damian.

To finalize the choice, you will confirm the photos that show Damian and reject the ones that do not.

TIP When confirming and rejecting photos in Faces view, iPhoto zooms into a picture to show you the matching face. If you want to see the entire photo, click the switch in the upper right of the window from Faces to Photos.

4 Click the first photo to confirm it as Damian. A green background on the title bar indicates this photo has been confirmed.

If you have more than one photo to confirm, you can speed up the process by dragging a selection box around them.

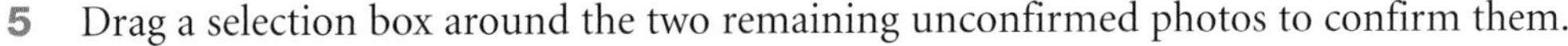

5 Drag a selection box around the two remaining unconfirmed photos to confirm them.

6 Click Done.

Using the confirmed photos as additional reference, iPhoto now has a better idea what Damian looks like. The message informs you that iPhoto has found still more photos that may include Damian.

7 Click Confirm Additional Faces.

8 Select the first three pictures in the top row because they all feature Damian.

The last photo in the top row, however, is not Damian. It has a resemblance because it's of his sister but you'll want to reject this photo.

9 Double-click the photo of Damian's sister, Maria, to reject it. A red highlight appears to indicate it is not Damian.

10 Click Done, then in the Source list, click Events.

TIP You can remove a subject from the Faces view by selecting the snapshot on the corkboard and pressing Command-Delete.

With all the photos of Damian located, you could proceed to the next snapshot on the Faces corkboard and have iPhoto locate more photos to confirm or reject. This face-recognition technology is still in its infancy, so be prepared to find some suggestions that are way off and even some instances when a face can't be found at all. The iPhoto recognition skills are remarkable but not yet infallible.

Adding Missed Faces

In some photos, people will be turned away from the camera or be wearing a hat and glasses, so iPhoto cannot recognize them. Still, you may want to identify those photos as including a particular person. iPhoto allows you to identify and name a face even when iPhoto can't.

1 In the viewing area, double-click The Krupps Family Event.

2 Scroll to find the photo of the two kids hugging and double-click the photo to display it in the viewer.

3 At the bottom of the window, click the Info button.

The info panel opens on the right displaying information about the selected photo's camera and including a Faces area.

Although iPhoto knows a face is in the photo, it doesn't recognize it as Damian. It also has missed Maria's face altogether, probably because her eyes aren't visible. Still, this is a beautiful photo that you would want to find when looking for a photo of either child. So you'll help iPhoto solve the mystery of who is in this picture.

4 Position your pointer over Damian's face. iPhoto shows you where the face is and leaves the name tag as "unnamed."

TIP At times iPhoto may incorrectly detect a pattern in your photo as a face. To remove a face detection box from a photo, click the X in the upper-left corner of the box.

5 In the name tag, type *D*. As soon as you type the letter D, all names in iPhoto and from your Address book that begin with D are displayed in a list.

6 Continue typing *Damian* and then select his name from the list. Selecting from the list ensures that you use the same name, spelled the same way, every time a photo includes that person.

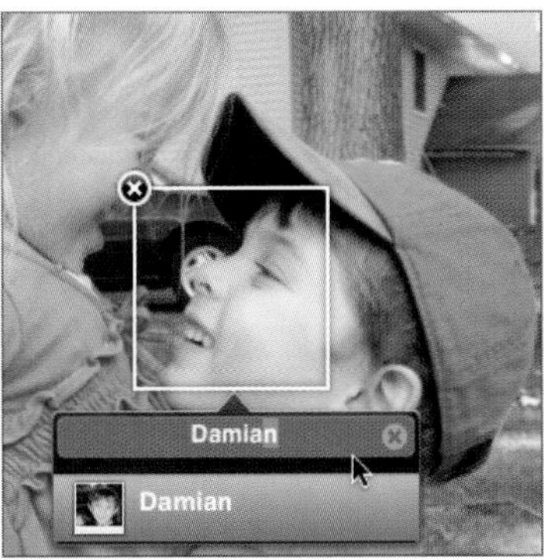

To add Maria's name you first need to identify her face for iPhoto.

7 In the Info panel, click "Add a face."

A rectangular outline appears on the photo. Use this rectangle to frame the face you want to identify in the photo.

8 Click in the center of the rectangle and drag it over Maria's face.

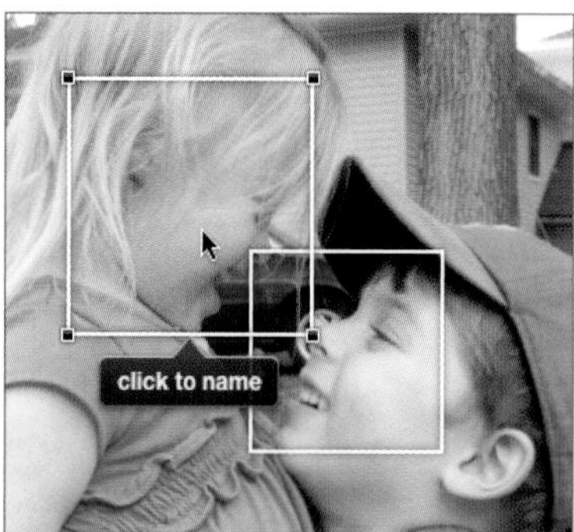

9 Add Maria's name to the name tag and then select her from the list.

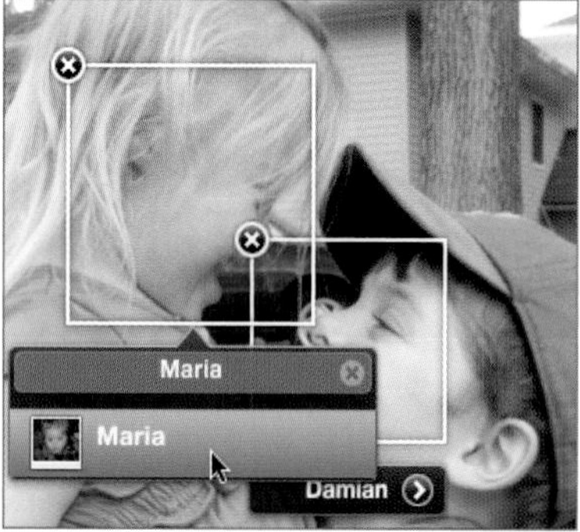

The payoff for all this naming is that you can find photos of your family members in an instant. No more searching for hours to dig up that one picture you know you kept somewhere. You can even make the searching easier by combining Faces with Smart Albums.

Creating a Faces Smart Album

After you have applied names to Faces, you can create Smart Albums based on the people in your photos.

1 In the Source list, select Faces.

2 Command-click Maria and Damian's snapshots.

3 Drag the two snapshots to an empty area of the library.

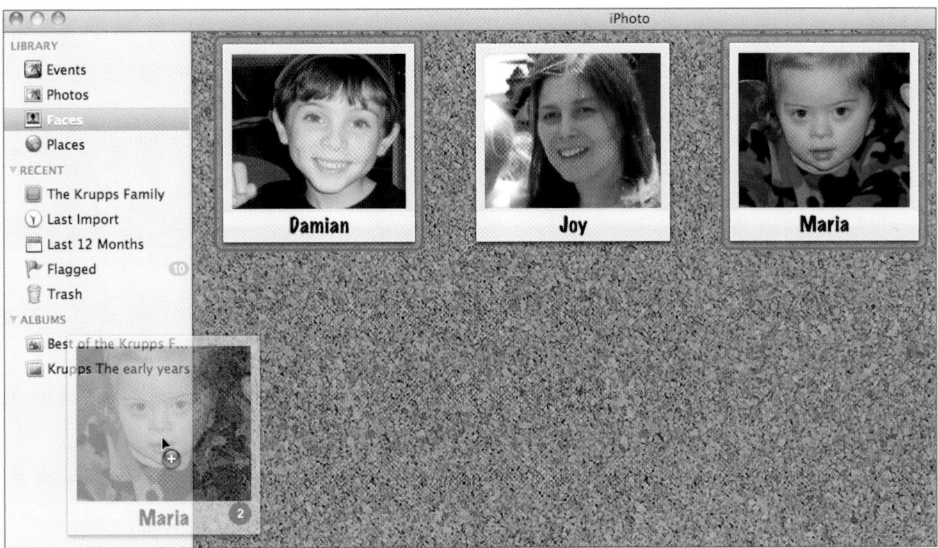

A Smart Album is automatically created with the name "Damian or Maria." The Smart Album will find all the photos featuring either child, or you can choose to edit the smart album's conditions as you did in Lesson 2.

Finding Places

Based on the last exercise, you can now find photos according to who is in them. Wouldn't it be just as nice to find photos based on *where* you took them? In iPhoto you can map the location where each photo was taken within mere feet of where you were standing.

Places uses GPS information to identify where photos were taken, or if GPS isn't available, you can add your own location information by typing a country, state, city or point of interest. iPhoto instantly gives you a list of locations to choose from.

NOTE ► To use Places, you must be connected to the Internet. The Places maps and list of locations are not stored on your hard disk, which enables them to be regularly updated.

Viewing GPS-Tagged Images in Places

You can now buy cameras with built-in GPS capabilities. GPS-equipped cameras will save the location where each picture was taken, just as transparently as they save the date a picture was taken. If you own an iPhone 3G or later, you already have a GPS-equipped camera that works with the iPhoto Places view.

In the Places view, you can look at a map that shows where all your photos were taken. If your pictures have GPS information already embedded, the entire process is done for you.

1 In the Source list, select Places.

   The viewing area changes to show a map of the world. The red pins on the map indicate where photos in your library were taken.

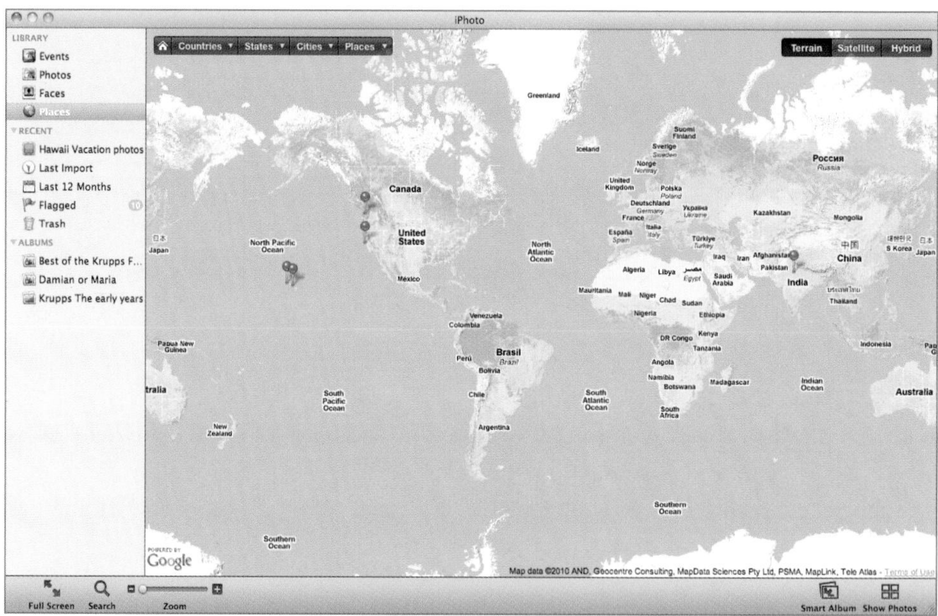

2 Place the pointer over the red pin in India.

When you place your pointer over each pin, a label appears showing the name of the location.

NOTE ▸ Multiple photos taken in one general area may appear as a single pin until you zoom further into the map.

3 Click the arrow to the right of the pin's label. The viewing area shows the photos taken at the Taj Mahal, and the Info panel shows the precise location of the photo in a small map pane.

TIP When using a Magic Mouse or a Multi-Touch track pad, you can zoom in and out of the map by moving the mouse over the area of interest and sliding two fingers up or down.

4 In the upper left of the viewing area, click the Map button to return to the Places view.

You can see a more detailed map of an area by dragging the Zoom slider, or choosing from Path Navigator pop-up menus at the top of the map.

5 From the Path Navigator pop-up menus, choose States > California.

The map zooms in to view only those pins located within the state of California. A few pins are located within San Francisco and a few pins are placed on the Golden Gate Bridge.

TIP You can change the map style by clicking the Terrain, Satellite, or Hybrid view buttons in the upper-right corner of the map.

6 To see all the photos for all the red pins currently displayed on the map, click Show Photos in the iPhoto window.

Instead of only seeing one pin's photos, using the Show Photos button shows the photos from all the pins displayed on the map.

7 In the iPhoto window, click the Info button, and select the first photo in the upper-left corner of the viewing area. The map updates to show you the location of the selected photo.

8 Click the last photo in the lower-right corner of the viewing area.

The map updates again. The title at the top of the map reads, "Bernal Heights Park," because iPhoto can locate specific areas within a city; or, as in the next case, a point of interest.

9 Click the center photo in the viewing area. The pin's location is the Palace of Fine Arts in San Francisco.

When photos include GPS information, the location information is saved with the photo as longitude and latitude. Instead of showing you the longitude and latitude values, iPhoto calculates the region, city, or point of interest that those numbers correspond to and displays that information. But what if you are using a regular camera without GPS? Even then, it doesn't take much more than a few clicks to get those photos on the map.

Assigning a Location in Places

Even without a GPS data attached to your photos, you can add them, and entire Events, to the Places map.

> **NOTE** ▶ If you have not completed Lesson 1, open and import Desktop > ATS iLife11 Book Files > Lesson 01 > Memory Card.dmg.

1 In the Source list, select Events, and then select the Cameron's Matches Event

   Because no location information exists for these photos, the Info panel map is empty. The easiest way to add a location is to add it to an entire Event. The Event and all the photos contained in it will be associated with a single pin that identifies the general area in which the photos were taken.

2 Above the Info panel's map, click "Assign a Place," and type *Atlanta*. iPhoto searches for Atlanta and provides a list of locations that match.

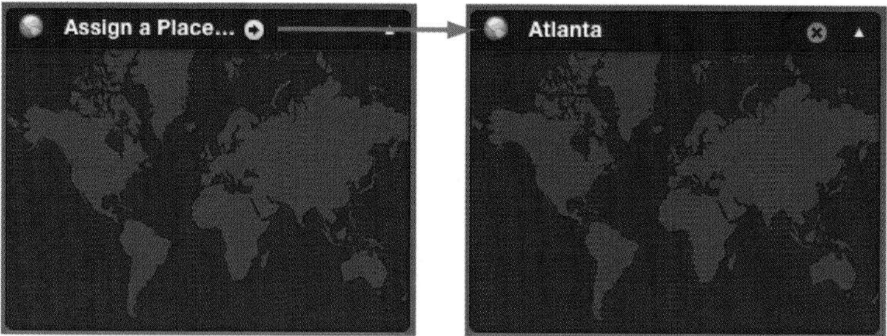

3 Select Atlanta Georgia, the first item in the list. The entire Event and all the photos in it are now represented by the single pin you just placed.

4 In the Source list, click Places to change to Places view.

5 From the Path navigator pop-up menus, choose Countries > United States.

The pin you assigned for Atlanta appears on the right side of the map. If your library is small or you have particular photos that you would like to locate more precisely, you can select those individual photos and follow the preceding steps to assign them to specific locations.

Moving a Pin

When you assign a location for pictures or Events, iPhoto places the pin at the center of the location. That's acceptable if you are at the Eiffel Tower, but not so great when you assign Alaska. Rather than choosing the dead center of a large area, you can move a pin to an exact location in just a few simple steps.

1 From the Source list, select Events, and then double-click the Greg and Caren's Wedding Event.

2 Select the last picture in the Event.

This picture's location is set as Oahu. While that's accurate, the map shows it in the center of the island even though it was taken at Pearl Harbor.

3 Drag the red pin down until it is positioned directly over the "P" in Pearl City.

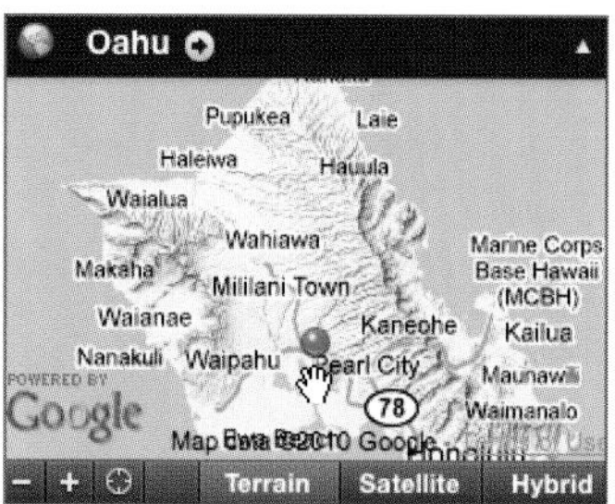

4 Triple-click the Zoom-in button (+) to make sure that you are within Pearl Harbor as shown in the figure below.

5 Refine the pin's position that so it sits just off the right coast of the island within Pearl Harbor.

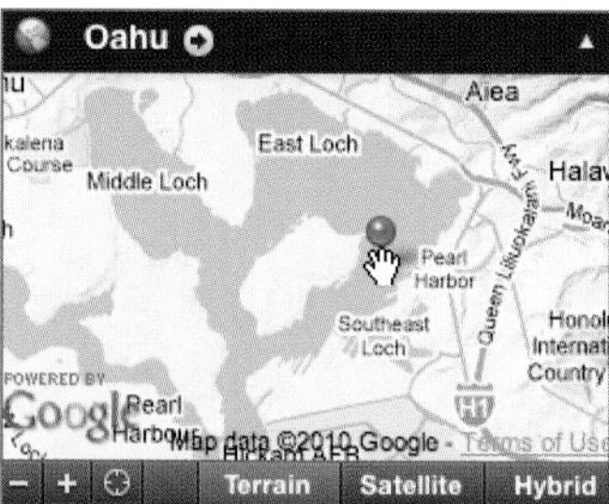

With the pin set correctly you are ready to name it more precisely.

Changing a Location Name

Most of the time when repositioning pins, iPhoto will identify the new location with its correct name. But occasionally you will want to change the name. For instance, if you take a picture at your friend's house, iPhoto will locate the house correctly, but you will probably want to call it "Bubba's House," rather than 1234 Elm St.

1 With the Pearl Harbor photo still selected, click the pin on the map to display the Location Name pop-up menu. Depending on where you actually set your pin, the Location name may be different.

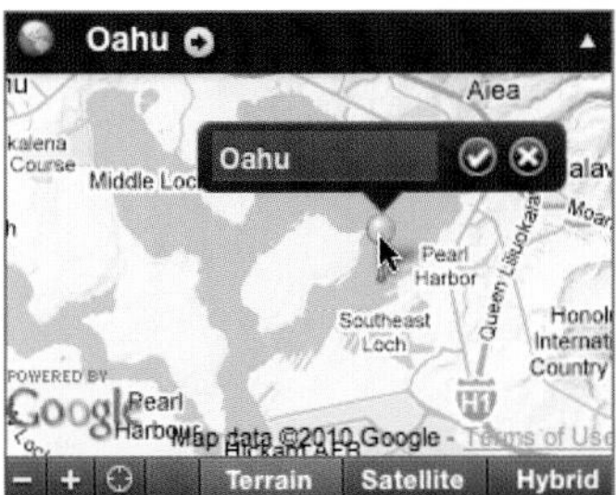

2 Double-click the name in the Location Name pop-up menu to select the word for editing.

3 Type *USS Arizona Memorial*, and then click the checkmark to confirm the new name of the pin.

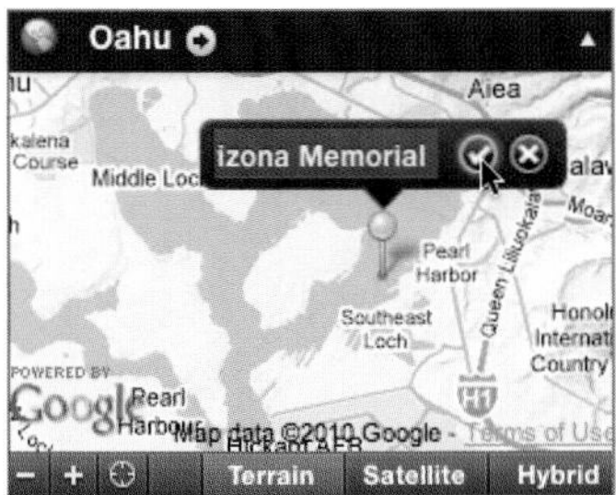

If you ever visit Pearl Harbor again and take new pictures, you can enter USS Arizona Memorial and it will appear because it's now defined in iPhoto as a location.

Managing Places

Because a single point can't always represent a large location, iPhoto allows you to set the vicinity as part of the pin's location. Any subsequent photos taken within that vicinity setting will be assigned the correct location.

1 Choose Window > Manage My Places.

The Manage My Places window shows the pin for the currently selected photo. The blue circle around the pin represents the location's area.

The circle should be large enough to encompass all the places nearby where you are likely to snap a picture, so it needs to be made larger.

NOTE ▶ Locations that iPhoto already knows have a defined area. Only places you create are shown in the Manage My Places window.

2 Drag out the circle's handles to increase its size and cover the entire channel and the land on both sides.

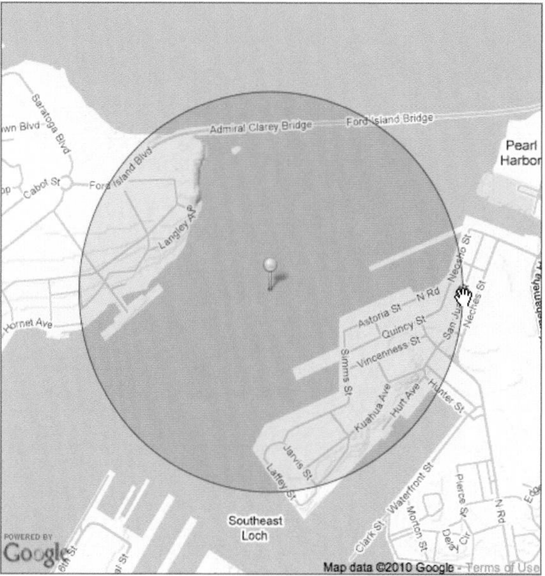

3 Click Done to close the Manage My Places window.

TIP To remove a location you have added, click the minus sign to the right of the Location name in the Manage My Places window.

You've now created an enlarged area for the location, USS Arizona Memorial. Next time you enter a new custom name for a pin, use the Manage My Places window to refine the area around it. The more precise you are in configuring Places, the more effectively it will help you find photos in the future.

Creating a Smart Album from a Map

Now that you have tagged your photos with location information, you can create geography-based Smart Albums.

1 From the Source List, select Places.

2 From the Path Navigator pop-up menus, click the Home button to view the entire world map.

3 Drag the Zoom slider to view just the western half of the United States.

4 In the lower-right corner of the window, click the Smart Album button.

A new Smart Album is created in the Source list, and the viewing area displays the photos from that Smart Album. The Info window shows the map that defined which photos are included in the Smart Album.

5 In the Source list, type *Western US* to name the new Smart Album.

In the future, when you add any images to your library that fall within the region defined for that Smart Album, as shown in the Info panel's map, the new photos will automatically be added to that Smart Album.

Posting to Facebook, Flickr, and MobileMe

Sharing photos these days is all about posting to the web. It's the easiest way to show your photos to all of your friends and family. iPhoto can seamlessly share photos on the most popular photo sharing sites: Facebook, Flickr, and MobileMe.

NOTE ▸ You must have an Internet connection and MobileMe, Facebook, or Flickr accounts to perform the next three exercises. If you don't, you can register for Facebook and Flickr at no charge. MobileMe offers a free 60-day trial at www.me.com.

Posting to Facebook

Facebook is the most popular photo-sharing site on the web. You can select a single photo, album, or an entire Event to post on Facebook.

NOTE ▶ The steps to share to Facebook are very similar to the steps for sharing to MobileMe and Flickr. Because the steps are so similar, we'll detail sharing to Facebook only, but later list some benefits of each site.

1 In the Source list, select the "Damian or Maria" Smart Album.

2 From the toolbar, choose Share > Facebook.

TIP When you share a single photo to Facebook, you have the option to make it your profile picture or add it to your Wall.

If you've never previously shared to Facebook from iPhoto, the login window opens.

3 In the login window, enter your Facebook name and password.

4 Select the "I agree to Facebook's terms" checkbox, and then click Login.

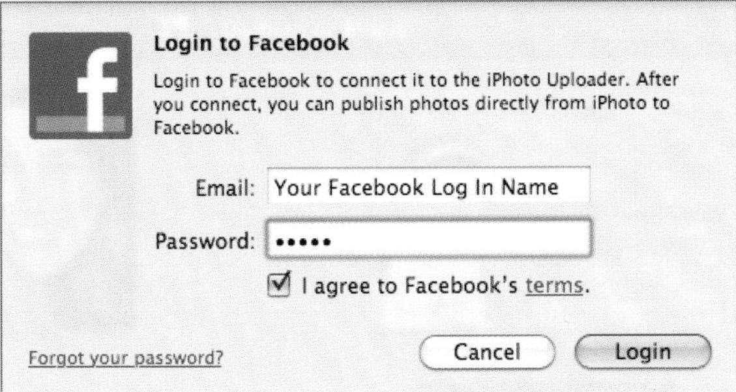

NOTE ▸ When you enter a user name and password for a Facebook, Flickr, or MobileMe account, the account is added to your Sharing Preferences so you will not have to log in again to share additional albums to these sites.

A side window slides in from the lower-right corner with a New Album button. The Source list also shows a Facebook album for the account you entered.

5 Click the New Album button to open the Publish window.

TIP To add photos to an existing album, log in to Facebook from iPhoto, select the photos, choose Share > Facebook from the toolbar, then select the existing album from the window.

6 Enter the album's name and who can view it, then click Publish.

TIP To remove a Facebook, Flickr, or MobileMe account from iPhoto, delete the account in the iPhoto Preferences Sharing tab.

When your photos are uploaded, you can select the Facebook album in the Source list to view all the albums you've posted to Facebook. In the Info pane, you can choose who can view the albums on Facebook.

TIP To delete an album from Facebook, Flickr, or MobileMe, select the published album in iPhoto, and then press the Delete key.

Now that you know how to share photos with Facebook, you can follow the same steps when you choose to share with either Flickr or MobileMe.

Differences in Posting to Facebook and Flickr

Flickr and Facebook each have unique benefits that may entice you to post your photos on one or the other. Here are the most important differences:

Flickr

- Flickr is the only site that will display iPhoto keywords.
- If the "Include location information for published photos" checkbox is selected in the Web section of Preferences, Places information will appear in Flickr.

Facebook

- If your friends and family comment on your Facebook photos, those comments will also appear in the iPhoto Info panel.
- If you've added an email address in the Faces view Info panel, when photos of that person are posted to Facebook, they are notified via a Facebook message.

Lesson Review

1. Describe a benefit that Facebook provides that the other two sharing photo gallery sites do not.
2. Where can you change the settings of an album you uploaded to Facebook, Flickr, or MobileMe?
3. In Faces, how do you reject a photo when the person iPhoto suggests is not correct?
4. Where do you find the button to create a new Smart Album based on the Places view?
5. How do you add a name to a face that has not been located by iPhoto?

Answers

1. If your friends and family comment on your photos in Facebook, those comments will appear in your iPhoto Info pane.

   Or, if you've added an email address in the Faces view Info panel, when photos of that person are posted to Facebook, he or she will be tagged and notified via a Facebook message.
2. When a Facebook, Flickr, or MobileMe gallery album is selected in the Source list, the Info pane will display a Change Settings button. Clicking this button will show the Album settings window. These settings are almost identical to the Album settings you find on your Facebook albums web page.

3. Double-click the photo you want to reject. Then, click Done.
4. When Places is selected in the Source list, the Smart Album button is found in the lower-right corner of the iPhoto window.
5. Display the photo in the Viewer. Click the Add Faces button, and position the rectangle over the subject's face. Finally, type the subject's name in the name tag.

4

Lesson Files	Pictures > ATS iPhoto Library: Greg and Caren's Wedding Event
Time	This lesson takes approximately 45 minutes to complete.
Goals	Understand a histogram Correct exposure Adjust contrast, saturation, and detail Improve highlights, shadows, and levels

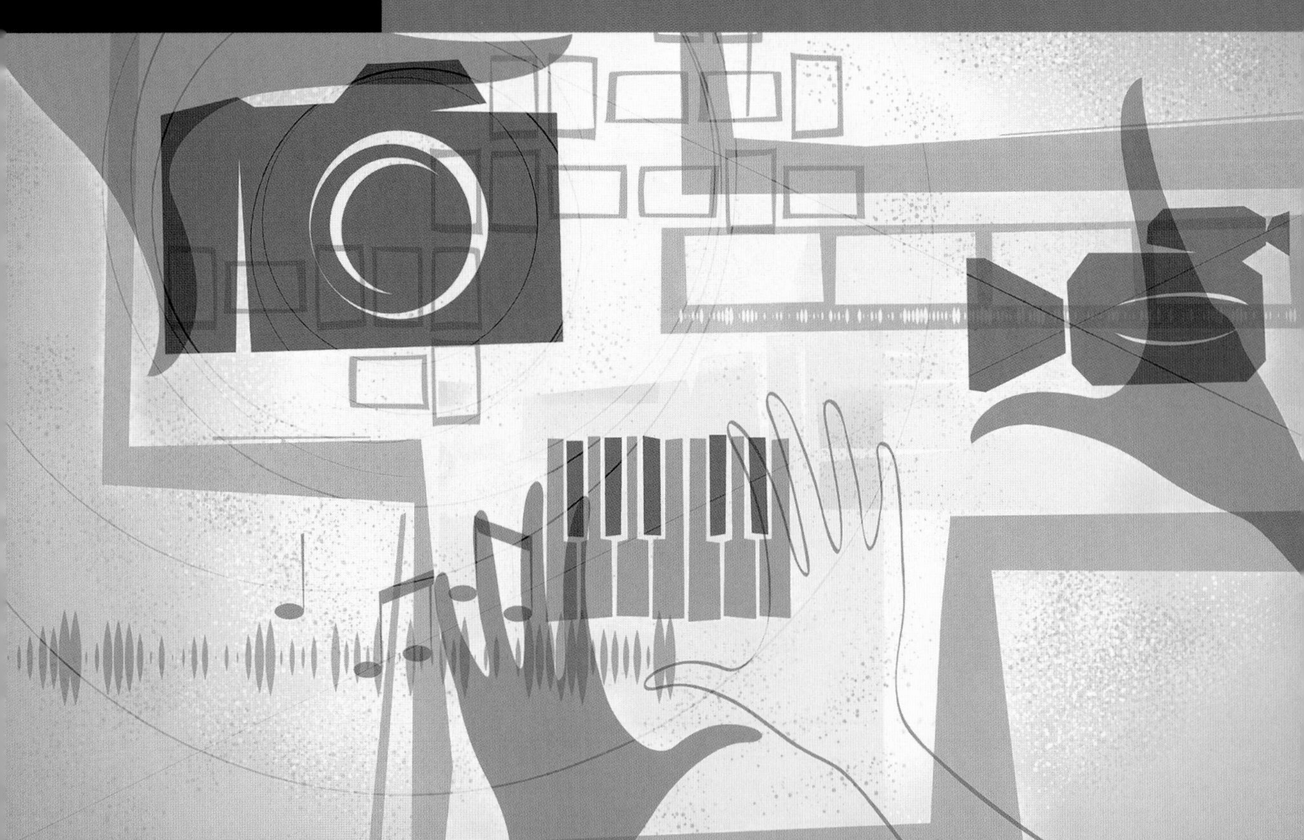

Lesson 4

Perfecting Your Pictures

In some cases, quick fixes and effects are all you will need to edit your photos. At other times, such as when you are creating a keepsake printed book, you may want a bit more control over the adjustments. iPhoto includes powerful tools for fixing common problems that have plagued almost everyone who has ever carried a camera.

In this lesson, you'll apply some of the advanced image adjustment tools in iPhoto to prepare photos for inclusion in a printed photo book that you'll create in Lesson 5.

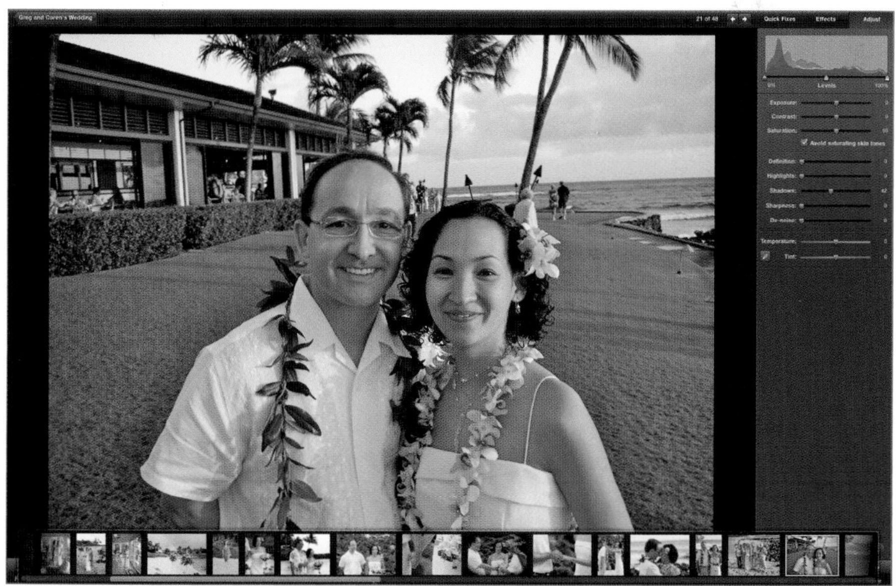

Understanding a Histogram

Before you begin making advanced adjustments to your photos, you must get familiar with a histogram because it's an important part of precision photo editing. A histogram is a graph that shows how much of your photo is in the dark range (shadows), the light range (highlights), and the middle range (midtones) of brightness.

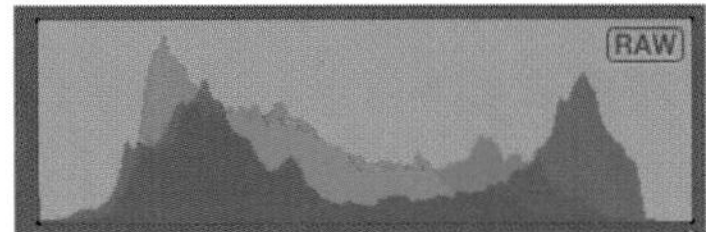

Let's look at some real histograms to see how they work.

1 Click the Full Screen button Full Screen. You'll use full-screen view because you can see the photo more clearly.

2 In the Source list, select Events, and double-click "Greg and Caren's Wedding."

   You'll find several perfect wedding photos here that you don't need to edit. The images you'll want to edit are flagged to make it easier to locate them.

3 Select the first photo in the Event.

4 Click the Edit button Edit and then click the Adjust tab. Examine the histogram and the photo.

The histogram can help you determine if your photo is "well exposed," which means that it has dark shadows and bright highlights, and that the majority of the image is located within the midtones. This scenic Napali coast photo is well exposed so the histogram extends broadly from left to the right, which indicates that the luminance range of this image includes very dark shadows and very bright highlights. That's a well-exposed photo.

5 In the thumbnails at the bottom of the screen, select the next photo to the right.

This photo is *underexposed.* The height of the graph to the left indicates that more of the image exists in the shadows than in any other range. Furthermore, the histogram graph doesn't extend all the way to the right, which shows that the photo has almost no highlights. This photo is not well exposed.

6 In the thumbnails at the bottom of the screen, select the next photo to the right.

This photo is *overexposed*. It is very bright all over with very few shadow areas. The histogram is very heavy on the right side to indicate the abundance of highlights. This is bad. If the graph is up against either the left or right edge, it means it is off the charts and the photo will suffer a loss of detail in the shadows or highlights, respectively.

Correcting Exposure

Now that you've detected exposure problems via the histogram, what can you do about them? The first and maybe most common adjustment is exposure. Exposure adjusts the balance of shadows and highlights, which influences how light or dark your photo looks. It's similar to setting your camera's exposure.

TIP If your camera can save pictures in RAW format, you will be able to adjust the exposure to a greater degree than if it saves in JPEG format.

You'll adjust this photo's exposure, and then see how the histogram reflects the adjustment.

1 In the Adjust tab, drag the Exposure slider left to about –1.15, until the graph is no longer crowded against the right edge.

2 Press and release the Shift key to compare the original photo and the adjusted photo.

3 Examine the histogram to observe the adjusted results.

   The photo no longer loses detail in the bright clouds. The graph is more centered overall, and consequently the photo is more pleasing. Using the same Exposure slider, you could also fix the underexposed photo. However, adjusting the exposure doesn't cure every problem, as you will see.

Original

Adjusted exposure

Adding Contrast

A similar problem to under- and overexposed photos is flat or low-contrast pictures in which highlights and shadows are dull and muddy. Adding contrast simultaneously extends the highlights to become brighter and the shadows to become darker.

1 In the thumbnails at the bottom of the screen, scroll to the far right and select the next-to-last flagged photo.

You may think this photo is perfect, but you would be mistaken. In the histogram the graph is squeezed into the midtone range, which indicates a low-contrast picture with no very bright or very dark areas. Using the Contrast slider, you can stretch the highlights and shadows to remedy this situation.

2 Drag the Contrast slider to about 70 to increase contrast and cause the histogram's graph to stretch wider.

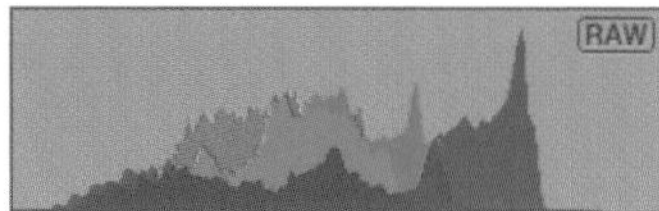

3 Press and release the Shift key to compare the original photo and the adjusted photo.

See what that tiny bit of contrast adjustment did? The photo has a greater range from shadows to highlights. Adding a bit of contrast is often the easiest way to improve those flat-looking pictures.

Original

Adjusted contrast

Adjusting Levels

The histogram includes Levels sliders that are among the most popular iPhoto tools. Using Levels sliders, you can individually fine-tune the shadows, midtones, and highlights to make precise and elegant corrections.

1 Drag the thumbnail slider to the right to select the last flagged photo.

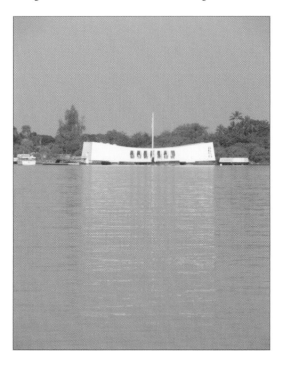

When using the Contrast slider, you do not have any control over how much of your photo gets darker or lighter because a contrast adjustment evenly modifies the darks and lights in your photo. With Levels sliders, you can independently set how much of your picture ends up in the darkest shadows or the brightest highlights, and even shift midtones. All of this will make more sense when you make those changes in the next exercise.

This photo has low contrast. If you drag the Contrast slider, the highlights in the monument will just get whiter, which will cause the photo to lose detail. You want to make the shadows darker without making the highlights lighter. That's what the Black Point Levels slider does for you. You'll find it against the left edge of the histogram.

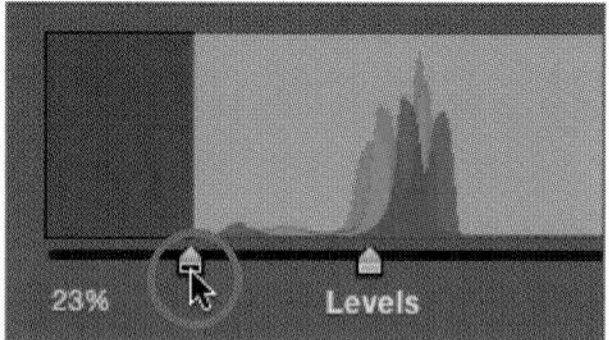

2 Note that a large gap exists between the slider and the darkest areas of the graph. Drag the Black Point Levels slider to a position under the darkest point of the graph.

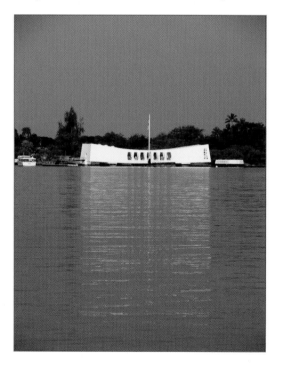

The shadow areas of the photo are now darker, which adds more contrast to the photo without altering the highlights. You could drag the White Point Levels slider on the right side of the histogram to lighten the highlights, but there is no need to do so in this photo.

NOTE ▶ When adjusting the Black Point Levels and White Point Levels sliders, watch your photo and decide whether it actually should have completely black or white areas. For instance, on a foggy day, the shadows probably won't be completely black, and the whites are probably duller, too.

When you adjusted the shadow levels, your midtones were shifted because you effectively shrunk the range of brightness. What previously was the midpoint has moved because you moved only the black point. Think of an accordion. When you expand the left side of the accordion, what is considered the middle of the instrument has moved as well. (I knew those accordion lessons would come in handy!) Unlike with an accordion, you can adjust the midtones levels without impacting the white or black points. This adjustment allows you to get a better balance between a darker or brighter picture without worrying about losing detail in your shadows and highlights.

3 Drag the Midtones Levels slider to the left, until the photo's brightness suits you.

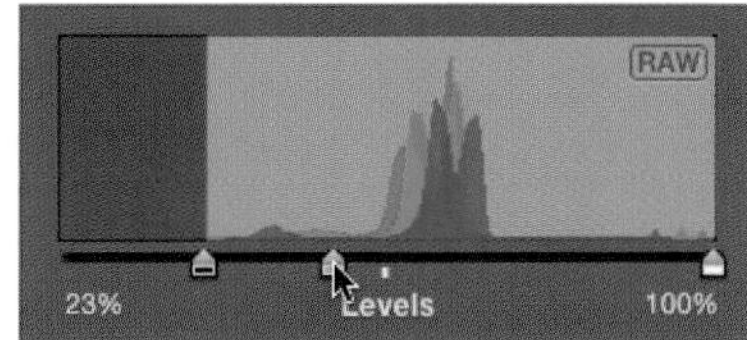

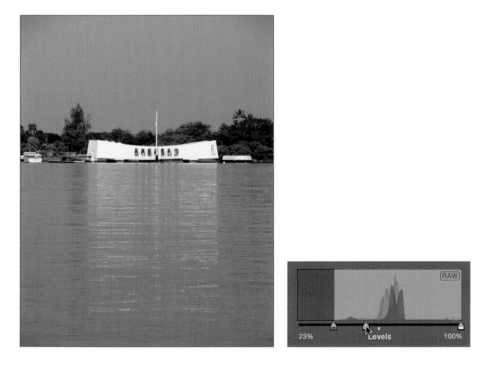

Making this midtone adjustment is mostly subjective. Set it however you think the photo looks the best.

The ability to modify your black point, white point, and midtones makes the Levels sliders a handy toolset to have around.

Increasing Color Saturation

Saturation is the intensity or vividness of color in your photos. Many people like the look of oversaturated colors, but oversaturation increases visual noise in your photos and has the nasty side effect of making skin tones look like the result of bad tanning creams. That being said, skies, grass, and water can sometimes benefit from a saturation boost.

1 Drag the thumbnail slider so you can select the fifth flagged photo from the left.

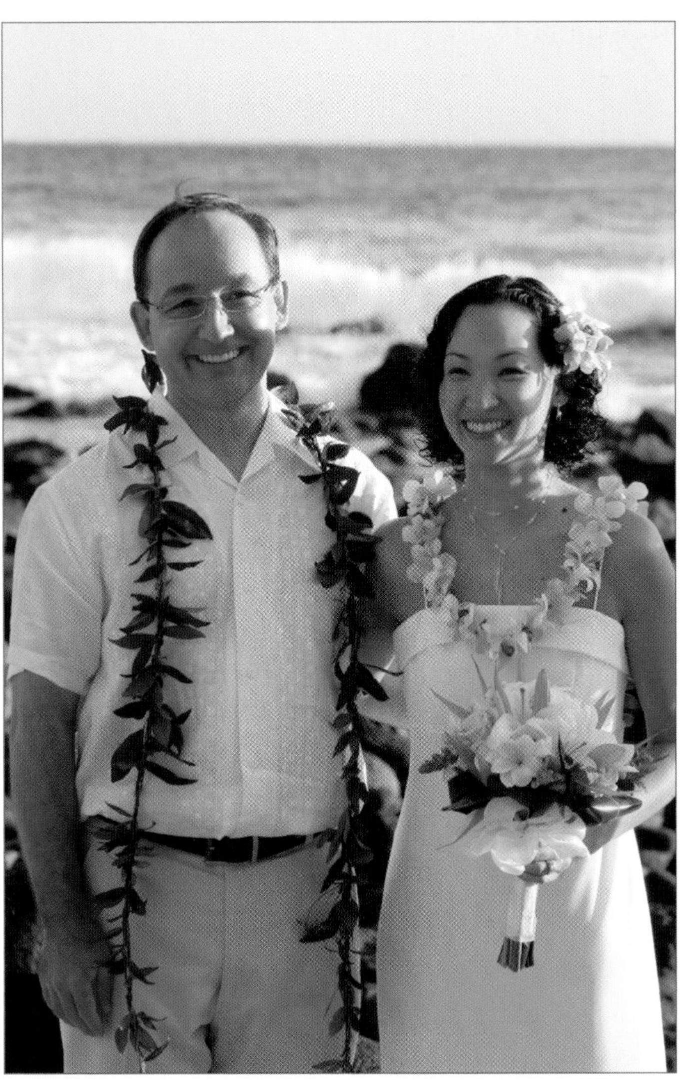

The couple looks great in this photo, but the sky and ocean look a bit faded and gray. Adding a bit of saturation can improve this.

2 Drag the Saturation slider to about 70.

This adjustment works well only because iPhoto limits skin tone saturation, by default. If you disable this option, you get a very different result.

3 Deselect the "Avoid saturating skin tones" checkbox. The couple becomes decidedly more orange in color. It's very unnatural.

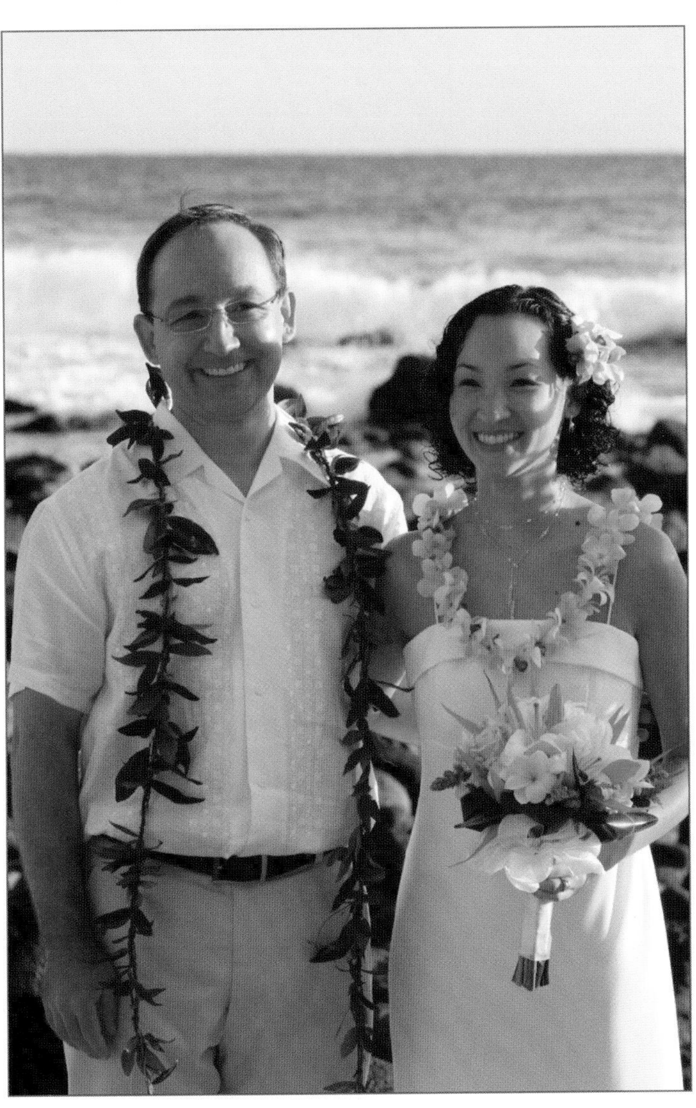

4 Select the "Avoid saturating skin tones" checkbox, and then press and release the Shift key to compare the original photo and the adjusted photo.

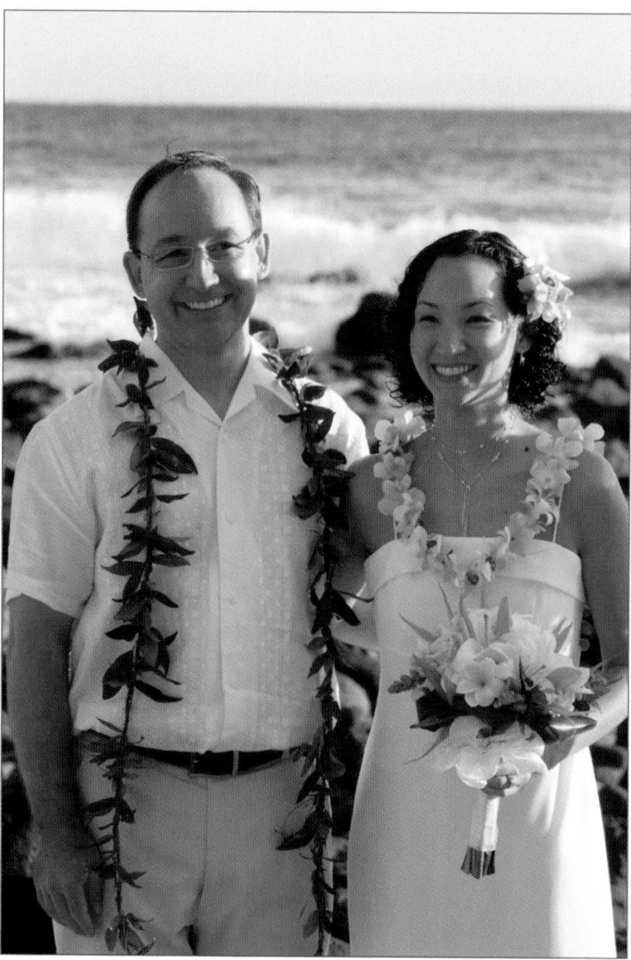

The adjustments you've learned are really the bread and butter of photo correction. The adjustments you'll learn next have less eye-popping impact and are used to address more-specific issues.

Applying Definition

Increasing definition adds pop to flat-looking pictures much like a contrast adjustment does. But definition does its magic by adding contrast in smaller areas rather than across the entire photo. That's why definition is sometimes referred to as *local contrast*.

1 Drag the thumbnail slider so you can select the third flagged photo from the right. There is so much detail in these carvings, but it doesn't show up as well as it could.

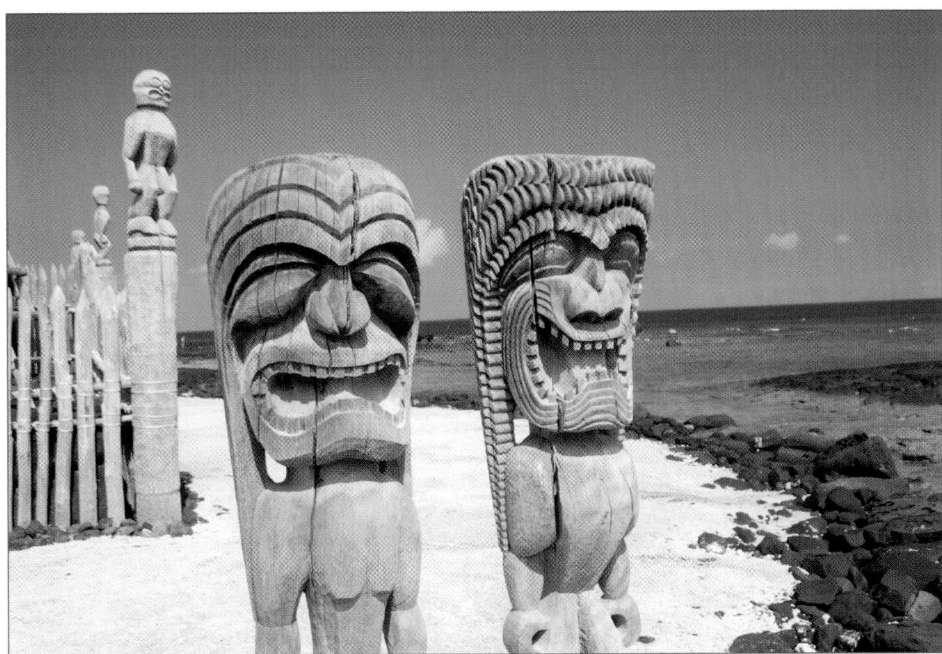

2 Drag the Definition slider to about 80.

It's as if someone wiped the screen clean of some mildew. You can see more detail in the wood carvings.

3 Compare the original photo and the adjusted photo.

Original

Adjusted definition

Although not every photo will benefit from increased definition, a definition adjustment can add noticeable clarity to landscape photographs. Definition is not always flattering in portraits because it can emphasize shadows under eyes and facial wrinkles.

Improving Highlight Detail

Adjusting the Highlights slider can increase the detail in highlights by slightly darkening the brightest areas of your image. This is helpful for restoring the textures of snow and clouds.

1 Drag the thumbnail slider so you can select the seventh flagged photo from the left.

2 Drag the Highlights slider to about 40 and watch as the sunset sky becomes more detailed and less like a wash of white.

   TIP Dragging the slider too far will cause the highlights to go flat.

3 Press and release the Shift key to compare the original photo and the adjusted photo.

Original

Adjusted highlights

By adjusting the Highlights slider, the bright areas of the sky and ocean now have better detail and more texture while leaving the shadowed couple unchanged.

Improving Shadow Detail

Adjusting the Shadows slider lightens the shadows, adding detail where there was none (or at least detail that you couldn't see).

1 In the thumbnails at the bottom of the screen, select the flagged photo of the couple.

   You can see harsh shadows on the left side of the faces. Increasing the Shadows slider a bit will fill in the light as if you had a fill flash when taking the picture.

2 Drag the Shadows slider to about 20.

3 Compare the original photo and the adjusted photo.

Original

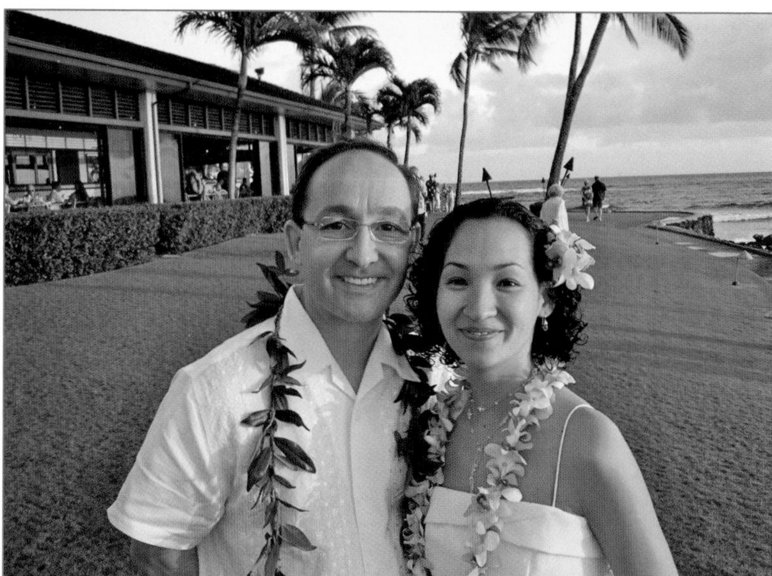

Adjusted shadows

The Highlights and Shadows sliders are great for trickier photos that don't respond well to Exposure or Levels controls. These sliders are simple to use, but the results are very impressive.

Applying Sharpening and Noise Reduction

One of the side effects of boosting shadows as you did in the previous exercise is that it often increases the visual noise in your picture. Although iPhoto has a De-noise tool, you must use it carefully because any noise reduction can tend to soften the focus of your picture. It's a cruel joke, isn't it? To get the best results, you'll usually want to apply sharpening and noise reduction at the same time to balance the two.

1 In the thumbnails at the bottom of the screen, select the fourth flagged photo from the right. This photo just has big black silhouettes of the hills in the foreground. It would be nice to see some detail in those hills.

2 Drag the Shadows slider to around 25 to reveal more detail in the dark hills.

When sharpening and reducing noise, it's often easier to zoom into a specific area of the photo and then make the adjustments.

3 Drag the Zoom slider to zoom into the photo. When you are zoomed into a photo, a Navigation window appears, in which you can pan to different parts of the picture.

4 Drag the small box inside the navigation window until you are viewing the parking lot in the lower-left corner of the viewer.

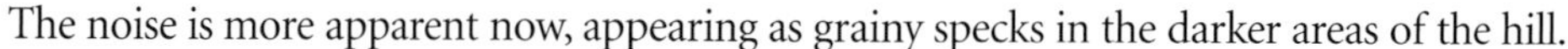
The noise is more apparent now, appearing as grainy specks in the darker areas of the hill.

5 Drag the De-noise slider to around 40.

A lot of the grainy noise goes away but the cars and the clouds have become less sharp. Now the fun begins. It's a back-and-forth process, adjusting the De-noise and Sharpness sliders until you get what you consider an acceptable result.

6 Drag the Sharpness slider to around 35. Watch the cars in the parking lot and the clouds to see some sharpness return to the photo.

7 Drag the Zoom slider all the way to the left to view the entire picture.

You can apply sharpness to many other photos to reduce softness. Softness can happen because of the zoom on your camera, the digital processing within the camera, or just the environment where you are taking the picture. Noise, on the other hand, can appear when you are taking pictures in very low light or when you increase the Shadows slider value. All these things work against getting a perfect photo, but with a little trial and error, the De-noise and Sharpness sliders can help fix very difficult problems.

Adjusting White Balance

Similar to using the Warmer and Cooler effects as you did in Lesson 2, dragging the Temperature controls adjusts the overall photo tint. Without going into a science lesson, this color value is called *temperature* because it alters a camera's color temperature setting, also called white balance. Correcting white balance/temperature problems can be done automatically by iPhoto or manually.

1 In the thumbnails at the bottom of the screen, select the fourth flagged photo. This image has a blue tone. You'll fix the temperature in this photo automatically by using the eyedropper.

2 In the Temperature controls, click the eyedropper tool.

When selecting an area in the photo with the eyedropper, look for an area that should be a medium gray tone. Medium gray could be a cement sidewalk, the dark shadowed, creased areas of someone's white shirt, or a wall that's painted gray. Just don't pick your brightest whites or your darkest shadows.

3 Click the ceiling of the photo.

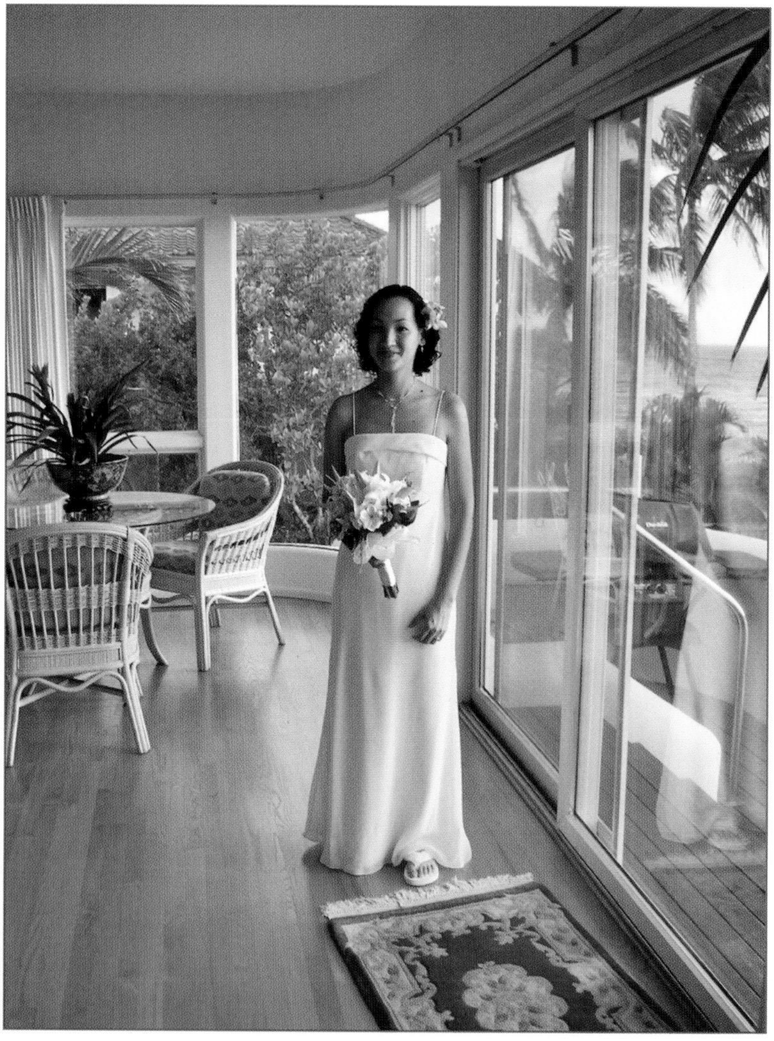

4 Compare the original photo with the adjusted photo.

If your personal taste is for warmer- or cooler-looking pictures, you can fine-tune the color using the Temperature and Tint sliders.

Your photos are now looking great and deserve to be preserved for posterity. You'll do just that in the next lesson by assembling them into a photo book to be printed and bound as a memento of this important event.

Lesson Review

1. If the majority of a histogram graph is up against the right side, what does it indicate about the picture?
2. What's the difference between exposure and contrast?
3. What is a side effect of increasing the De-noise slider?
4. True or false: The Shadows adjustment darkens the shadows in a photo.
5. What tone are you looking to click when setting the white balance/temperature with the eyedropper?

Answers

1. This photo is overexposed. It is generally bright with few shadow areas. If the graph is up against the right edge, it is off the charts and there is a loss of detail in the brightest parts of the photo.
2. Exposure adjusts how light and dark the photo looks. Contrast extends the highlights to become brighter and the shadows to become darker.
3. It softens the photo.
4. False. Adjusting the Shadows slider lightens the shadows, adding detail where there was none (or at least detail that you couldn't see).
5. When selecting an area in the photo with the eyedropper, look for an area that is a medium gray tone in the photo. Just don't pick your brightest whites or your darkest shadows.

5

Lesson Files Pictures > ATS iPhoto Library: Greg and Caren's Wedding Event

Time This lesson takes approximately 45 minutes to complete.

Goals Create a keepsake book

Edit photos in a book

Order books

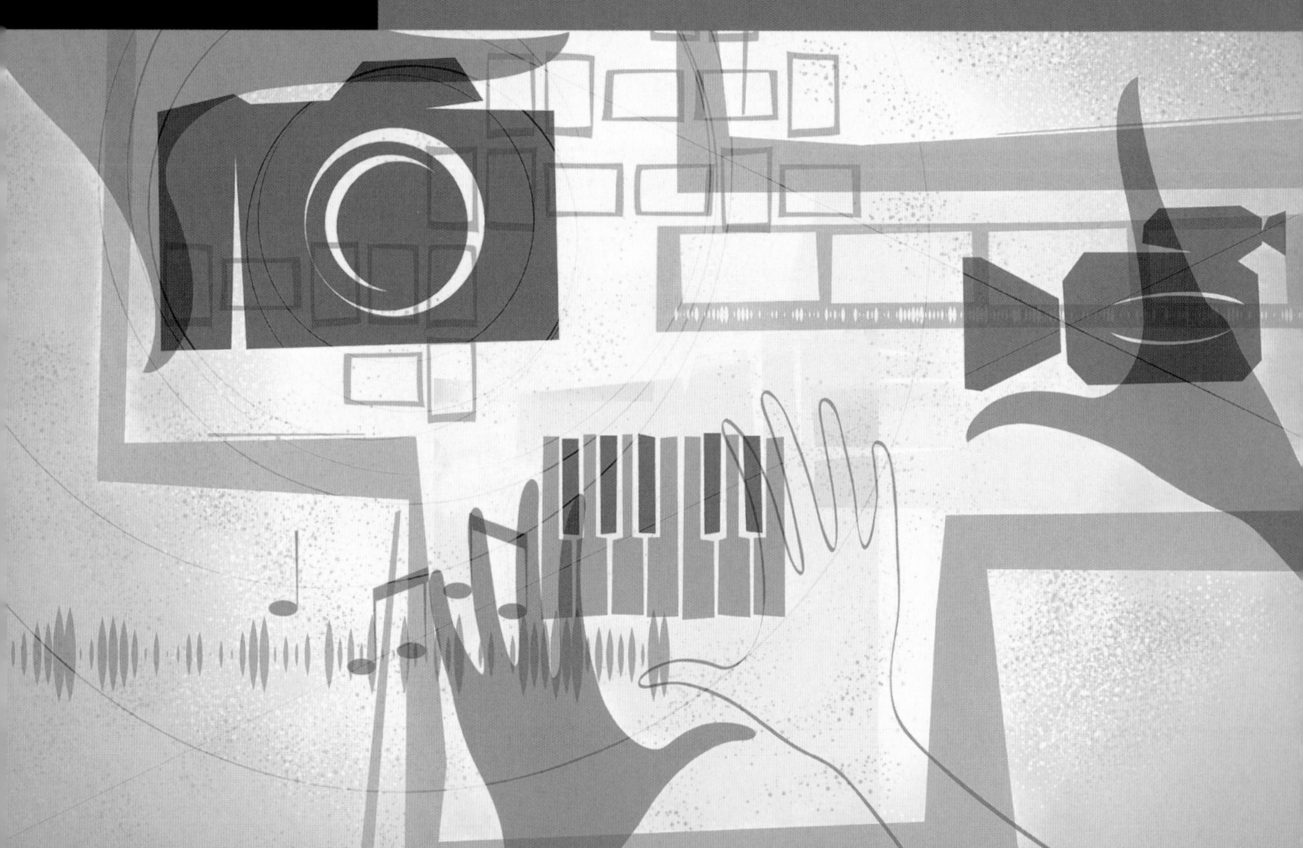

Lesson **5**

Designing a Photo Book

Weddings, graduations, and even some Irish wakes are times of celebration. They are times you want to keep with you forever. Smaller, yet no less cherished occasions like birthdays and family vacations are also times you'd like to remember. Making a printed coffee table book may seem like something far fetched or too expensive for you to do, but iPhoto makes it possible and very affordable to design and publish a wide range of photo books. In this lesson you'll take your perfected pictures to the next level by designing a professional-looking photo book, so you can enjoy your special occasions one vibrant page at a time.

Creating a Book Layout

In this exercise, you'll create a beautiful keepsake book from within iPhoto. You can quickly place photos into any one of the Apple-designed book themes, then professionally print it using Apple print services and have it delivered right to your house.

Exploring Book Themes

To begin creating a book, you'll select an Event that contains the photos you want to place in your book, and then select a theme.

1 While in full-screen view, click the "Greg and Caren's Wedding" button at the upper-left corner of the screen to display all the photos in this Event.

2 Press Command-Shift-A to ensure that no photos are selected.

TIP You can select which photos will be used in the book or leave photos unselected to include the entire Event or album in the book.

3 At the bottom of the screen, click Create > Book.

The Book Theme view fills the screen with several designs. In addition to selecting a theme, you can choose whether to produce a hardcover, softcover, or wire-bound book.

In the lower left of the viewing area you can also select a size for the book. Because this is a wedding book, you may want to make it in the Extra-large size.

4 In the lower-left corner of the viewing area, click the XL button.

NOTE ▸ The Extra-large book type is available only in hardcover. The Medium and Small book types are available only in softcover. The Large book type is available in both soft- and hardcover.

5 To choose a theme, click the book theme preview to the right of the centered theme in the viewing area.

Selecting a book to the right or left brings that selection to the center. The theme name is shown with its pricing information.

NOTE ▸ The printing cost is estimated for a 20-page book using the current size and style. The price is displayed in the lower-left corner of the viewing area. The Apple printing service is available in the USA, Canada, Japan, and selected countries in Europe and Asia.

6 Click the theme to the right until Modern Lines is the centered theme. This is a simple, elegant theme that will work nicely for these pictures.

You've selected your contents and theme and you're ready to make your photo book.

7 Click Create.

The book layout appears with all your photos presented. The pages are displayed from left to right and top to bottom with the cover placed in the upper-left corner.

Although a book is initially formatted with pictures on each page, you can change the photos, the layout, and even the theme at anytime. In the next few exercises, you'll modify a few of these options.

Changing Pictures on Pages

With all the pages of the book displayed in front of you, you can scan over them to see if you might want to make some changes.

1 Double-click the book's front cover.

   The photo of the Bride and her Maid of Honor may not be the best photo for the cover of the book. Let's look for an alternative.

2 Click the Photos button to display all the photos in the Event.

3 Scroll down to find the photo of the couple's hands.

TIP Hover the pointer over a photo in the side pane to see a photo's number.

4 Drag the photo on top of the current cover shots to replace it.

The cover photo highlights in yellow when you are directly over it. When you release the mouse button, your photo book has a new cover.

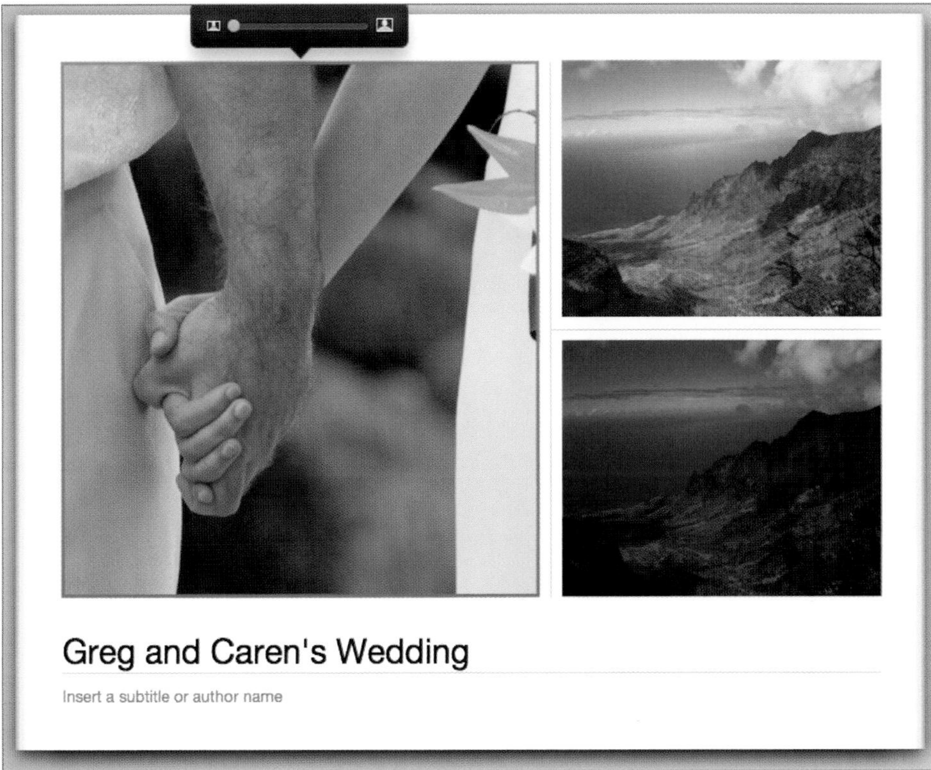

Selecting New Page Layouts

As you browse the pages, you'll notice that some have multiple photos. These page layouts can be changed to place fewer or more photos per page.

1 On the cover, click the white background to deselect the current photo. A blue highlight surrounds the cover page and the Design pop-up menu appears.

2 From the Design pop-up menu, click the Layout menu to the left to view the cover page layout options. A blue outline highlights the current selection.

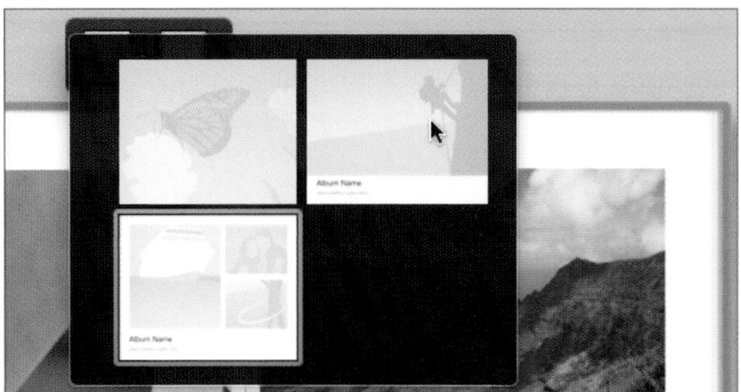

3 Click the cover layout in the upper-right corner to create a single photo cover with an area for a book title. The cover changes to a single-photo layout with text.

You have even more choices when changing page layouts.

4 Click the All Pages button to return to All Pages view.

5 Double-click page three to view it full-screen.

This page includes three photos, two of which are identical to the photo on page two. The photo of the couple is a good choice to fill this page.

6 From the Design pop-up menu at the top of page three, choose "1 Photo."

You have three available layouts for single-photo pages. In the upper left is the "full-bleed" option in which the photo covers the page without a border.

7 Click the "full-bleed" option. Two photos are removed from the page and one photo fills it. Unfortunately, it's the wrong picture!

8 To locate the removed photos, at the top of the Photo pane choose Show > Unplaced photos. This will display all the photos from the Event that have not been used in the book.

9 Drag the unused photo of the couple onto the photo on page three to replace it.

The couple's photo now fills the entire page and it looks perfect next to the scenic photo on page two. Let's go through a few more pages and see if there are other changes to make.

Adding, Deleting, and Rearranging Pages

When all your Event photos are placed in the book, you may find that some photos are too similar or just seem out of place. To address that situation, you can delete pages, add new ones, and rearrange pages at will.

1 Click the All Pages button to return to All Pages view.

   Page five looks a bit out of place. It is sandwiched between pages featuring indoor photos before the wedding. Let's remove page five to group together all the pre-wedding, indoor photos.

2 Select page six and then press the Delete key.

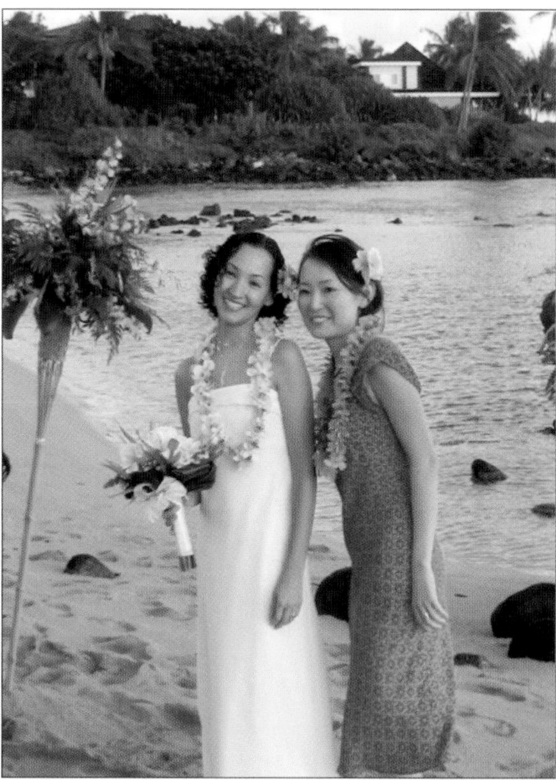

3 When a dialog warns you about having an even number of pages, click Yes. This warning will appear even when you have an odd number of pages.

The middle of the book has a number of dolphin photos that could be reduced, and near the end, a page of steaming volcanic rock is interesting but not central to the wedding.

4 Click page 17 (the dolphins) to select it.

5 Command-click page 19 (more dolphins) and page 27 (black volcanic rock) to select them.

6 Press the Delete key, and in the warning dialog, click Yes.

You can add pages just as easily as you delete them.

7 Under the Photos pane, click the Add Page button to insert a blank page after the currently selected page.

You can rearrange pages to place them in a better order. Let's use this page as a good transition between the wedding photos and the honeymoon vacation photos.

8 Drag the blank new page between pages 16 and 17.

As you drag the blank page, the pages separate to indicate where the page can be placed.

9 When the page can be located between pages 16 and 17, release the mouse button.

Now you have a page that divides the book between the wedding and the honeymoon photos. Because this wedding involved some unique travel, placing a map on the page could act as a nice divider.

Customizing Maps

Some themes can integrate maps into your book. If your photos already have locations assigned to them, the map can automatically be placed on the page, or you can manually add a map and locations.

1 Double-click the blank page 17.

2 In the Design pop-up menu, choose Map, and then choose the Map layout.

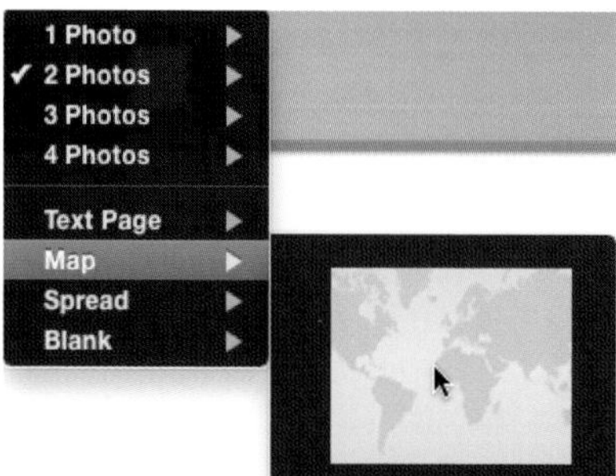

A map fills the page. Because these photos have places assigned already, locations are highlighted on the map.

3 In the viewer, select the map page.

4 Click the Design button.

You can customize the map in the Design pane. Let's first choose the style of map.

5 Click the second map in the top row to choose that map style.

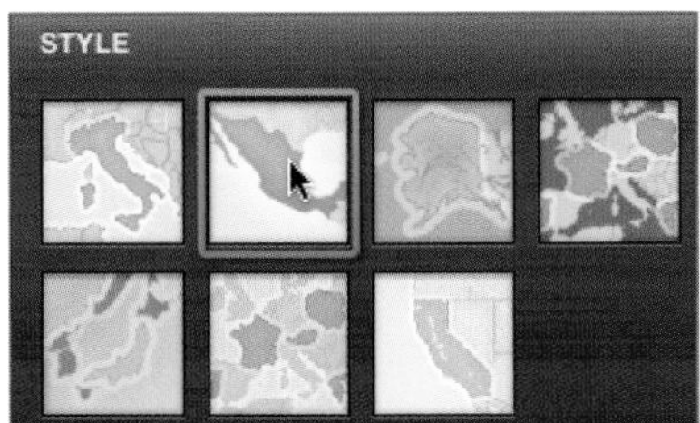

You can add and remove locations in the Places list. The big island Hawaii is the only one with two locations on it. You'll remove the second location to make this map more consistent with the others.

6 In the Places list, deselect Honaunau to remove it from the map.

TIP You can add or remove a location by clicking the Add/Remove Location buttons (+/-) under the Places list.

The map shows points where the couple visited, but you can do better than that. You can add travel lines to show the route they traveled.

7 From the Lines pop-up menu, choose Curved.

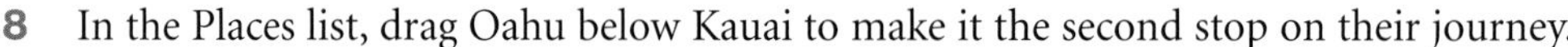

8 In the Places list, drag Oahu below Kauai to make it the second stop on their journey.

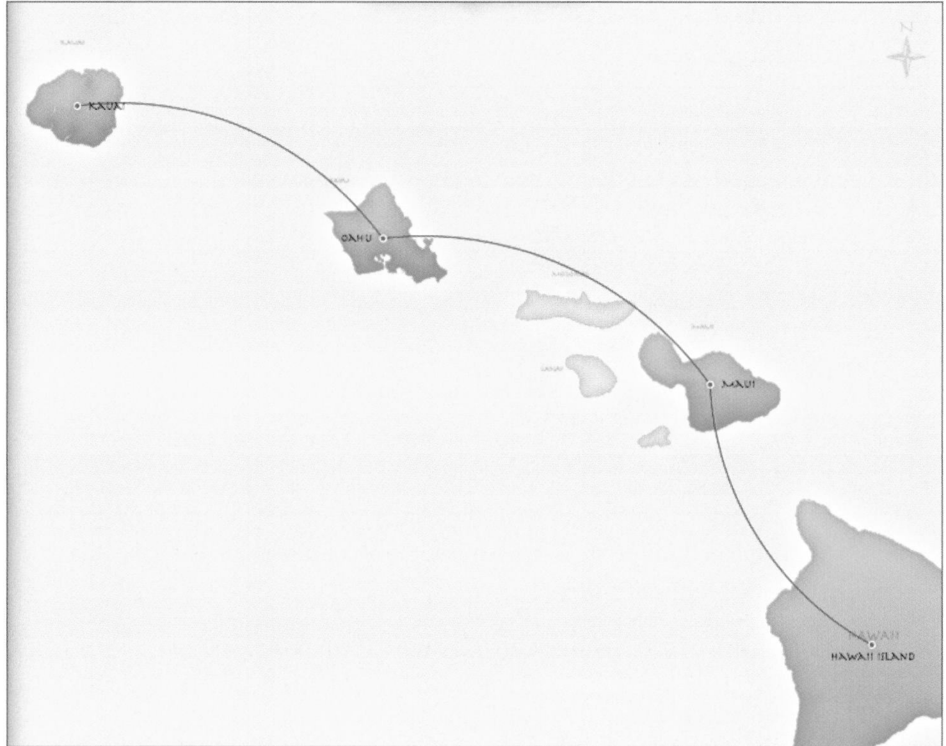

9 Click the All Pages button to return to All Pages view.

Using the other options in the Design pane, you can add a title to the map or remove some of the existing map details. It's a great way to supplement your photos with additional visual interest.

Framing Photos on a Page

With your basic book structure in place, it's time to perform a final image check. You'll see that some photos are used more than once and some don't fit comfortably on the page.

1 Double-click page 10.

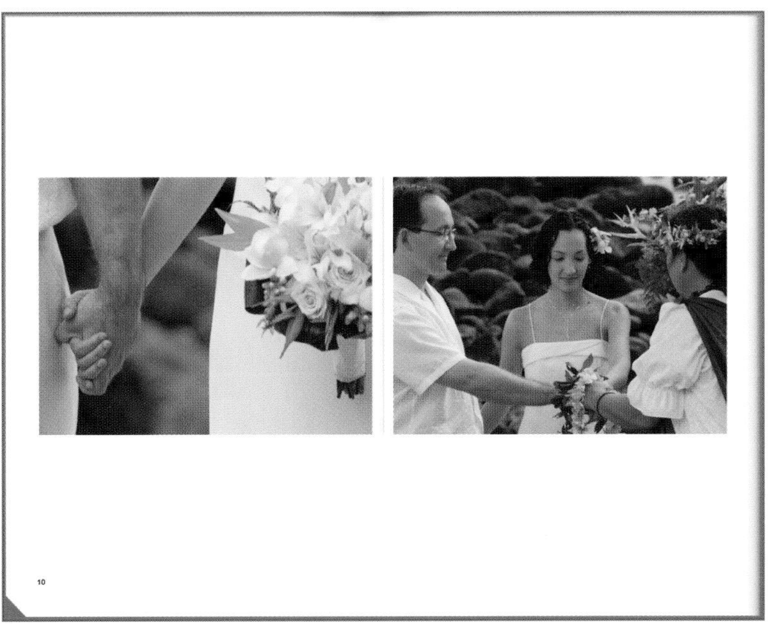

The photo on the left is already used on the cover. Although you can use a photo as many times as you like in a book, you have so many beautiful pictures that you don't need to use a photo twice.

In the Design pane you can see the same layout options as in the Design pop-up menu. You can change the layouts in the Design pane.

TIP Selecting text in a book will change the Design pane to show text formatting options.

2 In the Design pane, choose Layout > Spread.

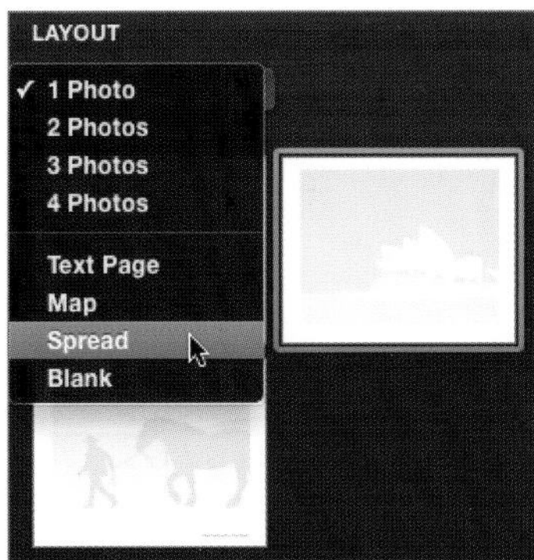

Spread extends a single photo across two pages. For very special photos this can create a stunning presentation.

3 Click the first spread in the list to apply it to the two pages. iPhoto uses the first photo on a page when it creates a spread; unfortunately, you want to use the second photo for your spread.

4 Click the Photos button to open the Photos pane, and from the Show pop-up menu, choose Unused Photos, if it isn't already selected.

NOTE ▶ You may have to reselect Unused Photos to refresh the display.

5 Drag the photo of the Groom,Bride, and Minister onto the Spread page in the viewer.

Well, the thought was nice but the execution leaves a bit to be desired. The page crease is right over the bride's face and the groom's head is mostly cut off.

6 In the viewer, drag down on the photo to reposition it until the top of the groom's head is no longer cropped off the page.

7 To move the bride out from under the crease, drag the Image Scale slider slightly to the right to increase the size of the image.

8 Drag the photo right to reposition the crease between the bride and groom.

9 Continue to reposition the image until you are happy with the framing.

When you are done, you'll have a nicely-framed photo that spans two pages.

You'll often adjust a picture's framing when fixing pages of your book.

Editing Photos in a Book

When you have all your photos inserted and arranged in your book, you may find that you want to tweak individual photos to increase their impact in context. To do this, some of the effects you used in a previous lesson can be applied directly to the photos in your book. In addition, you have instant access to all the Edit pane adjustments.

1. With the photo spread on pages 10 and 11 selected, in the Design pane, click the B&W effect.

   The photo changes to black and white. Applying the effects from the Design pane will not modify this photo outside of the photo book. If you need to perform more adjustments, you have access to all the iPhoto editing options.

2. In the Design pane, click the Edit Photo button to open the photo in Edit view.

   Any effects that you apply from the book's Design pane do not show up in the Edit view. The rule is that anything you do to a photo within the photo book is confined to the photo book. Anything done to a photo outside the photo book also affects the photo within the context of the photo book.

3. In the Effects tab, click the Vignette effects, and then click four times on the Edge Blur effect.

4. Double-click the photo to return to the wedding book.

You now have a soft, dreamy black and white photo that highlights this special moment.

Ordering Books

When you are done, you can use the Apple print service to have this book professionally printed. The end result is a vibrant, high-quality publication delivered to your doorstep. In this exercise, you'll use an Apple account in preparation for placing a book order.

> **NOTE** ▶ If you don't actually want to set up the account now, just follow along with the steps in this exercise.

1. In the viewer, click Buy Book.

   iPhoto quickly examines the book, and if it finds any problems such as unchanged placeholder text, it displays an alert.

2. Click Continue. (Although if you were preparing a real book order, you would fix any displayed problems.)

   The Your Order window appears with the price and shipping options.

   > **NOTE** ▶ If you are not ready to purchase the book, you can access any book or card you create by clicking the Projects button in full-screen view or the book or card in the Source list.

3. Enter your zip code, and from the Ship Via pop-up menu, choose a shipping method. The cost of your order is adjusted to include the price of the shipping method you've chosen.

4. If the order looks correct, click the Check Out button.

   The next window will require your Apple ID login information, the same ID you use in iTunes.

   After you log in, the final order form is shown with the shipping address and your payment method displayed.

5. If you currently wish to buy a photo book of someone else's wedding, click Place Order. However, you'll probably just want to click Cancel.

When you place an actual order, iPhoto uploads all of the photos and sends the book to the print service. In a few days, your book will be on its way.

Lesson Review

1. How do you start creating a photo book?
2. How do you locate all the unplaced photos in a book?
3. Do you change a page's layout from the Design pop-up menu, or in the Design pane?
4. Where are the book effects located?
5. True or false: The locations on a map in a book can only come from photos that have been assigned a location in Places.

Answers

1. Select your photos (or an Event or album) and then click the Create button in the toolbar.
2. In the photo's pane, choose Show > Unplaced Photos.
3. You can change a page layout in both places.
4. Book effects are located in the Design pane.
5. False. You can manually add locations to a map in a book.

6

Lesson Files	Pictures > ATS iPhoto Library: “Sara goes sky diving” Event
Time	This lesson takes approximately 45 minutes to complete.
Goals	Watch an instant slideshow Create a slideshow album Customize individual slides

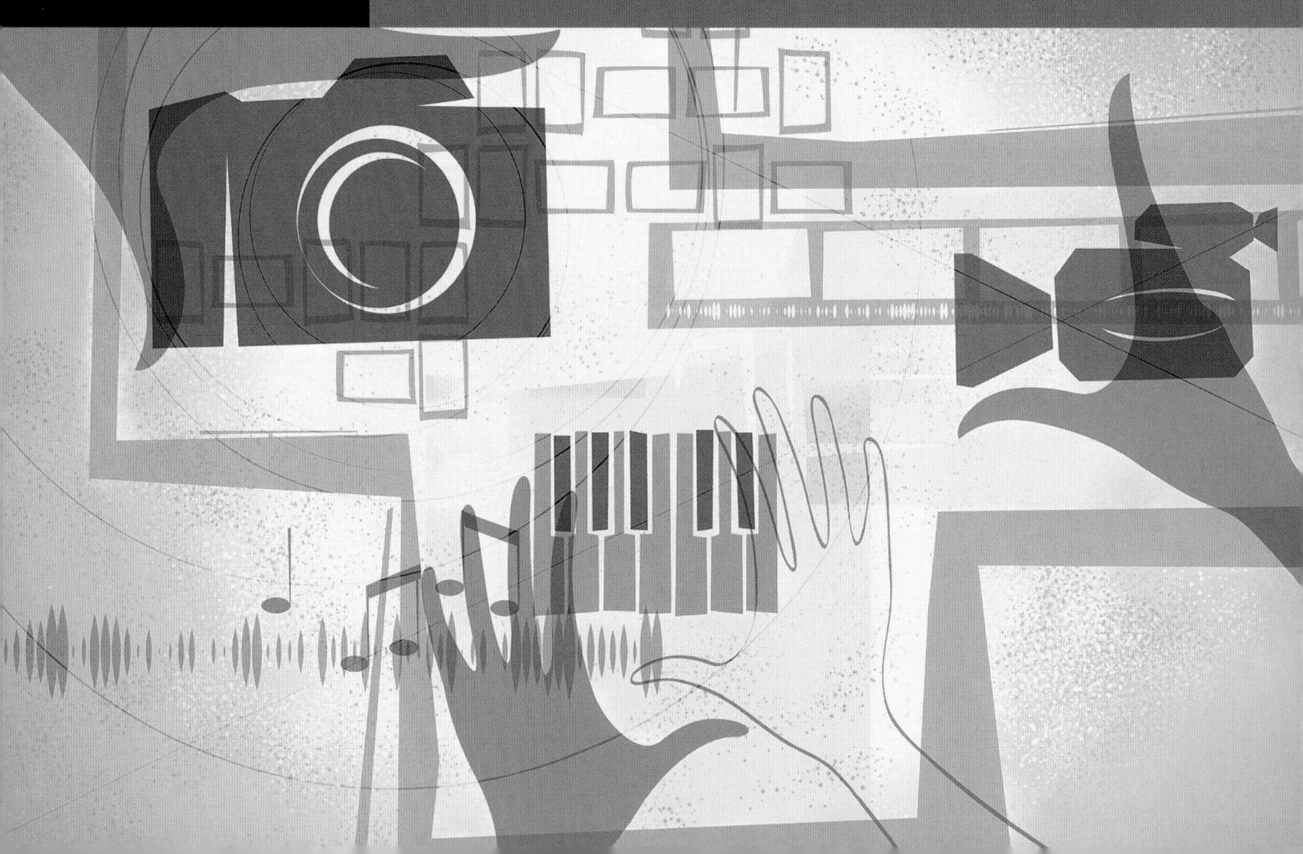

Lesson **6**

Making Photos Move with Slideshows

As great as online sharing and printed photo books are, they lack the cinematic excitement of a movie. Flipping pages or scrolling from shot to shot can never equal the immediacy of combining moving imagery, dramatic cuts from one visual to the next, and an emotional musical score.

Instead of sitting back and casually browsing your photos, you can go Hollywood and put them into a slideshow. Slideshows can assemble photos, videos, and music into high-impact multimedia presentations that you can play for friends at home, place online, or display on your Apple mobile device.

Using Slideshow Presets and Albums

You can create two kinds of slideshows in iPhoto: instant slideshows and saved slideshows. Instant slideshows are the quickest and easiest way to showcase your photos but can be viewed only within iPhoto and cannot be saved. Saved slideshows—come on, take a guess...Right!—*can* be saved in your library like an album or a book. You can export saved slideshows to your iPod or the web, or you can burn them to disc using iDVD.

Using Instant Slideshow

An instant slideshow is the easiest and fastest way to put your photos into a slideshow. It's perfect for impromptu gatherings when people are visiting and you want to quickly show off some photos, yet still make it a special viewing.

1 From Events, select the "Sara goes sky diving" Event. This Event contains exciting photos of the sky dive and a few video clips as well. You will use this event to create your slideshow.

TIP Photos in the Event are sorted in the order they will play in the slideshow.

2 In the toolbar, click the Slideshow button to create an instant slideshow. A slideshow panel appears, containing the slideshow themes you can choose.

3 From the Slideshow Themes, click Origami.

TIP Moving your pointer over any of the theme thumbnails will play a preview of that theme.

Themes combine a visual style with music. Although you could change a few options in the tabs at the top of the Slideshow window, the point of the instant slideshow is to create a slideshow in an instant.

4 Click Play to begin the instant slideshow. The screen goes dim and the slideshow plays full screen.

5 After the three video clips play, press the Esc (Escape) key to close the instant slideshow.

It's a great-looking theme with music that fits well with the fun they must have had sky diving (ahem, no thanks). As you watched the instant slideshow, you may have noticed a few things you wouldn't mind changing. You might also decide that it would be nice to share the show with friends or family members. Although you can't share instant slideshows, you can however create a saved slideshow that will do that and more.

Creating a Slideshow Album

Creating a saved slideshow is similar to creating a photo book. You begin by deciding which photos you want to use, and then you click the Create button in the toolbar.

1. From your Events, double-click the "Sara goes sky diving" Event. The Event's photos are shown in the viewing area.

   TIP Slideshows can use photos from albums or Smart Albums, as well as Events.

2. Press Command-A to select all the photos displayed in the viewing area.

3. Scroll down and Command-click the last video clip to deselect it.

   You can select which photos and video clips are included in the slideshow. The last video clip was a little long for the show; by deselecting it, the clip will not be included in the slideshow.

4. Click the Create button, and from the pop-up menu, choose Slideshow. A saved slideshow is created in the Source list with the name of the Event.

   The viewer now shows the first photo in the slideshow, and the photo browser at the top of the viewer shows the slides in the order they will appear.

   TIP You can double-click the text on the first slide to change it.

   The toolbar includes buttons for the slideshow options.

5 Click the Themes button, and choose Shatter.

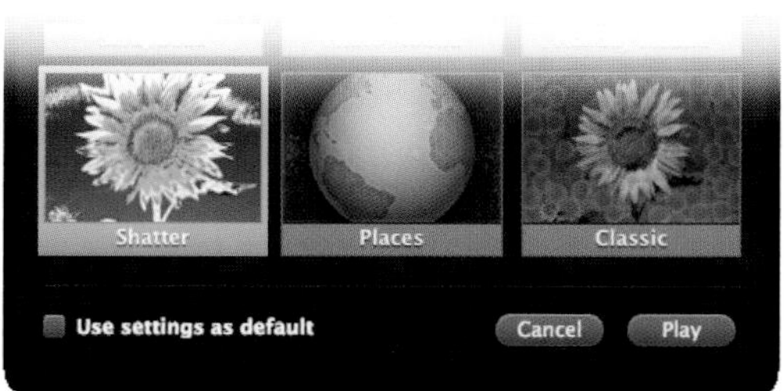

6 Click the Choose button to set the Shatter theme and close the window.

7 Click Play to begin the slideshow. The screen dims, and the slideshow plays full screen.

8 After the two video clips play, press the Esc key to close the saved slideshow.

You could decide that you are finished and export your slideshow now, but a few customizations could make your slideshow much more engaging.

Rearranging Slideshow Photos

Although you selected the pictures when you created the slideshow, you can delete and rearrange photos and video clips in the slideshow to improve the flow of your presentation.

> **NOTE ▶** You can add new photos to a slideshow by dragging them from your iPhoto library onto the saved slideshow in the Source list.

1 Scroll the photo browser to the right to view the last two video clips.

2 Double-click the last video clip to play it in the viewer. This clip is noisy and doesn't have much interesting in it. It's probably better to leave this one out of the slideshow.

3 In the upper left of the window, click the "Sara goes sky diving" button to return to the slideshow.

4 Click the last video clip and then press Delete to remove it from the saved slideshow.

The second-to-last video clip now becomes the last video clip and is selected and displayed in the viewer. This video clip is a nice introduction to Sara and the whole adventure, making it fit better near the start of the slideshow.

5 Drag the video clip to the left until the photo browser begins to scroll.

6 Place the video clip as the fourth item in the slideshow, after the photo of the three brave sky divers.

7 At the bottom of the iPhoto window, click the Play button.

That, my friends is a rockin' good slideshow! It took almost no work at all, and you ended up with something that's really fun to watch. But you can do a lot more!

Changing Settings and Options

Although the selection and presentation order of photos are probably the most important considerations in a slideshow, many other options can be applied to enhance the show's impact. While you can use the buttons at the bottom of the screen to change themes and music, the upcoming exercises cover options found in the Settings window.

Setting the Aspect Ratio

Because saved slideshows can be shown on a variety of devices, such as iPads, iPhones, computer screens, and HDTVs—all of which have different shapes and sizes—you may need to set the aspect ratio for your slideshow based on the device that will display it. In the next exercise, you'll format this slideshow for DVD delivery on a standard TV.

1 In the toolbar, click the Settings button.

2 In the Settings window, choose iPad/TV (4:3) from the Aspect Ratio pop-up menu.

3 Close the Settings window.

The viewer now shows the 4:3 aspect ratio and crops the pictures to fit them correctly within the frame. If you forget to set the aspect ratio, you'll still be able to play your slideshow on various devices but you will see letterbox or black columns on the sides of the movie. Next you'll explore a few more options before you burn this to a DVD.

Changing Themes and Music

Just as easily as you selected a theme, you can also change a theme at any time. Applying new themes to a slideshow can alter its entire feeling. The Ken Burns theme has the most options, so you'll try using it.

1 At the bottom of the iPhoto window, click the Themes button, and choose the Ken Burns theme from the dialog that appears.

NOTE ▶ Why is it called Ken Burns effect? Ken Burns is a filmmaker famous for his documentaries on PBS. Many of his documentaries use archival photographs, and he popularized a technique that focuses attention and creates movement by panning and zooming the camera on the photographs.

2 Click Choose.

3 Click the Preview button to preview the slideshow in the iPhoto window.

4 Click the Preview button again to stop the preview after you have watched a few slides go by.

The Ken Burns effect adds a nice, easy zooming and panning across the photos, but the music that comes with it doesn't fit the sky diving action.

5 At the bottom of the iPhoto window, click the Music button, select the **Incident at Gate 7** song, and then click Choose.

TIP From the Source menu in the Music Settings window, you can choose songs from your iTunes library.

As you play your presentation, you'll notice that the pacing feels more laid back and easy going. It's not just the music that does that, each theme has a default duration for photos. In the settings, you can set a new duration for all of your photos or just selected ones.

Changing Settings on a Single Photo

In a slideshow, you control the viewer's attention and focus by adjusting the timing of the entire slideshow, as well as individual slides.

1 Click the Settings button. The Settings window opens with the All Slides tab selected. Any setting in this window is applied to all the slides in the slideshow.

2 Click the This Slide tab. This tab has settings that are applied to only the selected photo.

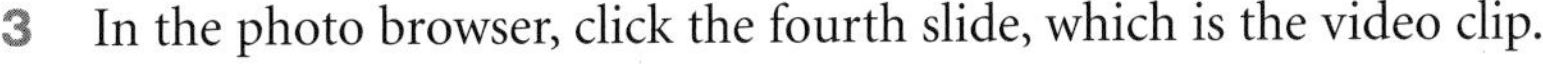

3 In the photo browser, click the fourth slide, which is the video clip.

This is a special section of your show. Not only is it a video clip, but it is also a transition point. Every photo after this shows the sky divers up in the air. To emphasize this change in scenery, you'll add a special transition between this video clip slide and the next one.

4 Select the Transition checkbox.

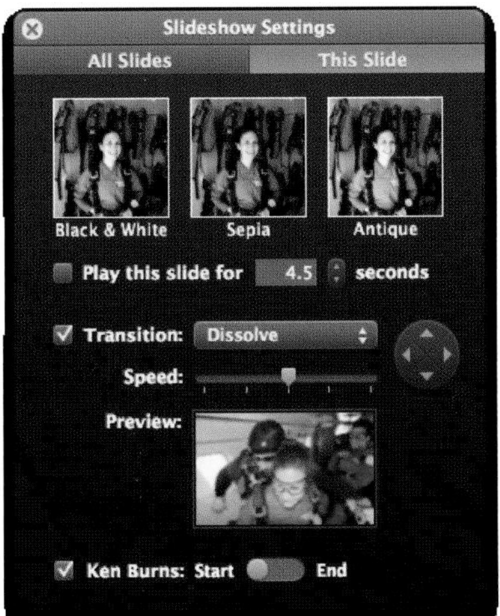

5 From the Transition pop-up menu, choose Flip. A preview of the Flip transition plays in the small preview window. You can use the circular direction button to select which direction the flipping goes in.

6 On the circular direction button next to the Transition menu, click the arrow on the right side.

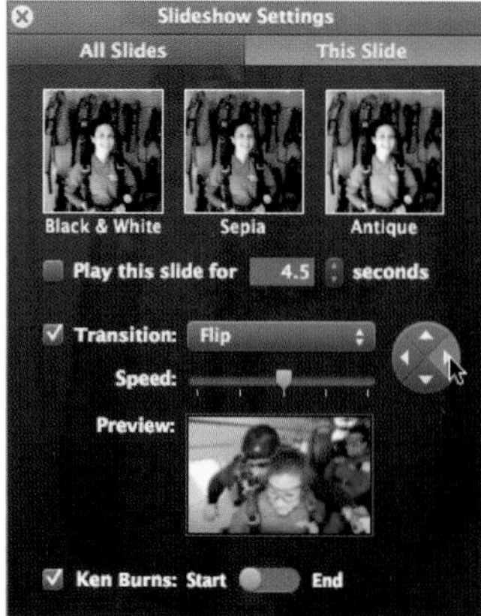

When you click the arrow, the small preview window now shows the flip transition going toward the right.

7 Click the Preview Slideshow button to play the slide with the new Flip transition effect.

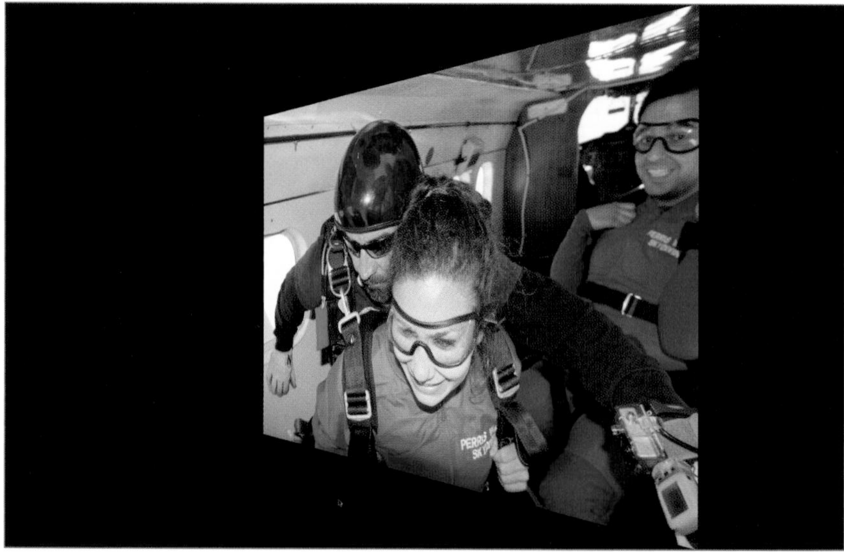

This Transition menu is not available in all themes, and the direction button is not available for all transitions. Some themes have more options than others, and some options are unique to a theme. You'll look at another one of those unique options in the Ken Burns theme.

Modifying the Ken Burns Effect

The Ken Burns theme applies a pan-and-zoom technique to your photos. Using the Settings window and the viewer you can modify that pan and zoom.

The seventh photo in the slideshow might be more exciting if you exaggerated the zoom-out so they appear to be falling farther away.

1 In the photo browser, click the seventh slide.

2 If the Settings window isn't open already, click the Settings button in the toolbar and click the This Slide tab.

The Settings window has a Start and End selector for the Ken Burns effect.

When set to the Start position, the view shows how the slide will start in the slideshow. Set the Ken Burns selector to End and the viewer shows how the slide will end in the slideshow.

3 Make sure the Ken Burns selector is set to Start.

4 In the bottom of the iPhoto window, drag the Zoom slider to the right (about halfway) to zoom in to the photo.

5 Drag the photo to reposition it so that the sky divers are in the center of the window.

6 Click the Ken Burns selector to set it to End. The photo in the viewer jumps to a zoomed-out view.

7 In the bottom of the iPhoto window, drag the Zoom slider to the left so the image is zoomed out all the way.

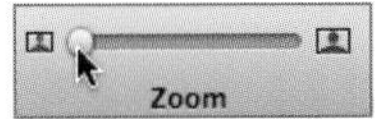

8 Click the Preview Slideshow button to play the slideshow with the customized Ken Burns effect.

Although you have applied the Ken Burns theme, you are not required to apply a pan-and-zoom effect to every slide. You can deselect the Ken Burns setting in the Slideshow settings to turn it off.

Sharing Your Slideshow

The slideshow is essentially a short movie, so when you want to share it with others, you have several options to consider. You can click the Export button to place it on your iPad, iPhone, or iPod; or you can use the Share menu to send it to iDVD.

Exporting a Slideshow

As you learned in Lesson 2, you can use iTunes to copy photos to your iPad, iPhone, or iPod Touch. You can do the same with a saved slideshow.

1 With the saved slideshow selected in the Source list, click the Export button in the toolbar.

The Export window opens in order to convert your saved slideshow into a movie. You can select various movies sizes for the devices that sync with iTunes. To the left are checkboxes to select the sizes you want to create. The supported devices are displayed at the top of the window, and below them you can view the sizes they support.

TIP You can select as many sizes as you like in the Export window. Although exporting multiple sizes will increase the export time and the storage space required, doing so also ensures that each device gets the best quality movie that it can play.

You'll choose a Medium size because that supports the widest range of devices.

NOTE ▸ Although the Export window shows the iPhone supporting only the Mobile setting, you can select Medium if you plan on syncing the movie with an iPhone 4. The iPhone 3G or 3Gs has a screen resolution of only 480 x 300, so higher-resolution video files waste space and battery life on those devices.

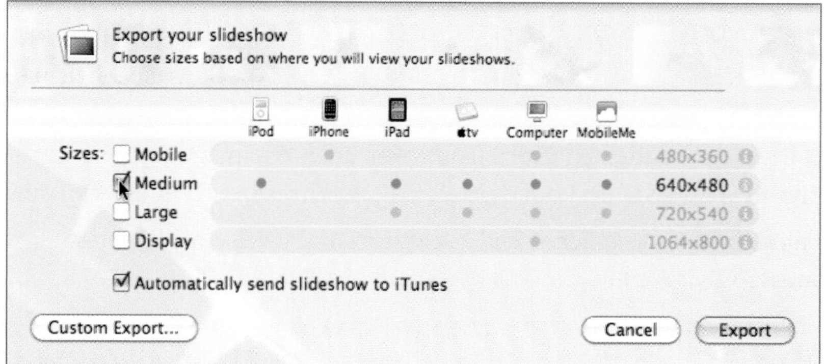

2 Click the Medium checkbox.

TIP If you want even more control over the movie file format, click the Custom Export button. Use this option only if you are familiar with QuickTime compression settings.

3 Click Export to open the Save window, and select a location to save your slideshow movie.

TIP You can deselect the "Automatically send slideshow to iTunes" checkbox if you don't want iTunes to open after exporting your slideshow. This is useful if you are going to sync your slideshow with iTunes on another Mac.

iPhoto creates an iPhoto Slideshows folder in your Pictures folder and defaults to saving your slideshow movie there.

4 In the Save window, click OK to save the movie to your iPhoto Slideshows folder.

Once the movie is created, the Finder opens with the iPhoto Slideshows folder open and the movie selected. Double-clicking the movie will launch iTunes and play the slideshow. The next time you sync your iPhone or iPad you can select this slideshow movie in the Movies tab and place it onto your Apple mobile device.

Lesson Review

1. Why would you choose to use an instant slideshow rather than a saved slideshow?
2. How do you customize the transitions between slides?
3. How do you play a video clip from the photo browser?
4. Why and when would you need to set the aspect ratio of your slideshow?
5. If you are not sure which device you will be syncing with, which single movie file size would be best to export?

Answers

1. Instant slideshows are the quickest and easiest way to showcase your photos in a slideshow if you do not want to save the slideshow.
2. First, select a theme that allows that option. Second, select a slide in the photo browser and click the Settings button. Finally, click the This Slide tab and select the Transitions checkbox.
3. Double-click the video clip in the photo browser.
4. You set the aspect ratio for your slideshow because slideshows can be shown to a variety of devices such as iPads, iPhones, computer screens, and HDTVs, all of which have different screen shapes and sizes.
5. The Medium option for movie file size is the best single choice because it supports the widest range of devices.

7

Lesson Files	ATS iLife11 Book Files > Lesson 07 > Weekend Zoo Trip folder
Time	This lesson takes approximately 60 minutes to complete.
Goals	Understand photo formats Import from a folder Merge and split Events Assign keywords Create backups

Lesson **7**

Importing and Managing Photos

Now that you have a firm grasp on using iPhoto to make fantastic pictures, books, and slideshows, it's time to turn your eye toward the essentials of managing and backing up photos in your library. These photos are not replaceable. You can't go back in time and take them over again. Think of all the moments that are captured in these photos that can never be recovered.

It's sobering to think that you could lose your photos, but don't lose sleep over it. iPhoto has great ways to manage and back up your library. Because this lesson goes over backing up files to an external hard drive and DVD, readers without those devices won't be able to follow every step-by-step instruction. Still, it is well worth following along to better understand how iPhoto manages your library.

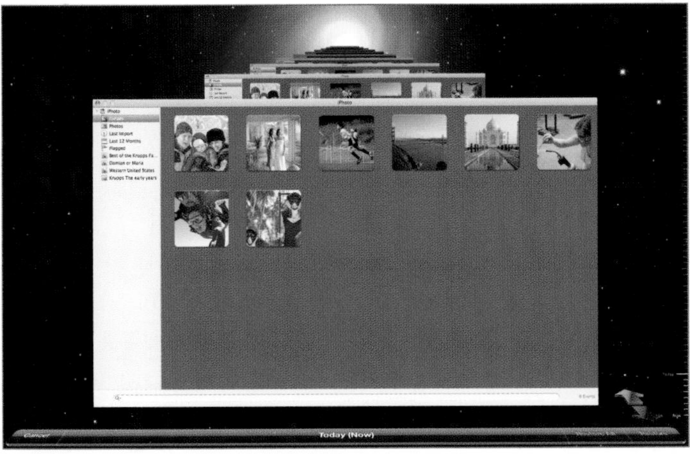

Understanding Photo Formats

Some cameras give you a choice between two photo file types: JPEG and RAW:

- JPEG is a file type that compresses the amount of information that makes up a picture. It reduces detail that the eye can't ordinarily see so that you can store more photos in a camera.
- A RAW file type retains nearly all of the detail captured by the camera when you took the picture. As a result RAW photos take up considerably more storage space than the same picture compressed with JPEG. The advantage of RAW files is that they offer you finer exposure control when you edit photos.

For everyday pictures or when you want to fit more pictures into your camera, JPEG is a good file format choice.

However, if you plan to make professional use of your pictures or want to have the maximum amount of editorial control, you should consider using RAW format if your camera supports it.

Importing a Photo Folder

If someone gives you a folder of photos or you download photos from a friend or family member's website, you'll need to import them into iPhoto from your Mac, which is a bit different from importing from a camera (as you did in Lesson 1.)

1 If you just performed the steps in Lesson 1, click the Full Screen button to exit full screen, then in the Source list, select Events.

2 Choose File > Import to Library. The navigation window opens so you can locate the folder of photos you want to import.

   TIP If iPhoto is open, you can drag the folder to the iPhoto window.

3 In the top half of the Import Photos window, navigate to ATS iLife11 Book Files > Lesson 07 > Weekend Zoo Trip.

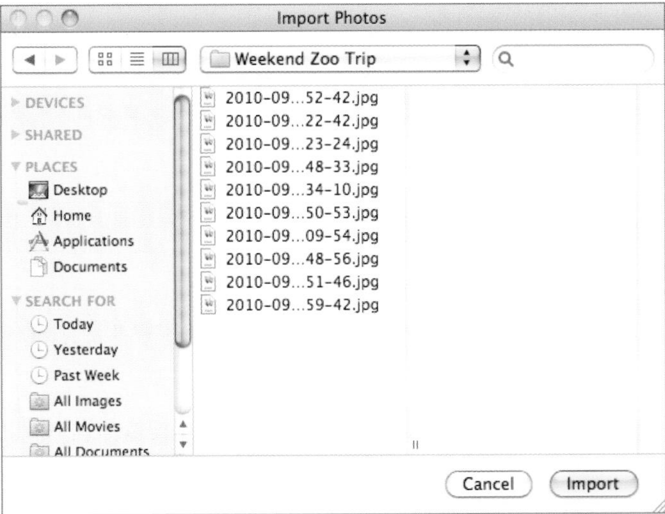

4 Click Import.

A status bar appears at the top of the import view to show the import progress. When the process is completed, the Last Import album is selected in the Source list so you can view the photos you just imported.

Importing from Photo Booth

Some Macintosh applications can send photos directly to your iPhoto library. For example, you can send email photo attachments directly from Mail to iPhoto, and send a photo directly from the Photo Booth application.

1 Open Photo Booth and take a picture with your Mac iSight camera.

2 In the tray at the bottom of the Photo Booth window, click the photo you just took, and then click the iPhoto button above the tray at the left.

iPhoto opens and imports the photo.

Organizing Your Events

As the number of Events in your library increases, you may discover that you have difficulty remembering the contents of each Event. Fortunately, you can add descriptions and customize the photo used to represent the Event in the library.

Adding Event Descriptions

When an Event's title isn't enough to jog your memory, you can add a more detailed description to the Event.

1 In the Source list, click Events and then select the Weekend Zoo Trip Event.

2 In the toolbar, click the Info Pane button to display the Info pane.

3 Click in the description area just under the title and date of the Event.

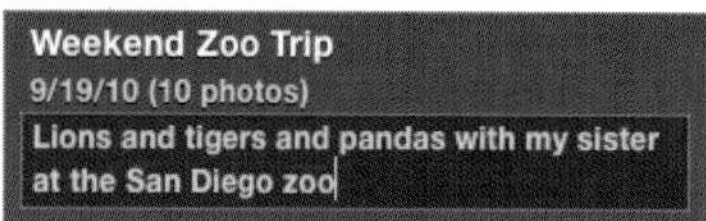

4 Type a description, *Lions and Tigers and Pandas with my sister at the San Diego Zoo.*

5 Click anywhere outside the description area to apply your changes.

Providing an informative caption for the entire Event can be useful when you later search for photos.

Changing an Event's Key Photo

A more visual way to remember what's in an Event is to change the picture iPhoto uses as the representative key photo in the Event view.

1 Double-click the Weekend Zoo Trip Event.

2 Click the last photo in the Event, the women with the masks.

3 Choose Events > Make Key Photo.

4 Click the All Events button. The viewing area now shows the photo you selected to represent that Event.

Splitting Events

iPhoto creates Events according to the date photos were created. Sometimes, though, you'll find that the photos in one iPhoto Event actually represent two or more occasions. For example, if you shoot some photos at a soccer game in the morning and more photos at a birthday party in the afternoon, iPhoto will put all the photos into one Event because they were taken on the same date. If that happens, you can split the Event into two Events. In the wedding Event, you may want to split the ceremony pictures from the honeymoon vacation photos.

1 Double-click Greg and Caren's Wedding Event.

2 Select the photo of the burning tiki torches.

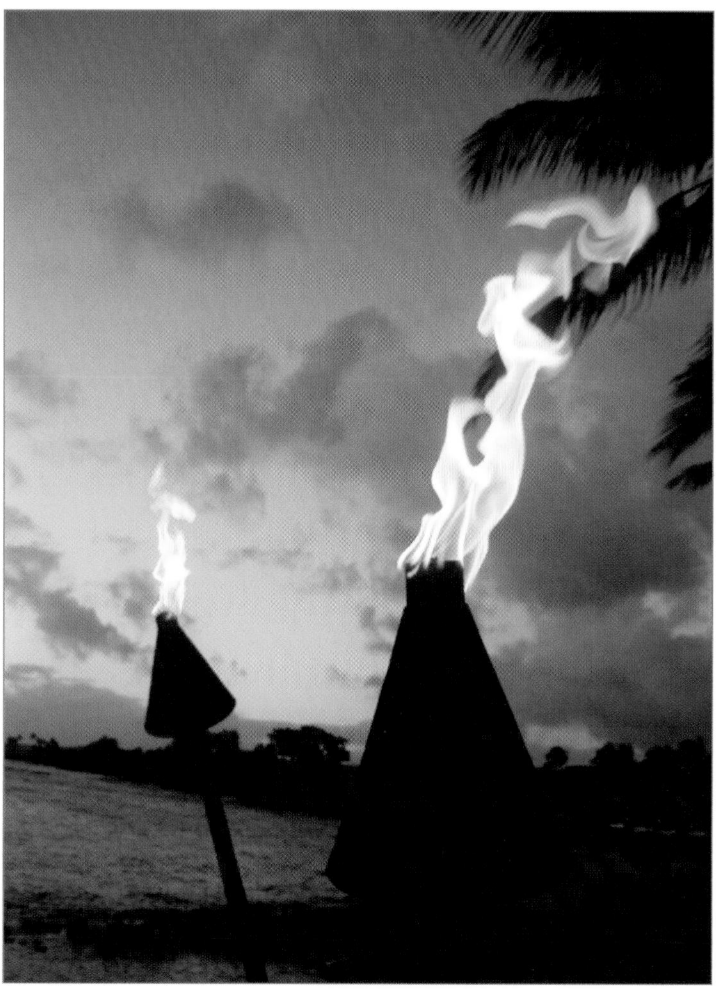

3 Choose Events > Split Event. The viewing area becomes a split view showing the original Event above and a newly created untitled Event below. The untitled Event contains the photo you selected and all the photos that were taken after it in the original Event.

4 Click the All Event button.

5 Double-click the untitled event placeholder title, type *Hawaii Honeymoon Vacation*, and press Return.

All the Events in your library are displayed, including the new Hawaii Honeymoon Vacation Event.

Moving a Photo Between Events

When you split Events, a photo will sometimes be left behind, or you might include too many photos in the newly split Event. In either case, you'll want to move one or more photos from one event to another. Although this is easy to do, it's not quite as obvious a task as you might think.

1 Click Greg and Caren's Wedding Event.

1 Choose iPhoto > Preferences, and then click Sharing.

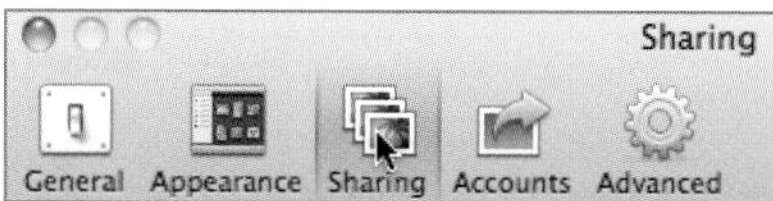

The iPhoto preferences window displays its Sharing pane.

2 Select the "Share my photos" checkbox.

Sharing begins immediately after you select the checkbox. You can choose to share all the photos in your library or just the photos in selected albums.

3 Select "Share selected albums," and then scroll down the album list and select the "Best of the Krupps Family" album.

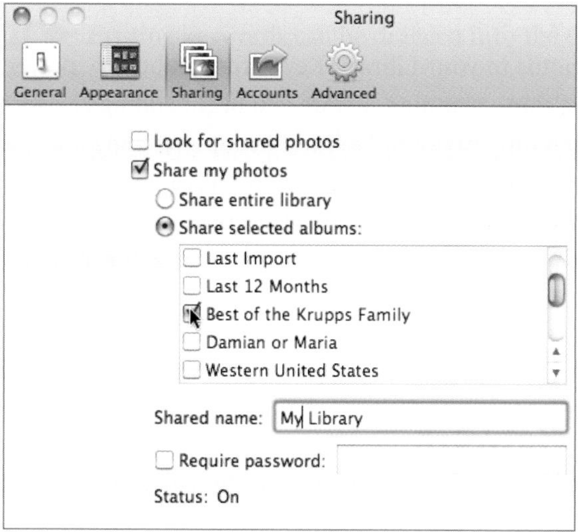

You can type a name in the "Shared name" field or use the name iPhoto has provided. This is the name other people will see in their iPhoto Source list.

4 Select "Require password," and then enter a password you want to use. When you assign a password to your shared photos, other iPhoto users on the network can see that you've shared photos, but they cannot view the photos unless they enter the password.

5 Close the preferences window.

If you have access to another Mac on your local network, you can open iPhoto and see the shared collections in the Source list. Although you cannot edit the photos while you view them as a shared library, you can select them, make an album, create a photo book, or create a slideshow with them. At that point, the photos are imported into your Library and they no longer need to be shared for you to view them.

Backing Up Your Photos

iPhoto is completely integrated with Time Machine, the Apple backup software. All you have to do is make sure Time Machine is turned on in the System Preferences. Time Machine automatically backs up your library along with other changes that you make on your Mac.

If you are not using Time Machine or don't have an external hard disk, you can still back up your iPhoto library. You can easily and quickly burn all or part of your iPhoto library to a recordable DVD. You should consider doing this regularly. Recordable discs are cheap, but the time you've spent creating, arranging, and cleaning up your photos isn't.

Backing Up to a Recordable Disc

When you burn your library to a disc, iPhoto puts an iPhoto library onto the disc that contains the albums, Events, and folders from the iPhoto library of your Mac. In essence, you're taking a snapshot of your library at the moment you burn the disc.

You can use this snapshot to recover from mistakes—such as accidently deleting the wrong Event—or to store photos and albums that you want to save but no longer need in your iPhoto library.

1 In the Source list, click Events to see all your Events in the viewer.

When iPhoto burns a library to disc, it copies only the selected items. When no photos are selected, it backs up the entire library. In this exercise, you will back up your entire iPhoto library.

2 Choose Edit > Select None to make sure no photos are selected.

3 Choose Share > Burn. A dialog appears instructing you to insert a blank disc in your Mac.

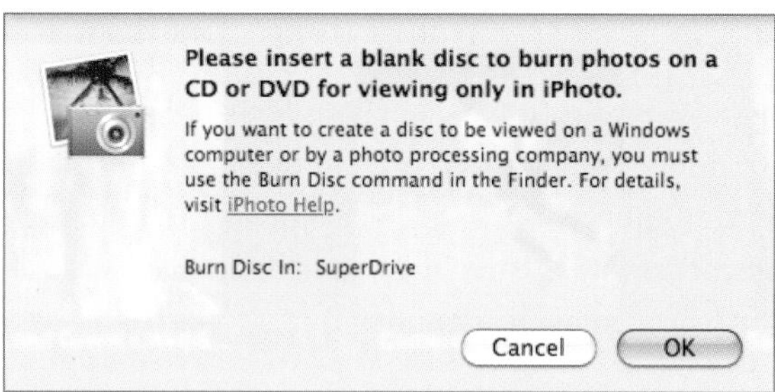

4 Insert a recordable disc in your disc drive, and click OK.

Disc information appears at the bottom of the iPhoto viewing area. After you click Burn, a dialog appears in which you can confirm your decision and click the Burn button again.

Restoring Photos with Time Machine

Backing up with Time Machine is the easy part. Open Time Machine, pick your backup hard disk and let Time Machine go to work. From then on, changes to your iPhoto library are backed up automatically, along with everything else on your Mac. The only time you need to return to Time Machine is when you want to retrieve a deleted file or restore your entire Mac from a backup.

NOTE ► You must have a Time Machine set up with your system to follow the steps in this section.

1 Choose File > Browser Backups. Time Machine opens and displays the iPhoto window for each available backup.

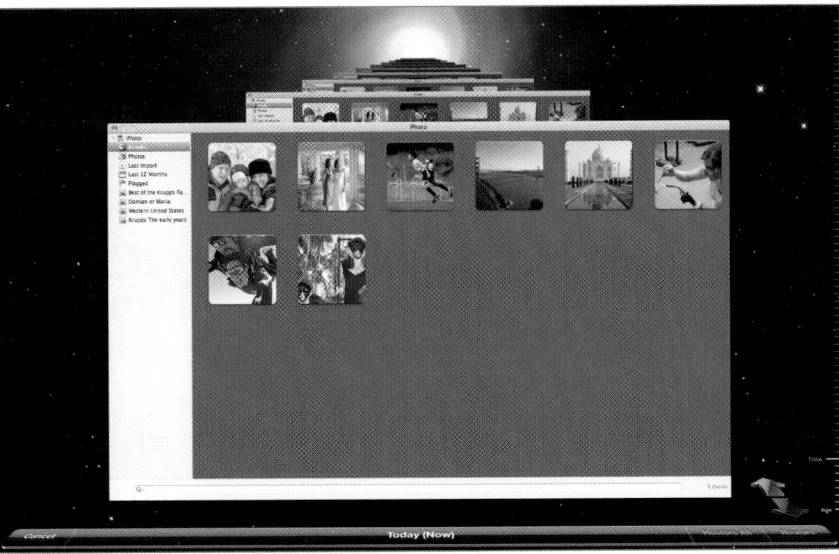

2 Click an iPhoto window from some previous date.

3 Select a photo, and then in the lower right of Time Machine, click Restore.

iPhoto will import any photo that is no longer in the iPhoto library. If the photo is still in the library, iPhoto gives you a chance to decide whether to import the duplicate or not. If you've restored multiple photos, you can also apply your decision to any other duplicates that iPhoto encounters.

4 Click Don't Import or Cancel to return to iPhoto.

With your Library safe and secure, you can close iPhoto and relax. Or you continue to play with iPhoto to discover some of the other things it can do. You can always use your backups to recover from any mishaps.

Lesson Review

1. How can you save a snapshot of your iPhoto library?
2. What do you have to do to back up your iPhoto Library with Time Machine?
3. When splitting an Event, what happens to the photo you select?
4. When sharing photos over a local network, when does sharing begin?
5. How do you assign a keyboard shortcut to a keyword?

Answers

1. Record a copy of it on a recordable DVD by choosing Share > Burn.
2. Make sure Time Machine is turned on and automatically backing up your Mac to a backup hard disk. Time Machine automatically backs up your library along with other changes that you make on your Mac.
3. The photo you select and all the photos that come after it end up in the new split Event.
4. Sharing begins immediately after you select the "Share my Photos" checkbox.
5. When you add a new keyword or drag an existing keyword into the Quick Group window, a keyboard shortcut is assigned automatically.

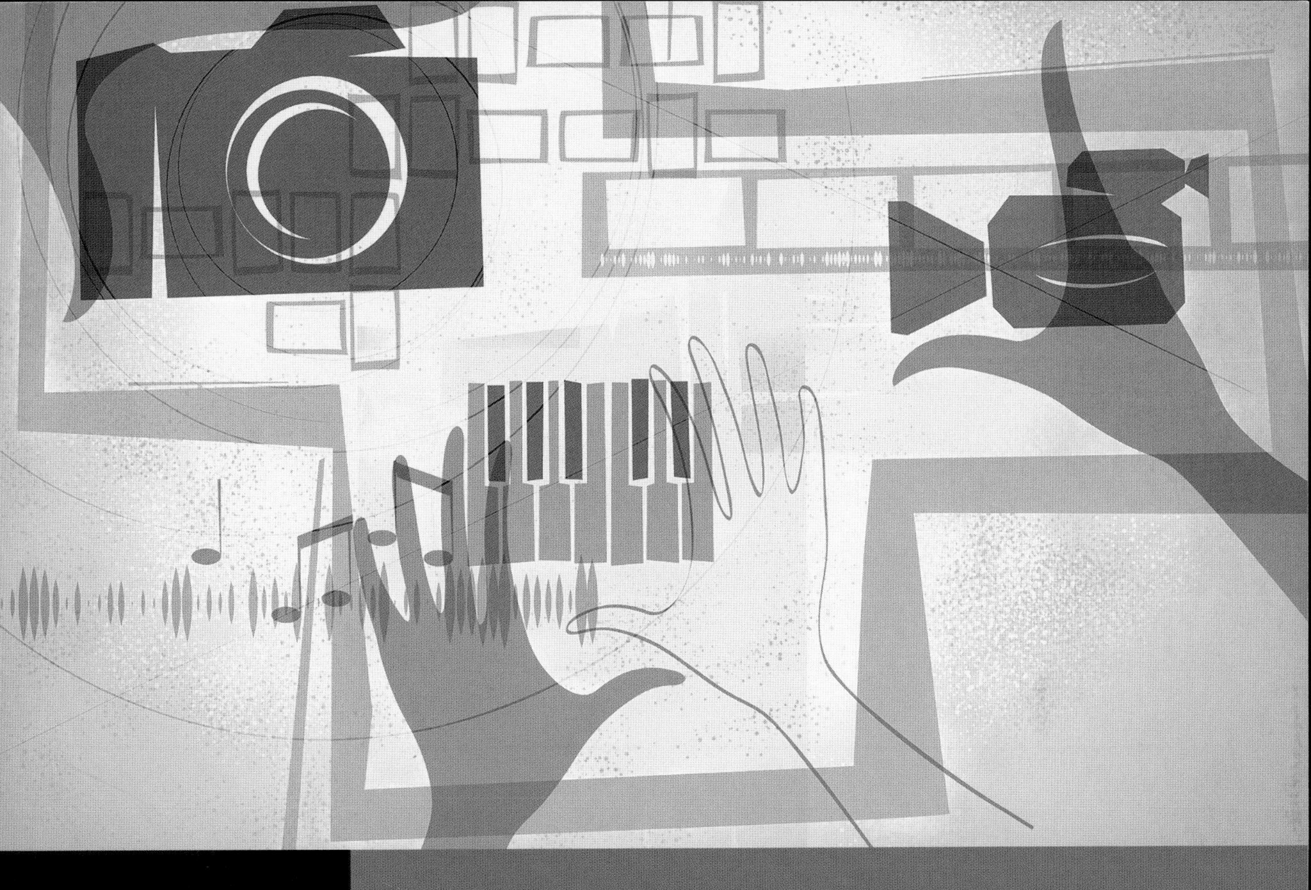

iMovie: A Little Slice of Hollywood at Home

8

Lesson Files — Desktop > ATS iLife11 Book Files > Lesson 08 > Old Holiday Movies

Time — This lesson takes approximately 90 minutes to complete.

Goals — Import from the Finder

Skim and play video clips

Marking favorites and rejects

Making your first project

Choosing themes

Adding video and music to a project

Syncing a movie with your iPad, iPhone, and iPod

Lesson **8**

Moviemaking Made Easy

Are you the family's hotshot gadget owner with the latest HD camcorder? The sideline screaming soccer mom taking video clips of her kid with an iPhone or iPod Touch? Perhaps you dress in all black, read Jack Kerouac, and make art movies with a digital still camera. Or maybe you just have a lot of cats and sit by the flickering pale blue light of the TV. No matter who you are, you've probably told yourself that you just never have enough time to watch your home videos, much less make a movie from them.

Well, iMovie is about to change all that for you. You'll be making great-looking movies in a very short period of time with fun surprises around every corner. So let's dive right in and learn how easy it is to make movies with iMovie.

Opening iMovie

You can open iMovie in two primary ways:

- In the Dock, click the iMovie icon.
- In the Applications folder, double-click the iMovie icon.

NOTE ▶ iMovie is one of the default icons in your Dock. If the iMovie icon isn't there, you can drag it from the Applications folder onto the Dock.

1 In the Dock, click the iMovie icon.

When you open iMovie for the first time, the welcome screen appears. The welcome screen contains links to online video tutorials and includes information about iMovie and other Apple applications.

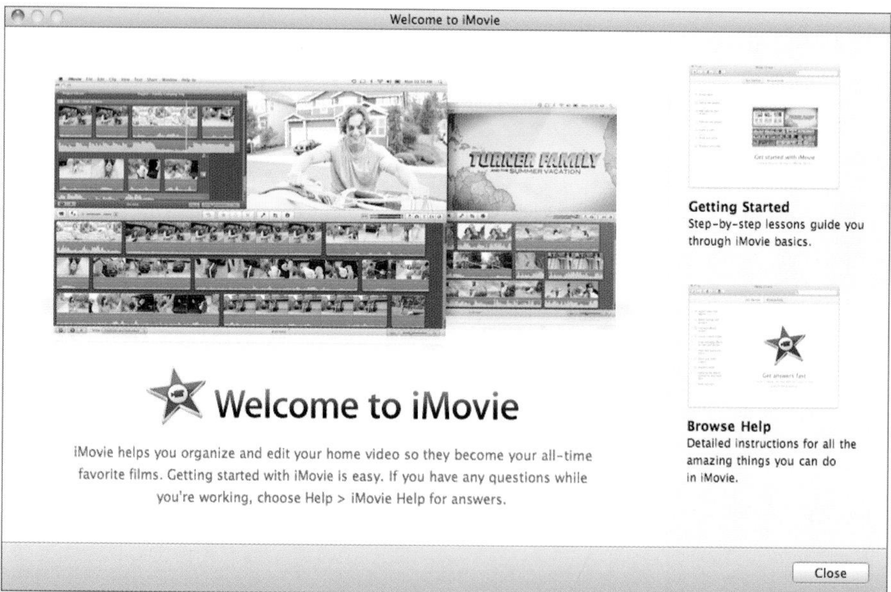

2 Click Close to close the welcome screen.

NOTE ▸ If you've previously opened iMovie, you can open the welcome screen from the Help menu.

Now you're ready to bring clips into iMovie. But before you do that, let's take a quick look at the iMovie window and its controls.

Looking at the iMovie window

The iMovie window is divided into sections for Events, Projects, and the viewer. In the toolbar you can access media, including music, photos, and titles, as well as commonly used movie making tools.

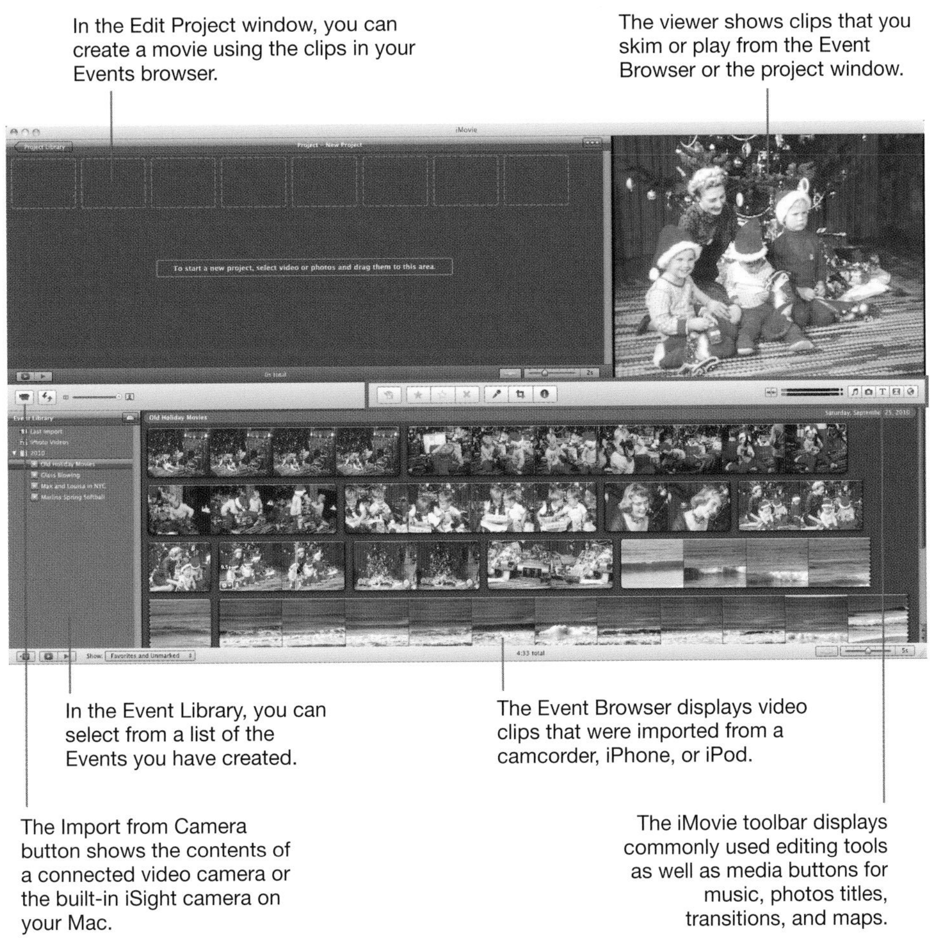
In the Edit Project window, you can create a movie using the clips in your Events browser.
The viewer shows clips that you skim or play from the Event Browser or the project window.
To start a new project, select video or photos and drag them to this area.
In the Event Library, you can select from a list of the Events you have created.
The Event Browser displays video clips that were imported from a camcorder, iPhone, or iPod.
The Import from Camera button shows the contents of a connected video camera or the built-in iSight camera on your Mac.
The iMovie toolbar displays commonly used editing tools as well as media buttons for music, photos titles, transitions, and maps.

With an understanding of the iMovie window, you're ready to import some movie clips.

Getting Clips into iMovie

Much like iPhoto, you import video clips into iMovie Events and store them in a library.

In this lesson, you'll import clips from a Mac hard disk, but iMovie offers several other methods for importing video clips. Here's where you'll find these other methods described:

- Accessing movie clips from iPhoto—Lesson 12
- Importing clips from a tape-based camcorder—Lesson 14
- Importing clips from a tapeless camcorder—Lesson 14
- Importing clips from a digital still camera—Lesson 14

NOTE ▶ Analog VHS or 8mm camcorders cannot connect directly to your Mac. A detailed list of supported camcorders can be found on the iMovie support website: http://help.apple.com/imovie/cameras.

Importing Clips from Your Mac

In some cases you may want to import clips on your Mac hard disk into iMovie. You use the File > Import menu to do so.

1 Choose File > Import > Movies.

If this is the first time you've imported into iMovie, the HD Import setting window prompts you to select the default video size for HD importing. Camcorders record HD video in a variety of file formats, such as H.264 or MPEG-4. iMovie can convert these files into an optimized video format that improves playback performance and creates smaller files.

You have two choices for optimizing video format:

Full—Maintains the best HD video quality but requires large amounts of hard disk space and a fast Mac.

Large—Optimizes the HD video to a smaller size, so files use less hard disk space and play smoothly on all Macs.

NOTE ▶ You can use H.264 or MPEG-4 files in iMovie while retaining most application functions. However, if you want to apply fast or slow motion, iMovie must convert your clips before applying speed changes.

2 Choose Large - 960x540 to get the best playback performance. If you've imported into iMovie previously, the HD Import Setting window will not appear and you will see the import navigation window.

3 In the HD Import Setting window, click OK.

The navigation window opens and includes options for where to store the clips on your hard disk. In the top half of the window, you can locate the video clips you want to import.

4 In the Import window, navigate to Desktop > ATS iLife11 Book Files > Lesson 08 > Old Holiday Movies.

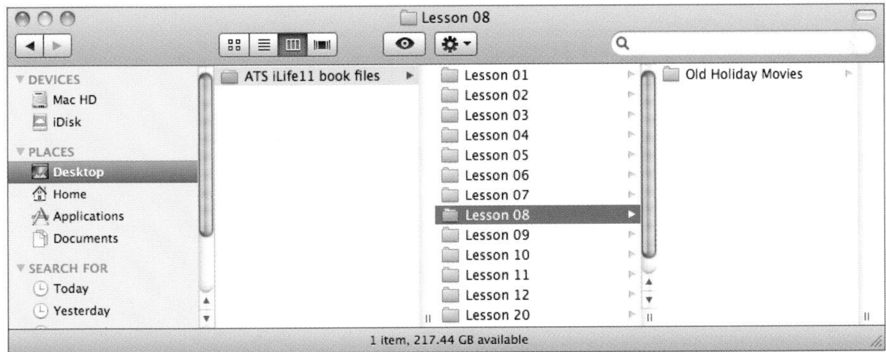

TIP Video can take up a lot of space on your hard disk, so if you plan to record more than one hour of HD video or three hours of standard video annually, you should think about investing in a large (and fast) external hard drive.

In the "Save to" pop-up menu in the navigation window, you can select the hard disk on which you want to store your imported video clips.

5 If you have more than one hard drive connected to your Mac, make sure your main Macintosh HD is selected in the "Save to" menu.

Next, you can create a new Event to contain all the clips you are about to import, or you can import the clips to an existing Event. Events group captured video clips inside iMovie, much like a folder groups documents. Typically, you will create a new Event for each special occasion you record.

6 Select "Create new Event," and then type the name *Old Holiday Movies.*

The clips you will be importing are not HD video clips, so the "Optimize video" setting has no effect. Because you are importing from the Finder, you can choose to copy or move the clips into iMovie.

TIP Copied files use twice as much storage space but retain a duplicate backup set of files.

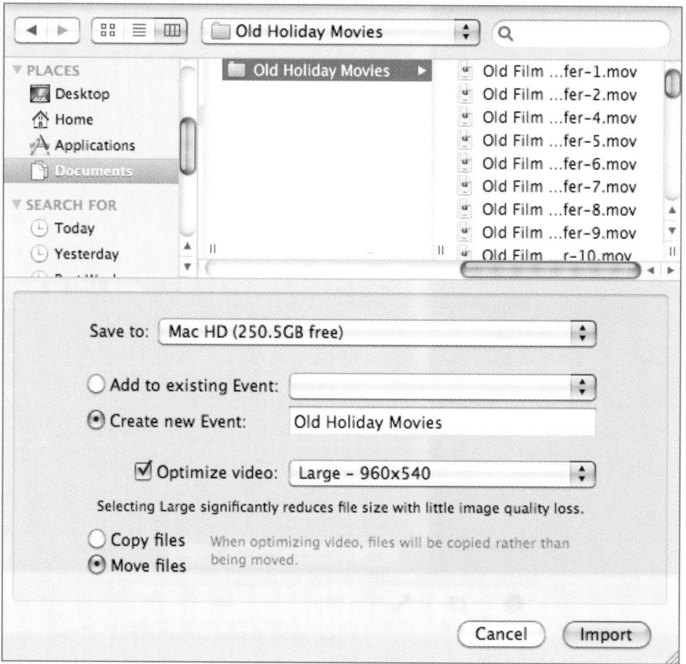

7 Select "Move files," and then click Import. A dialog asks if you want to import all the files in the Old Holiday Movies folder.

8 Click OK.

After finishing the import process, the Event and all its imported video content is displayed in the lower half of the iMovie window, ready for you to watch and enjoy.

Skimming and Playing Clips

After you import video clips, they are displayed in the Event Browser as *filmstrips*. Filmstrips are created using multiple representative frames, called *thumbnails*. Using the filmstrips, you can quickly see, jump to, preview, and play any portion of any clip.

1 Move the mouse pointer left and right over the first filmstrip of the perfect holiday setting complete with dog and bike. As you do so, the viewer updates to show the corresponding location in the video clip. This process is called *skimming*—a way to quickly find specific parts of your Event.

TIP When a filmstrip breaks at the end of the Event Browser, it continues on the line below. You can skim continuously through the break by holding down the Shift key as you move the pointer, or by pressing the Caps Lock key.

Once you skim to an area you are interested in watching, you can play the clip in the viewer.

2 Position the pointer at the start of the first filmstrip in the Event.

3 Press the Spacebar to play the clip.

4 Press the Spacebar again to stop playing.

Skimming and playing is a good beginning technique, but you can do a few more things to more easily find the best parts of your Events.

Marking the Best and Worst Clips

Not all clips are created equal. Some clips are filled with heartwarming, fuzzy goodness, and others are a big waste of time. iMovie provides simple tools to differentiate the two, making it easier for you to find and enjoy the best parts of your Event.

Selecting a Range and Marking Favorites

With the skimming technique firmly in your grasp, you're one step away from selecting a range within a clip. Selecting a range is the basis for many activities in iMovie. First and foremost, it allows you to identify portions of a clip and to mark them as favorites.

1 Position the pointer at the start of the first clip in the Event.

2 Skim to the point where the dog turns his head to look into the camera, and then click the mouse button on the filmstrip to select a few seconds of the clip, indicated by a yellow outline.

If your life can't be reduced to a few seconds in each clip, you can extend the selected range to ensure that your best memories are fully included. Drag the handles on the left and right sides of the yellow selection range to extend or reduce the range.

TIP In the Browser tab of iMovie Preferences, you can modify the default selection range size.

3 Skim to the right edge of the yellow outline until your mouse pointer changes to a resize pointer.

4 Drag the edge of the selection range to the end of the clip.

You've now made a selection within the first filmstrip. So what? It may not seem like a big deal, but it becomes bigger with one click.

TIP If you accidently select the wrong range, you can deselect it by choosing Edit > Select > None, or by selecting another range.

5 Click the "Mark as Favorite" button to mark the selected range.

The green line at the top of the selected range identifies it as a favorite.

TIP When you press the Spacebar to play a clip, you can press keyboard shortcuts to quickly mark favorites. Press the Right Arrow key to increase playback speed and press F to begin marking the Favorite range. Press the Left Arrow key to restore normal playback speed and press F again to mark the end of the favorite range.

Changing a Favorite Range

It's easy to get overzealous and mark too much of a clip as a favorite. You can remove a portion of the favorite range by selecting a range and clicking the Unmark button.

1 Skim to the yellow selection handle on the left side of the filmstrip.

2 When your mouse pointer changes to a resize pointer, drag to the right to shorten the selected range.

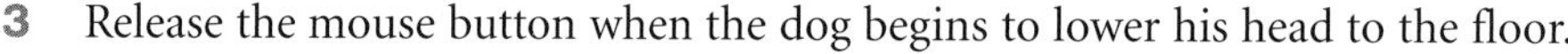

3 Release the mouse button when the dog begins to lower his head to the floor.

4 In the toolbar, click the Unmark button.

The selected area no longer has a green line at the top. You've neatly and efficiently identified the best portion of this clip.

Think of it like highlighting a book. Highlight too much of the book and the highlight is useless, highlight too little and you miss many of the important parts. The same standard applies when marking favorites.

Rejecting Clips

So far you've identified two portions of a clip: your favorite part and a less interesting but still valuable part. A third portion is the part of a clip you have no interest in. It's the portion you want to reject and maybe delete. Identifying a rejected range is similar to identifying a favorite.

1 On the second clip in the Event (the machine gun–toting tots), drag from the start of the filmstrip to the end. You may not want this clip in your wholesome family Event Library.

2 With the entire filmstrip selected, click the Reject button (the red X).

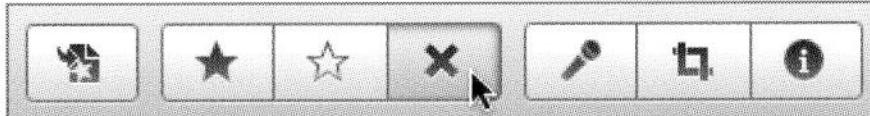

The entire clip is removed from the Event Browser but it hasn't been deleted, just hidden from view.

You aren't limited to rejecting entire clips. As with favorites, you can also reject portions of clips.

3 On the fourth clip in the Event Browser—the kids opening presents—drag from the start of this filmstrip until the boy in the red hat stops grabbing his brother's presents and goes offscreen.

An easy way to identify where to stop is to watch the duration indicator next to your mouse pointer as you drag the selection range. This number displays the length of the selection in seconds.

4 Stop dragging when the selection range duration is around 4.0s.

5 Click the Reject button.

TIP You can also press Delete to mark a range as a reject.

You've successfully rejected a portion of a clip. The rejected ranges are still available if you want them back, but they are now out of the way and no longer cluttering your Event.

Filtering Events

After you've marked some ranges as favorites or rejects, you can filter the Event to show only one group or the other.

1 From the Show pop-up menu at the bottom of the Event Browser, choose Favorites Only.

The Event Browser now displays only the Favorite ranges.

2 From the Show pop-up menu, choose Favorites and Unmarked. You can now see all your clips except the rejected ones.

Playing an Event in Full Screen

With a tidier Event Browser, you can sit back and really enjoy watching the remaining clips. Although watching them in the viewer is enjoyable, you can play your clips full screen for an even better viewing experience.

1 In the lower left of the Event Browser, click the Play Full Screen button to start playing the first clip in the Event.

2 Press the Spacebar to pause playback.

3 Position your pointer at the bottom of the screen to display a filmstrip of the entire Event.

4 Click the filmstrip and then skim over it to preview the Event.

5 Press the Spacebar at any time to start playback.

6 Press the Esc key to exit full screen.

In the first half of this lesson, you learned a basic way to use iMovie. Watching your favorites in full-screen mode is the easiest way to enjoy the best parts of your home video. In the upcoming sections, you'll learn how to make a great-looking movie.

Creating a New Project Using a Theme

In an iMovie project, you combine clip selections from an Event with titles, transitions, and music to make a full-fledged movie. By applying an iMovie theme, you can automatically place titles and transitions into your project.

1 Choose File > New Project.

NOTE ▸ When you open iMovie for the first time, a new project is created for you, but you can still choose New Project as in step 1.

When you create a new project, a Project Settings window appears in which you can name the project and select a theme.

2 Type the name of the project, *A Holiday to Remember*.

3 Click the Photo Album theme to select it. Preview the selected theme on the right side of the Project Settings window.

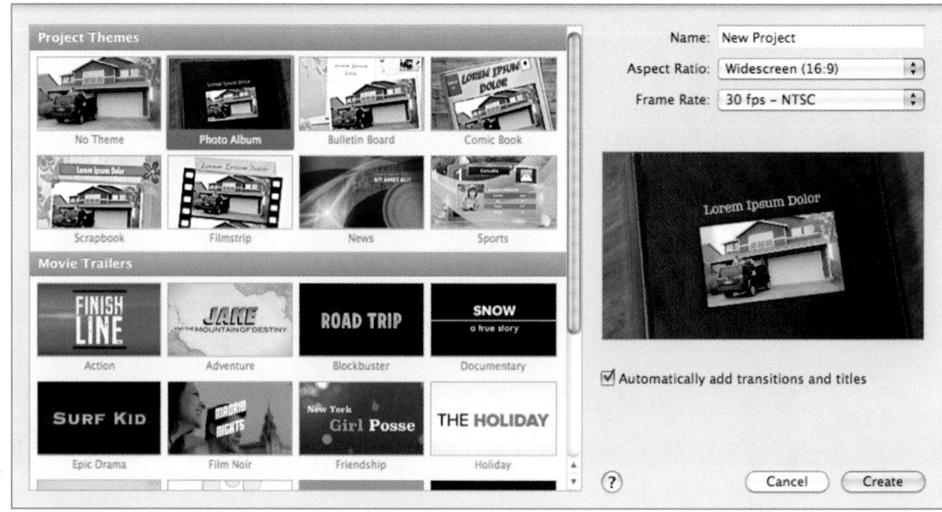

A theme is a collection of titles and transitions that conform to a specific style, such as sports, travel, or comic book. Because the checkbox to automatically add transitions and titles is selected by default, as you create your project, opening titles, ending credits, and transitions are added automatically according to the theme's style.

On the right side of the Project Settings window, you'll find settings related to the clips you are going to use.

The first setting under the project name is for Aspect Ratio, which determines the shape of your video clips. An HDTV has a rectangular, widescreen aspect ratio of 16:9 (pronounced 16 by 9). That is, the screen is 16 units wide by 9 units high. The familiar standard definition TV has a more nearly square shape with an aspect ratio of 4:3.

Typically you'll set the Aspect Ratio value to match your captured video. In this example, the old holiday clips are in a 4:3 aspect ratio.

4 From the Aspect Ratio menu, choose Standard (4:3).

The Frame Rate setting under Aspect Ratio sets the speed at which the video was recorded. Generally you can leave this setting unchanged because iMovie will correct it when you add the first video clip to your project.

TIP Be aware that camcorders made for use in different parts of the world operate at different speeds.

All the holiday video content was created at the same speed, so you will leave this setting at its default value and let iMovie set it correctly.

5 Click Create to create your new project. An empty project is created and displayed in the upper-left corner of the iMovie window.

TIP You can change themes at any time by choosing File > Project Theme. You can also change the aspect ratio by choosing File > Project Properties, but you cannot change the speed of a project once you've selected it.

Dragging Selections to a Project

Now, all you need to do is select the best parts of your videos and add them to the project window. If you've already marked your favorites, you're good to go. In the current Event, some clips are marked as favorites and some you will need to mark.

Adding clips to a project begins by selecting a range and then dragging that selection into the project window.

1 Skim over the first clip in the Event, which shows the dog.

2 Click the green favorite bar to select the favorite-marked area.

3 To verify that you've made the right selection, choose View > Play Selection, or press the / (slash) key. The selected area plays once.

   This selection is a nice way to start a movie. It instantly lets your audience know the season and the setting.

4 Skim to the center of the selected range in the Event Browser. The pointer changes to a hand to indicate that you can drag and move the selected range.

5 Drag the selected range into the project window to add the first clip to your project. In the project window, iMovie automatically places a gold title bar over the clip's thumbnail. When using a theme, the first clip in a project always gets a title.

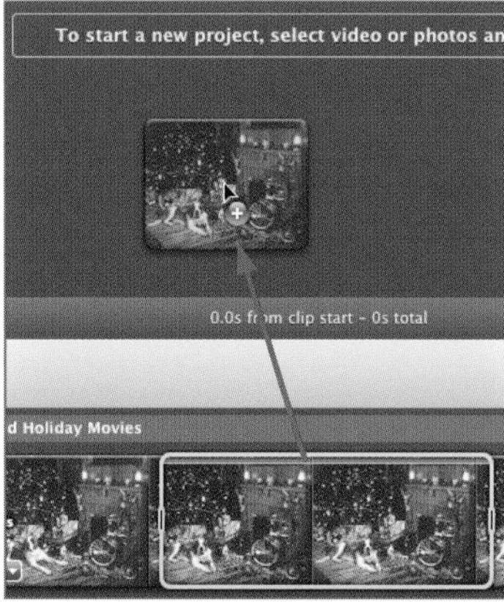

NOTE ▸ When you drag clips into the project window, you are not copying the actual movie files from your hard disk. The project just points to the clips in your Event. As a result, you can use a clip in multiple projects without using additional disk space.

6 Skim over the clip in the project window. The viewer shows the clip with the photo album's opening title style. It uses the name of the project as the title's text.

Next you'll add a few more clips to make this project a bit more fun to watch.

7 Skim over the second clip in the Event Browser.

8 Click at the start of the second clip to make a quick selection.

9 Drag the selected range into the project window. When you drop a clip over the gray background of the project window, it will always appends the new clip to the end of the project.

10 Skim over the third clip in the Event Browser. When the child on the left removes the wrapping paper, click to make a four-second selection.

11 Drag the selected range into the project window and release it anywhere over the gray background.

As you add more clips, notice that the last clip in your project has an ending title and iMovie adds transitions between each clip.

12 In the Event Browser, skim over the fourth clip, a close-up of the mother, and click at the start of the clip to make a quick selection.

13 Drag the selected range into the gray background of the project window.

Dragging clips is the most basic way to add selections to a project, but you will learn how to speed up the process in the next section.

Adding Selections to a Project

If you are adding several clips to the end of a project, you have a faster way to do it than dragging them into the project window. You can click the "Add to Project" button, or press a keyboard shortcut, to add a selected range to the end of your project.

1 In the Event Browser, skim over the clip of the grandmother sitting with the children, and click at the start of the clip to make a four-second selection.

2 Click the "Add to Project" button, or press the E key, to add the selected range to the end of your project.

You'll use the "Add to Project" button and the keyboard shortcut again in this project.

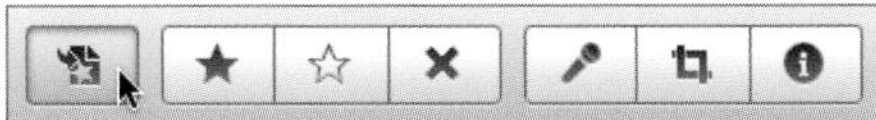

TIP When a clip is added to the current project, an orange line is added to its filmstrip in the Event Browser to indicate the range that is used in the project.

3 In the Event Browser, skim over the clip featuring another shot of the grandmother and kids. Click to make a quick selection.

4 Click the "Add to Project" button, or press the E key, to add the selection to the project.

5 In the Event Browser, skim to the shot of the tree.

6 Click at the start of the clip to make a quick selection.

7 Click the "Add to Project" button, or press the E key.

TIP A keyboard shortcuts document can be found in the iMovie Help menu.

To this point, the clips you've added have been appended to the end of your project. Next, you'll add a clip to the middle of the project.

Placing Clips in the Middle of a Project

As you now know, when you drop a clip into the gray background of the project window, or add it using the "Add to Project" button, it is placed at the end of a project. But when you drag a clip between two clips in the project, it is placed at that spot.

1 In the Event Browser, skim over the clip that shows the toys.

2 Click near the start of the clip to create a quick selection.

3 Skim to the center of the selected range.

4 Drag the selected range into the project window and hover just to the right of the second clip and the transition icon until a green insert line appears, indicating where the clip will be placed.

5 Release the mouse button to place the clip into your project.

The project opens up to make room for the newly inserted clip.

You just completed your first movie! As you can see, it's incredibly easy to make a movie. But before you get the popcorn, let's look at it again and make sure its worthy of your filmmaking genius.

Playing a Project in Full Screen

When playing a project you can press the Spacebar to start and stop playback at the current position, but often you'll want to play the project from its very beginning. Instead of skimming to the start, you can click the Play button to play a project from the beginning.

1 In the lower-left corner of the project window, click the Play button.

You can also view the project full screen in the way you played the Event earlier in this lesson.

2 Press the Spacebar to stop playback, if necessary.

3 To the left of the Play button, click the Play Full Screen button.

4 Press the Spacebar to stop playback, and then press the Esc (Escape) key to exit full-screen mode.

After viewing your project, you may have noticed a few things you want to change. In the following exercises, you will make some common changes, starting with removing clips from a project.

Removing Entire Clips from a Project

Sometimes you will want to remove a clip from your project. In this example you have too many similar clips. Removing one will make your movie seem less repetitive.

1 Skim over the two grandmother clips. These two clips are very similar, but the second clip is preferable because the boy doesn't start to run away. That's the one to keep.

2 Click the first clip of the grandmother and children.

3 Press the Delete key to remove the clip from the project.

NOTE ▶ Deleting a clip from a project does not delete it from the hard disk, or mark it as rejected.

Rearranging Clips in a Project

Your project shouldn't be a random sequence of clips; it should convey a logical short story. On many occasions, you will have the right clips in your project, but in the wrong locations. You can rearrange clips to place them in the best story-telling order.

1. In the project window, skim over the clip of the mother.

   Juxtaposing this close-up with the wider clip of the grandmother makes it appear that Mom instantly aged about 30 years.

2. In the project, click the clip of Mom and then drag it to the left, until the green vertical insert bar is displayed on the right side of the toys clip, and release the mouse button.

   TIP ▶ You can Shift-click multiple contiguous clips in a project to select them, and then you can delete or move them as a group. To select noncontiguous clips, Command-click them one by one.

3. Skim back to the left, over the clip of toys.

4. Press the Spacebar to play the project and review the changes.

Don't be afraid to try different clip arrangements. You can always move clips back to their original positions, or use Edit > Undo to reverse your changes.

Auditioning and Adding Music

Music plays a large part in setting the mood for your video. A head-banging metal song might work with the retro vibe of this project, but something nostalgic would be more likely to cause a few teary eyes in the crowd.

NOTE ▶ If you're creating a movie for personal use, you can feel free to use copyrighted music, such as files from your iTunes library. However, if you're planning to distribute your movie, it's best to choose from the iMovie royalty-free music library.

1 In the Browser, click the “Music and Sound Effects” button.

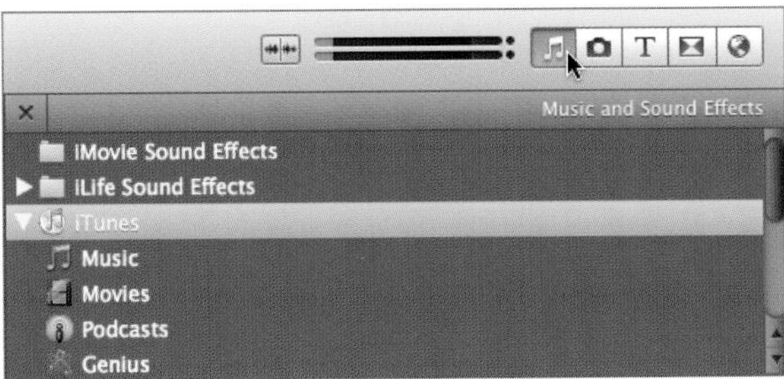

The browser contains audio media organized into three groups: iTunes contains music found in your iTunes library, iMovie Sound Effects contains sound effects, and iLife Sound Effects contains both sound effects and royalty-free music.

2 Click the disclosure button next to the iLife Sound Effects folder to display its contents.

3 Select the Jingles folder to view the royalty-free music clips.

TIP You can select any folder to display its contents in the lower half of the “Music and Sound Effects” pane.

Instead of listening to every song, you can sort songs by time to determine which songs most closely match your movie’s length.

4 In the lower half of the “Music and Sound Effects” pane, click the Time column heading to sort the songs by their durations.

Name
Artist
Time
Sprightly.caf
Apple Inc.
0:05
Perspectives Short.caf
Apple Inc.
0:06
Sideman Strut Short.caf
Apple Inc.
0:06
Island Short.caf
Apple Inc.
0:06
Highlight Reel Short.caf
Apple Inc.
0:07
Bossa Lounger Short.caf
Apple Inc.
0:07
Breakbeat Short.caf
Apple Inc.
0:07
Red Velvet Short.caf
Apple Inc.
0:07
Greasy Wheels Short.caf
Apple Inc.
0:07
Electric Rodeo Short.caf
Apple Inc.
0:07

Just below the project window and above the toolbar, iMovie displays the total length of your movie. This movie should roughly be 37s (37 seconds).

5 Scroll through the songs until you come to songs with a duration of 39 seconds or more. You don't want to select a song shorter than your project, but if it's a little longer that's OK—iMovie will stop the music when the video ends.

6 Double-click the song, **Curtain Call Long.caf**, to listen to it. It's not a holiday song per se, but it has a nostalgic feel. Let's add it as background music.

7 Drag **Curtain Call Long.caf** to the left over the browser, then up over the project window. When your pointer is hovering over the gray background of the project window, the background turns green, indicating that you can release the mouse button to add the music to the project.

You don't have to precisely place a background music track; just drag it over the gray background of the project window. iMovie will automatically position it at the start of the project and end it after the last clip finishes or when the music concludes, whichever is shorter.

8 Hover your mouse pointer over the project window until the background turns green, and then release the mouse button.

9 Click the Play button, or press the \ (backslash) key, to hear the results. That music works perfectly!

You can use this method to add as many songs to a project as you like. The additional songs will be added to the end of the project and will play until the video content ends.

Using Transitions

Transitions can create a more dramatic contrast between clips or smooth the movement from one clip to another. iMovie comes with 24 standard transitions, and addition transitions are available with each theme.

Adding Transitions

Even though iMovie is set to automatically place transitions in the project, you can override those decisions and add your own.

Because you moved a few clips and deleted others, your project now lacks a transition between the last two clips. Although you don't necessarily need a transition there, it might look nicer.

1 Click the Transitions button.

The Transitions pane replaces the "Music and Sound Effects" pane to show all the transition options available with the currently selected theme. Hovering the mouse over a transition thumbnail will show a preview.

NOTE ▸ If no theme is selected, the first row of transitions is removed and the Transitions pane starts with the second row of transitions.

The Cross Dissolve transition is the standard transition. The others are more like novelty transitions and should be used sparingly.

2 Drag the Cross Dissolve between the last two clips in the project. A green insert line appears on the left side of the last clip.

Because iMovie adds transitions automatically by default, a dialog appears. You can choose to turn off automatic transitions and manually apply all future transitions, or click Cancel to close the dialog and continue to have iMovie insert transitions.

TIP ▸ If you turn off automatic transitions, the existing transitions and titles in the project will remain.

3 Click the "Turn off Automatic Transitions" button. With automatic transitions turned off, you can continue to change titles and transitions without viewing the dialog.

4 Click the Play button or press \ (backslash).

5 After you see the dissolve transition, press the Spacebar to stop playback.

TIP You can delete transitions by selecting them and pressing Delete.

You are now in control of adding and deleting transitions. Feels good doesn't it?

Replacing Transitions

If you don't like the style of a transition in your project, you can change it at any time while making your movie.

1 Skim over the transition between the mom clip and the kids clip. Let's make this more interesting by using one of the themed transitions.

2 From the Transitions pane, drag the Photo Album 4 transition to the second transition in the project window.

When you release the mouse button, a pop-up menu appears with three choices:

- Replace the one transition you are targeting.
- Replace all the transitions of a similar style.
- Replace all transitions.

Overusing a themed transition can cause it to lose its appeal, so let's replace only this transition.

3 From the pop-up menu, choose Replace to replace the transition.

4 To review what you've done, click the Play button, or press \ (backslash).

5 After you have viewed the new transition, press the Spacebar to stop playback.

Changing the Length of a Transition

You now know quite a bit about transitions. But you should also know how to make them longer or shorter in your project. Changing a transition length is easy to do but sometimes tricky to understand when it doesn't turn out as you expected.

To blend two clips, the transition must overlap the clips in the project to cover the blending. That's easy enough, but the trickery is required when you don't have enough captured video to extend the clip and cover the blending. When this happens, iMovie tries to extend a clip as far as it can but it doesn't announce that it can't give you what you want. It just does its best and moves on.

1 Click the transition you just replaced to select it, and in the toolbar, click the Inspector button.

The inspector appears with a data field in which to enter the duration of the transitions. You can enter any value.

2 Deselect the "Applies to all transitions" checkbox so that the adjustment is applied only to this one transition.

3 Set Duration to 10 seconds, and click Done.

4 Skim just before the transition in the project and then press the Spacebar to play through the transition.

5 After you have reviewed the transition, press the Spacebar to stop playback. The transition is longer, but it doesn't last 10 seconds.

6 Skim over the transition.

The duration of around 4.8 seconds is displayed above the transition. The duration is highlighted yellow to indicate that this is not what you entered, but it's the maximum iMovie can do with the clips that are captured.

Modifying a Themed Transition

Themed transitions are specially designed transitions that have more graphics in them and also permit more customization.

1 Slowly skim over the themed transition you modified in the preceding exercises. As you do so, in the viewer notice that pictures from your project are in the surrounding graphics of the transition. These are randomly selected frames from clips that you can customize, thereby allowing you to select more interesting images.

NOTE ▶ Themed transitions have different icons than the simple black-and-white icons of standard transitions, which makes them easier to locate when skimming through a project.

2 Click the themed transition to select it. The transition is highlighted, and two number tags are displayed in the project. The viewer displays the transition's graphic layout.

Each number tag in the project window corresponds to the same number in the viewer. You can drag the number tags in the project window to change the frame that appears in the viewer.

3 Drag tag 2 to the left until it is over the clip of the presents.

4 Drag tag 1 to the left until it is over the second clip in the project.

5 When the frame appears as you want, click Done in the upper-right corner of the viewer.

6 Click the Play Full Screen button to watch the entire project.

7 When the project is finished playing, press the Esc key to leave full-screen mode.

Some transitions have more frames and tags to adjust, but this one is relatively simple. You now have a more meaningful transition.

Getting a Movie to Your iPad, iPhone, or iPod

You will probably want to view your projects outside of your Mac and iMovie. Sharing movies is often part of a big presentation at a party or family gathering, but these days sharing is also a spur-of-the-moment occasion when you run into a friend on the street. With iMovie it's simple to place your movies on a mobile device and show them wherever you are.

Movies from iMovie are placed onto iPads, iPhones, and iPods using iTunes.

1 Choose Share > iTunes.

The iTunes Share window opens. You can select different movies sizes for the several devices that sync with iTunes. To the left are checkboxes to select the sizes you wish to create. At the top the supported devices are displayed, and below them you can choose from the sizes they support.

Although iPads and iPhones support the HD 720 size, the video clips you're using in this project were captured only at a smaller size, so you are limited to the smaller sizes.

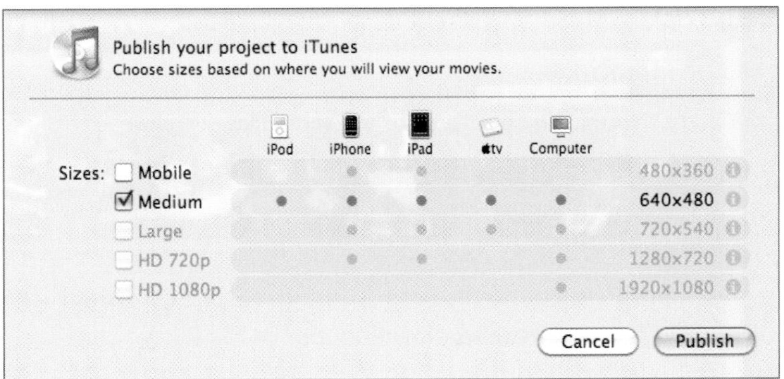

2 Select Medium because this size works with most devices.

3 Click Publish to create the movie file and send it to iTunes.

Once the movie file is in iTunes, the next time you sync your iPhone or iPad you can select this movie in the Movies tab and place it onto your mobile device.

Lesson Review

1. How do you import clips from the Mac?
2. What button do you click to remove a favorite or reject marking from a selected range of a clip?
3. How do you view clips that have been rejected?
4. How do you view the filmstrip for an Event in full-screen mode?
5. Name two of the three ways you can add clips to a project.
6. True or false: When you add clips to a project, you are duplicating the movie files on your hard disk.
7. How do you change the length of a transition in a project?
8. What button do you click to access your iTunes music library from within iMovie?
9. True or false: You get a movie onto your iPhone by choosing iPhone from the Share menu.

Answers

1. Choose File > Import > Movies.
2. In the toolbar, click the Unmark button.
3. From the Show pop-up menu at the bottom of the Event Browser, choose Rejected Only.
4. Position your pointer at the bottom of the screen to display a filmstrip of the entire Event.
5. Drag clips from the Event Browser into the project window. Select clips and click the "Add to Project" button in the toolbar. Select clips and press the E key.
6. False. You are not copying the actual movie files on your hard disk. The project window just references the selections from the Event, it doesn't duplicate files. The project file

is actually a small text document that point to clips in your Event. As a result, you can use a clip in multiple movies without using much disk space.

7. Select the transition and click the Inspector button in the toolbar to enter the duration in the Duration field.
8. In the toolbar, click the "Music and Sound Effects" button.
9. False. No iPhone item is present in the Share menu. Choose iTunes and then sync your iPhone with iTunes.

9

Lesson Files — iMovie Event: Max and Louisa in NYC

Time — This lesson takes approximately 30 minutes to complete.

Goals — Choose a new Event

Select a trailer

Change to the outline

Fill in the storyboard

Remove clips from a trailer

Customize a storyline

Lesson **9**

Having Fun with iMovie Trailers

Creating iMovie trailers is another simple way to produce an enjoyable, if short, movie. *Trailer* is a term used in Hollywood to describe the coming attractions you see before a feature presentation. iMovie trailers are a slick, creative way for you to turn your clips into bigger-than-life Hollywood-style Coming Attractions.

In this lesson, you'll select a movie genre and then customize a story line to fit your home video. Finally, you'll add clips according to the iMovie storyboard directions.

Selecting a New Event

Before you begin creating a trailer, you'll open a different Event, with footage somewhat more contemporary than the clips you used in the previous lesson.

1 From the Event Library list, select "Max and Louisa in NYC." This is an Event filled with clips that mom and dad took of their children, Max and Louisa, over the course of two years.

You'll use clips of Louisa, already marked as favorites, to make the trailer.

2 From the Show pop-up menu, choose "Favorites only."

The Event is sifted to show only the favorite clips. You can skim over a few clips to get an idea of what the Event contains.

Selecting a Trailer Genre

Movie trailers are a specific project type that you create in the same way you created the project in the previous lesson.

1 Choose File > New Project.

In the Project Settings window, instead of selecting from the themes, you'll preview and select one of the available trailers.

2 Scroll down until you can see all the movie trailers.

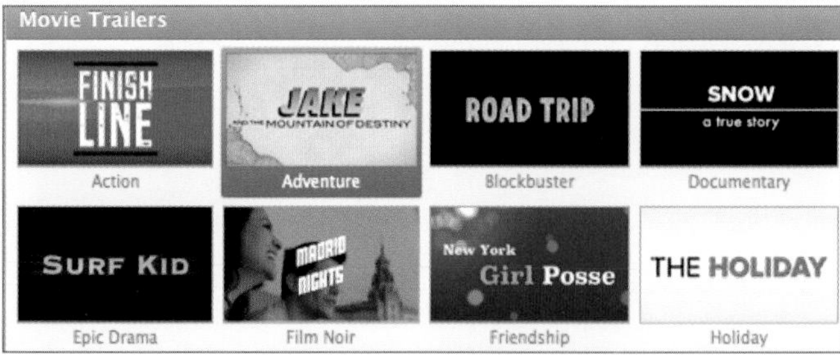

3 Click Adventure to select it. The trailer's preview appears on the right side of the window.

Below the preview is a brief suggestion concerning the type of video content you might use and how many "cast members" this trailer requires.

TIP The Blockbuster, Friendship, Sports, Supernatural, and Travel trailers allow you to change the number of "cast members".

4 In the Name field, type *Louisa's Adventure Trailer*.

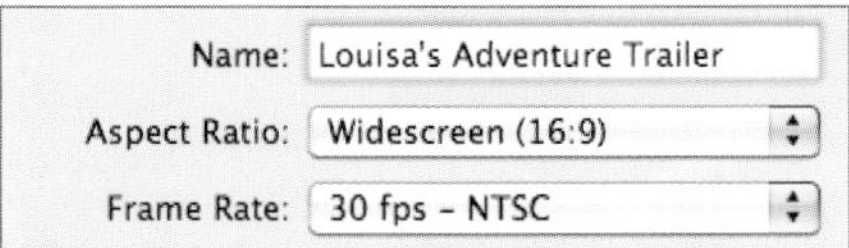

5 Set Frame Rate to "30 fps –NTSC."

6 Click Create.

The Trailer project window appears, but instead of a standard project window such as the Theme project window, the Trailer project window has a tabbed interface that guides you through the process of creating the trailer.

Changing the Outline

When you create a trailer, you'll first encounter the Outline tab. Here you can personalize the storyline text that accompanies your trailer. You'll be able to customize elements such as the cast list, the release date of your movie, and a studio name and logo. Although every line item in the outline can be changed, you'll start by changing the name of the lead character.

1 On the Movie Name line, click Jake. The movie name splits into three sections, and the name Jake is highlighted.

2 With the name Jake highlighted, change the name by typing *Louisa*.

3 On the Cast Star line, change Jake to *Louisa*.

4 Click twice on the name Callahan to highlight it, and then type Louisa's last name, *Blakely*.

You will also need to change the gender so that any titles using pronouns will use the correct pronoun.

5 Click the Male label under Louisa's name and choose Female.

6 To change the studio logo, place the mouse pointer over the Snowy Mountain Peak. The viewer shows the Snowy Mountain Peak studio logo, which—due to international copyright laws—looks similar but is clearly different from the logo of an Actual Large Hollywood Movie Studio.

7 Click the Snowy Mountain Peak text. A menu of alternative imitation studio logos appears.

8 Select Spinning Earth in Space to change the current logo. You could also change the name of the studio, but you'll leave it as it is.

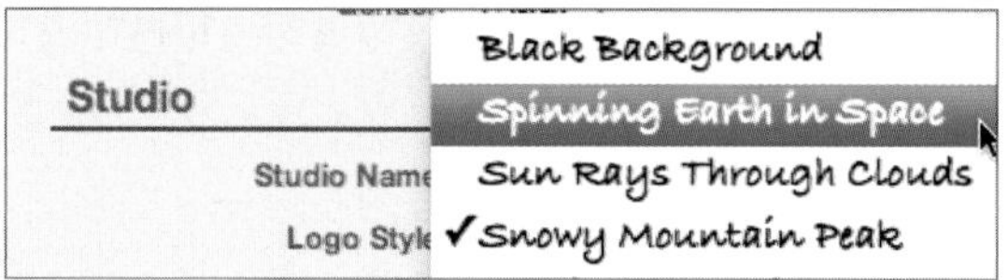

9 In the Outline pane, scroll down to view the credits that will appear at the end of your trailer.

10 Skim over the credit text to preview the credits in the viewer.

By default, iMovie fills in the credit list using the "me" card in the address book of your Mac, but you can change each credit as necessary. You'll leave that part for later, and move on to adding clips.

Filling in the Storyboard

With the Outline personalized, you can move on to the storyboard.

1 Click the Storyboard tab.

   The storyboard contains placeholders that describe the types of clips to add, how long those clips should be, and an appropriate order for the clips. It's good to start by playing the trailer without adding any clips to get a sense of what you are creating.

2 At the top of the storyboard, skim to the start of the HighDef Films title.

3 Press the Spacebar to play the trailer.

   The trailer includes titles, music, and all the placeholders you need to create a complete coming attraction. All you need to do is select your best clips to match the placeholder descriptions.

4 When the trailer finishes playing, scroll the storyboard to the top.

   The first placeholder is highlighted yellow to give you an indication of the type of clip you need to find. In this case, you want a 2.7-second landscape clip. Clips with a shorter duration will not work. The first clip in the Event is a 3-second NYC street clip, so you'll use that.

5 Make sure that "Favorites only" is still selected in the Show pop-up menu. Skim over the first clip in the Event, which shows NYC taxis passing by.

   Adding clips for trailers works a bit differently than adding clips to other projects because the placeholder predefines the length of the clip.

6 Skim along the first clip in the Event until you see about half of the taxis coming in.

7 Click the mouse button to add this to the trailer. The placeholder is filled in with the selected clip, and the yellow highlight moves to the second placeholder in the storyboard.

This next placeholder requires a clip of Louisa. This is the first time she'll appear in the trailer, so it should be a clip that clearly introduces her.

8 Skim over the second clip of Louisa putting on her shoes. There is a nice point in this clip where she turns to face the camera.

9 Skim to the point where Louisa starts to turn and face the camera, and then click to add this clip to the trailer.

Now you'll take a short break to review your trailer.

10 Skim to the start of the HighDef Films title at the top of the storyboard.

11 Press the Spacebar to play the trailer.

12 After the second clip, press the Spacebar to stop playback and get ready to add more clips.

13 Skim over the third clip of Louisa zipping up her coat.

14 Click at the very start of that clip to add it to the trailer.

The next placeholder suggests a medium clip. A medium clip is usually framed so the bottom of the shot begins at the knees or waist of the subject. The fourth clip in the Event is just a landscape of some leaves, but the fifth clip in the Event shows Louisa swinging on the rings. This works as a good medium clip.

NOTE ▶ The placeholder clip description (medium, close-up, long shot) is just a suggestion. You can select any type of clip composition, but the duration cannot be shorter than the placeholder.

15 On the fifth clip in the Event, click when Louisa looks toward the rings.

The next placeholder suggestion is for a landscape clip. Now you can return to the fourth clip in the Event.

16 Add the fourth clip of Louisa kicking leaves.

Next, you'll fill in the remaining trailer placeholders using the remaining clips in the order that they appear in the Event.

17 Add the remaining clips in the Event by clicking at the start of each one, beginning with Louisa on the rings and ending with the Louisa wearing a pink tutu on her head.

Start with the sixth clip.

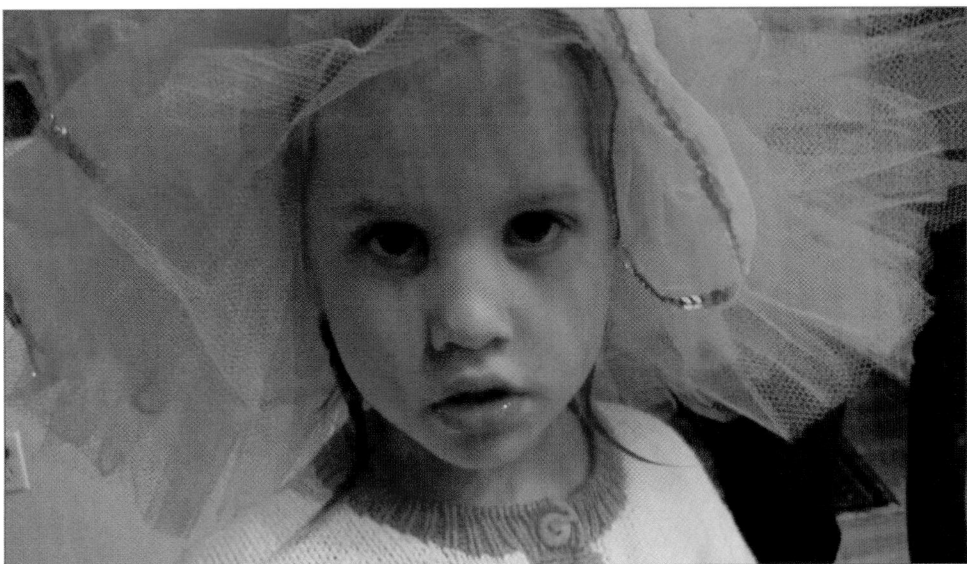

End with clip of Louisa wearing a tutu.

Your exciting adventure trailer is complete, and you can play it to see what you've created. It's a fun movie to watch and really simple to create, but you can still make some changes to improve it.

Replacing Clips in a Trailer

In some cases you may want to replace one clip in the trailer with another one.

1. In the Storyboard, skim to the last clip (Louisa with a tutu on her head).

   TIP You can turn off audio playback while skimming by choosing View > Audio Skimming.

   You have a more playful clip you can use here, so you'll remove this clip and then add another one in the placeholder.

2. In the upper-right corner of the clip's thumbnail, click the Undo button.

3. Click the empty placeholder to select it. The yellow highlight appears.

4. In the Event, skim to the last clip of Louisa wearing the tutu.

5. Click at the very start of the clip to fill in the empty placeholder.

6. In the upper-right corner of the project window, click the Play button.

Knowing that you can change your trailer even after all the placeholders are filled relieves the creative pressure when you're producing your first few cinematic masterpieces.

Using the Clip Trimmer

Although each clip in the trailer has a predefined length, you can change the range used by adjusting it in the Clip Trimmer.

1 In the Trailer window, skim to the clip of Louisa dancing outside. The clip ends a bit too soon—we never get to see her pose at the end. You can correct that in the Clip Trimmer.

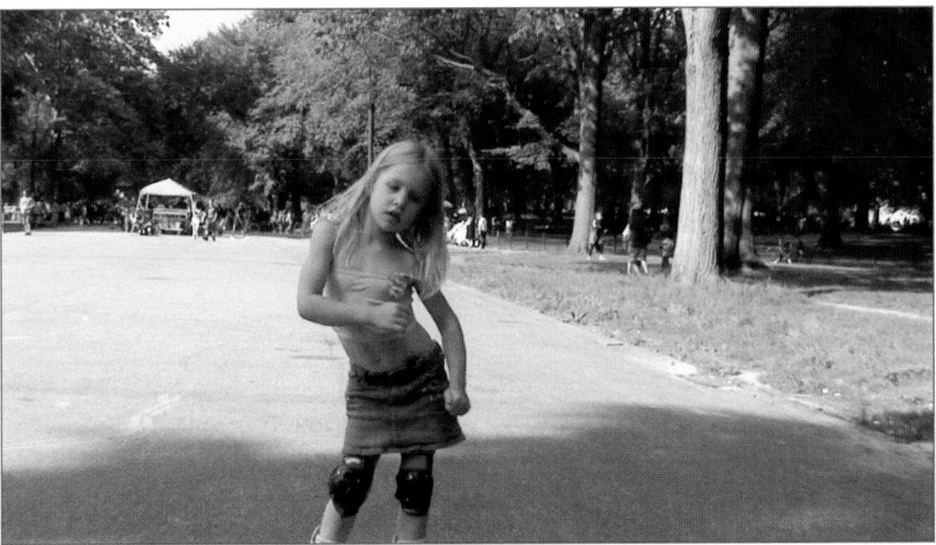

2 Click the Clip Trimmer button. The Clip Trimmer replaces the Event Browser and shows a more detailed view of the entire clip, as well as the selected range in the trailer.

3 In the Clip Trimmer, skim past the right edge of the selected range to see Louisa's little dance. As you can see, the best part wasn't included, so you'll reposition the selected range to include the ending of the dance.

4 Position the mouse pointer in the center of the selected range so that it changes to a hand icon.

5 Drag the selected range to the right.

6 Control-click (or right-click) the selected range.

7 From the shortcut menu, choose Play Selection.

8 In the upper right, click Done to close the Clip Trimmer.

> **TIP** If you want to add more clips than the trailer allows or change a clip's length, you can convert the trailer to a project by choosing File > Convert to Project. After you convert to a project, you cannot convert back to a trailer, so it's wise to duplicate the trailer by choosing File > Duplicate Project.

The trailer is complete, and you can play it to review what you've created. It's a delightful movie to watch, but you could still improve it.

Personalizing the Storyline

You can personalize the trailer's story line by changing its text. Every line of text in the trailer can be rewritten. In this trailer, the main title at the end reads, "Louisa and the Mountain of Destiny." That's a dramatic title, but because there aren't that many mountains in New York City, you'll change the name to something more appropriate.

1 Skim down to the movie title at the end of the storyboard.

2 Click the words "Mountain of Destiny." If the words aren't selected, double-click them in the storyboard.

3 Replace "Mountain of Destiny" by typing *Big Apple.*

4 Click the Credits shaded text box to stop text editing.

TIP After you change text in the storyboard, the right side of the text box displays an Undo button. Click the Undo button to restore the orignal text.

The changes made in the Storyboard tab can be seen in the viewer as you type, and you can play the trailer to see the entire movie.

5 In the upper-right corner of the project window, click the Play button.

Trailers offer a unique way to show off your video clips in style. And just like the movie you made in the previous lesson, you can share it to your iPad, iPhone, iPod, or any other device supported in iMovie.

Lesson Review

1. Where do you find the choices for movie trailers?
2. How can you change the studio logo at the beginning of the movie trailer?
3. What determines the length of a clip added to the trailer?
4. True or false: It is possible to extend or shorten the length of a clip in a trailer.
5. True or false: You can change the trailer style at any time while you are making the trailer.

Answers

1. Movie trailers are located in the Project Settings window when you choose File > New Project.
2. Once you create a new trailer, you can select a studio logo from the Outline tab.
3. A clip's length is determined by the placeholder in the trailer.
4. False. You cannot change the length of a clip in the trailer. You can change which part of the clip is used by adjusting it in the Clip Trimmer.
5. False. Once you begin creating a trailer, you must start over again if you want to select a new trailer style.

10

Lesson Files

iMovie Events: Marlins Spring Softball

Desktop > ATS iLife11 Book Files > Lesson 10 > Leopards Logo.jpg, Marlins Logo.jpg, Damian.jpg

Time

This lesson takes approximately 30 minutes to complete.

Goals

Switch projects in the Library

Use the Sports theme

Create sports-oriented video effects

Lesson **10**

Creating Your Own Sports Highlights Video

Sports are among the most popular events for families to capture on video. But endless hours of T-ball smack down don't always make for good popcorn eatin' video. Why can't our home sports videos look like the highlights we see on TV? We all want to add dramatic slow-motion replays and have flying sports graphics. Why not us? Why not indeed! The Sports theme in iMovie is more than a theme—it's a true game tracking, player highlighting machine!

Switching Projects in the Library

iMovie allows you to make as many projects as you want, and you can access them at any time using the Project Library. You'll begin this exercise with a project that already has all its clips in place.

1 To access other projects, click the Project Library button.

In the Project Library, every project is listed with a filmstrip. When a project is selected in the Project Library, you can watch or skim it using the filmstrip.

2 Click the First Game project to select it.

TIP After you select a project in the Project Library, you can click the Play Full Screen button to play the project in full-screen mode.

3 Skim over the filmstrip of the softball game to see it in the viewer.

4 Press the Spacebar at any time to play the project.

5 Click the Edit Project button to open the project.

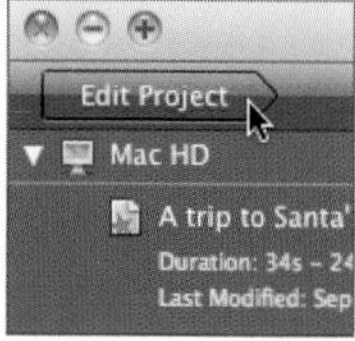

The Project Library slides away to reveal the full project showing a kids' softball game. You are going to finish this project by creating some impressive sports-oriented effects.

Applying a Theme to an Existing Project

Most of this project is already completed, but no titles or transitions have been added. When you apply a theme to an existing project, titles and transitions can instantly be applied.

1 In the toolbar, choose the Title Browser.

2 At the top of the Title Browser, click Set Theme. The Project Themes Browser opens to display all the themes.

3 Select the Sports theme and select the "Automatically add transitions" checkbox.

4 Click OK.

5 Click the Play button.

By enabling automatic transitions, the Sports theme titles and transitions are added throughout the project and also become available in the Title and Transitions panes.

Using the Sports Team Editor

You can use the Sports theme as you would any other theme, but if you have a passion for a sports season and record all the games, you can go a few extra yards to make your movie into a real champion. The Sports Team Editor is a database that can track all the teams and players in a season, so when it comes time to make your game highlights video, all that information is at your fingertips.

Entering Team and Player Information

You can start entering information into the Sports Team Editor at any time, so don't worry if the season is half over and you have a few projects already started.

1 From the Window menu, choose Sports Team Editor.

The editor is organized into two sections. In the top half, you add and delete teams in the league. The lower half displays the players for a selected team.

You'll start by adding your team to the roster.

2 At the bottom of the Teams section, click the Create New Team button.

A copy of the Leopards team, Leopards 2, is created and ready for you to customize. You can leave the Season as Spring '10 and change the other information.

3 Double-lick Leopards 2 and type *Marlins*. Press Tab to add Marlins as the second team in the league.

Now you'll change the sport from baseball to softball.

4 Click the word "baseball" in the Marlins' team entry. A list of common sports is displayed, but softball isn't there. You'll have to modify the sports list to correct this heinous omission.

5 At the bottom of the Sports Team Editor, click the disclosure triangle next to Sports. A list of sports appears, as well as the stats columns you want displayed for the players in each sport.

6 At the bottom of the Sports section, click the Create New Sport button. A new sport entry appears for you to customize.

7 Type *Softball* as the Sports Name, and then press Tab to move to the next column title.

The columns you create will contain statistics you want to see for each player.

8 Type *Position*, press Tab to move to the next column, and type *Age*. You can add whatever stat you want, but using more than 20 letters will cause the text to be very small in your movie.

9 Press Tab again and type *Nickname*.

10 Press Tab to move to the last column and type *Favorite Pro Player.*

Volleyball	Position	Age	Height	Weight
Softball	Position	Age	Nickname	Favorite Pro Player
+ -				

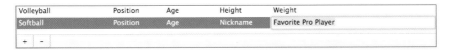

You can now change the sport that these teams play.

11 In the Teams section of the editor, set the Sport to Softball for both the Leopards and the Marlins.

Now that the teams and sport are set up, you can add players.

12 In the Teams section, make sure that Marlins is selected.

13 At the bottom of the Players for Marlins section, click the Create New Player button to add a new player entry to the Marlins lineup, ready to be customized.

14 Type *26* as the player's number, then press Tab and type *Damian Krupps* as the player's name.

15 Press Tab again to enter his position as *Shortstop*.

16 In the next three columns, set Age to *9*, Nickname to *Prime Time*, and Favorite Pro Player to *Big Papi*.

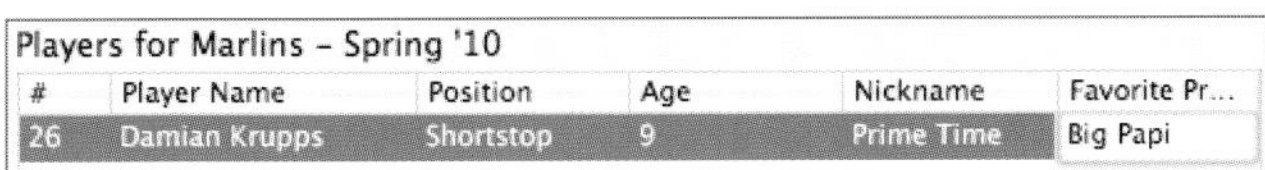

Players for Marlins – Spring '10

#	Player Name	Position	Age	Nickname	Favorite Pr...
26	Damian Krupps	Shortstop	9	Prime Time	Big Papi

OK, you've entered the stats for the player, now you can add the team logos and player photos.

Adding Graphics and Player Photos

What would a slick sports highlight show be without personalized graphics of your players and team logos?

1. In the Teams section of the Sports Team Editor, select the Leopards.
2. In the Team logo area, click the "Add" button.

3. Navigate to Desktop > ATS iLife11 Book Files > Lesson 10 and open **Leopards Logo.jpg**.
4. In the Teams section, select the Marlins and repeat steps 2 and 3 to open Documents > Desktop > ATS iLife11 Book Files > Lesson 10 > **Marlins Logo.jpg**.

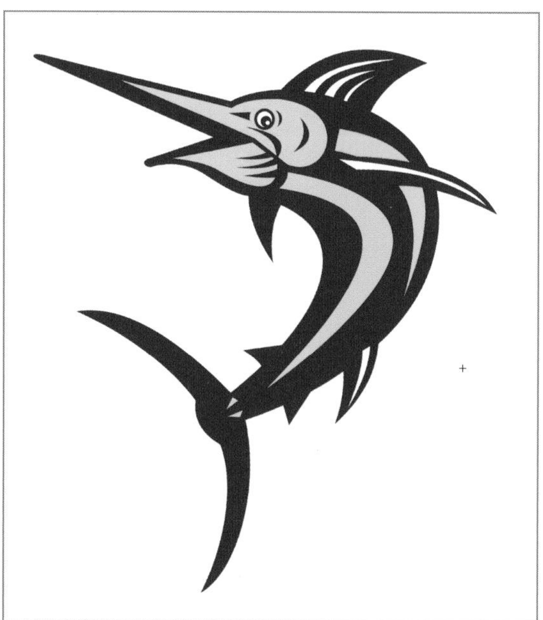

Now you'll add a picture for one of the players.

5 In the Players section of the Sports Team Editor, select Damian Krupps.

6 In the Player photo area, click the "Add" button.

7 Navigate to Desktop > ATS iLife11 Book Files > Lesson 10 and open **Damian.jpg**.

TIP You can drag photos into the Team Logo well or the Player Photo well instead of using the Add buttons.

You now have the beginnings of a full league database with team logos and player photos and stats. When you assemble your sports project, you can use all of this information to create championship graphics just like those you see on TV.

Customizing a Team vs. Team Graphic

It's time to put your database to work in a project. The opening of this project should show the two competing teams, and with the Sports theme, you have a title that does just that. Unlike in Lessons 8 and 9 where iMovie added the titles for you, in this lesson you'll add a title on your own using the Title browser.

1 In the toolbar, click the Title Browser button.

The Title Browser places theme-specific titles at the top and displays the standard titles available to every project below them.

2 Drop the "Team vs. Team" title to the left of the first clip to make it the starting clip in the project.

Because iMovie is set to add transitions automatically, applying a transition opens a dialog, just as in Lesson 8.

3 Select "Turn off Automatic Transitions."

A background selection window now opens. This step is really a formality because the title design includes its own background. So, whatever you choose here will not be seen in your movie.

NOTE ▶ For more information about adding titles, see Lesson 12, "Moviemaking with Photos and iPhoto Clips ."

4 Click any background style.

The "Team vs. Team" title is added to the project and displayed in the viewer. Because you had only two teams in the Sports Team Editor, those two teams are displayed. To change the participating teams, you would select them in the viewer from the Team pop-up menu.

You could also choose to add a new team or edit the names of existing teams by selecting the appropriate item in the Team pop-up menu.

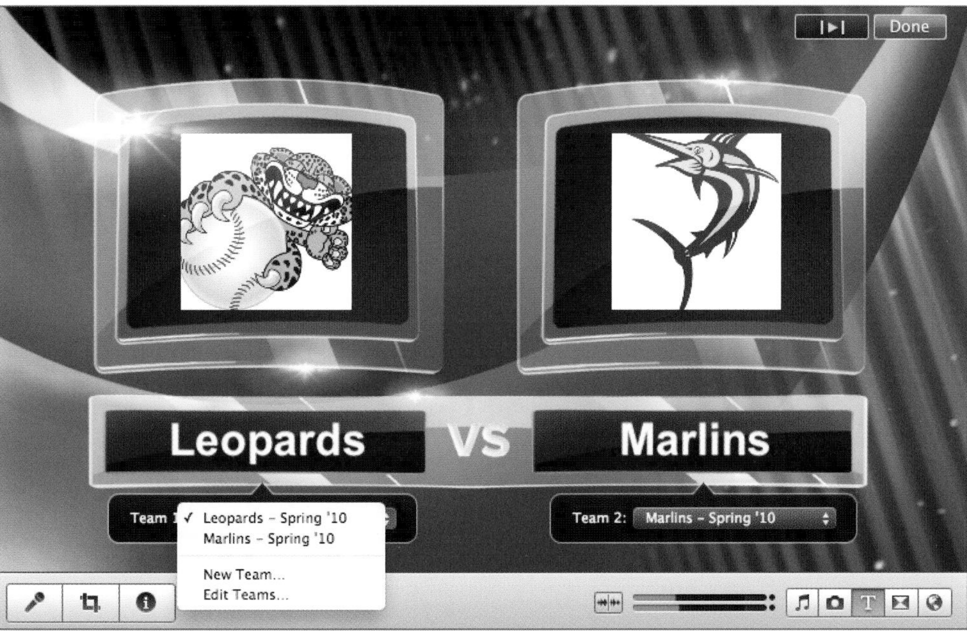

5 In the viewer, click the Play button to see the title in action.

Titles are a major part of any sports video and many of the titles in the Sports theme take advantage of the team and player information you add into the Sports Team Editor. Some titles combine with visual effects to give you the feel of a network sports program.

Creating an Instant Replay Effect

The instant replay should be a key part of any well-produced sports highlights show, including yours. An instant replay (for the sports-lingo deprived) is a clip that is repeated at a slower pace to show the action in greater detail and, of course, to increase the drama of a play. Your first step toward creating an instant replay is to find that game-changing event in your project.

1 Skim over the seventh clip in the project. This is a good highlight clip of the star player at bat. You can select just the portion of the clip where he swings his bat as your instant replay.

2 Select a range that starts just before the ball enters the frame in the upper-right corner and ends just before he begins to run. This selection range marks the area that will repeat in slow motion.

3 Choose Clip > Instant Replay > 25%.

This percentage dictates the playback speed. Choosing 25% reduces the normal playback speed by 75%.

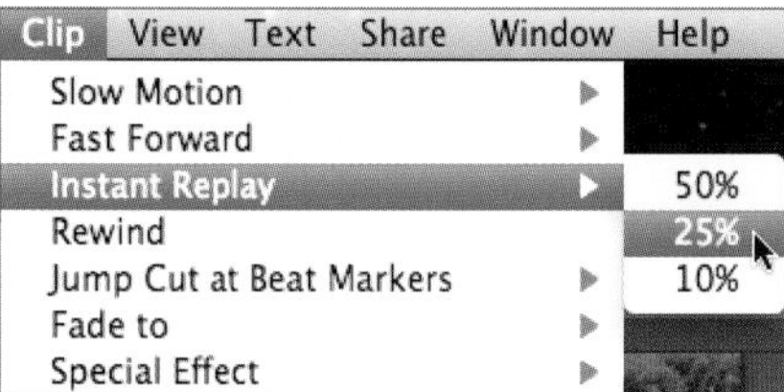

In the project, the clip splits and the instant replay is inserted with a title.

4 Skim before the instant replay begins and press the Spacebar to play your new effect. Stop playback once you have seen the entire effect.

That's a classic sports effect that every player wants to see herself in.

Highlighting a Player

You can also single out specific players with graphics that highlight him and his stats to create a special thrill for the kids on a team. Once you've entered all of a player's information in the Sports Team Editor, you can make a Player Stats title to highlight that player.

1 Skim to the start of the clip from which you created the instant replay.

   Before the instant replay begins, the clip has a long introduction. This long section before the replay is a good place to show the player's stats.

   NOTE ▶ You can add titles over clips as well as backgrounds.

2 Click the Title Browser button if the titles aren't already visible.

3 Drag the Player Stats title to the third clip from the end, so that the first third of the clip is highlighted in blue. The blue highlight indicates the portion of the clip in which the title will appear. You want to display the title in only the first third of this clip.

   When the title is applied, you can select the player you want to highlight.

4 In the viewer, select the Marlins as the Team and Damian as the Player. Click Done.

Earlier, you entered information for only one player so that's all that appears in the list. Now you'll adjust the title placement and see how it looks.

5 To start the title a little later in the clip, drag it to the right until the title ends about halfway through the clip.

6 Play the clip to view your title.

Your sports theme movie is complete. Next, you might share your movie with all the players and their families by placing the movie on your iPad, iPhone, or iPod. However, you could also upload your movies to an online sharing site for everyone to access. You'll learn more about posting movies to video sharing sites in Lesson 12.

Lesson Review

1. True or false: Instant replay is available only when using the Sports theme.
2. How do you enter the information for the Player Stats title?
3. How can you access other projects you've created in iMovie?
4. How do you add a logo of your team to the Sports Team Editor?
5. What sports can be used in the Sports Team Editor?

Answers

1. False. Instant replay fits naturally with a Sports theme but can be used in all projects, with or without a theme.
2. The Player Stats title gets its information from the Sports Team Editor. You must enter all the players and their stats into the Sports Team Editor for the Player Stats title to acquire and display player information.
3. When you want to move from one project to another, open a project from the Project Library.
4. In the Sports Team Editor, under the Team Logo well, click the Add button to import the photo from your Mac.
5. You can add any sports you desire by clicking the Create New Sport button at the bottom of the Sports section in the Sports Team Editor.

11

Lesson Files	iMovie Events: Max and Louisa in NYC
Time	This lesson takes approximately 60 minutes to complete.
Goals	Make a project without a theme
	Edit a project
	Enhance clips
	Work with multiple audio tracks
	Stabilize a clip

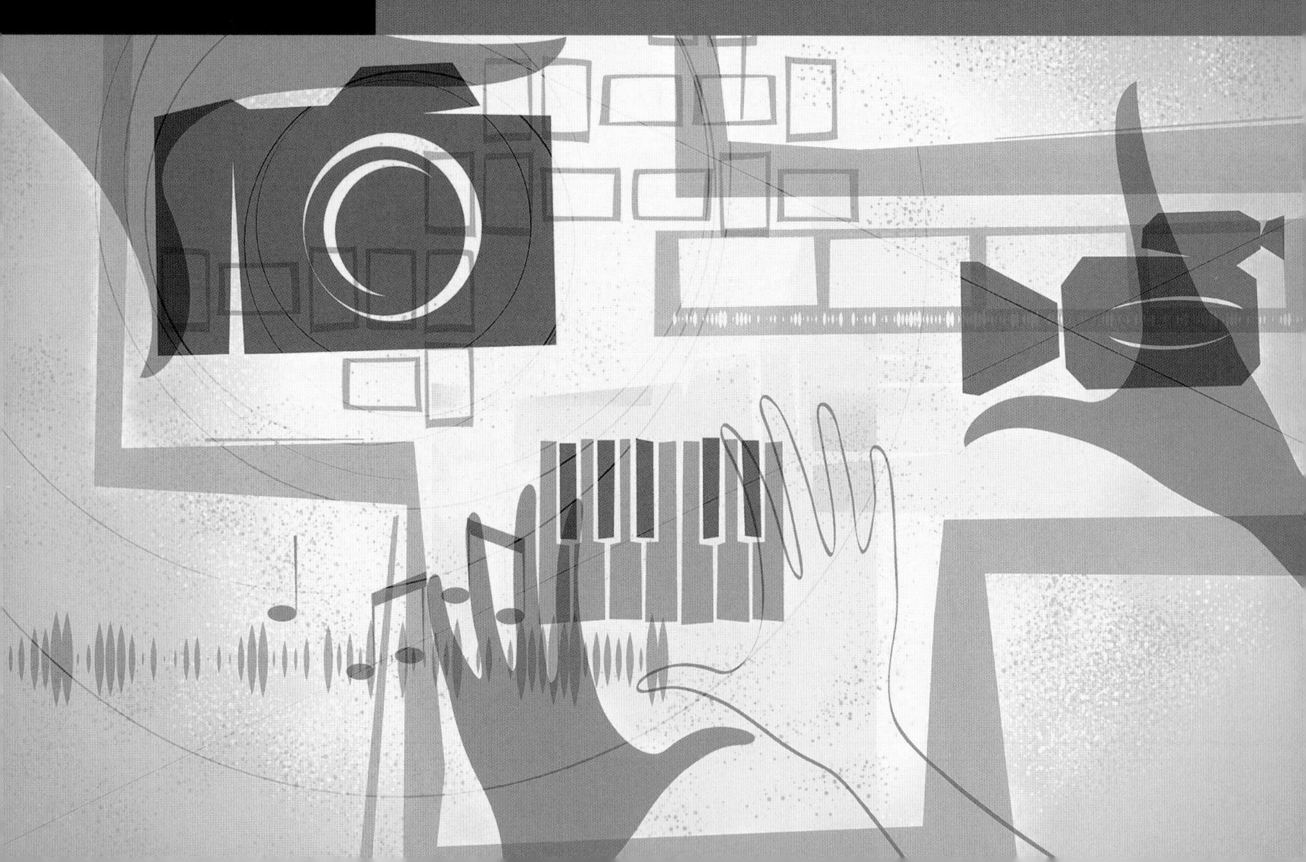

Finish with the sixth clip from the end.

TIP Each filmstrip thumbnail represents five seconds of the clip, by default. A filmstrip with six thumbnails is around 30 seconds in length. You can change the length that each thumbnail represents by dragging the Thumbnail Duration slider in the lower-left corner of the Event Browser..

5 Click the Edit button, or press the E key.

A dialog appears to suggest that selecting more precise ranges in a clip might make a better movie. In general this is a good rule to follow, but most of these clips are short and you'll be trimming some of the longer ones.

6 In the dialog, click Continue to add the clips to the project.

7 Make sure your pointer is not over the browser, and then click the Play Project button, or press the \ (backslash) key to play the project.

As you play through this short project, you'll notice that when you add multiple clips at once, you will probably want to make multiple changes.

Editing a Movie

Okay, someone needs to say it. Not everyone likes to watch your home movies. It's not that your kids aren't cute, or your dog isn't incredibly smart, or your vacation wasn't beautiful. It's because home movies tend to drag on and on. Here's the good news: It's easy to fix.

Taking the time to refine and tighten your project will make the difference between a boring movie and something people will truly enjoy watching.

Deleting Portions of a Clip

Removing sections of clips that are just too long or unimportant is a fundamental way to refine clips in your project.

Although you have more precise ways to remove portions of a clip, let's start with the easiest and quickest way.

1 In the project, skim to the clip of Louisa chasing a remote control car. It's in the middle of the project and is the 13th clip from the end.

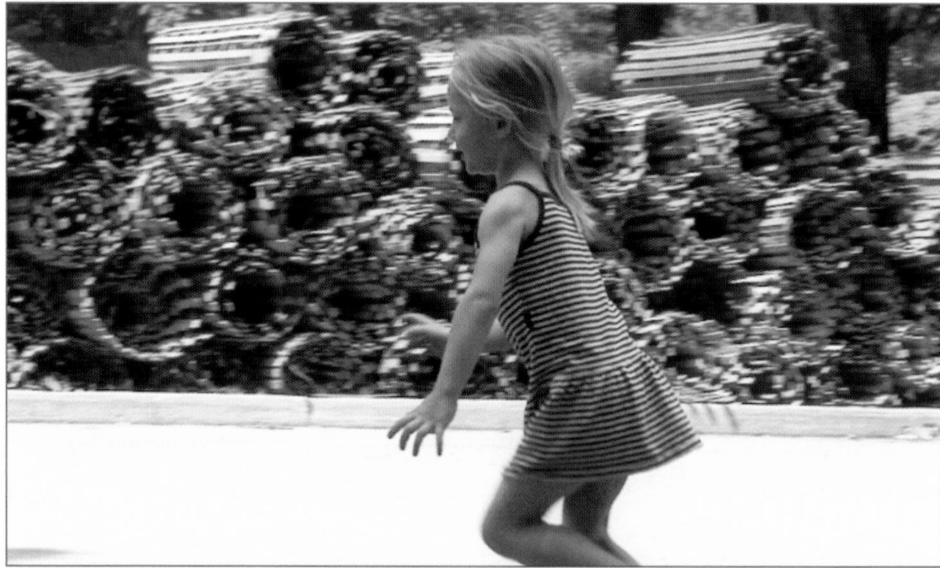

This clip is a good candidate for editing. All the interesting action happens at the start of the clip, so why not remove the less-interesting ending?

2 Skim to the point where Louisa is no longer on screen and then back up a tiny bit until you can see Louisa again.

3 Drag a selection range to the right from this point to the end of the clip. You should now have a 2.7-second selection range that you can remove from the project.

4 Press the Delete key to remove the selected range.

TIP In this example, you selected the range you wanted to delete. You could also select the range to keep and then choose Clip > Trim to Selection to delete the unselected portion of the clip.

As when you delete an entire clip, the deleted portion of the clip isn't removed from your Event, it's just removed from the project.

Using a Replace Edit

Another common refinement is simply replacing clips that may have looked nice in the Event but don't work well in your project. Instead of deleting the offending clip and separately inserting a new clip, you can perform a single step to achieve both goals.

1 Skim over the first clip in the project.

This clip doesn't work as the opening to your movie. The second clip in the project is a classic NYC street scene—a clearer way to introduce the setting. Let's replace the first clip with the NYC street clip.

2 Skim over the clip of a rainy New York scene to see the clip. You may need to scroll the window.

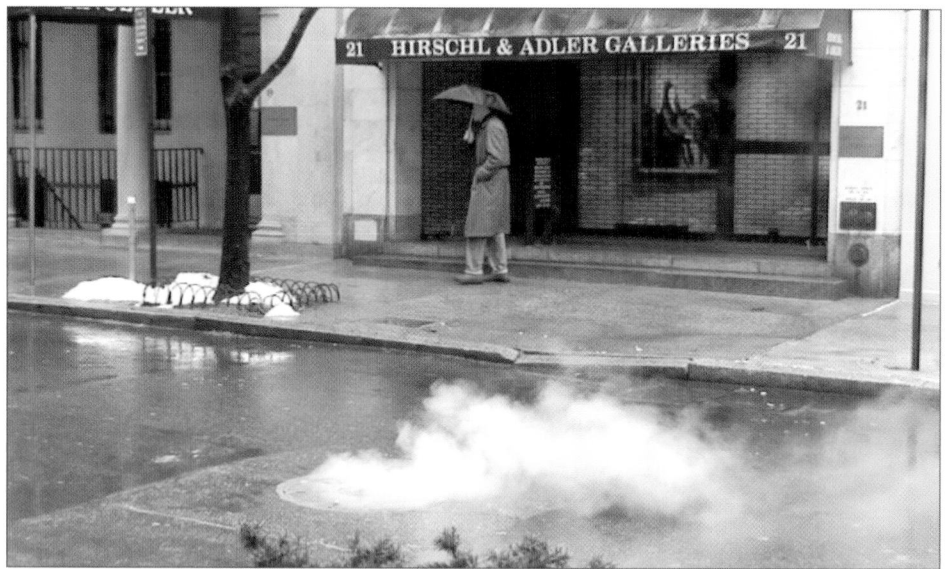

This clip is exactly the type you are looking for; a nice, rainy NYC street scene. Because it is only 2.4 seconds long, you'll use the entire clip.

3 Drag this clip in the Event over the first clip in the project and release the mouse button.

   When you drop a clip from your Event directly on top of a clip in your project, the Edit pop-up menu appears with a few simple editing choices.

4 From the Edit pop-up menu, choose Replace.

The new clip replaces the old clip in the project. Replace is a simple yet common edit that you'll use often.

Inserting and Splitting a Clip

The Edit pop-up menu also contains Insert edits, useful for splitting a single clip into two parts and placing a new clip between those parts.

1 In the project, skim over the long clip of Louisa playing in the snow.

This is a very long clip to show uninterrupted. You could use a shorter portion of the clip but its delightful quality is the long, seemingly oblivious back-and-forth traipsing in the snow. You can preserve the fun in this clip and still sustain interest by breaking it up with other clips.

2 In the Event Browser, skim over the snowy park shot which is the next-to-last clip. This similarly snowy scene is a good clip to insert.

3 From the browser, select the entire snowy park clip and drag it into the project window about one-third of the way into the long clip of Louisa.

4 From the Edit pop-up menu, choose Insert.

The snowy path clip splits the longer clip into two sections. You'll insert one more clip to break up the second half of the clip.

5 Skim over the last clip in the Event browser. This is a seven-second clip of Louisa dragging her snow-filled sled. Let's select a shorter range.

6 Skim to the point at which the tip of the sled enters on the right.

7 Drag the selection range to the right until Louisa is near the left edge of the frame. This creates a selection range of about 3.3 seconds.

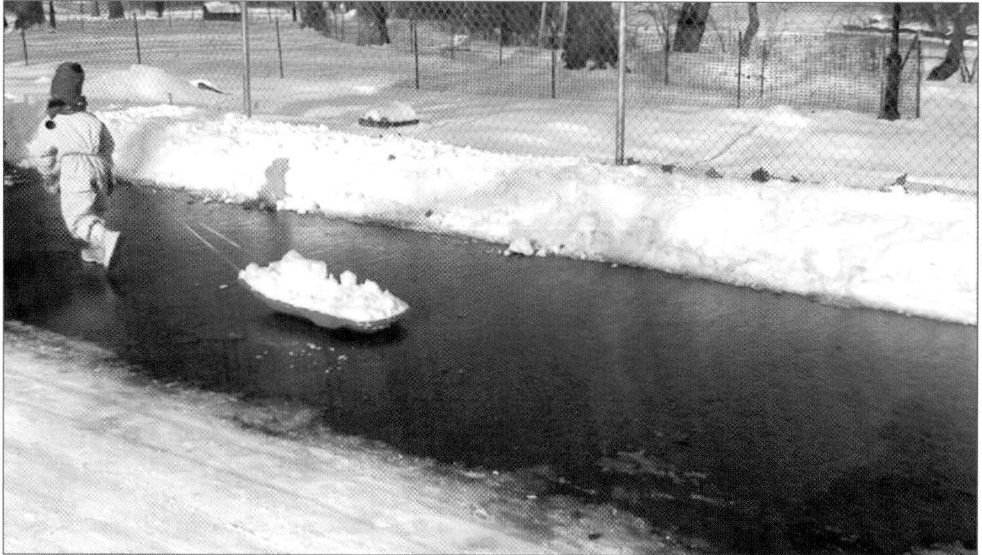

8 Drag the clip up into the project window, about one-third of the way into the longer, second clip of Louisa in the snow.

9 Release the mouse button when you are roughly between the second and third thumbnails on the filmstrip.

10 From the Edit pop-up menu, choose Insert.

The clip of Louisa and the Sled is inserted, splitting the longer clip into two sections. This creates three shorter eight-second clips of Louisa in the snow, split by other snowy clips.

11 Play the project to see how the clips flow together. Even though this creates a good winter-in-the-city section, sometimes you can give a sequence of clips a little extra distinction using effects and enhancements.

Enhancing Clips

Until now your focus has been on placing clips within your project. Although that is a fundamental technique of moviemaking, another aspect deals with enhancing those clips. Much like you brighten, add contrast, and boost image saturation in iPhoto, you can enhance video clips in iMovie.

Speeding and Slowing Clip Playback

Let's begin enhancing your clips with speed changes. Changing a clip's playback speed can enhance a dramatic or comedic situation; but, as with all jokes, it's funny once or twice and embarrassing if you use it all the time.

1 In the project, skim over the first clip of Louisa playing in the snow.

   This is already a fun clip, made more fun by splitting it into three parts. You can even give it more impact by speeding up Louisa's frolicking.

   Select the clip, and then in the toolbar, click the Inspector button.

   In the inspector the Clip tab includes many functions that can be applied to the clip, including speed changes.

   Drag the speed slider to the right two notches to increase the speed to 400%.

   TIP Some camcorders record in video formats that cannot accept speed changes. Clips in those formats will display a button in the inspector that you can click to convert the clips prior to applying a speed change.

   In the project window, the clip is displayed using only one thumbnail because its duration has changed from eight seconds to two seconds.

2 Press the Spacebar to review the speed change, and then press Spacebar again to stop playback.

3 Click Done to close the inspector.

   The second clip of Louisa playing in the snow needs the same speed change applied, but you'll apply it in a different way.

4 In the project, select the second clip of Louisa playing in the snow.

5 Choose Clip > Fast Forward > 4x.

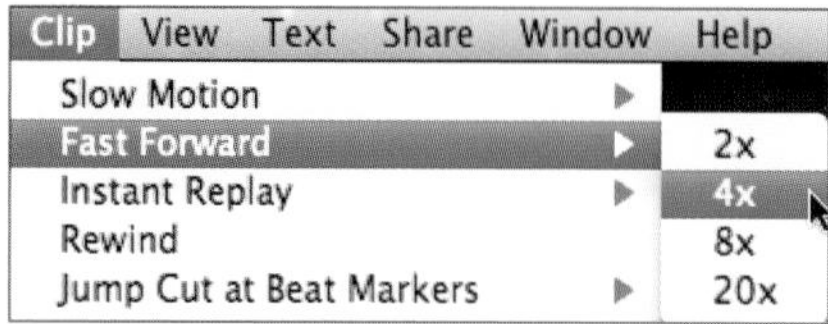

The Clip menu has settings for fast and slow motion but the results are the same as in the inspector.

6 Press the / (slash) key to play the selected clip and review the speed change.

As you may have noticed, iMovie often provides more than one way to achieve the same result. Your choice of method may depend on how quickly you can get the result, the adjustment precision available, or merely which one pops into your head first.

Using the Action Menu

One more clip of Louisa playing in the snow should be sped up. To do so, you'll use the very handy Action menu. The Action menu saves you the steps of selecting the clip and opening the inspector. Anytime you can save a step or two during editing, you'll finish the movie quicker and enjoy it sooner.

1 In the project window, skim over the third clip of Louisa playing in the snow.

The Action menu is displayed in the lower-left corner of a clip only as you skim over the clip.

2 Click the Action menu gear icon on the clip. When you click the gear icon, the Action menu appears. One of its options opens the Clip Adjustments tab of the inspector.

3 Choose Clip Adjustments.

4 Drag the speed slider to the right to increase the speed to 400%, then view your results by pressing the Spacebar to start and stop loop playback.

5 Click Done to close the inspector.

You'll use the Action menu a number of times in future lessons. It's a convenient way to get to the inspector while saving a few clicks.

Previewing and Applying Video Effects

Video effects can change the look of clips to mimic the appearance of Hollywood movies. Simple color effects, such as Sepia or Black & White, can be applied. Or you can use more sophisticated effects such as Dream and Bleach Bypass. You can apply only one video effect at a time in iMovie, but it's easy to try them out using the Preview Palette.

Your current project starts out with both New York City and the kids slowly waking up. Then, with a burst of energy, we move outside. To embellish the contrast, you'll apply a video effect to the first part of the project. Let's start by applying an effect to one clip.

1 Open the Action menu on the first clip in the project, and choose Clip Adjustments.

2 Click the Video Effect button that currently reads None.

The Preview Palette appears with all its effects. To try one, you can skim over them and watch the clip in the viewer.

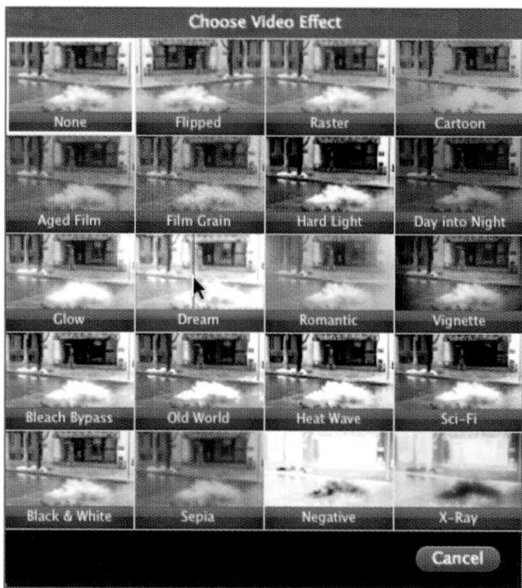

3. Skim over Aged Film, Dream, and Romantic. You are not limited to skimming. You can preview the effect by playing the clip.

4. While skimming over Dream, press the Spacebar.

   The current clip plays with a preview of the video effect applied.

5. Click Black & White to apply the effect to the clip and confirm your choice.

   The Preview Palette flips over to display the Clip Adjustments tab.

6. Close the inspector.

   TIP As with transitions, enhance the story with video effects; don't let them become the center of the story.

The filmstrip thumbnails in the project will not show the video effect, but if you skim or play the clip in the project you'll see that the video effect is applied.

Copying and Pasting Adjustments

The Black & White effect should be applied to the next eight clips that make up the opening of your movie. iMovie has a fast way to apply a video effect from one clip to many clips using Copy and Paste.

1. Select the first clip in the project, if necessary.

2 Choose Edit > Copy.

3 Click the second clip in the project to select it.

4 Shift-click the clip of the key turning in the door lock. Holding down the Shift key selects all the clips between the two clips you click.

5 Choose Edit > Paste Adjustments > Video Effect. In the Paste Adjustments submenu you'll see the options you can paste to the selected clips.

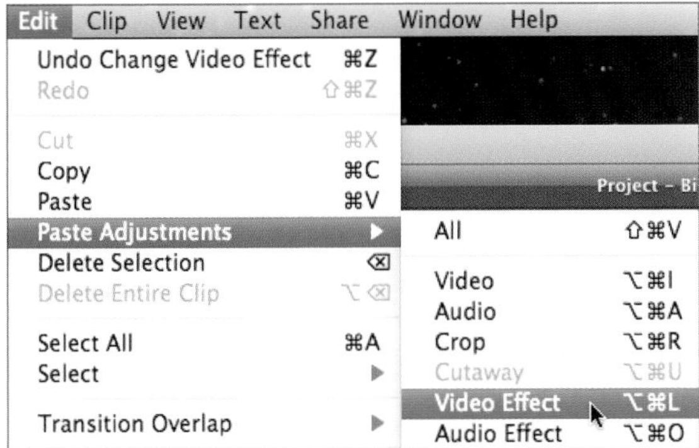

The Black & White effect is copied from the first clip and pasted to all the selected clips.

6 Click the Play button, or press \ (backslash) to play the project.

7 Press the Spacebar to stop playback when the black-and-white section ends.

Using Paste Adjustments can obviously save a lot of time. Next time you use it take a moment to view the other enhancements that it will work for.

Previewing Transitions

You used the Transition Browser earlier to place a new transition over an existing one. That's a fine way to replace transitions if you already know which transition you want; but if you aren't sure which transition to select, you can preview transitions in the Preview Palette, just like you previewed video effects.

1. In the toolbar, click the Transition Browser button.
2. Drag the Cross Dissolve transition between the clip of the door being locked (clip 7) and the first color park clip (clip 8).

3. Skim to the start of the door being locked, and press the Spacebar to view the cross dissolve. Press Spacebar again to stop playback.

   This is a good place for a transition from the black-and-white interior clips to the color clips of the outdoors; but let's explore some other transition options.

4. In the project, click the Action menu under the Cross Dissolve transition, and choose Transition Adjustments to open the inspector with the adjustments visible.
5. Click the Cross Dissolve transition button.

   The Preview Palette appears, allowing you to skim over any transition and see a preview in the viewer.

6. Skim over the Circle Open transition, and then click to apply it. Close the inspector.

The Preview Palette is very helpful for previewing transitions in the context of your video. It works similarly for titles and audio effects.

Adjusting White Balance

Your video camera has a setting called *white balance,* which essentially tells the camera if you are in sunlight (blue light) or indoor light (yellow light). Knowing this, the camera can correctly adjust the color.

There's just one problem. If you forget to set the white balance, or the automatic white-balance setting is misadjusted, then you get blue-tinted images outside and yellowish images inside. That's why iMovie includes a White Balance adjustment that you can apply to your clips.

1 Skim over the last clip in the project, depicting the two kids sitting outside.

   Do you notice this clip has a decidedly bluish tint? You might conclude that their skin tone looks blue because they are freezing outside on a cold day, but that wouldn't explain the blue tint on the sidewalk or in Louisa's cap. Let's fix it.

2 On the last clip in the project, choose Action Menu > Video Adjustments.

   The inspector opens with the Video tab selected. The Video tab includes sliders to control the Brightness, Contrast, and Color of a clip. It also has a White Balance control.

3 In the viewer, move the pointer over the clip. The pointer changes to an eyedropper icon. Using the Eyedropper tool you can correct the clip's white balance by selecting a part of the image that should be gray.

4 Click the eyedropper over the sidewalk, near the chair behind Louisa.

5 Click Done to close the inspector.

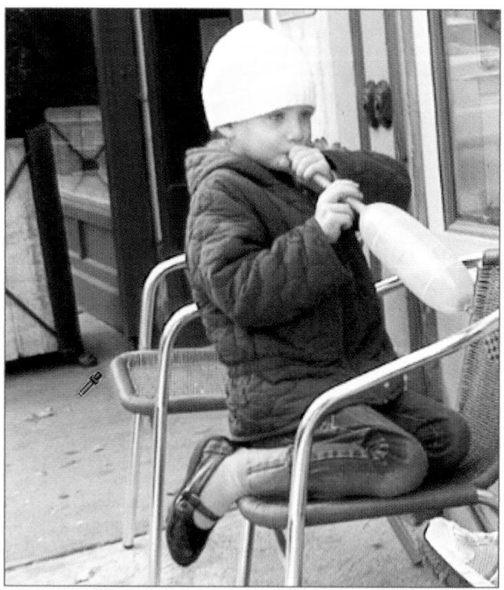

This sidewalk should be a medium gray color instead of a slate blue. When you click in the viewer, the clip shifts to a warmer, less bluish tint.

TIP You can drag the small circle in the inspector's color wheel to manually adjust the image tint, or click the Revert button to remove your white-balance adjustment.

Working with Audio

Always remember that an audience listens to your movie as much as they watch it. Audio is sometimes underestimated, but it remains a significant element in your movie. In this exercise, you'll enhance your project by adding audio tracks that work well with the video.

Pinning Music Tracks

When you added a background music track in Lesson 8 it was automatically placed at the start of the project, but it doesn't have to start there. This time you'll add music that starts when Max opens his eyes in bed.

1 In the toolbar, click the Music and Sound Effects button.

2 Click the Time column to sort the music tracks according to length.

3 Scroll down to 1.36 seconds and find the song called **Piano Ballad.caf**.

4 Drag the song into the project, being careful to drop it over the gray background on the far right and not over a clip.

The background music track is green, which makes it easy to see where it starts and stops. By dragging the background music track you can begin it somewhere other than the start of the project.

5 In the project, move the pointer over the Piano Ballad title bar. The pointer changes to a hand icon to indicate that you can drag the music track to a new location.

6 Drag the title bar so that the song begins over the third clip, as Max opens his eyes. The music track turns purple to indicate that it is now a pinned music track.

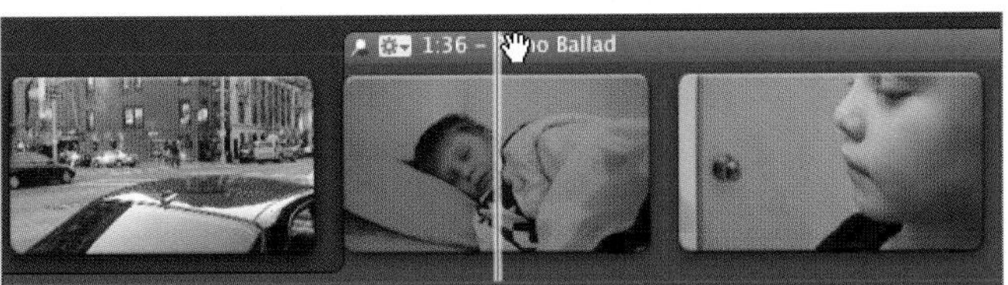

TIP You can unpin a track by choosing Clip > Unpin Music Track. The music track will then play from the start of the project.

Let's hear how it sounds.

7 Click the Play button, or press \ (backslash). After you hear some of the music, press the Spacebar to stop playback.

Pinned music tracks are connected to the clip to which they are pinned. In this project, your music track will always start when the clip of Max starts. If you move the clip of Max to a different location in the project, the music will move with it.

Adding Multiple Audio Tracks

While iMovie can play only one background music track at a time for obvious reasons,, it can play multiple audio tracks at a time.This enables you to layer sound effects into your movie. The start of this project could use some audio to make it sound more consistent.

1 In the Music and Sound Effects Browser, select iLife Sound Effects.

The iLife sound effects include a number of categories for sound effects such as animals, booms, sci-fi effects, and many others. The first clip in your project is a rainy outdoor NYC street scene, so let's search for some rain storm sounds.

2 Click in the search field at the bottom of the browser and type *Rain*.

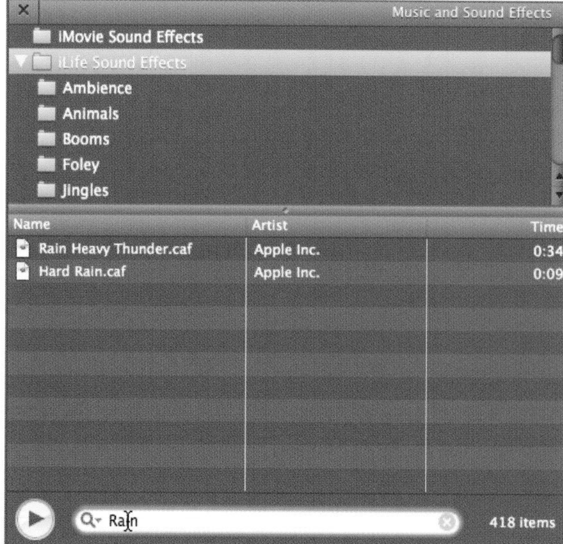

The browser displays all of the items in the iLife Sound Effects folder that contain the word "rain."

3 Double-click **Hard Rain.caf** to audition it. This sounds like it would go well at the start of your project.

4 Drag the Hard Rain sound effect on top of the first clip in the project. This time, instead of dropping it in a gray area of the project, you will drop it directly over the first clip to add it as a secondary audio track and not as a background music track.

5 Release the mouse button when the pointer is over the beginning of the first clip in the project.

A single green strip is placed in your project to indicate the secondary audio track that contains the rain sound effect.

6 Press \ (backslash) to play the rain sound effect. After you've previewed the effect, press the Spacebar to stop playback.

You can add as many secondary audio tracks in a project as you want. Let's also add some street sounds to enhance the movie.

7 Double-click in the search field in the browser and type *traffic*. The browser now shows all of the items that contain the word "traffic."

8 Double-click **Traffic.caf** to audition it. It will work well when played with the rain effect.

9 At the bottom of the Music and Sound Effects Browser, click the blue Stop button to stop playing the traffic sound effects.

10 Drag the traffic sound effect to the same location that you placed the rain sound effect.

Two green audio tracks now represent the sound effects.

11 Press \ (backslash) to play the project, and press the Spacebar to stop playback after you've heard the combination of music and sound effects.

This is a good start at creating the right atmosphere for your movie, but the sound can still be improved.

Trimming Audio Tracks

One of the first things you'll notice about both of the sound effects tracks is that they last longer than the two outdoor street clips. In this exercise, you'll trim these two sound effects clips to match the video.

1 Move the pointer over the end of the Hard Rain audio track. The pointer changes to a resize pointer when the track can be trimmed.

2 Drag the end of the audio track to the left until it is under the clip at the point Max opens his eyes.

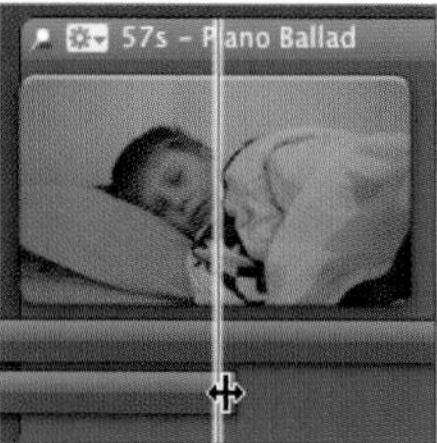

You've now trimmed the rain track to last a bit beyond the opening two street scene clips. You'll do the same to the traffic track.

3 Scroll down in the project window until you find the end of the traffic sound effects track.

4 Move the pointer over the end of the Traffic audio track until it changes to a resize pointer.

5 Drag the end of the traffic track until it aligns with the end of the rain track.

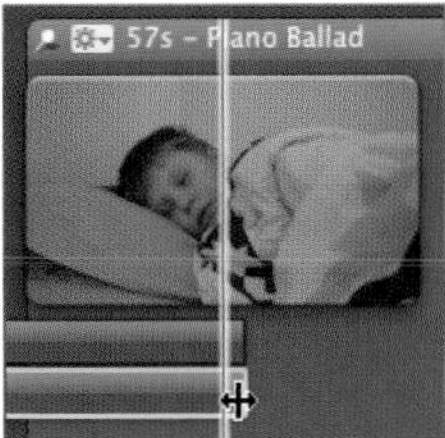

NOTE ► You may have to scroll the project window and then continue dragging to reach the start of the project.

6 Play the project to hear the results, then stop playback.

You now have consistent rain and street sounds that unite the two opening clips in the project. With that, you have essentially replaced the less dramatic sound from the video clips.

Muting Audio

Some sequences will have a stronger impact if you reduce or entirely remove the clips' original audio. When you lower the sound until it can no longer be heard, it's called *muting*.

1 Select the first clip in the project.

2 Shift-click the second clip in the project to highlight both clips.

3 From the Clip menu, choose Mute Clips.

TIP The Mute Clips menu item changes to Unmute Clips when you select clips that have been muted.

4 Play the project to hear the difference, then stop playback.

Now the sound is embellished and clear because all you hear are the sound effects that you added to the sequence.

Using the Clip Trimmer for Audio

During the opening, cars go by but the traffic sound effect just doesn't match up with those passing vehicles. Just because the sound effect is placed at the start of the project, it doesn't mean that you have to use the first part of the sound effect clip. You can use the Clip Trimmer to select a different portion of the sound effect to play in the project.

1 In the Traffic sound effect track in the project, click the Action menu and choose Clip Trimmer.

The Clip Trimmer for the sound effect track is displayed below the project. The spiky light-blue shape represents the audio that is playing—the *audio waveform*. The taller the waveform, the louder the audio is during that portion of the audio clip.

The darker areas outside the yellow selection lines are the remaining portions of the audio clip.

2 Place the pointer in the center of the highlighted selection range and drag the selection range to the right until it is centered over the first tall section of the audio waveform.

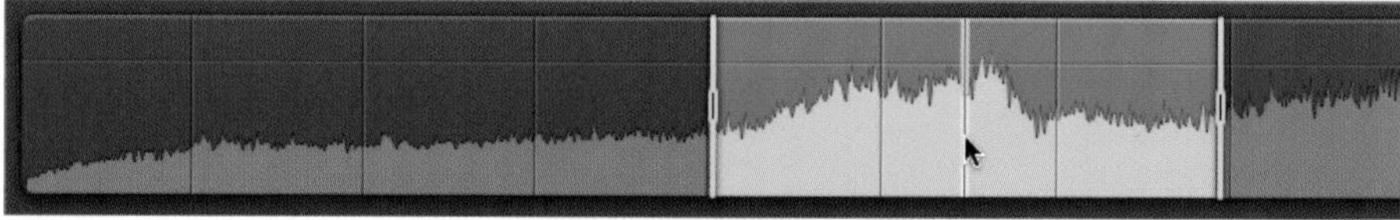

Because this is a traffic sound effect, you can assume that the taller parts of the audio waveform are louder traffic sounds.

TIP This is a good example of a situation when it would be helpful to enable Audio Skimming in the toolbar. You would hear the traffic noise as you skimmed over the clip trimmer.

3. Click Done to close the Clip Trimmer.
4. Play the project to hear the results, and stop playback when you're done.

   Small, detail-oriented adjustments like these changes to the sound effects tracks can really make a movie feel polished.

Setting a Clip's Audio Level

Not every clip's audio needs to be muted and replaced. Some background sounds, such as the key turning in the lock and the leaves being kicked, add to the ambience of the movie. Still, these aren't the ype of sound effects that you play at full blast. You can adjust the level of any clip using the Audio Adjustments in the inspector.

1. Play from the start of the project and stop playback when you hear the sound of the leaves being kicked.

   This is a good, natural sound that suits the video, but it is very loud and drowns out the soothing music.

2. On the kicking leaves clip, from the Action menu, choose Audio Adjustments to open the inspector with the Audio tab selected.

3. In the inspector, drag the Volume slider down to around 25%, then click Done.
4. Skim to the clip before the kicked leaves and press the Spacebar to start playback.
5. Press the Spacebar again to stop playing after you hear the new audio level.

You may find other locations in the project where a clip's audio level could be lowered, still other places where you could mute the audio. Go through your project and practice adjusting clip levels and muting clips where you think it is appropriate.

Stabilizing a Project Clip

When you shoot video without a tripod or monopod, you're going to wind up with shaky video. iMovie's Stabilization feature can help reduce and sometimes eliminate that video shake. It can be performed on an entire Event or on a single project clip, as you'll do in this exercise.

1 Play the ninth clip from the end of the project, showing Louisa walking with her dad.

Notice that the clip is shaking because the person with the camera is walking. This is a great candidate for stabilization because while the camera is bumpy, we're not seeing footage of the clouds or the cameraperson's feet. Clips that move quickly from subject to subject are less likely to be good candidates for stabilization.

2 Click the shaky clip to select it.

3 Click the Inspector icon to open the inspector.

4 Select the Stabilization checkbox to begin the stabilization analysis. This analysis examines each frame and compares it to the frames before and after to calculate the camera movement. It's sophisticated stuff.

5 When the analysis is complete, press the Spacebar to play the stabilized clip. When you have finished watching the clip, click Done in the inspector.

The stabilized clip plays back smoothly. You may also notice that the clip is slightly zoomed in. This is one of the side effects of stabilization: The shakier a clip is, the more it is zoomed to provide a little "elbow room" to perform the stabilization. You'll learn more about stabilization in Lesson 12.

NOTE ▶ You can turn stabilization on and off to compare the results by selecting and deselecting the checkbox in the inspector. Once the clip is analyzed, turning stabliza-tion off and on does not repeat the analysis.

Lesson Review

1. Where can you choose Replace and Insert edits?
2. Would you use the Clip menu or the inspector to change the playback speed of a clip?
3. True or False: You can apply an unlimited number of simultaneous video effects to a clip.
4. Is the Preview Pallete used to try out different video effects or different transitions?
5. How do you add additional audio tracks in iMovie?

Answers

1. When you drop one clip from your Event directly on top of a clip in your project, the Edit pop-up menu appears with Replace and Insert edit choices.
2. The Clip menu has different settings for fast and slow motion, but it does the same thing as dragging the speed slider in the inspector.
3. False. Only one video effect can be applied to a clip at a time.
4. You can try out both video effects and transitions in the Preview Palette. It will display the options depending on what is selected in the project.
5. iMovie can feature only one background music track at a time but can play multiple audio tracks. Dropping a music or sound effects clip directly over a video clip in a project adds it as a secondary audio track.

12

Lesson Files	ATS iPhoto Library: "Sara goes sky diving" Event
Time	This lesson takes approximately 45 minutes to complete.
Goals	Use photos and videos from iPhoto Apply and modify the Ken Burns effect Add and change titles Create cutaways Use beat markers to edit to music Enhance audio with EQ and noise reduction Duck music while someone is talking Analyze an entire event for stabilization Share online with friends and family

Lesson **12**

Moviemaking with Photos and iPhoto Clips

Many of us take video clips with digital still cameras, iPods, and iPhones. They are handy, lightweight, and very simple to use. But more often than not, those video clips end up in iPhoto, along with the photos. And there they sit. Relegated to being viewed like still photographs instead of blossoming into full-blown movies. It's high time to stop treating them like secondary clips. You can do something with those clips, as well as all the photos in your iPhoto library. iMovie can use any photo or video clip stored in your iPhoto library and make spectacular-looking movies from them.

Accessing iPhoto Clips

NOTE ▸ This lesson requires that you have opened and are using the ATS iPhoto library that came with this book. To ensure you have the right library, follow the instructions on installing and opening the ATS iPhoto library in the Getting Started section of this book.

Many video clips are captured using iPhones and digital still cameras. If this is the case with your video clips, you can still access them directly inside iMovie and use them to make a movie.

1 In the Event Library, click iPhoto Videos.

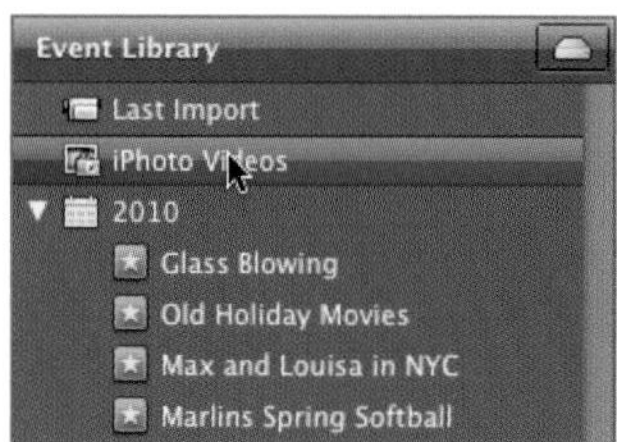

TIP If you do not have any video clips in your iPhoto library, iMovie will not display an iPhoto library item in your Event Library. For this lesson, make sure you have installed and opened the iPhoto library on the DVD provided with this book.

All the iPhoto video clips are shown in your Event Browser. iMovie accesses them from your iPhoto library without moving them.

The iPhoto clips in the library have been included in a partially completed project that you can open from the Project Library.

2 Click the Project Library button.

3 Click the "Sara's sky dive" project to select it.

4 Skim over the sky diving filmstrip to preview it in the viewer.

5 Click the Edit Project button to open the project.

You are going to finish this project by adding some photos and editing them to the beat of a music track. You'll then learn how to upload a movie to a video sharing site.

Finding and Using Photos

This project starts with an abrupt introduction to Sara. To create a smoother introduction you'll add a photo from the iPhoto library.

1 Click the Photo Browser button to open it and view your iPhoto library.

2 To view only the photos taken at the same time as your video, select the Show Photos checkbox near the bottom of the photo browser.

   The photo browser filters out all the photos that were not taken on the same date as the video in your Event Browser.

   NOTE ▶ Be aware that the Show Photos checkbox has nothing to do with the iMovie project that is open. It filters based only on the iMovie Event you are viewing.

   The first photo in the browser would start our project nicely.

3 Drag the photo to the left of the Fade Up transition icon on the first clip in the project. Release the photo when a green insert bar appears to the left of the transition.

TIP ▶ Photos have a default length of four seconds. You can change this default length by choosing File > Project Properties. You can also change the length of photos already placed in a project by double-clicking any photo in a project to open the inspector.

4 Play the clip to view the results, and press the Spacebar to stop playback when you're through.

You may have noticed that a slight pan and zoom were added to the photo. This pan and zoom combination is called the Ken Burns effect and you can modify it to get the effect you want.

NOTE ▶ Why is it called the Ken Burns effect? Ken Burns is a filmmaker famous for historical documentaries. Many of them use archival photographs, and to focus attention and create visual interest, he pans and zooms the camera on them.

Modifying the Ken Burns effect

The Ken Burns effect never seems to get old and always looks great on photos. It is enabled by default when you add photos to a project, and you can modify its movement very easily.

1 Play the photo in the project. It would engage the viewer more effectively if you created a subtle zoom-in using the Ken Burns effect.

2 From the toolbar, choose the Crop tool.

Three Crop buttons are available near the top of the viewer, including one for the Ken Burns effect. Are you wondering why this effect is grouped with the Crop buttons? It's because you are essentially creating a crop window that moves over the photo.

Two other crop buttons are available in the viewer.

- Fit ensures that the entire photo can be seen in the viewer.
- Crop trims the photo to cut out extraneous parts or focus attention on a particular area.

A small green start label appears with a green rectangle around the image. The green rectangle determines which part of the image will be displayed at the start of the clip. The red rectangle determines which part of the image is displayed at the end of the clip.

In this case, you can start showing as much of the image as possible and move to focus more on the nose of the plane at the end.

3 Click the green line to make sure it is selected in the viewer.

4 Move the pointer to the lower-right corner of the green rectangle until the pointer changes to a crosshair.

5 Drag the green rectangle down and to the right until the right side of the rectangle is against the right side of the viewer.

6 Click the Play button in the upper right of the viewer to see the results. It's not bad, but simply pans from right to left. Let's add a subtle zoom.

7 In the viewer, click the "*End*" text in red to select the ending rectangle.

8 Move the pointer to the lower-right corner of the red rectangle until it changes to a crosshair.

9 Drag the corner up until the left edge touches the letter A on the plane.

10 Click the Play button in the viewer to see the results.

11 Click Done in the viewer to close the Crop tool.

TIP If you want the pan and zoom to move faster, create a greater difference between the size and placement of the two rectangles. A smaller difference between their size and placement will cause a slower, smoother zoom and pan.

The result is a beautiful, subtle pan and zoom that adds visual interest to an otherwise static picture. If you wanted to remove the Ken Burns effect you could choose a different crop button .

Choosing a Title

Let's place an opening title over the photo you just added.

1 Click the Title Browser button. Because no theme is applied, the Title Browser displays only the standard titles.

2 Skim your pointer across the third row of titles in the Title Browser. A small preview of the animation plays for each title thumbnail.

Position your pointer over the first title in the third row, Drifting.

TIP You can add a title over a colored background if you drop a title between clips or at the start or end of a project. A background Preview Palette is used to select the background.

3 Drag the title over the plane photo at the start of the project and move your mouse until the blue highlight appears over the entire photo, then release the mouse button.

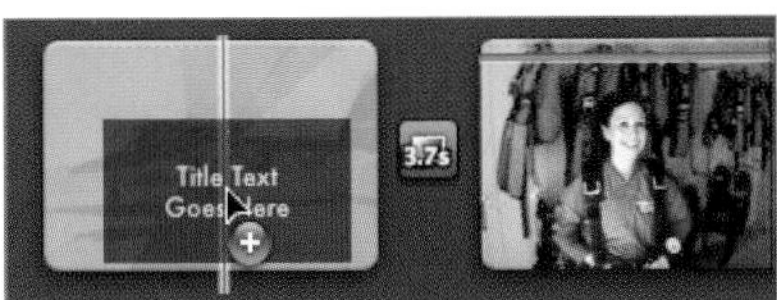

TIP Although a title can straddle two clips, placing an animated title over a transition will disable the transition.

The last step is to change the text of the title.

4 In the viewer, the words "Title Text" should be highlighted in blue. If not, triple-click the words to select the entire line.

5 Type *Sara's First*, then press Tab to go to the next line of text, and type *Sky Dive*!

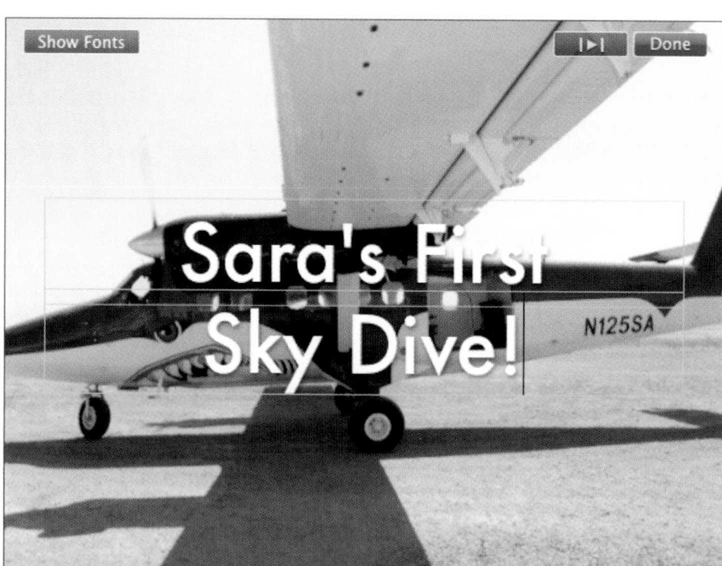

6 Click the Play button in the viewer to play the title.

You have a selection of animated and static titles that you can use in iMovie. Although you can insert only one title onscreen at a time, you can place titles anywhere in your project, over any type of clip, or over a plain background.

Creating a Cutaway Shot

When you are making a movie, you sometimes decide what footage to use based on its audio and not its video content. That's the approach you are going to take to trim this first clip in the project. There is some extra talking going on that just isn't needed.

1 In the project, after the title, play the first video clip, which introduces Sara.

Most of this clip is good, but in the middle she explains that she has no special occasion for the sky dive, saying that they are "just doin' it," and then she utters, "Cooool." It's a bit of a letdown and doesn't add to the movie, so let's cut it.

2 Skim just after she answers the question, "Is this your first time sky diving?" Just after Sara says, "Yes," drag a selection to the right, ending when Karen, the camera operator, says, "Cool."

3 After you've made the selection, press Delete to remove it.

4 Skim after Karen says, "Hi, guys." Just before Karen says, "All right," drag a selection to the right, and end the selection about 9.5 seconds later, before the interviewer asks, "Anything you want to say?"

5 Once you've made the selection, press Delete to remove it.

6 Play the project to hear how the two cuts sound.

After Sara says, "Yes," it should start cleanly with the interviewer asking, "Who are you here with?" If it doesn't, choose Edit > Undo twice and try the edit again. If you just listen to the audio without watching your movie, it should naturally sound like one continuous conversation.

The video, however, has issues. Cutting out the middle of a clip creates what is called a *jump cut*, a cut in which the camera position varies only a tiny bit between two adjacent clips. Jump cuts are usually considered bad (except in music videos, where they are considered *edgy*.) One way to avoid a jump cut to insert a *cutaway*. A cutaway is when you insert new video content into a sequence while continuing to play the audio of the preceding clip.

To create a cutaway, you'll need to display some of the less common yet very useful moviemaking features in iMovie by enabling the Advanced tools in iMovie's Preferences.

7 Choose iMovie > Preferences.

8 Click the General tab and select the Show Advanced Tools checkbox. Then close iMovie Preferences.

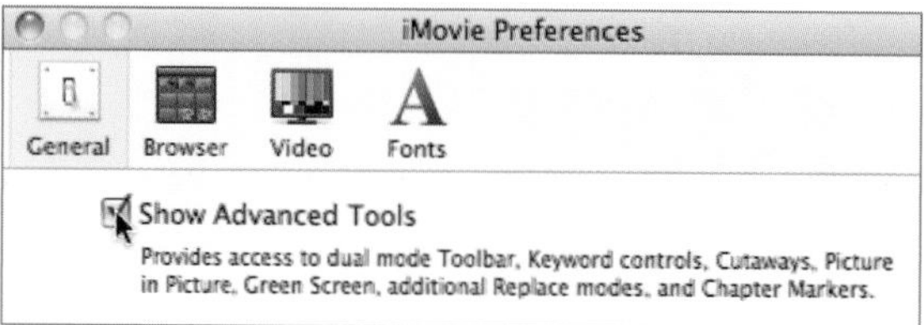

You are now ready to create a cutaway. Instead of using a video clip as our cutaway, let's use a photo.

9 Click the Photo Browser button to display pictures from iPhoto.

10 Drop the picture of the three sky divers, **EPPAJQK 0002**, onto the first clip of Sara. The Edit pop-up menu appears showing a much-expanded list of editing functions, including the Cutaway option.

11 From the Edit pop-up menu, choose Cutaway.

The cutaway is added above the main clips in your project which helps give you some idea which clips are involved, as well as where the cutaway starts and ends.

Moving a Cutaway

The cutaway begins wherever your pointer was when you released the mouse button. Depending on that location, you may need to move the cutaway so that it covers your jump cut.

1 Place the pointer over the cutaway clip in the project window until it changes to a hand icon.

2 Drag the cutaway clip until it starts at the end of the first clip of Sara.

3 Play the project to watch the cutaway. Stop playing after the cutaway ends.

The cutaway ends too soon, revealing the end of the clip that should be covered. You'll extend the cutaway to fix the problem.

4 Position the pointer over the right edge of the cutaway clip until it changes to a resize pointer.

5 Drag the edge of the clip to the right until it is located at the start of the Sara's third clip.

6 Play the project through the cutaway and then stop.

7 Choose iMovie > Preferences.

8 Click the General tab and deselect the Show Advanced Tools checkbox, then close Preferences.

You've assembled a smooth series of clips as a pre-jump introduction to your movie. You'll now create an exciting sky diving sequence that perfectly syncs photos to the beat of high-energy music.

Editing to a Musical Beat

When music is a significant part of your movie, you can edit clips and photos to the beat to give it a more consistent pace. You'll have an easier time editing to the beat if you place beat markers to identify the beats in the soundtrack.

1 Skim to the end of the project.

2 In the lower-right corner of the project browser, drag the thumbnail size slider left until it reads 2S, making it easier to see the background music track

3 On the background music track, from the Action menu, choose Clip Trimmer.

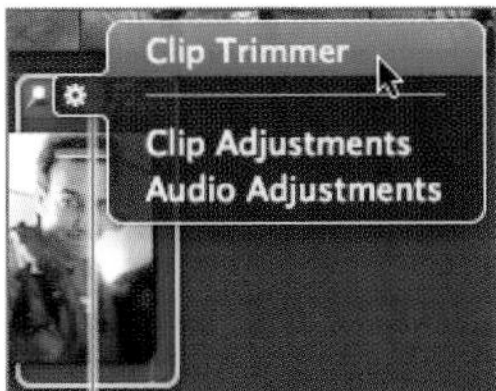

The entire background music track is displayed in the Clip Trimmer. The next step is to tap out the beats of the song to add beat markers. At the top of the trimmer is a musical note icon that you could drag and place on the music track; but an easier way to place beat markers is to play the music and tap out the beats in real time.

4 At the top of the Clip Trimmer, click the Play button. While the music plays, press the *M* key in time to the music until the song ends.

TIP If you feel a marker is not exactly on the beat, you can drag it to a new position or drag it into the project window to remove it entirely. You can remove all the beat markers by Control-clicking the Clip Trimmer track, and from the contextual menu, choosing Remove All Beat Markers.

With the beat markers in place, you'll now add a few photos of the sky diving adventure.

5 Click Done in the Clip Trimmer window when you finish marking beats with beat markers.

6 Click the Photo Browser button if the photos are not already visible.

7 Click the third photo in the browser, **EPPAJQK_0021.**

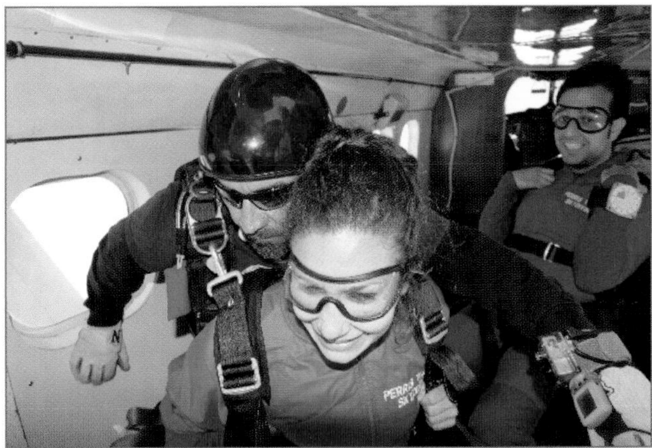

8 Shift-click the next-to-last photo in the browser—Sara landing—then release the Shift key and drag all 17 selected photos to the end of the project.

When beat markers are added to a background music track, clips and photos added to the project will automatically align to start on one beat and end on the next.

9 Click the Play Project button in the project window to review your results.

That's a fantastic little movie you have there. It really catches the excitement of the sky dive. Having the photos snap to the beats makes it easy to edit to music, but not every clip works as effectively. At times you will want to turn off that feature and set a clip to last as long as a range you select. In the next exercise, you'll disable the "Snap to Beats" feature and add the last clip to your project.

Disabling 'Snap to Beats'

The photos show Sara's landing and that's where your video clips pick up again. You'll now add Sara's parting words of wisdom. But you'll turn off the "Snap to Beats" feature so that her statement isn't cut off at the next beat.

1 On the last clip in the Event Browser, select a range matching the Favorite mark.

The selection should start at the sentence, "So what do you have to say to all your friends and family?" and it should end after Sara says, "Awesome."

2 Choose View > Snap to beats to disable the feature.

3 Click the Edit button to add the selection to the project.The clip is added to the end of the project, crossing over a number of beat markers that are displayed in the pinned music track.

Enhancing Audio

In the next few exercises, you'll enhance your project's audio quality by mixing audio levels, reducing noise, and equalizing the sound.

Reducing Background Noise

Noise can be a problem when you record video outdoors, in a room with machinery, and especially in a sky diving plane! You can, within reason, reduce noise using iMovie's Audio Adjustments inspector.

1 In the project window, play the clip of Sara in the plane. Then, when the clip ends, press the Spacebar to stop playback. You'll hear lots of humming and hissing in this clip. Although you can't remove all of the noise, you can improve the fidelity of this track.

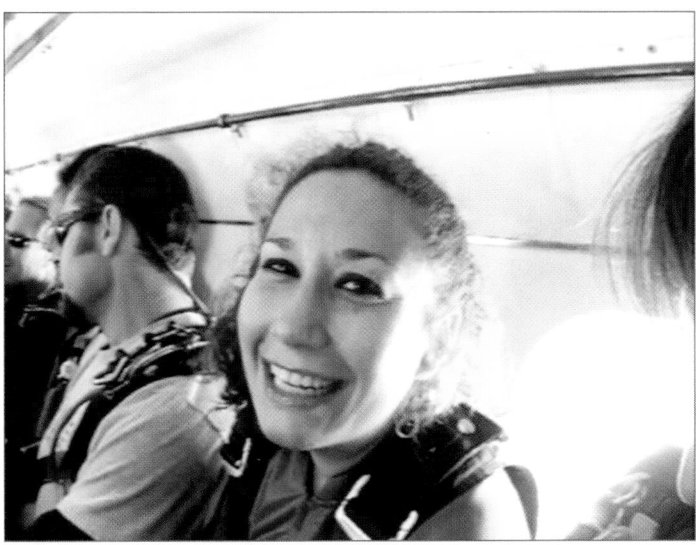

2 Select the clip in the project, and from its Action menu, choose Audio Adjustments.

3 In the Audio Adjustment inspector, select the Enhance checkbox.

You now can drag the slider to control how much background hissing is reduced. It's tempting to drag the slider all the way to the right to impose maximum reduction. Alas, the more you increase noise reduction, the more muffled the voice in your clip becomes. So, while carefully listening to the clip, try to find a compromise between reduced hissing noise and vocal clarity.

4 Press the Spacebar to play the selected clip.

5 As the clip plays, drag the Enhance slider slowly to the right until you find an acceptable balance between noise and dialog.

TIP As the clip plays, you can compare your adjusted mix to the original audio by clicking the Enhance checkbox to select and deselect noise reduction..

6 When you have found the optimal setting, press the Spacebar to stop playback.

This type of noise reduction processes a very specific high hissing and does it quickly and easily.

Equalizing Audio Clips

The equalizer allows you to boost or reduce a range of audio frequencies. Rather than just providing bass and treble adjustments like your sound system at home, the equalizer divides the sound into 10 ranges, or *bands*, that allow you to hone in on the audio frequency you want to adjust. While you already removed a great deal of the hissing noise, you still have a loud, deep buzz noise in your audio track.

1 Make sure the clip is still selected and the Audio Adjustments inspector is still open.

  The sliders to the right of the equalizer boost or reduce the treble frequencies. Sliders to the left boost or reduce bass frequencies. But instead of adjusting all the sliders, you can use one of the equalizer's nine handy presets to set those sliders.

2 Press the Spacebar to play the clip, and from the Equalizer menu, choose Bass Reduce.

  This preset should help remove more of the low noise.

3 If the results are close but not optimal, you can further adjust the equalizer's sliders to refine the results of the preset. Try adjusting the sliders with the current clip to improve your results.

4 When you have a sound that you like, press the Spacebar to stop playback. Click Done.

In almost all cases, music tracks from iTunes and sound effects clips from iMovie do not need equalization. You'll also find many other situations that don't require audio adjustments. But when you need more bass or treble or must remove extraneous noise, the equalizer is very handy.

Ducking Music

When you combine background music and dialog, setting the audio level as you did in the previous lesson is often too limited. The easiest, and most automated, way to mix speech and music is called *ducking*. That is, you force the music to "duck under" the speech.

1 Skim to the last photo in the project and press the Spacebar to preview the last clip.

The music is loud and you can't clearly hear Sara speaking. If you lowered the music, it would be lowered for the entire project, which is not what you want. This is where ducking comes into play. It allows you to reduce the music volume to mix more compatibly with the other audio tracks. Let's try it.

2 In the project window, choose Action menu > Audio Adjustments on the last clip.

3 In the inspector, select the Ducking checkbox.

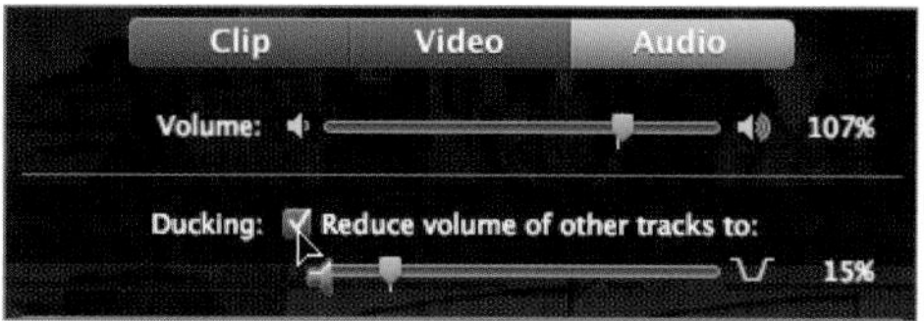

4 Click Done to close the inspector.

By selecting this checkbox, the music volume is reduced to 15 percent of its normal volume for the length of the video clip. Then the music returns to its normal volume.

5 Begin playing the project at the last photo before the video clip.

This sounds better. The music smoothly ramps down to a lower volume when the video clip begins. Now let's see what happens when you add another clip, or in our case, an ending photo.

6 Click the Photo Browser button if the photos are not visible.

7 Add the last photo of Sara and her instructor to the end of the project.

8 Play the project and watch the last few clips.

By enabling ducking on Sara's interview clip, the music ramps back up to its normal volume after the video clip ends. If you wanted the music to stay quieter during the photo, you could also enable ducking on the photo. Ducking makes it easy to achieve consistent results when mixing background music with other audio tracks.

Analyzing for Stabilization

In the previous lesson, you stabilized a single clip. If you have the time, you can analyze an entire Event for stabilization. When you do so, all the stabilization processing is performed before you begin adding Event clips to a project. When you add those clips to a project, they stabilize instantly. The key phrase here is, "if you have the time." Analyzing can take as long as five times the length of the clip. That is, if you have a one-minute clip it could take five minutes to analyze. Depending on the contents of an Event, that analysis could take hours, a process you'd want to initiate only when you will be away from the computer for a reasonable length of time.

> **NOTE ▶** The time cited above is a rough estimate. Depending on the power of your Mac and the size of the video content, the analysis time can vary greatly.

1 In the Event Browser, select the first clip in the "Sara goes sky diving" Event.

2 Choose Edit > Select Entire Clip, or press Command-A; then press Command-A again, or choose Edit > Select All.

With all the clips selected, you can analyze them for stabilization.

3 Choose File > Analyze Video > Stabilization.

NOTE ▶ Analyze and stabilize are two different processes. That's why iMovie makes a distinction between them. Analyze is the process of stepping through a video clip frame-by-frame and identifying the camera's motion. After that information is gathered, it is stored inside iMovie. Stabilization is the act of applying that camera motion information to steady the movement in your video clip. You cannot stabilize clips in an Event but you can analyze them. Clips are stabilized only when you place them in a project.

Lucky for you, this Event already has been analyzed, or you would be waiting for a few minutes. One way to tell if Event clips have been analyzed is to view the information on a clip as you skim it.

4 Choose View > Playhead Info, or press Command–Y, then skim over clips in the Event.

As you skim, a tooltip displays useful information. One bit of information it displays is whether a clip has been analyzed for stabilization.

5 Choose View > Playhead Info to turn off the tooltip.

6 In the Event, play the portion of the last clip with the orange line. The orange line indicates the area used in the current project. This clip is a bit shaky and perfect for stabilization.

7 In the project, play the same clip. Note that the clip's camera movement is much smoother. When you add an analyzed clip to a project, stabilization is applied.

TIP When you skim over stabilized clips in a project, a badge with a hand appears in the upper-left corner of the clip. A black badge means the clip is optimally stabilized. An orange badge means stabilization has been only partially applied because fully applying stabilization requires zooming the clip in to a level that would visibly degrade the video quality. You can override this setting by increasing the Zoom slider in the Clip Adjustments inspector, but the badge will turn red as a warning.

What do you do with clips that are extremely shaky? If a clip is so extremely shaky that stabilization cannot work effectively, a red squiggly line is displayed over the clip in the Event.

8 Skim to the red squiggly line in the middle of the first clip of the Event.

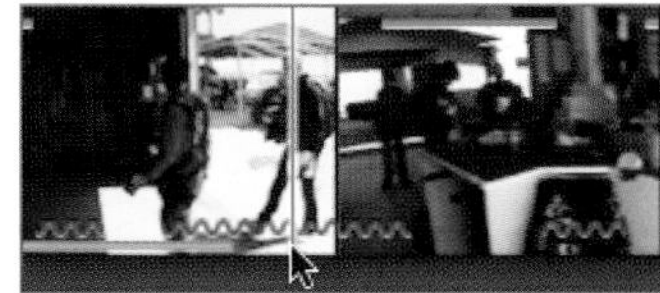

9 Skim to the red squiggly line at the end of the second clip.

On both of these clips, the red line appears over areas where the camera moves so erratically that the video is unusable. You probably shouldn't add these portions of the clip to your project; but if you do, it is usually best to deselect Stabilization in the Clip Adjustments inspector.

TIP You can hide/unhide these excessively shaky parts of your video by clicking the button with the red squiggly line on it at the bottom of the Event Browser.

Stabilization can help in many cases but it can't perform magic. Don't expect it to stabilize a clip in which your dog grabs the camcorder and swings it around the room.

TIP Most new camcorders use a CMOS sensor to capture the digital video file. These sensors can create slanted and wobbling distortion effects often called *rolling shutter* artifacts. They are especially noticeable in a stabilized clip. If you notice that your clips appear skewed or slanted after stabilization, adjust the Rolling Shutter setting in the Clip Adjustments inspector.

Sharing Movies Online

With your project complete, you can now share it with friends and family no matter where they are in the world. iMovie can upload to a number of very popular web-based video sharing sites including the most popular video sharing site, YouTube.

Let's learn how to post to YouTube. (The other choices work in a similar way.)

Sharing to YouTube

YouTube is the most popular web destination for sharing video. It allows the world easy access to your movies. To share the current project to any site from within iMovie, you begin in the Share menu.

1 Choose Share > YouTube.

The YouTube publishing dialog appears with a few fields you must fill in, and a few optional fields.

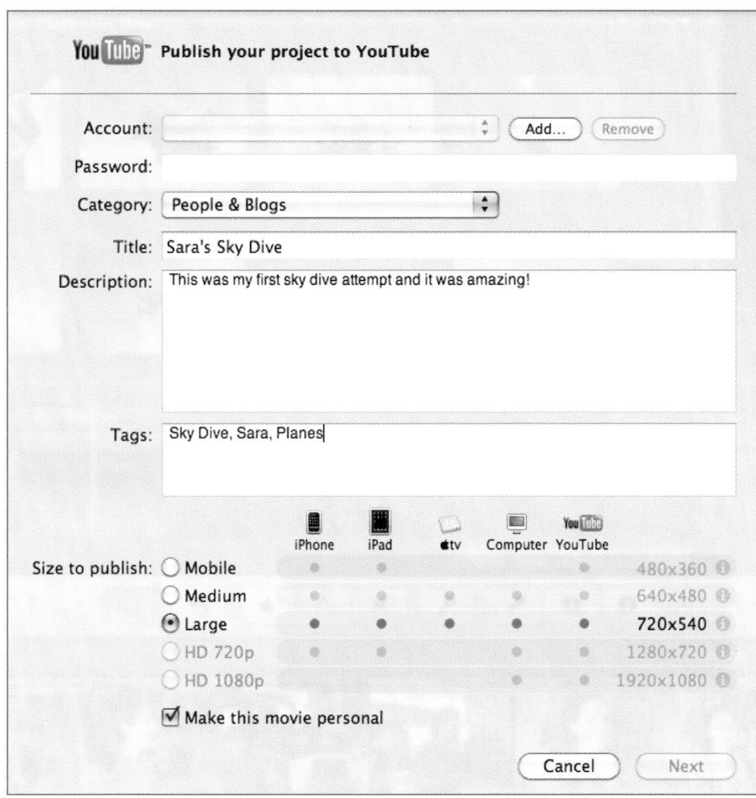

2 If this is your first time sharing to YouTube from iMovie, click Add to enter your YouTube account information.

NOTE ► If you don't have a YouTube account, then you need to create one on the YouTube website, www.youtube.com.

3 Select your account name and enter the account password.

4 Select a category that best represents the movie you are posting. This will make it easier for people to find your movie.

5 Enter the title if you want a title that is different from your project's title.

6 Add any description and tags that will help viewers on YouTube find your movie and understand what it is about before they view it.

7 Select the upload size of your movie. Larger sizes such as HD 720 or HD 1080 will create higher-quality video but will also take much longer to upload.

8 Finally, choose who is allowed to view your movie. The YouTube dialog in iMovie includes a checkbox to make your movie “personal.” This limits the viewing to 25 people to whom you send a special linked email.

9 Deselect the “Make this movie personal” checkbox so that anyone on YouTube can view your movie.

10 Click the Next button to view the YouTube Terms of Service. After reading the terms, click the Publish button make your project into a movie and upload it to YouTube.

You can prepare your movies for distribution on other online sharing sites such as Facebook, Vimeo, and MobileMe. You can also Remove your movies from a site using the Share > Remove from menu.

Lesson Review

1. In iMovie, can you use video clips that are saved in an iPhoto library?
2. If you didn’t want a photo to have a Ken Burns effect on it, how do you remove the Ken Burns effect?
3. If cutaway is not listed in the Edit pop-up menu, how do you find it?
4. Where is a beat marker located?
5. Can you reduce noise with the equalizer?
6. What does the red squiggly line mean on clips in an Event?
7. Where do you find the Facebook sharing option?

Answers

1. Yes, iMovie accesses all the video clips saved in your iPhoto library using the iPhoto videos event in the Event Library.
2. If you want to remove the Ken Burns effect, you can choose the other cropping options, Fit and Crop.
3. Cutaway is found in the Edit pop-up menu when Show Advanced tools is enabled in the iMovie Preferences.

4. Beat markers are located in the Clip Trimmer for any audio track.
5. Yes, when you need to enhance the sound by adding more bass or treble or having to remove the noise from an air conditioner, the equalizer can come in very handy.
6. If a clip has been analyzed and it is extremely shaky, to the point where even stabilization will not work, a red squiggly line is displayed over the area.
7. All sharing options are found under the Share menu in the main menu bar.

13

Lesson Files	iMovie Event: Glass Blowing
Time	This lesson takes approximately 60 minutes to complete.
Goals	Apply themed titles and transitions manually Add maps to a project Use the Precision Editing view Understand advanced editing techniques Record a voiceover

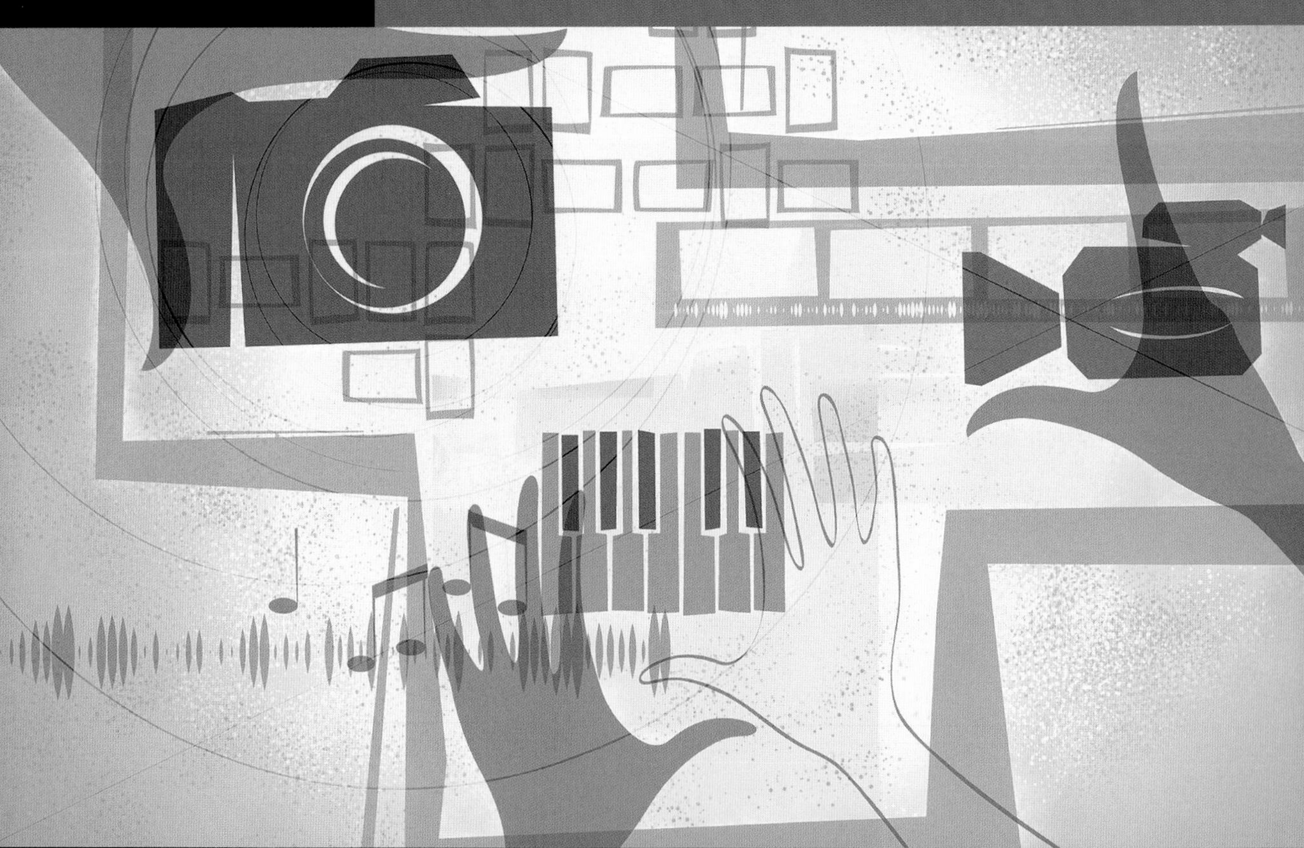

Lesson **13**

Advanced Moviemaking

Is your creative appetite whet? Have the previous lessons been fun, but you burn for something more? Maybe you are looking for ways to finesse your movie's story or maybe you desire something more visually intriguing. The editing features you'll explore in this lesson are aimed at assisting you in refining your storytelling, not just assembling your best clips and adding music and titles. After this lesson, you may find that you have aspirations of submitting to Sundance or premiering at Cannes, or not.

Choosing Projects from the Library

Once again, you need to begin by opening a project that already has been started.

1. Click the Project Library button, then click the "Glass blowing 101" project to select it.

   Let's watch some of the project before you open it.

2. Skim to the start of the Glass Blowing filmstrip.

   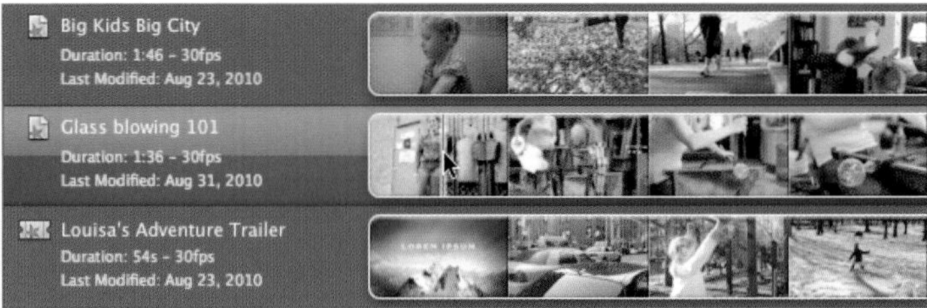

3. Play the project, and when the project ends, click the Edit Project button to open it.

The project demonstrates glass blowing. In this lesson, you will finish this project using some advanced iMovie features and sophisticated moviemaking techniques.

Setting a Location Using Travel Maps

Once again, you are faced with the question of how to start this project. You've used various techniques and content including titles, photos, and sound effects; but one of the most engaging ways to start a project is to show a map. iMovie's maps can point out a single location or show a travel route for your vacation video.

1. In the toolbar, click the "Maps, Backgrounds and Animatics" Browser button.

   The maps in the browser are broken down in to three categories containing four styles each. The Globe and Map categories are the two that allow you to add travel lines and pinpoint locations.

2. Drag the Blue Marble Map to the left of the first clip to make the map the first clip in the project.

When you add a map, the Map inspector appears so you can choose a location. In this project, you'll use the map to highlight Seattle, the location of the glass blowing studio, The Pratt Center.

3 Click the Start Location button, which currently is set to a location in your time zone.

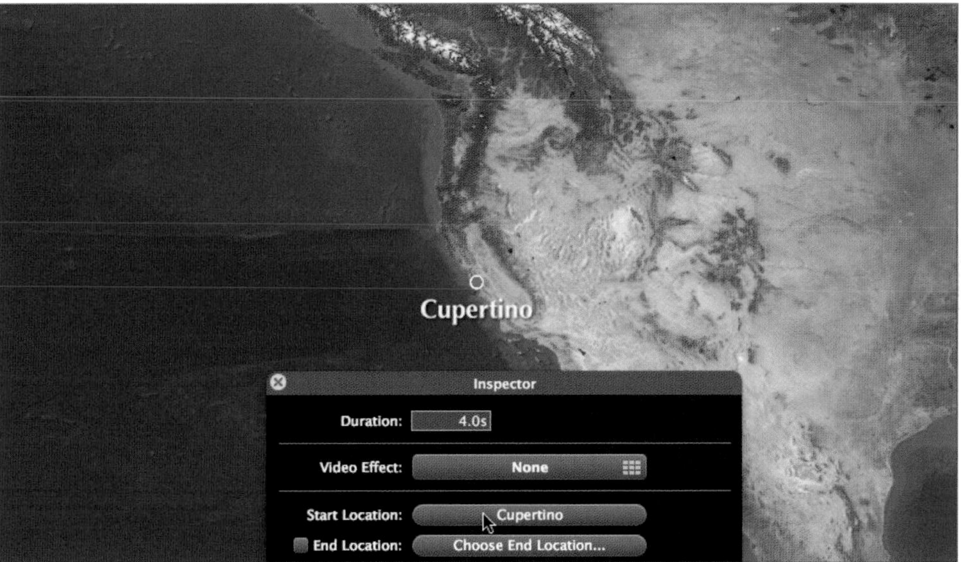

4 In the search field, type *Seattle*. Three matching locations appear in the area below the field.

TIP Setting an end location will produce an animated line that travels from the start location to the destination when you play the project.

5 Choose the third entry, Seattle. The bottom of the window displays the text as it will appear on the map. You can customize the text to more specifically identify the location.

6 Double-click the word "Seattle" in the "Name to Display on Map" text box.

7 Type *The Pratt Center, Seattle Wa*, click OK, then click Done in the inspector.

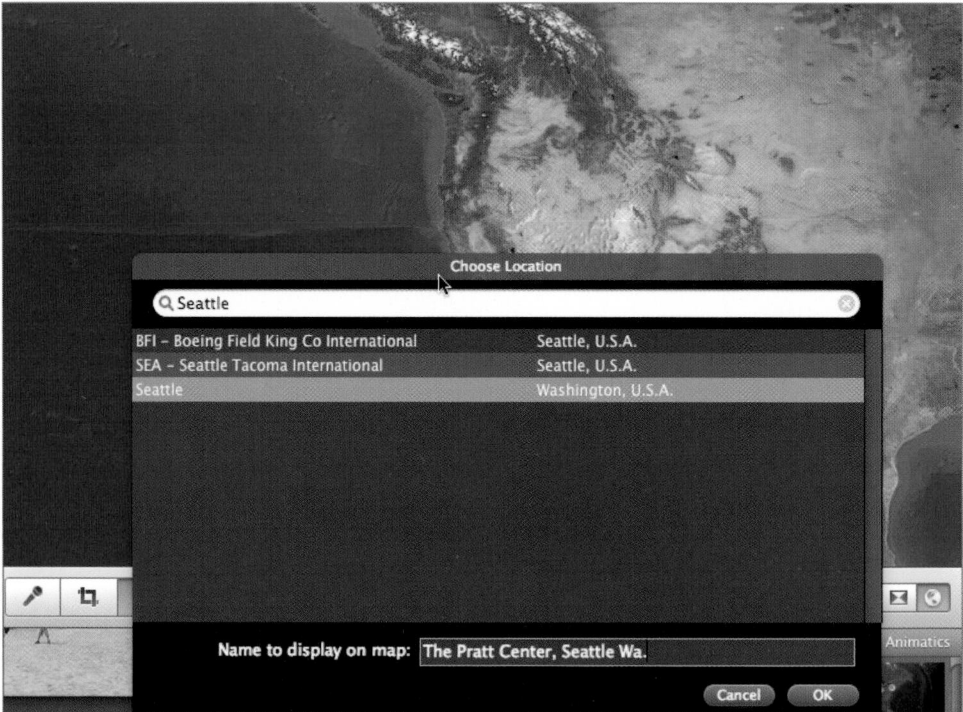

8 Click the Play button in the lower left of the project window to review the result, and press the Spacebar to stop playback after you've seen the map.

Maps can add informative visual interest for educational videos, vacation movies, or even small businesses videos. If your movies don't take place in an iconic setting that's easily recognizable in your clips, then maps offer a great scene-setting alternative.

Trimming with the Precision Editor

The process of removing a few frames or seconds from clips in a project is called *trimming*. You did a bit of rough trimming in previous lessons, but now you'll employ a more precise method. The Precision Editor is designed specifically for fine tuning the start and end points of project clips.

1 Click the Play Project button, or press \ (backslash). You may notice a few clips that need refinement.

2 Press the Spacebar to stop playback after the glass blower picks up the giant tweezers (in the fourth clip in the project.)

3 Skim the third and fourth clips in which the glass blower sits down, and then examine the close-up of her picking up the giant tweezers.

In the third clip, notice that she sits, reaches, and then you cut to a long pause before you see her hand in the next clip. You can use the Precision Editor to improve the continuity of movement in these two clips.

4 From the tweezer clip's Action menu, choose Precision Editor.

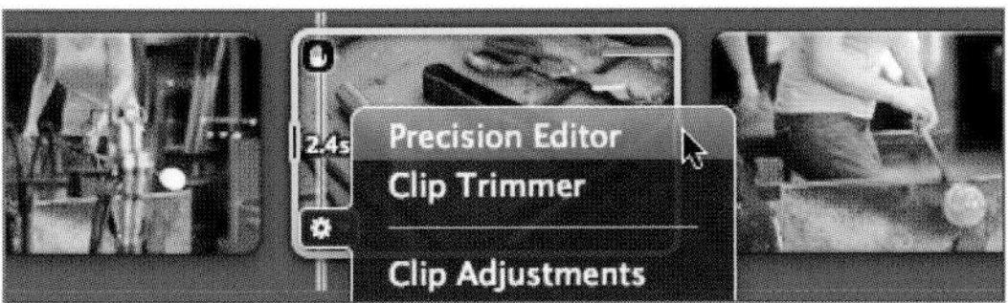

The Precision Editor appears below the project. It is a magnified view of the transition between the two clips. The blue bar in the center indicates where the cut occurs between the first clip displayed in the top filmstrip (also called the *outgoing clip*) and the second clip displayed in the bottom filmstrip (called the *incoming clip*).

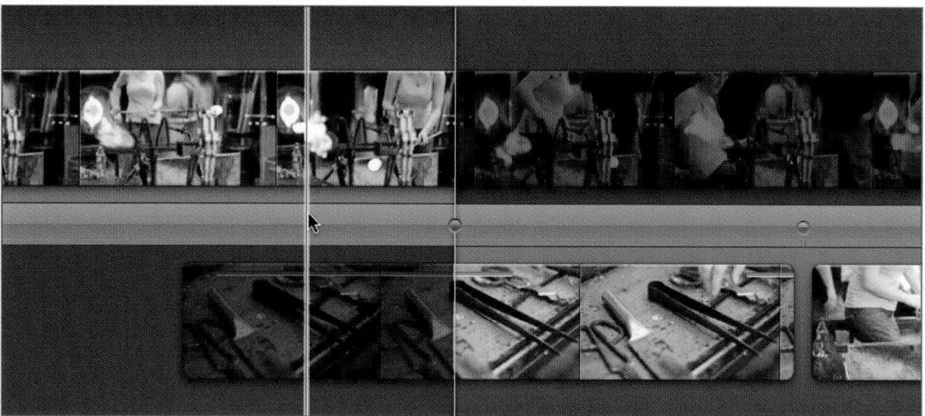

5 With your pointer positioned in the gray area of the Precision Editor, skim back and forth to preview the transition. Skimming in the gray area of the Precision Editor is identical to skimming over the transition in the project window.

The filmstrip in the upper left of the Precision Editor shows the portion of the project clip that plays before the transition, and the filmstrip in the lower right shows the clip that plays after the transition.

The shaded parts of the filmstrips, in the lower-left and upper-right areas of the clips, show portions of the clips that aren't used in the project.

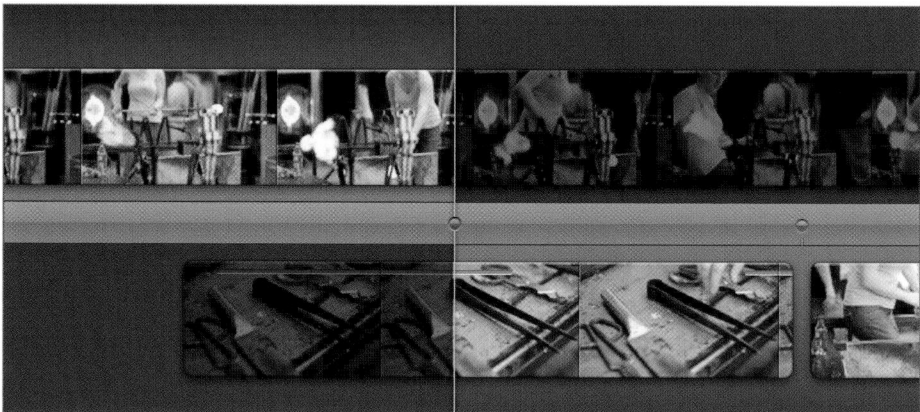

6 In the upper-right corner of the Precision Editor, click the Play button.

The first thing you'll correct is the long delay before the hand enters the frame on the incoming clip.

7 Move the pointer over the bottom filmstrip near the blue bar, and skim slowly to the right until you see the hand enter the frame.

8 Skim slowly to the left until the hand leaves the frame and then click the mouse button. This chooses a new starting point for the incoming clip. The filmstrip slides over to indicate the adjustment.

9 Click the Play button to review the change.

You can refine the outgoing clip by extending it to include the glass blower sitting down and reaching for the tweezers.

10 Move the pointer over the top filmstrip near the blue bar.

11 Skim slowly to the right until you see the glass blower sit down and reach, being careful not to extend too far where she looks into the camera. When she is reaching, but not looking into the camera, click the mouse button.

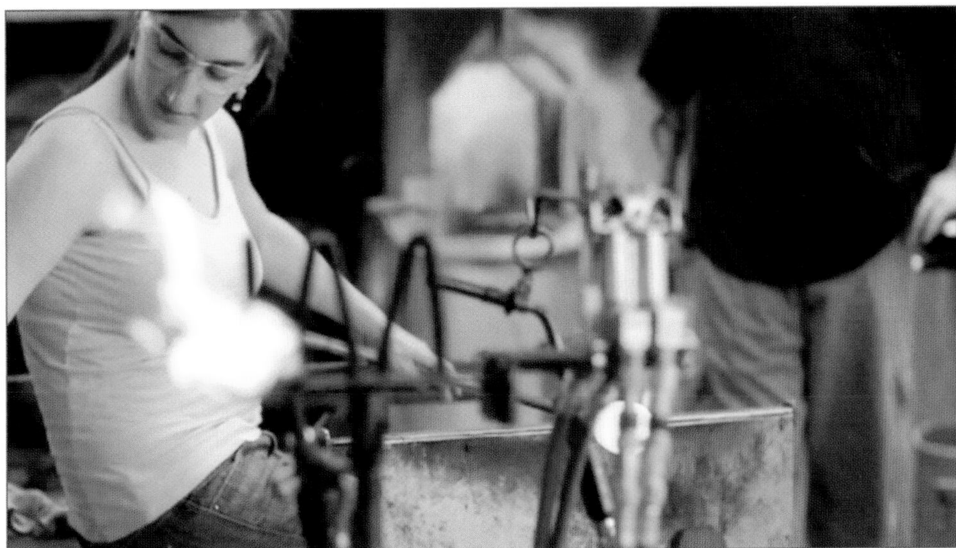

12 Click the Play button to review the change.

You could have achieved the same results by selecting and deleting ranges, but the Precision Editor is a more adept refinement tool. It allows you to see the unused portions of each clip, as you will see in the next section, because it also edits audio.

Trimming Audio in the Precision Editor

You can create more sophisticated transitions between clips by having video and audio content start at different times. Why would you want to do this? It can be a helpful way to hide content imperfections or to create a smoother flow through a transition.

1 In the Precision Editor, click the Show Previous Edit button twice to select the transition between the map and the first video clip.

2 Click the Play button to review the transition.

You could improve a few things here. First, a long pause exists between the end of the map and when the glass blower speaks. If you attempt to trim out the pause before she speaks, the edit may seem very abrupt. In addition, the map just seems out of place without music or some audible introduction. By playing her audio greeting, "Welcome to Seattle," with the map and then switching to her video, you improve the transition and smooth the sequence of clips.

3 Skim over the bottom filmstrip to where the glass blower says, "Welcome to Seattle".

4 Click the filmstrip between "Seattle" and her next sentence.

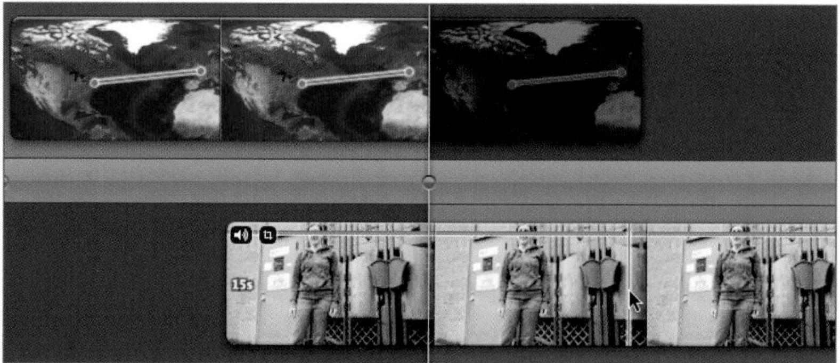

5 Click the Play button to confirm that you cannot hear "Welcome to Seattle" and that you can clearly hear her say, "The best thing to do here." If you trimmed too close to the next sentence (so that it sounds cut off), click again where you think the clip should start.

6 In the Precision Editor, click the Show Audio Waveforms button. The Precision Editor's Show Audio Waveforms button is different from the Projects button of the same name.

The audio waveforms are displayed in the Precision Editor, where you can trim the audio independently of its associated video.

TIP The button to the left of the Show Audio Waveforms button can be clicked to show titles, background music tracks, beat markers, secondary audio tracks, and voiceover tracks in the Precision Editor.

7 Move the pointer to the audio waveform display below the bottom filmstrip.

8 Skim near the blue bar until your pointer changes to a resize pointer.

9 Drag to the left, just before the glass blower says, "Welcome."

10 Click the Play button to hear your change.

11 Click Done to close the Precision Editor.

You have created what is commonly called an *L cut*. Regardless of what you call it, this is a sophisticated edit that has connected the first two clips of your movie in a more fluid and polished manner.

Recording Narration

In "how-to" movies such as the current project, it's helpful to include narration to help viewers understand what they are watching. You have three ways to record narration for your iMovie project:

- Record it at the same time you shoot the video
- Record it with your Mac's built-in iSight camera
- Record it using iMovie's Voiceover tool

Recording Using the Voiceover Tool

The Voiceover tool allows you to record narration directly into your project. Your first step is to find the location in your project where you want to place narration.

1 In the project, skim to the start of the third clip.

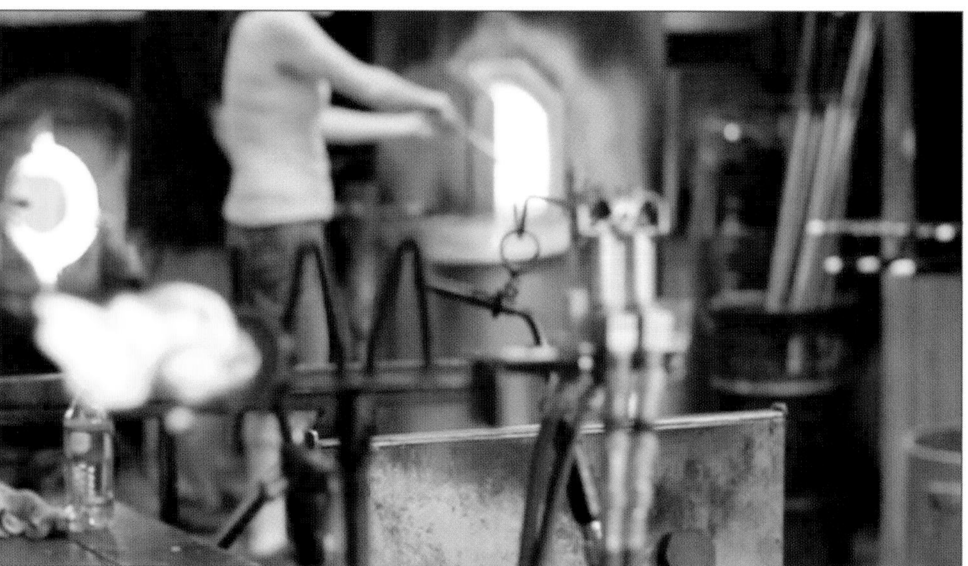

The narration line will be, "First, we heat the glass." This third clip will fit nicely with that line so you'll start recording here.

2 In the toolbar, click the Voiceover button.

The Voiceover window opens so you can test the recording levels.

3 Practice saying the line of narration as if you were recording it. While practicing, watch the input meters in the Voiceover window.

A good level primarily displays green lights, with yellow appearing only briefly during the loudest audio.

Red lights are bad. If you commonly see red lights, you should decrease the input volume until they no longer appear.

4 In the project, skim to the middle of the third clip's first thumbnail.

The recording stops when you press the Spacebar.

5 Click the clip to begin recording. A three-second countdown begins when you click the clip, giving you a cue to begin speaking. When you have completed the first line of narration, press the Spacebar to stop recording.

6 If you aren't happy with your recording, select the narration track that appears in the project and delete it. Then repeat steps 4 and 5 to try recording again.

7 Close the Voiceover window.

You now have your first voiceover track. Just like any audio track in a project, you can move its location and change its volume level.

Using Audio from a Video Clip

If you have a video clip that includes the narration, recorded either by a camcorder or directly into your Mac's iSight camera, just drag it into the project. In this exercise, you'll use the prerecorded video clips in the Event to add the second and third lines of narration.

> **NOTE** ▶ You can record video using your Mac's iSight camera by clicking the Camera Import button. The recorded iSight clip will be located in the Event with your other clips.

1 At the bottom of the Event, skim slowly over the second clip of Taryn the glass blower, speaking into her iSight camera.

She is speaking the second line of narration. You'll locate a good spot in your project to place this narration, but instead of adding the video clip in its entirety, you'll use only the audio.

2 Drag the clip of the second narration line over the sixth clip in the project. This clip shows an assistant in the process of glass blowing.

3 Release the mouse button to place the narration clip directly over the sixth clip and display the Edit pop-up menu.

4 Choose Audio Only.

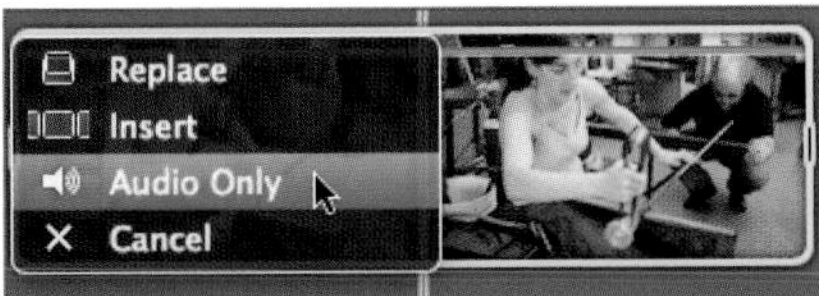

Only the audio from the clip is added to the project precisely where you released the mouse button. The green audio track can be moved, trimmed, and modified just like any audio track.

Enhancing Audio

As you now know, placing the audio in your project is only the first part of working with it. You'll improve the audio mixing over the next few exercises using a few new audio tools.

Ducking, The Sequel

As you did in Lesson 12, you need to ensure that voices can be heard over music. Again, you'll use ducking to do this.

1 Play the project just before the second narration line and stop playback after the narration clip ends.

   It's a very quiet narration compared to the other tracks, so you'll use ducking to lower the volume on both the video clip and the music.

2 Select the narration clip, then click the Inspector button.

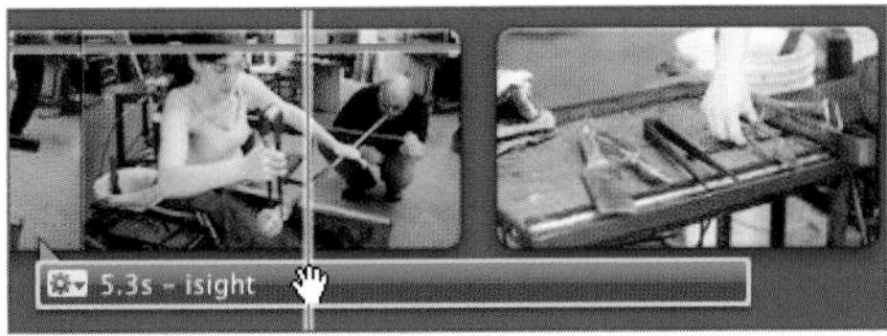

3 In the inspector, click the Audio tab and select the Ducking checkbox.

4 Play the project to listen to the second narration track.

This mix is better, but the narration is still too quiet. You need to make the narration as loud as it can be.

Normalizing the Audio Volume

Previously, you adjusted audio volume using the Volume slider. In this case, you will *normalize* the narration clip's volume. Normalizing finds the loudest part of a clip and raises the overall audio level so the loudest part of the clip is as loud as it can be without distorting. This gives you the maximum possible clip volume.

1 With the second narration track still selected and the inspector open, click Normalize Clip Volume.

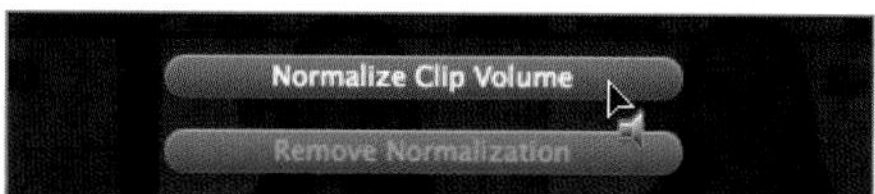

A quick analysis is performed to locate the loudest point and raise the clip's level.

2 Skim just before the second narration clip and press the Spacebar to begin playback. Stop playback when the narration clip is finished. The clip is now significantly louder.

You can find the third narration line in the Event, add it, duck it, and normalize it. You may need to move the inspector to make it easier to select the third narration clip.

3 When normalizing is complete, click Done to close the inspector.

4 Press \ (backslash) to hear the results.

You now have nearly perfect audio levels throughout your project. If you are wondering when to use the volume slider and when to normalize a clip, it's not always easy to decide. Both methods do much the same thing. In general, start using the Volume slider. If you can't get acceptable results—perhaps because the audio has lots of contrasting loud and soft levels—it might be easier to get the right level settings using Normalize Clip Volume.

Varying Audio Levels Within a Clip

For more advanced mixing situations in which you can't remove an offensive noise and ducking the volume adjustment is too limiting, you can set varying volume levels within a single clip.

1 At the bottom of the project window, click the Show Audio Waveforms button.

Audio waveforms are displayed under every clip in the project. Note that a thin black line runs through the audio waveforms. Dragging the line up or down is identical to dragging the Audio inspector's Volume slider.

The last third of the first clip is just wind noise. Using equalization to remove the wind noise would make the glass blower's voice sound bad. Your only real solution is to limit the wind noise by lowering the volume in only that section of the clip.

2 Skim to see the glass blower reach for the door knob.

3 Move the pointer down over the audio waveform.

The wind noise starts just before she reaches the door, and this is where you want to lower the volume level. Just as you would select a range on a clip, you can select a range within the audio waveform.

4 Drag a selection to the right until the wind noise is completely selected, just after you hear the music start.

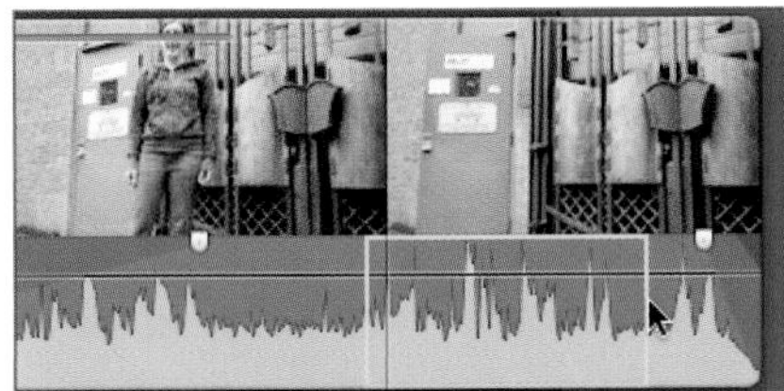

With an audio range selected, you can change the audio level of that range.

5 Move the pointer over the thin black line within the selected range.

6 Drag the line down until the tooltip displays 10 percent.

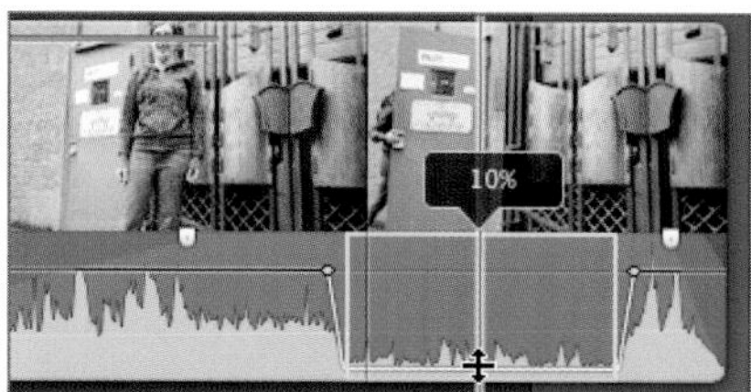

TIP You can reset the audio level adjustments by selecting the clip and choosing Remove Volume Adjustments from the Clip menu.

7 Play the project to review the audio level change.

8 Press the Spacebar to stop playback.

Changing the level has definitely reduced the wind noise but it is an abrupt change. You'll now smooth the transition between the two levels.

9 Drag the yellow control point on the left side of the selected range until the glass blower turns to face the camera.

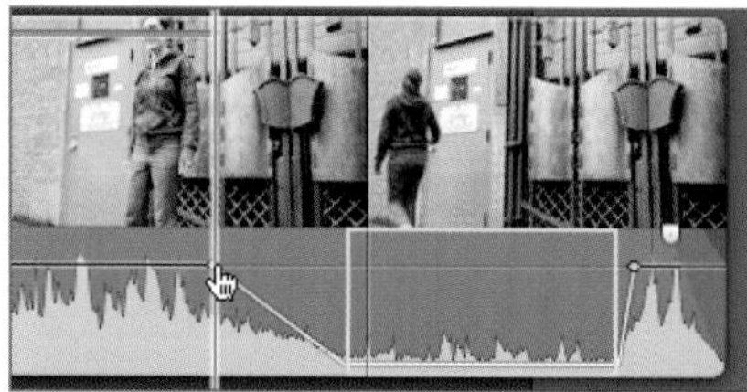

10 Play the project to review to the change, then press the Spacebar to stop playback.

That's a much better transition from the voice level to the much quieter wind noise level. If you like you can do the same thing on the right side of the range and extend the transition to the right.

11 Click the Show Audio Waveforms button to hide the waveforms in the project.

TIP Each clip has control points at its start and end that can be used to fade the audio in and out. They are similar to using Fade sliders in the Audio inspector.

Enabling Advanced Tools

With your audio mix sounding pretty good, you can return your focus to the video. Next, you learn about more of the advanced tools you enabled when you created a cutaway. Advanced tools can more easily solve some editing issues and provide additional layering effects.

Using the Dual Mode Toolbar

When you enable advanced tools, it subtly changes the way some toolbar tools work.

1 Choose iMovie > Preferences.

2 In the General tab, select the Show Advanced Tools checkbox, then close Preferences.

   The toolbar now includes more tools. You have a Selection tool as the currently chosen tool. The former "Add to Project" button now works slightly differently to save you time; and it's now called the Edit tool to signify its change in behavior.

3 Click the Edit tool to choose it.

4 At the bottom of the Event Browser, skim over the glass blowing clip shown in the following figure.

5 Place your pointer just before her hands appear in the viewer, then drag to the right until the end of the clip.

As soon as you release the mouse button, the clip is added to the end of the project. This method also works for the Favorite, Reject, and Unmark tools. Drag a range and the chosen tool is applied. It's a simple change but saves considerable time.

Creating a Split Screen

Split screen effects are similar to picture-in-picture effects in which one video clip shares the screen with another. It can be a nice moviemaking technique when you are trying to show two separate events at the same time or representing a lengthy process in a short amount of time.

1 Skim over the clip shown in the following figure.

At this point in the project, we've seen our fill of stretching and shaping glass. It might be nice to condense the final steps and add some visual interest, using a split screen.

2 In the Event Browser, create a six-second selection on this clip.

3 Drag the selection from the Event directly on top of the next-to-last clip in the project.

4 From the Edit pop-up menu, choose Side by Side.

The clip is placed in the project as a layer on top of the existing clip. You may need to move the added clip so that it starts almost at the same time as the existing clip.

5 Move the pointer over the newly added clip until the it changes to a hand icon.

6 Drag so that the new clip is centered over the existing clip.

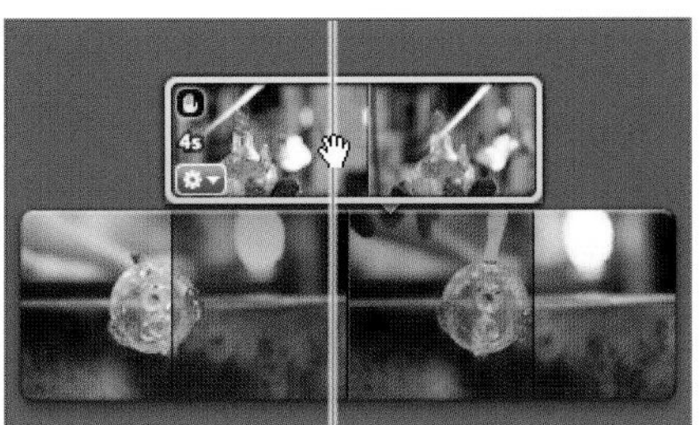

7 Skim to the clip before the side-by-side effect and press the Spacebar to review the result. Press the Spacebar to stop playback when you you've seen enough.

   It's not bad, but it could be better. The inspector allows you to customize the effect.

8 In the toolbar, click the Inspector button, and then click the Clip tab.

9 In the Side by Side section of the inspector, click the Slide Manual button.

10 Press the Spacebar to view the results, then press the Spacebar to stop playback.

11 Click Done to close the inspector.

You can use the techniques you just learned to create a picture-in-picture effect, which is also available in the Edit pop-up menu. The side-by-side and picture-in-picture effects are simple ways to dress up a clip or two in the right situations; but like all effects, they lose their impact when overused. You've been warned.

The project is mostly complete. By now you are a sophisticated moviemaker and ready to add titles and transitions on your own to complete your movie.

Lesson Review

1. Where do you find maps in iMovie?
2. What does the top filmstrip in the Precision Editor represent?
3. How do you start recording a voiceover?
4. Which method is best for boosting or reducing specific audio frequencies: normalization or equalization?
5. If you do not see Side by Side as an option in the Edit pop-up menu, what must you do?

Answers

1. In the "Maps, Backgrounds and Animatics" Browser in the toolbar.
2. The top clip represents the first clip in the transition, also called the outgoing clip.
3. With the Voiceover tool open, click the location in the project where you want the recording to be placed.

4. The equalizer, because it divides the sound into ten sections, or "bands," that let you hone in on the frequency you want to boost or reduce.
5. Select the Advanced Tools checkbox in iMovie Preferences.

14

Lesson Files

Lesson 08 > Old Holiday Movies

Lesson 08 > Marlins Spring Softball

Time

This lesson takes approximately 90 minutes to complete.

Goals

Understand video formats

Capture video from cameras and camcorders

Create and name new Events

Merge and split Events

Save disk space and consolidate projects

Adjust clips' date and time stamps

Use keywords

Backup projects and Events

Reclaim space on your hard disk

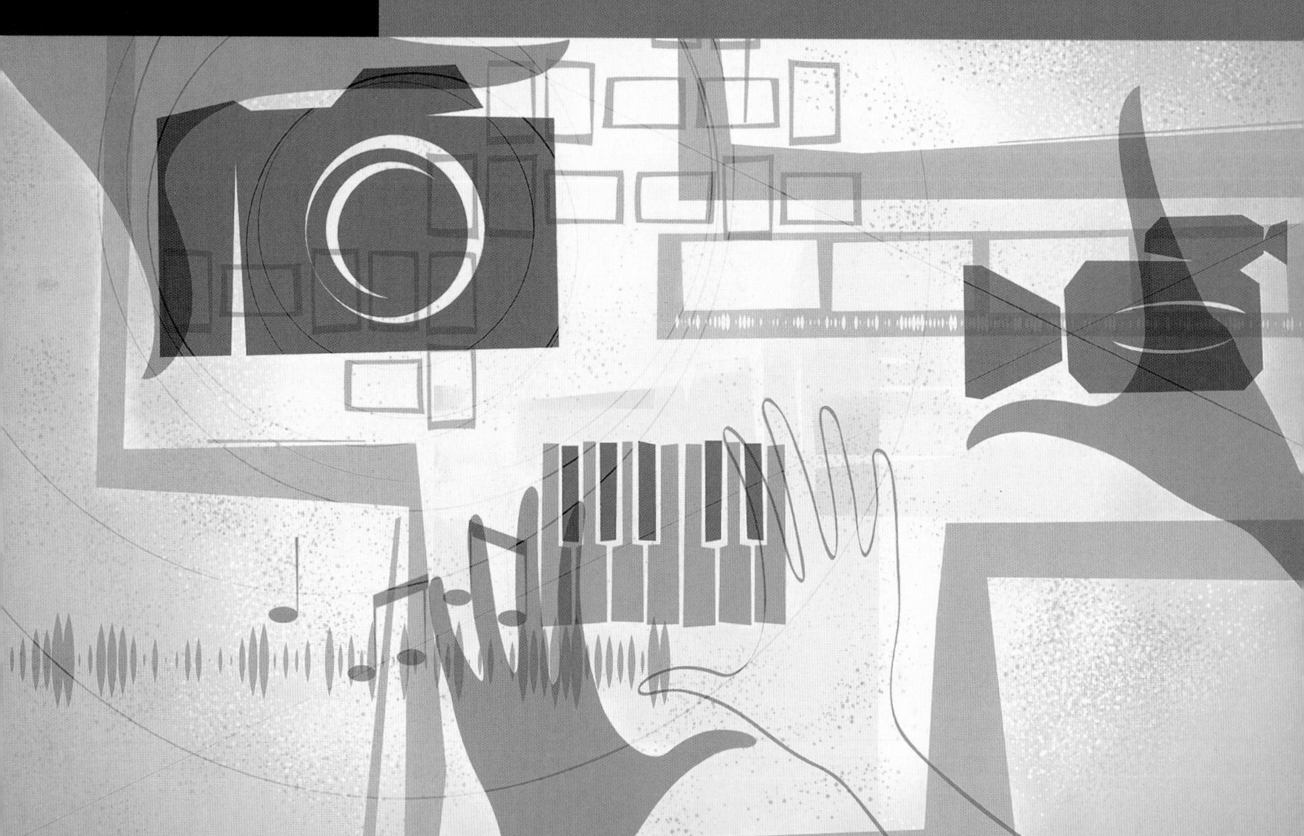

Lesson **14**

Capturing and Managing Media

Now that you have a firm grasp on using iMovie to make fantastic movies, it's time to turn your eye toward the essentials of capturing and managing the video in your library. iMovie not only captures clips from different devices, it also assists in keeping them in a neat and orderly library. Since this lesson goes over capturing from different devices and then how to manage them across multiple hard drives, not every reader will be able to follow the step-by-step instructions. Still, it is worth reading along to get a better understanding of how iMovie manages your library.

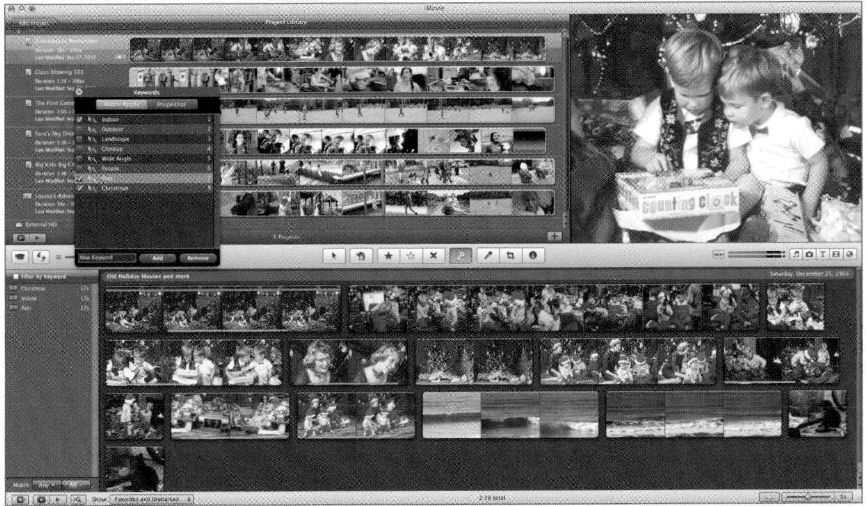

Understanding Video Formats

The process of transferring video from a camcorder to your Mac's hard disk using iMovie varies slightly depending on the type of camcorder you own.

Although the process of transferring video varies slightly from one camcorder to the next, the good news is that iMovie is designed to work with the majority of camcorders. Here's an overview of the camcorder types and video formats and how you transfer their content into iMovie.

Sizing Up Standard and High Definition

The most significant distinction in video formats is standard definition (SD) versus high definition (HD). It's a distinction similar to that of SD and HD television sets. Simply put, HD video provides a more detailed, sharper image than SD video. iMovie works equally well with SD and HD video formats, and you can even use them both in a single project.

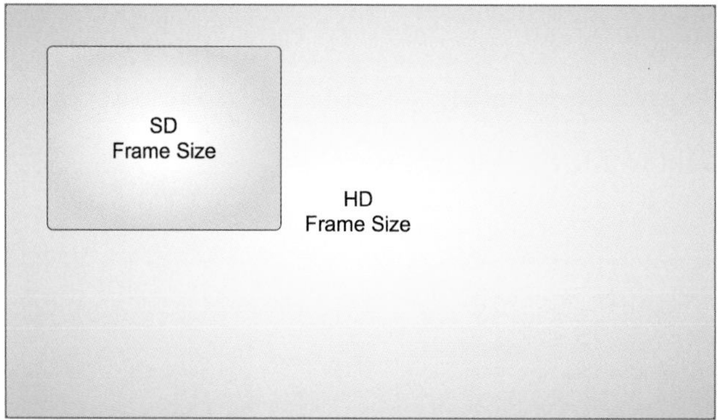

HD video comprises 1920 pixels horizontally and 1080 pixels vertically. SD video consists of 640 horizontal pixels and 480 vertical pixels. Because HD video contains more pixels, it requires more hard disk storage space and faster hard disk performance.

Also, video is recorded in a wide variety of file types including DV, HDV, AVCHD, and many others. Some types are SD and some are HD, but iMovie handles the differences and allows you to concentrate on your movie.

Understanding Frame Shapes

HD and SD have different frame shapes, or *aspect ratios*. HD's cinema-like, widescreen aspect ratio is 16:9. SD's almost square aspect ratio is 4:3 (four by three), the familiar shape we've watched since the beginning of TV.

In iMovie, you can choose whether you want to frame your project in a 16:9 or 4:3 aspect ratio, depending largely on the frame shape of your video clips. If you put HD video in a 4:3 project or SD video in a 16:9 project, iMovie will automatically pad the tops or sides to make the video fit.

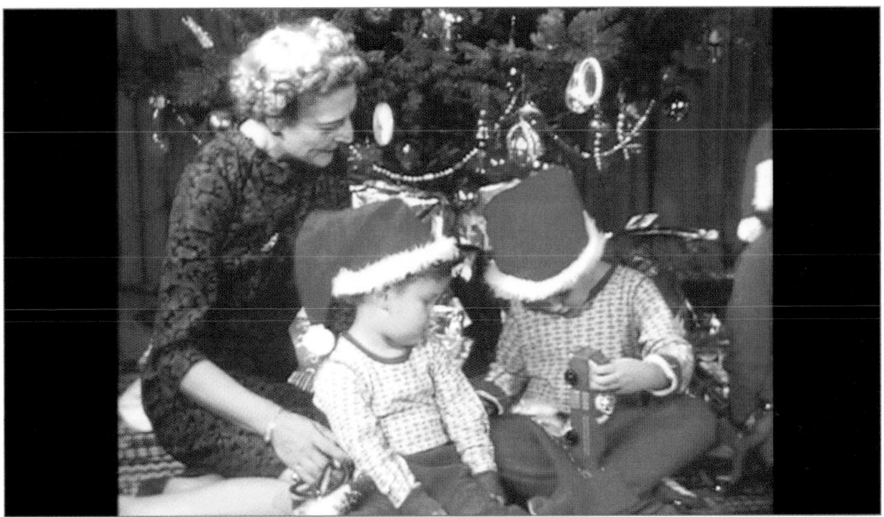

A 4:3 standard definition clip placed in a 16:9 widescreen frame. Black pillars are added to the sides to fill in the empty frame space.

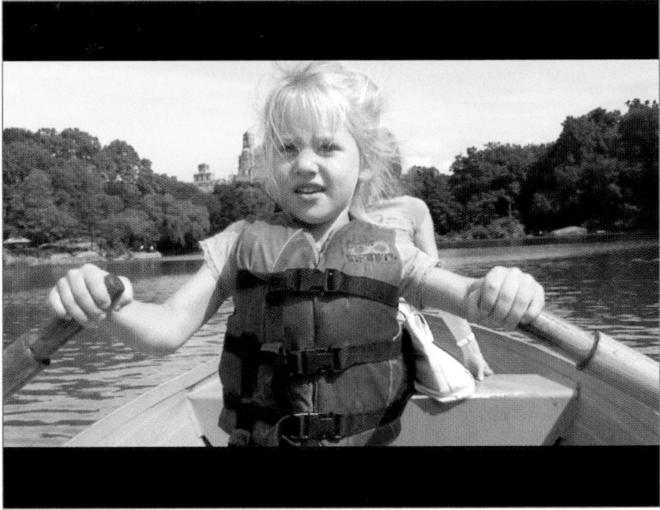

A 16:9 HD clip placed in a 4:3 SD frame. Black letterbox bars are added used to fit make the widescreen clip fit into the narrower frame without cutting off the sides of the image.

Choosing HD Size Options in iMovie

When you import an HD video into iMovie, can choose between two sizes: Large and Full.

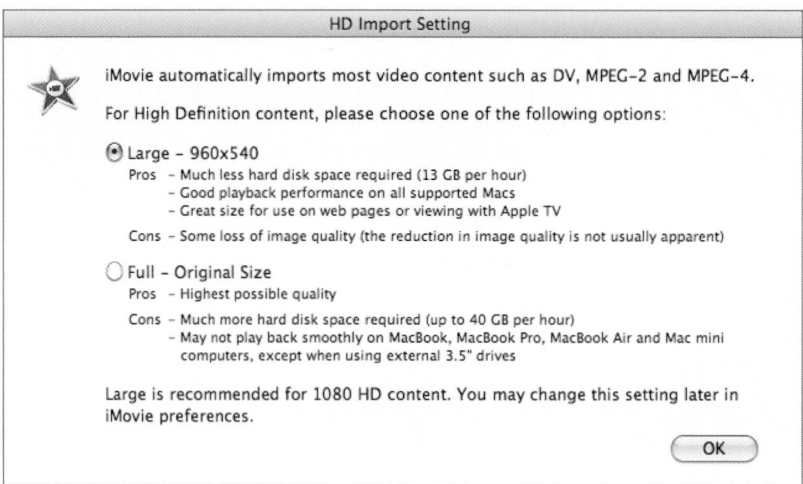

HD Import Setting
iMovie automatically imports most video content such as DV, MPEG-2 and MPEG-4.
For High Definition content, please choose one of the following options:
Large - 960x540
Pros - Much less hard disk space required (13 GB per hour)
- Good playback performance on all supported Macs
- Great size for use on web pages or viewing with Apple TV
Cons - Some loss of image quality (the reduction in image quality is not usually apparent)
Full - Original Size
Pros - Highest possible quality
Cons - Much more hard disk space required (up to 40 GB per hour)
- May not play back smoothly on MacBook, MacBook Pro, MacBook Air and Mac mini computers, except when using external 3.5" drives
Large is recommended for 1080 HD content. You may change this setting later in iMovie preferences.
OK

Large is a good choice when using HD video on older Macs or slower hard disks. iMovie optimizes the HD video down to a size of 960x540 pixels. You may lose some video quality; however, if you are mainly going to watch the video on DVD or the web, Large is an excellent choice.

Full maintains the original size and quality of your video clips. If you have a fast hard disk and a fast iMac or Mac Pro, Full size retains the highest-quality video. However, if your Mac and hard disks are older or slower, you may encounter stuttering playback.

Getting Clips into iMovie

When you're ready to put your videos into iMovie, your digital recording device and its recording medium are the main considerations. Some digital camcorders use videotape, while others use memory cards or hard disk drives. Some even record directly to DVD.

To import from a camera that records to a memory card, hard disk drive, or DVD, use a USB connector.

> **NOTE ►** Analog VHS or 8mm camcorders cannot connect directly to your Mac. A detailed list of supported camcorders can be found on the iMovie support website: http://help.apple.com/imovie/cameras

Whichever type of camcorder you own, in most cases iMovie will automatically recognize your camera and connection type once you attach them to your Mac and open the "Import from" window.

The window for capturing from a camcorder differs depending on whether you've connected a digital tape camcorder (such as HDV or DV) or a tapeless digital camcorder (which records to a hard disk, DVD, or memory card).

Importing Clips from a DV or HDV Camcorder

If you have a DV or HDV tape-based camcorder, use a Firewire or IEEE 1394 cable to connect the camcorder to your Mac. You can follow the directions below to connect your camcorder and capture a few of your own clips.

> **NOTE ▶** Not all Macs have a Firewire port, and some have only a Firewire 800 port. Check your Mac's configuration to confirm that your Mac includes Firewire support (and the connector type) before attempting to connect a DV or HDV camcorder.

1. Plug in your camcorder and connect the Firewire cable to your camcorder.
2. Set your camcorder to the Play or VCR setting.
3. Connect the other end of the Firewire cable to your Mac's Firewire port.
4. In the Dock, click the iMovie icon to open the application.
5. Wait a few seconds for the "Import from" window to open automatically.

> **NOTE ▶** If the "Import from" window does not open, disconnect and reconnect the camcorder and make sure it is set to Play or VCR.

The "Import from" window has very simple controls for capturing from a tape-based HDV or DV camcorder.

The Automatic setting rewinds the tape, imports all of the tape's contents, and rewinds the tape. The Manual setting allows you to rewind, fast-forward, and import any parts of the tape you want. You control the playback of the camorder using the transport controls.

The Camera pop-up menu is used to choose the device from which you want to import. Typically, this will be set automatically to the camcorder connected to your Mac.

The Import button starts the automatic or manual import process. The Done button closes the window.

After clicking the Import button, the import settings appear.

If you have created an existing Event in which you would like these clips to be kept, you can select "Add to existing Event," and then choose the Event name from the pop-up menu.

Alternatively, you can create and name a new Event by selecting "Create new Event."

The "Split days into new Events" will automatically make a new Event for every day that clips were recorded.

The "Save to" pop-up menu chooses the hard disk to store the video.

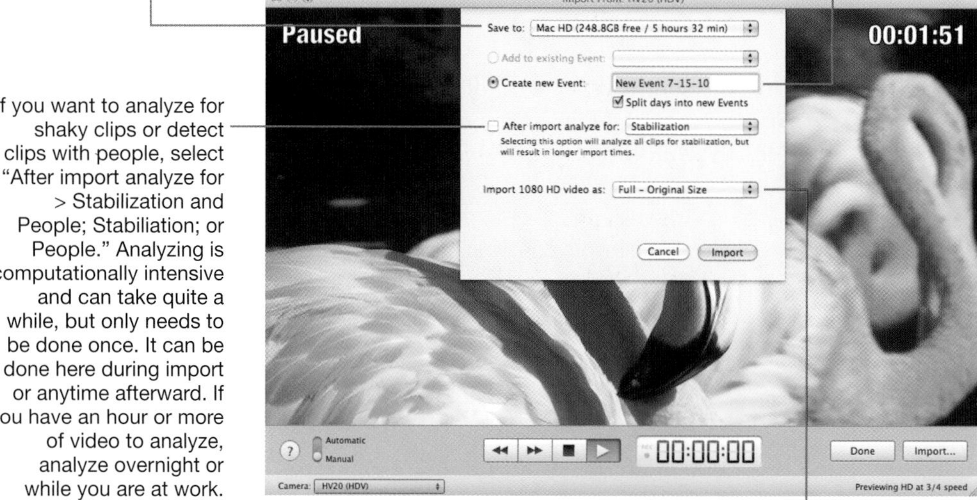

If you want to analyze for shaky clips or detect clips with people, select "After import analyze for > Stabilization and People; Stabiliation; or People." Analyzing is computationally intensive and can take quite a while, but only needs to be done once. It can be done here during import or anytime afterward. If you have an hour or more of video to analyze, analyze overnight or while you are at work.

If you are importing HDV video, you have the choice to keep it at its original HD size or choose a smaller size that will give better performance and take up less hard disk space.

After you click Import, *do one of the following*:

- ▶ If you're importing automatically, you can leave your computer and camcorder and return when the capture is finished and the tape is automatically rewound.
- ▶ If you're importing manually, click Stop when the section of video you want to transfer has been imported. You can continue to start and stop importing as the tape plays through until you have imported all the video you want.

NOTE ▶ One hour of SD digital video requires about 13 GB (gigabytes) of hard disk storage space. One hour of HD digital video optimized for iMovie requires about 50 GB of hard disk storage space. The amount of free space on each available disk is shown in parentheses next to the disk's name in the "Save to" pop-up menu.

Importing Clips from a Tapeless Camcorder

Tapeless camcorders connect to your Mac using a USB cable. In some cases, when a tapeless camcorder is connected to your Mac, iPhoto opens automatically. You can set iPhoto Preferences so the application does not open automatically.

When iPhoto opens, from its File menu, choose Quit.

1. Connect the AC adaptor to your camcorder.
2. Connect the USB cable to your tapeless camcorder.
3. Set your camcorder to the PC or USB setting.
4. Connect the other end of the USB cable to your Mac's USB port.
5. In the Dock, click the iMovie icon to open the application.
6. The "Import from" window opens automatically in iMovie.

   The "Import from" window displays thumbnails to represent every clip you captured from the camcorder.

If you connect an AVCHD camcorder, you can click the Archive All button to save a copy of the clips on the camcorder and to a hard disk to save as a backup, or to import at a later date.

The Automatic setting imports all the clips on the camcorder. The Manual setting allows you to select which clips to import by selecting the checkbox under each clip.

The Camera pop-up menu is used to choose the device from which you want to import. Typically, this will be set automatically to the camcorder connected to your Mac.

The Import All button starts the automatic or manual import process. Click the Done button to close the window.

When you click the Import All button, you'll see the following import settings:

NOTE ▶ AVCHD camcorders use a highly complex file format to record video. iMovie converts AVCHD video files into an optimized format that improves playback and performance on your Mac and other devices. Some tapeless camcorders record video in H.264 or MPEG-4 formats. These file formats do not need to be optimized for iMovie, but they do benefit from better playback performance when they are optimized.

If you choose not to convert H.264 or MPEG-4 files, you can still create a movie with all the same functionality as when you use optimized clips, except any fast- or slow-motion speed changes. iMovie will need to convert an H.264 or MPEG-2 clip before it can apply a speed change.

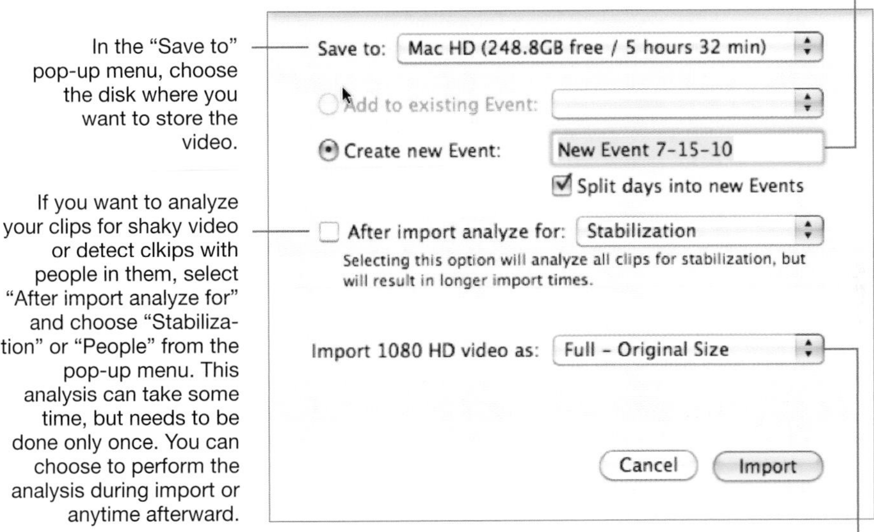

If you have created an existing Event where you would like these clips to be kept, you can select "Add to existing Event" and then choose the Event name in the pop-up menu. Alternatively, you can create and name a new Event by selecting "Create new Event" and typing a name for the Event in the data field. Select "Split days into new Events" to automatically make a new Event for every day on which clips were recorded.
In the "Save to" pop-up menu, choose the disk where you want to store the video.
If you want to analyze your clips for shaky video or detect clkips with people in them, select "After import analyze for" and choose "Stabilization" or "People" from the pop-up menu. This analysis can take some time, but needs to be done only once. You can choose to perform the analysis during import or anytime afterward.
Save to:
Mac HD (248.8GB free / 5 hours 32 min)
Add to existing Event:
Create new Event:
New Event 7-15-10
Split days into new Events
After import analyze for:
Stabilization
Selecting this option will analyze all clips for stabilization, but will result in longer import times.
Import 1080 HD video as:
Full - Original Size
Cancel
Import
You can choose to keep the video content at its original HD size or choose a smaller size produce smaller files and provide better playback performance.

After you click Import, you can leave your Mac and return when all the clips are imported.

Importing Clips from a Digital Photo Camera

When you want to import clips from a digital photo camera. use the File > Import menu to transfer them into iMovie.

1 Choose File > Import > Movies. The import settings window opens and includes the same options that were available during the previous two camcorder exercises.

2 Navigate to the mounted disc image that appears on the desktop, and in the DCIM folder, locate the movie files.

NOTE ▶ Not all digital still cameras are compatible with iMovie. Check the iMovie '11 Supported Cameras page on the iMovie website to see if your camera is supported. If your camera is not supported, you may still be able to access the clips in iMovie by importing the clips into iPhoto.

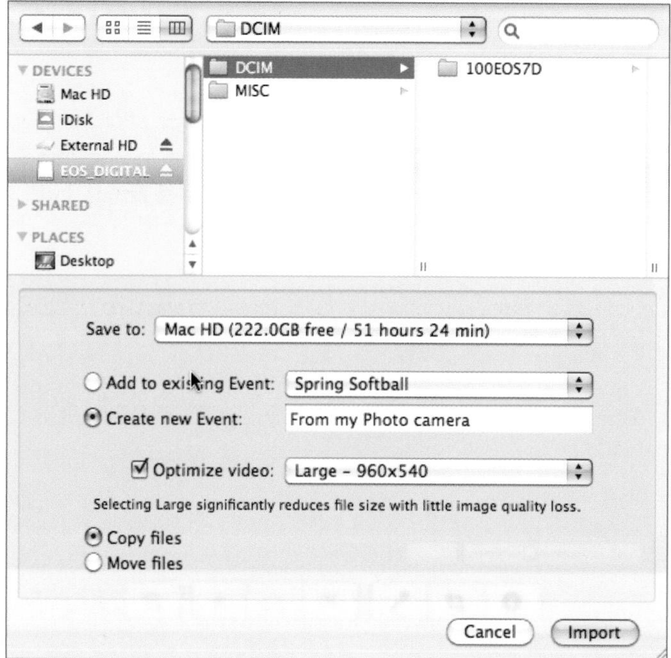

3 In the "Optimize video" pop-up menu, choose a size for your clips.

4 Click Import.

After the import process is finished, the Event and all the imported video content are available in the lower half of the iMovie window, ready for you to watch.

Managing Events in your Library

Events are at the heart of your Library. The more your Library grows, the more Events you'll have, so although you don't really create anything new in this lesson, it's important to know all the ways Events can be created, used, and organized.

NOTE ▶ The exercises in this lesson assume that you have imported the clips in Lesson 8 and created a few projects. In addition, a few features are discussed that require an external hard disk. If you haven't completed the earlier lessons or you do not have an external hard drive, you can still follow the steps but you will not be able to fully perform them.

Creating and Renaming Events

Events are created automatically when you import clips from the Finder or from a camcorder. But you also may want to create empty Events, perhaps because you want them in place before you import content, or you want to separate some clips from an existing Event. Whatever your reason, creating a new Event is simple.

1 Choose File > New Event. The Event is added and highlighted in the Library ready to be named.

2 Type a name for the Event. For this exercise, let's name the Event *Spring Soccer*. Then press Return to save the new title.

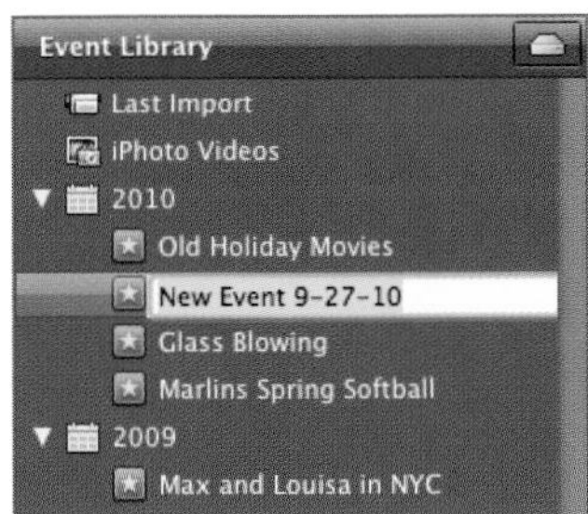

TIP If the Event isn't highlighted for renaming, double-click it.

Moving Clips Between Events

When you import clips from your camcorder, you may have clips spanning a period of days to months and including multiple special occasions. If you decide not to organize these clips into separate Events when you import them, you can always do so later.

1 In the Event Library, select the Marlins Spring Softball Event.

The first four clips here have nothing to do with Marlins Spring Softball. These feature a soccer game between eight–year-olds. These clips don't belong in the same Event as the softball game.

2 Select the first clip in the Event.

3 Shift-click the fourth clip in the Event to select all the clips between the first and the fourth clips.

4 Drag the first clip over the Spring Soccer event in the Event Library. When the clip is directly over the Spring Soccer Event and highlights in blue, release the mouse button to move the clips to that Event.

5 When the warning message appears, click OK to confirm that you want to move the clips to that Event.

NOTE ▶ If the Events exist on different hard disks, the clips will be copied, not moved, and will exist on both drives in both Events. You can delete whichever copy you no longer want.

Splitting and Merging Events

Instead of creating a new Event and moving clips to it, you can split an Event into two Events and choose the point where the clips are separated.

1 In the Event Library, select the Old Holiday Movies Event. The last three clips do not belong with the holiday clips, so that's a good place to split the Event.

2 Command-click the first ocean waves clip in the Event.

3 Choose File > "Split Event before selected clip."

In the Event Library, you now have a new Event called Old Holiday Movies 1 in addition to your original Old Holiday Movies Event. The clips before your selected ocean waves clip remain in the original Event. The clip you selected and the two clips that follow are moved to the new Event.

If you want to merge Events, that's also done through the File menu.

4 In the Event Library, Command-click both the Old Holiday Movies and Old Holiday Movies 1 Events to select them.

5 Choose File > Merge Events. A dialog opens in which you can name the merged Event.

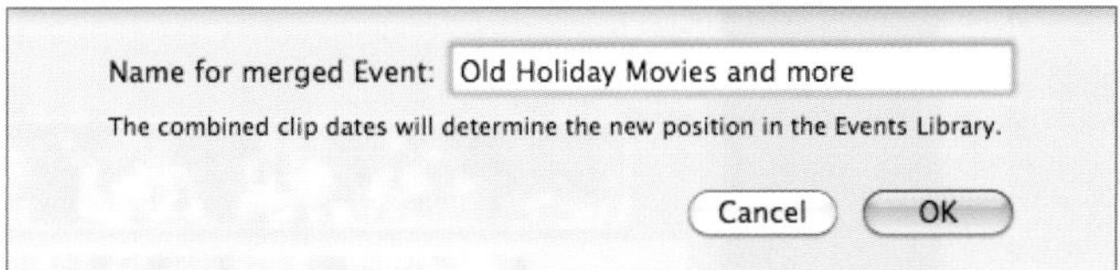

6 In the "Name for merged Event" field, type *Old Holiday Movies and more* and click OK.

The Events are now merged into a single Event with the new name.

Reordering Events in the Library

By default, Events are listed in the Library by date. However, you can list them in other orders as well.

1 Control-click (or right-click) in the empty gray space in the Event Library. In the contextual pop-up menu you can change how Events are listed.

2 Choose "Group Events by Month" to list the Events according to the month and year they were recorded.

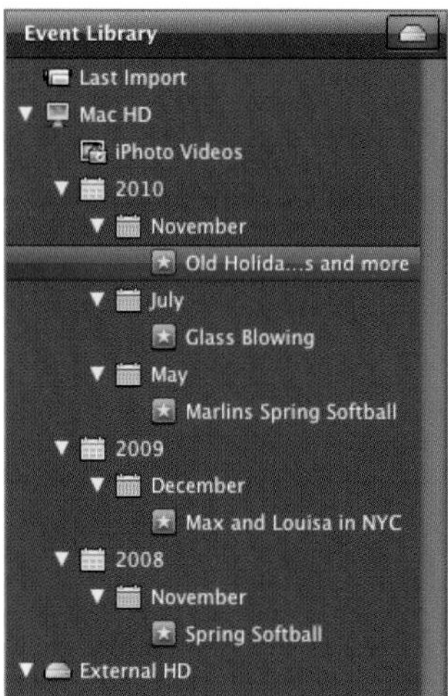

3 Choose "Group Events by Disk" to list the Events according to the disk where they are stored.

TIP You can also click the disk icon in the upper-right corner of the Event Library to group Events by disk. This is useful when you want to move Events from one hard disk to another.

4 Choose "Group Events by Month" again to return viewing Events grouped by month and year.

As your Library grows, you may not be able to settle on one way you sort your Events. You may find yourself changing the sort depending on what you are looking for and what you want to do.

Adjusting a Clip's Date and Time

In some cases you may find that the date was set incorrectly on your camcorder, or like the Old Holiday Movies and more Event, your clips have incorrect date information. In those cases, you can enter or modify the dates for every clip.

NOTE ▸ If you have not completed Lesson 8, then import the Old Holiday Movies folder in Desktop > ATS iLife11 Book Files > Lesson 08.

1 Select the "Old Holiday Movies and more" Event, if necessary.

2 Choose View > Playhead Info. The Playhead Info makes it easy to see the date and time for each clip.

3 Skim over the first clip to see that this clip was created on September 25, 2010, at 11:08 AM.

Hmmm, I think not. These clips are obviously very old, and even back then, Christmas didn't take place in September. The listed date is probably the date these clips were created, not the date they were shot.

The actual date these clips were filmed was December 25, 1965. Let's fix these dates.

4. Click the first clip in the Event.

5. Choose Edit > Select Entire Clip, and then choose Edit > Select All. All the clips are selected and you can now change their creation dates.

6. Choose File > Adjust Clip Date and Time.

   A window appears displaying the time and date of the first clip. The other clips will be offset based on how you set the first clip.

7. In the To field change 11/3/2010 to *12/25/1965.*

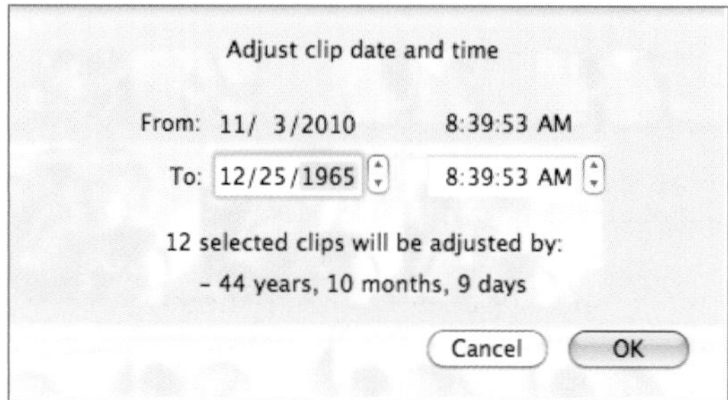

8. Click OK.

   The Event in the Event Library now correctly shows that this event has a new, 1965 date. As you skim over each clip in the event, the playhead info displays the correct date.

Analyzing an Event to Detect People

Because clips with people are often the clips you want to use first, iMovie can find ranges within clips that feature people. To locate and mark these ranges, iMovie must analyze the clips much like it did for stabilization.

1. Select the "Old Holiday Movies and more" Event.

2. Choose File > Analyze Video > People.

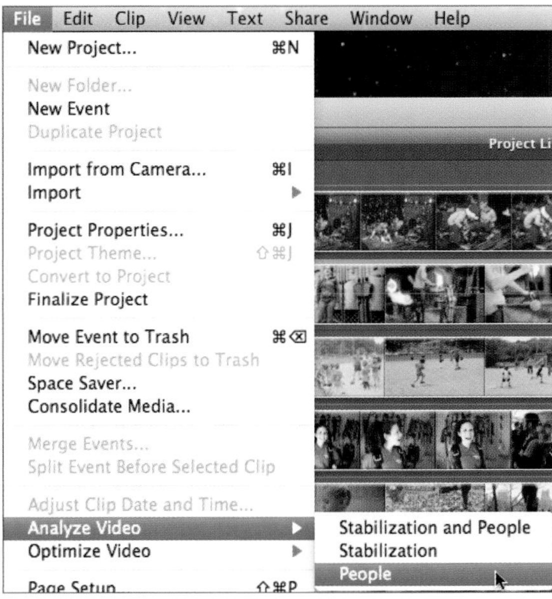

The analysis takes some time, so in many cases it's a good idea to choose to analyze for stabilization and people at the same time. For iMovie to detect people, they have to be facing the camera. iMovie won't find people if they are turned away or looking straight down. It also won't find people if they cock their head too far to one side, as Mom does in clip 4 of the Event.

As iMovie performs its people analysis, you'll notice that a purple line is drawn cross the top of certain clips to indicate the clip ranges that include people.

3 When the analysis is completed, skim over the clip of Mom in the Event. Notice how the purple line breaks when Mom cocks her head to one side and resumes when she straightens up again.

4 Choose View > Playhead Info if it's not already enabled.

5 Skim over the purple lines in the Event.

When you skim over a range in which people are detected, the Playhead Info shows the word "people." The word goes away when you skim over an area in which people were not detected.

Using Keywords

Keywords, or Tags, are text labels that you assign to areas of a clip to help you find certain areas more quickly. Although adding this information to your clips takes a bit of work up front, it can pay off when you need to find all the clips of Aunt Millie at the bocce ball court, and fast!

Auto-Assigning Keywords to Clips

The first step is to add keywords to your clips. To do that, you must enable the Advanced Tools to gain access to the Keyword button and the Keywords Palette.

1 Choose iMovie > Preferences, and select the Show Advanced Tools checkbox, if necessary. Then close Preferences.

In addition to expanding the Edit pop-up menu and changing the toolbar functionality, Advanced Tools also adds a Keyword button to the toolbar.

2 Choose View > Playhead Info if it's not already enabled.

3 In the toolbar, click the Keyword button to display the Keyword Palette. Here, you can select the keywords to apply to any given area of a clip.

4 Select the "Indoor" and "Pets" checkboxes. The first clip in the Event is recorded indoors and it includes a pet, so it makes sense to add those two keywords to the first clip.

5 Drag across the entire first clip in the Event to select it.

TIP The Inspector tab in the Keywords Palette changes the selection behavior so that you make the selection first and then select the keywords you want to apply. Which method you use is your choice.

As you skim over the clip, notice that the keywords Pets and Indoor show in the Playhead Info. Next you'll add your own keyword.

Adding Your Own Keywords

iMovie includes a short list of keywords, but you can add your own, and they'll remain in the list until you remove them.

1 In the Keywords window, in the New Keyword field, type *Christmas*, then click the Add button.

Christmas is added to the Keyword window and is ready to be applied to a clip.

2 In the Keywords window, select the checkbox next to Christmas.

3 In the Event, drag across the clip of the children opening presents to select it.

TIP Keywords can be applied to ranges within a clip. If you want to add the keyword to a clip but the dog appears only at the start of a clip, select only the range in which the dog is seen.

Removing Keywords

Skim over the clip and notice that while you have assigned your own keyword to the clip, along with the two previously added keywords, there's still one small problem. No pets appear in this clip. Let's remove that inaccurate keyword.

1 In the Keywords window, click the Inspector tab.

2 Select the clip that just received the keyword.

3 Deselect the Pets checkbox to remove the keyword from the selected range.

Filtering an Event Based on Keywords

Now that all the hard work is done, it's time for the payoff. You can use keywords to filter out clips that don't meet certain criteria.

In addition to the Keyword button, a "Filter by Keyword" pane is added to choose the criteria for sifting the Event.

1 In the lower left of the iMovie window, click the Keyword Filter button.

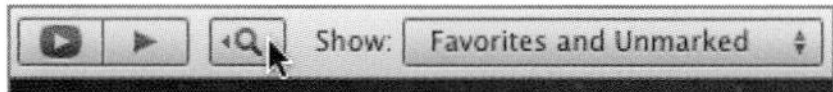

The "Filter by Keyword" pane lists all the keywords that have been assigned to this Event. Most of the keywords were created when you analyzed to detect people but the three keywords you added manually are also listed.

To filter an Event, select the keywords that you want to find, or want to avoid.

2 Click the green button to the left of the word Indoor. This indicates that you are looking for all the clips in the Event with the keyword Indoor.

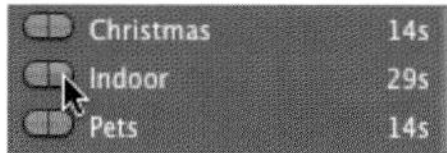

Two clips appear in the Event, the two clips to which you applied that keyword.

3 Click the red button to the left of the keyword Pets.

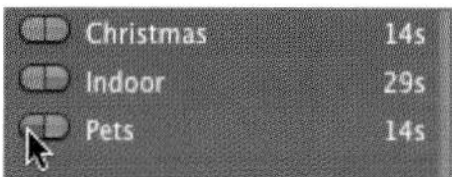

By selecting these two buttons you sifting for all clips with the keyword Indoor but without the keyword Pets. Consequently, the Event shows only one clip that matches your sifting criteria.

OK, let's get a little more sophisticated.

4 Click the red and green buttons again to deselect them.

5 Click the green button next to the word "People", then click the green button next to the word "Closeup."

Are the sifting results not quite what you expected? The People keyword visibly filtered the Event, but nothing changed when you selected the Closeup keyword. Certainly not all the people clips in this Event are close-ups.

6 At the bottom of the "Filter by Keyword" pane, click the All button.

Now the results show two close-ups of Mom. That seems more like it. When the "Filter by Keyword" pane is set to Any, the clips can match *any* of the keywords, so in this case your sift could match either People *or* Close-up. Clicking All requires the clips to match *all* keywords (or in this case, both keywords). Only two ranges match that criteria.

7 To reset the keyword filter and see all the clips again, select the "Filter by Keyword" checkbox at the top of the "Filter by Keyword" pane.

You can imagine applying this filtering to an Event containing a much larger number of clips. Filtering can come in very handy, making it much quicker to find the clips you need to make a movie.

Making Backups

If you are using a digital camcorder that records to a hard disk or a memory card, then you really should be backing up your projects and Events to another hard disk (or two!). With digital files, all it takes is one hard disk failure to lose all your clips and all your video memories. Even if you have a tape-based camcorder, it's still a good idea to back up your Projects and clips. iMovie gives you several ways to create backups.

NOTE ▶ Do not copy projects and Events from one drive to another in the Mac Finder. Always use iMovie to move projects and Events as described in the following exercises. Moving projects and events on the desktop while iMovie is closed will often result in projects not reconnecting to the clips in the Event.

Making a Camera Archive

iMovie has a Camera Archive backup feature especially for AVCHD camcorders. This feature copies clips from your camcorder to a hard disk of your choice to create a backup. With most other tapeless camcorders you can drag files from the camcorder to your hard drive to create a simple backup. Because AVCHD files are more complex, a customized backup feature is required.

1 Connect your AVCHD camcorder to your Mac. The Import window will open.

NOTE ▶ If you don't have, don't plan on purchasing, or just don't care about AVCHD camcorders, you can skip this section.

2 In the lower-left corner of the window, click Archive All.

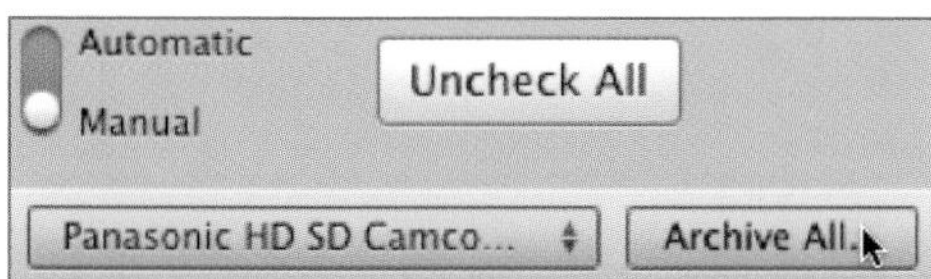

A Save As window opens in which you can enter a name for the archive.

3 Enter a name that indicates of the archive's contents (such as Sam's 8th Birthday). Then choose a destination to save the archive, and click Create.

When creating any archive or backup, it's best to save it to a hard disk other than the hard disk storing your imported import clips. Creating an archive or backup for your video clips is the same as creating a backup of any document. It should be located somewhere safe and separate from the copy you use every day.

Moving Events to an External Hard Disk

If you don't have an AVCHD camcorder or you forget to archive your AVCHD files from the camcorder, you can easily move your entire library to a backup drive within iMovie.

You can move a single Event, a project, or both a project and an Event at once. Let's first move an Event because it's so easy.

1 If it's not already highlighted in blue, click the "Group Events by Disk" button in the upper-right corner of the Event Library.

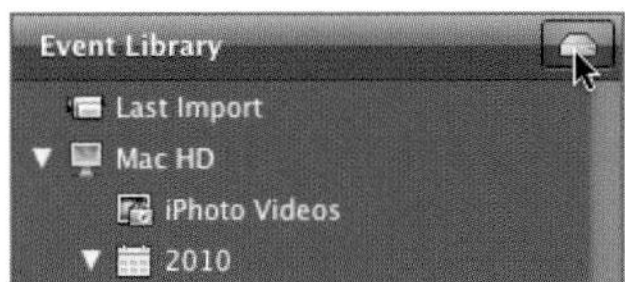

Clicking the "Group Events by Disk" button displays all the hard disks connected to your Mac, and under each hard disk name, lists the Events stored on that hard disk.

2 In the Event Library, drag the "Old Holiday Movies and more" Event to the external hard disk icon in your Event Library.

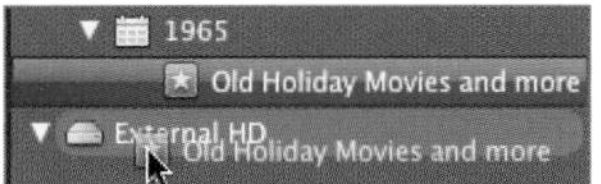

The Event and all its clips (even rejected clips) are copied onto the external hard drive. When the process is complete, two "Old Holiday Movies and more" Events exist. The original is still located on your Mac's hard disk and the copy is located on the external hard disk. The "Holiday to Remember" project will still use the clips from the Mac hard disk on which it was created.

TIP After you follow the preceding steps, if you delete the original Old Holiday Movies Event from the Event Library, the project will automatically access the clips on the external hard disk the next time you open that iMovie project.

Moving Projects to an External Hard Disk

Moving Events also moves all of your clips, which is what takes up most of the space on your hard disk. It's the simplest way to create a backup. To create a more complete backup of Events and projects or to move everything to another Mac, you start by copying the project.

1 At the top of the project window, click the Project Library button.

By clicking the disclosure triangles next to each hard disk icon, you can view the projects that are stored on that hard drive.

2 In the Project Library drag the "First Game" project to the external hard disk in your Project Library.

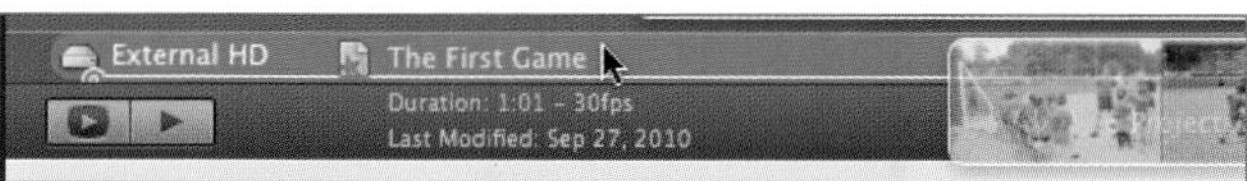

A dialog appears with two options.

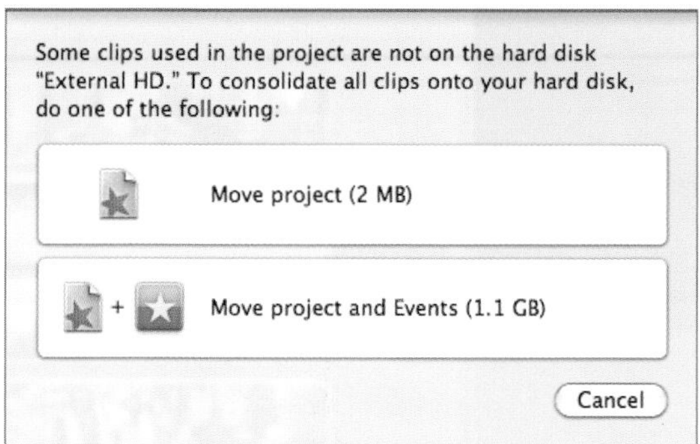

The first option is to copy the project. The amount of storage the project occupies is in parentheses. Because projects don't take up a lot of space, I can't think of many situations in which you would want to do this. (However, there is one that we'll discuss later.) The second option is to copy the project and the Events used to create the project. When you choose this option, the project, Events, and all associated clips (including the rejected clips) are copied to the external hard disk. When the copy is completed, two "First Game" projects and Events exist: the original project and Event still located on their Mac's hard disk, and their copies located on the external hard disk.

3 To avoid copying anything in this exercise, click Cancel.

A copy created on the external hard disk could be used as your backup or connected to another Mac and copied to its internal hard drive using the same procedure. This is the one case in which copying only a project makes sense. When the project and Events are on an external disk, if you're moving them to another Mac, you may want to copy only the small project file to the new Mac and leave the Event and all its clips on the external disk. This saves a lot of space on that Mac's internal disk.

Finalizing a Movie

When you finalize a movie, you can still watch it in iMovie even after you disconnect the external hard disk that contains the Event or after you delete all the clips in the Event. It's a good way to save your past work, yet restore room for your next creation.

1 In the Project Library, select the "Louisa's Adventure Trailer" project.

2 Choose File > Finalize Project.

TIP This can take a while so sit back or go get a beverage as iMovie does the work.

A status window appears to indicate the progress and show what size movie is being created. When you finalize a project, you essentially make movies of the project in multiple sizes. The movie is stored within iMovie so that you can still watch and share the movie on YouTube, iDVD, or elsewhere. You cannot change the project in any way. If you need to make changes to the project after finalizing it, you will have to restore the clips from your backup drive.

Consolidating Media

This final method of creating a backup is a bit more complicated and arguably not a desirable way to create a backup at all. But it does help in collecting your media in one location, thereby making it much easier to create a backup.

If any of the video clips, music, and other media used in a project are stored on a hard disk (or multiple hard disks) other than disk that contains the project itself, you can consolidate items to collect all that media onto the same disk as the project.

1 In the Project Library, select the "Glass Blowing 101" project.

2 Choose File > Consolidate Media.

TIP If the Consolidate Media menu item is dimmed, the media in your project are already located on the same disk as the project.

A Consolidate dialog appears with three options.

- Choose "Copy the events" to copy entire Events containing project clips to the same disk as the project.
- Choose "Copy the clips" to copy only the video in the clips used in the project to the same disk as the project. This saves you the most space since it does not copy your entire Event, only the clips it needs.
- Choose "Move the events" to copy content, as with the first option, and then have it automatically deleted from the source location.

TIP With all three options, any iTunes songs used in the project are also copied to the same disk as the project. If you move the disk to another Mac, some iTunes songs may need to be authorized to play on that Mac.

3 For this exercise, click Cancel so nothing is copied or moved.

By choosing any of the three options, the consolidate process begins copying or moving content. After consolidation, the project will reference the media at its new locations on the project disk. Consolidating doesn't inherently make a backup but it does collect all of your media into one location, thereby making it much easier to copy everything to a backup drive.

Reclaiming Hard Disk Space

If you need more free disk space but have only a single hard disk, you can quickly recover some available storage by applying Space Saver to remove clips that haven't been used in a project and haven't been marked as favorites.

1 In the Event Library, select the Old Holiday Movies and more Event.

NOTE ▶ Selecting a project will not work with Space Saver, which functions based on the selected Event. If no Event is selected in the Event Library, Space Saver is dimmed and unavailable.

2 Choose File > Space Saver. Before you continue, you might want to make sure you made a backup.

A Space Saver sheet appears with several options.

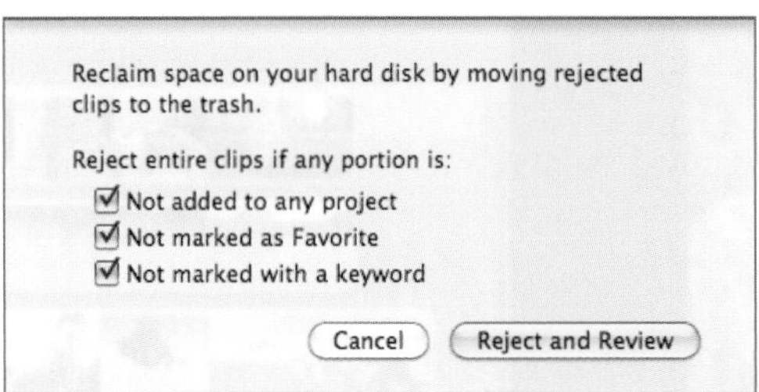

Space Saver works by marking clips as rejected based on the three checkboxes in this sheet.

- Select "Not added to any project" so that clips used in a project are not rejected.
- Select "Not marked as Favorite" so clips marked as favorites are not rejected.
- Select "Not marked with a keyword" so clips marked with a keyword are not rejected.

NOTE ▶ The keyword checkbox will not appear unless keywords have been applied to a clip in the Event.

3 Make sure that all checkboxes are selected, and then click "Reject and Review."

TIP If the clips are used in a project that is stored on an external hard disk and that disk is not currently connected to your Mac, then that project is not figured into Space Saver's calculation. This can be dangerous since Space Saver will not know if clips have been used in those remote projects.

The Event view is changed to show the rejected clips for your review.

At this point you can choose to "Delete the Rejected clips" or remove the Rejected marking and place them back in the Event.

Moving Clips to the Trash

After you reject clips or specific portions of clips, you can move them to the Mac's trash to free up disk space.

1 Click "Move Rejected to Trash."

The rejected clips are removed from iMovie and placed in the Mac's trash. They still are using space on your hard disk, so if you want to recover them into iMovie, you can do so. But you are just one Empty Trash away from completely deleting them.

NOTE ▶ Always doublecheck that the rejected clips are actually clips you want to delete. If you aren't sure, select the Unmark tool to and remove that clip from the rejected group.

2 On the warning dialog, click "Move to Trash."

iMovie will begin processing the clips. Because you rejected only a portion of a longer clip, iMovie must extract the rejected portion from the longer clip to move it to the trash.

When the processing is complete, you can take the final step to delete the clips from your hard disk.

3 In the Dock, click the Trash icon.

4 From the Finder menu, choose Empty Trash.

5 In the warning dialog, click Empty trash.

6 In the Dock, click the iMovie icon to return to iMovie.

The rejected clips are now deleted from your hard disk. In iMovie the view changes to show the favorites and unmarked clips in your Event browser.

You've come to the point where it's time to dig out your camcorder and put some of your moviemaking skills to use on your own home videos. It's time for the world to see your child playing t-ball in a flashy sports highlights video, you and your friends in an Adventure movie trailer, or even your eccentric uncle babbling into your iSight with a few nice titles and background music. You've completed the iMovie section of this book so you have the skills to create all those movies and a whole lot more. So with your new-found knowledge, go create memorable home movies.

Lesson Review

1. True or False: If you select a single clip in an Event and adjust its date or time, then all other clips will change based on the new date or time of the selected clip.
2. What do you need to do if the Keyword button is not displayed on the toolbar?
3. Why does Archive All not appear when a camcorder is connected and the Camera Import window is open?
4. Is Consolidate the best way to copy clips and projects to an external drive?
5. True or False: Space Saver marks all clips as Rejects based on the selected checkboxes and then moves the non-rejected clips to a backup drive.

Answers

1. False. Only selected clips are changed. If you want to change the date and/or time of all clips, you must select all clips.
2. To display the Keyword button on the toolbar, you must enable Advanced Tools in iMovie Preferences.
3. Archive All is available only for AVCHD camcorders.
4. No, Consolidate only moves or copies clips or events to the same disk as the project. The best way to copy a project along with its Event and clips is to drag the project to the external disk icon in the Project Library and then choose to copy the clips or the entire Event.
5. False. Space Saver does not move clips. It just marks them as rejects based on the selected checkboxes.

GarageBand: Making Great Sounding Music

3 In the control bar, click the Cycle button to create a yellow cycle region in the selected section.

The selected section title turns yellow to indicate that a cycle region has been created. It will cycle continuously (repeat/loop) until playback is stopped, another section is selected, or the Cycle button is turned off.

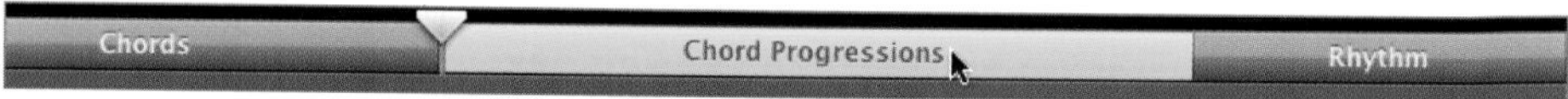

NOTE ▸ If all of the section titles turn yellow at once, the entire lesson was included in the cycle region. Click any specific section title to limit the cycle region to that selected section.

4 Press the Spacebar twice or double-click the Play/Stop button to stop, and then restart playback. Notice that playback always starts at the beginning of the cycle region.

5 Press C or click the Cycle button to turn off the cycle region.

6 Stop playback.

Now that you've learned how to select, navigate, and cycle through sections within the lesson, let's move on to some of the cool customizing features.

Customizing the Lesson Workspace

One of the most helpful lesson features is the ability to customize a lesson's appearance at any time to suit your specific needs. For example, you can show or hide the animated instrument, or turn on subtitles. All of the customizing choices are available in the Setup menu near the upper-right corner of the screen.

1 Click the Setup menu button. The Setup menu appears with choices for instrument setup, notation, language, and appearance.

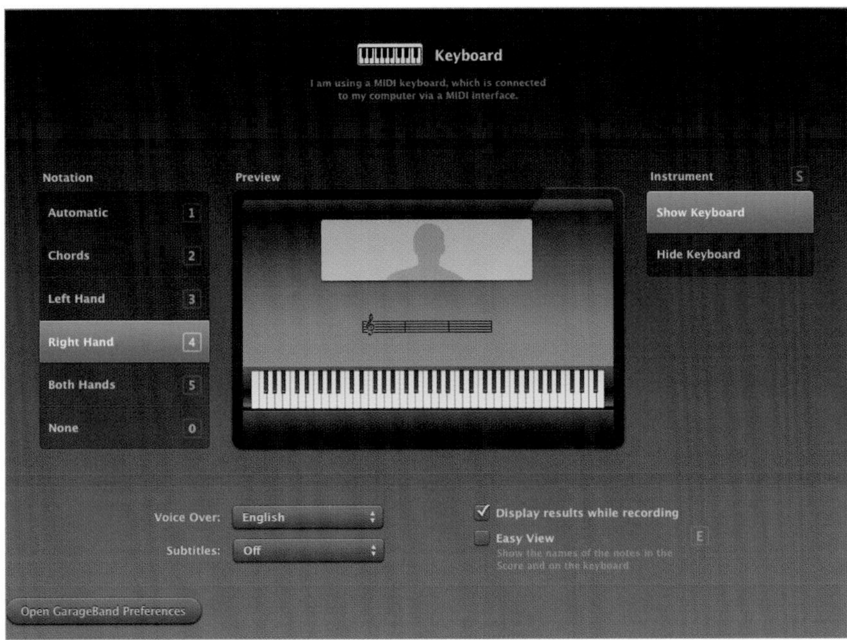

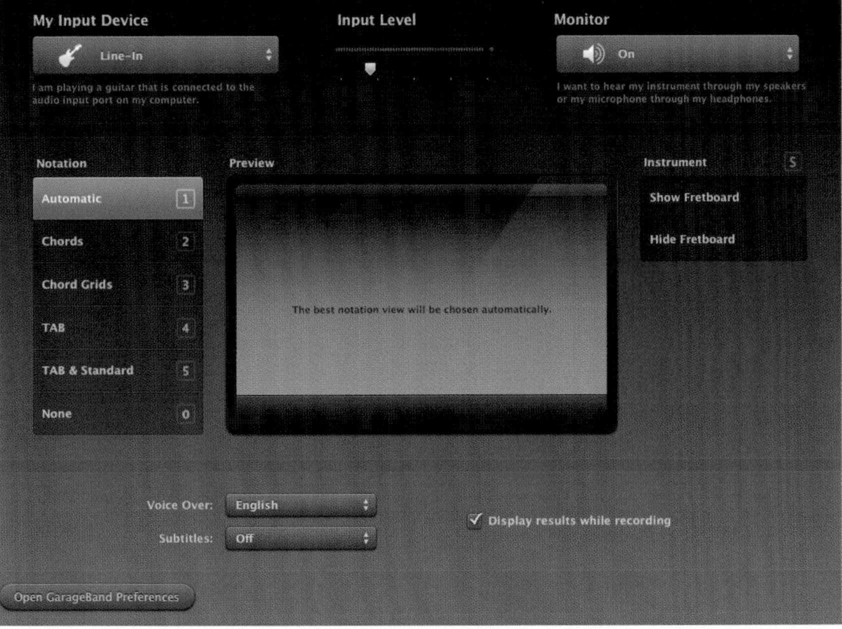

If you are following the Guitar lesson, the top of the setup interface includes Input Device, Input Level, and Monitor settings for connecting your guitar or for changing settings when the lesson is open.

2 Near the bottom of the interface, click the Voice Over menu to see the languages available for the lesson.

3 Select the the "Display results while recording" checkbox, if necessary, to display mistakes you may make as you record your practice in the next section.

4 Click the Setup menu button again, or click the arrow in the upper-left corner of the screen, to return to the lesson.

Tuning During a Lesson

In addition to taking a lesson, you can also tune your guitar and record your performance during the lesson.

NOTE ▸ Because both of these features require a guitar or keyboard connected to the computer, they won't be detailed in step-by-step exercises in this book.

The Tuner is located next to the Setup menu button near the upper-right corner of the screen.

To tune your guitar, click the Tuner button and play the string that you want to tune. The visual tuner works the same as most professional guitar tuners. Red lines appear on either side of the note name to indicate how sharp (right) or flat (left) the string is out of tune.

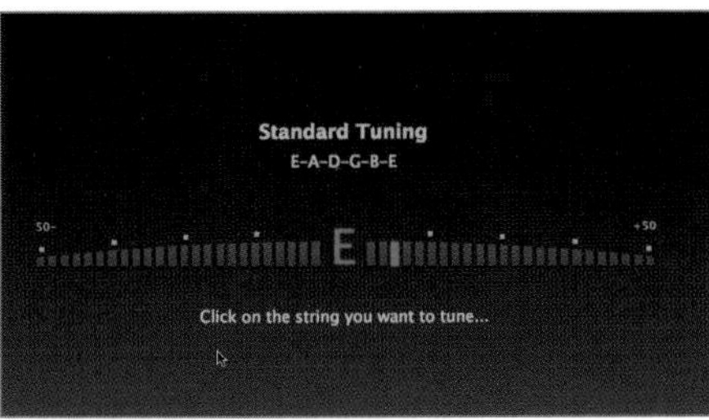

Out of tune (red)

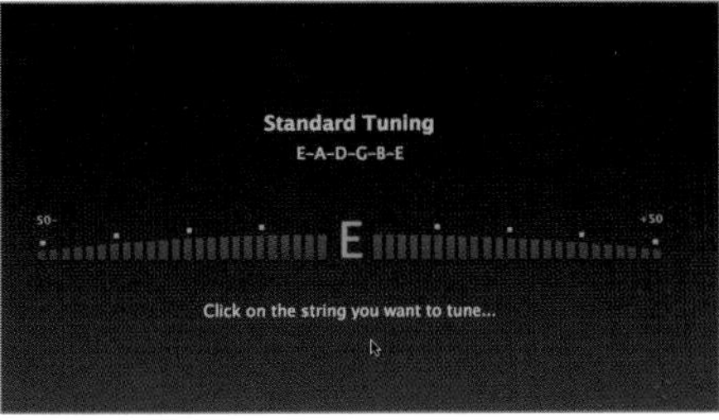

In tune (blue)

Recording and Reviewing Your Practice

It's time to meet your personal musical coach, motivator, and friend who will not only grade your work, but also chart your progress and give you instant feedback on your performance.

"How Did I Play?" is an exciting new GarageBand feature that offers the personal attention to detail and praise (or criticism) that can empower you to improve your playing beyond the instruction of the lesson itself.

To analyze your playing and see how you did, you first need to record the practice music in the Play chapter of your lesson.

To record your practice, *do the following:*

- Open the Play chapter of the lesson.
- In the control bar, click the Record button.

- Play your guitar or piano along with the music.

The multicolored bar is a visual representation of your recording. Correctly played notes are colored green; missed or wrong notes are red; and notes you played almost correctly are yellow. The percentage displayed in the lower-left corner of the control bar indicates the general accuracy of your playing.

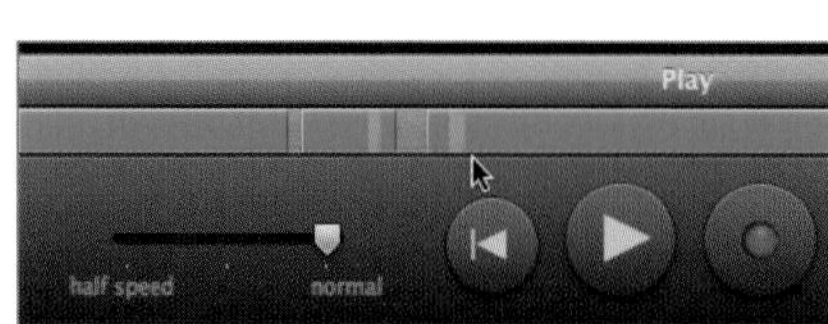

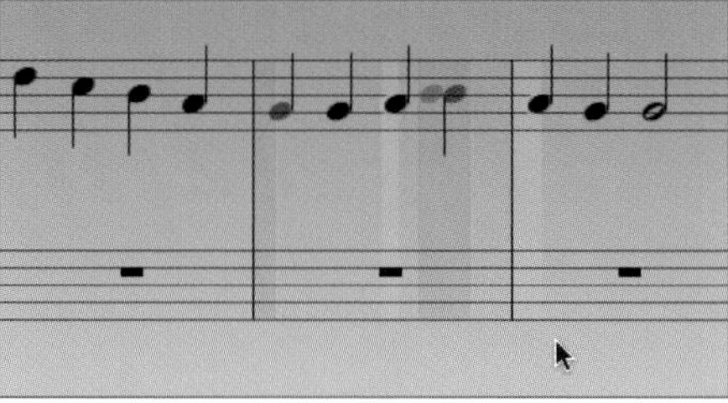

If musical notation is displayed, you will see red marks on the notation for note misses, and yellow for nearly accurate playing.

Don't worry if you see a lot of red the first time through. You know the adage "practice makes perfect." Well, it's true.

When you're finished, press the Spacebar to stop playback and recording. For a guitar recording, a purple Real Instrument region appears below the playhead; for a piano recording, you'll see a green Software Instrument region. You'll learn more about these region types in the next lesson.

Tracking Your Progress

The more practice sessions that you record, the better you will be able to track your progress. Few motivators are better than a graphic view of your performance and high scores. To see your progress, click the History button on the far-right side of the control bar.

History

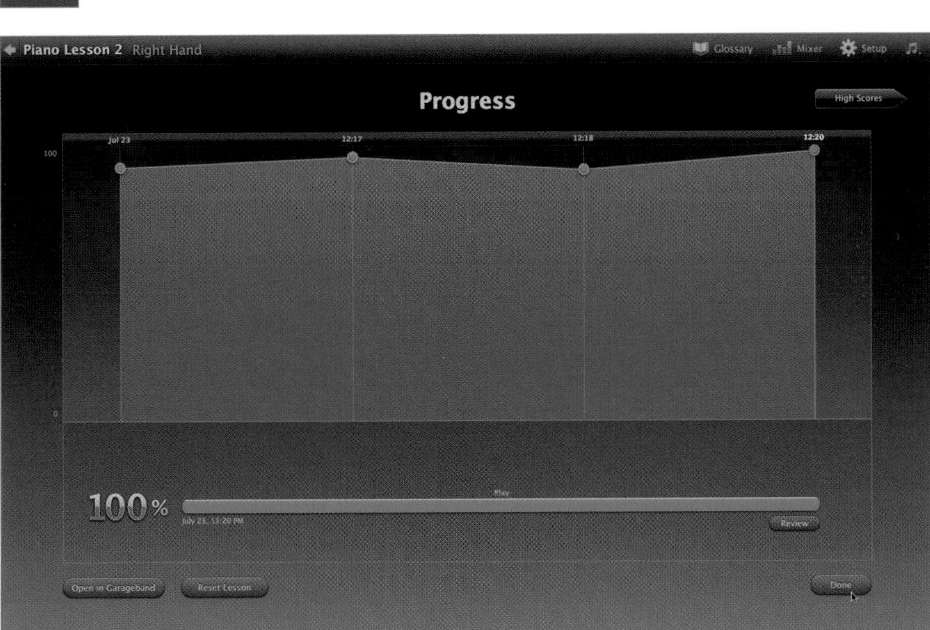

To see your high scores, click the High Scores button in the Progress window.

Changing a Lesson Mix

Because practice, practice, and more practice is an important part of any successful music study, you may want to adjust the lesson mix as you progress to best suit your practice needs. For example, you might grow tired of the instructor's voice saying the same thing over and over when all you want to focus on is the sound of his (or your) guitar or piano. Let's look at the Mixer and see how to change the lesson mix.

1 Click the Mixer button, located in the upper-right corner of the screen.

The Mixer appears as an overlay in front of the lesson window.

Each track includes a Mute button to silence a track, a Solo button to play only that track, and a Volume slider to adjust the track's volume.

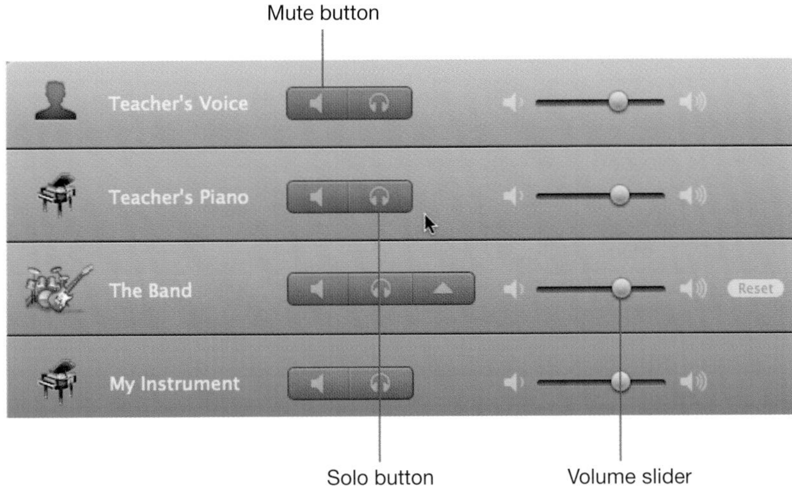

NOTE ▶ The Mixer for the Play chapter includes a My Recordings track if you have recorded your instrument during the lesson.

2 For the guitar lesson, play the Picking and Strumming section.

3 For the piano lesson, play the Chord Progressions section.

4 While the lesson plays, click the Mute button on the Teacher's Voice track to mute the track. The Mixer buttons, like other controls within GarageBand, turn blue to indicate that they're on.

5 Click the Mute button again to unmute the track. It may take a moment for Tim's voice to return after you unmute the track.

6 Experiment using the Mixer controls. When you're finished, click the Mixer button to hide the Mixer.

7 Close the lesson window to close the lesson.

That's it. Now you know your way around a Learn to Play lesson.

Downloading Additional Learn to Play Lessons

So you've finished the first Learn to Play lesson. Are you ready for more? GarageBand has 21 more Learn to Play basic guitar or piano lessons that you can download right to your Mac—and they're free!

To download your next lesson, you'll need to choose it from the Lesson Store.

> **NOTE ▶** If you don't want to download another lesson, you can still follow along with this exercise; just don't click the Download button when prompted to do so.

1 In the GarageBand project window, choose the Lesson Store.

The Lesson Store home screen appears in the project window. To download lessons, you first need to select the type of lesson.

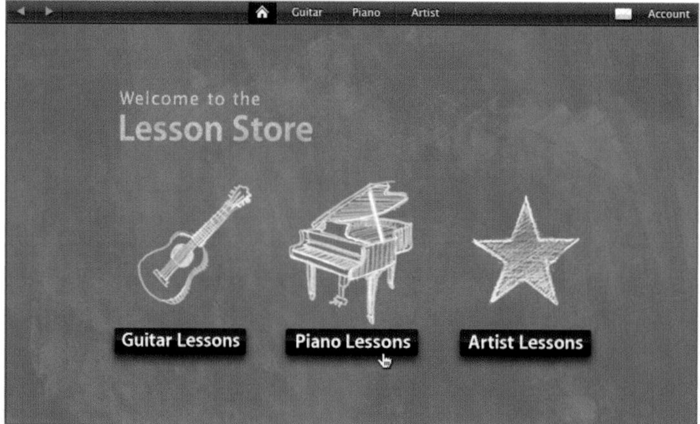

2 Choose Guitar Lessons or Piano Lessons from the Lesson Store home screen to open that instrument's lesson screen.

3 When the screen features the instrument of your choice, choose the series of basic lessons that you'd like to download.

A list of lessons available for download appears. You can download one at a time as needed, or click the Download All button to download the entire set. Keep in mind that downloading can take some time, so if you want to start a lesson right away, start by downloading just one.

4 Click the Download button for the basic guitar or piano lesson you want.

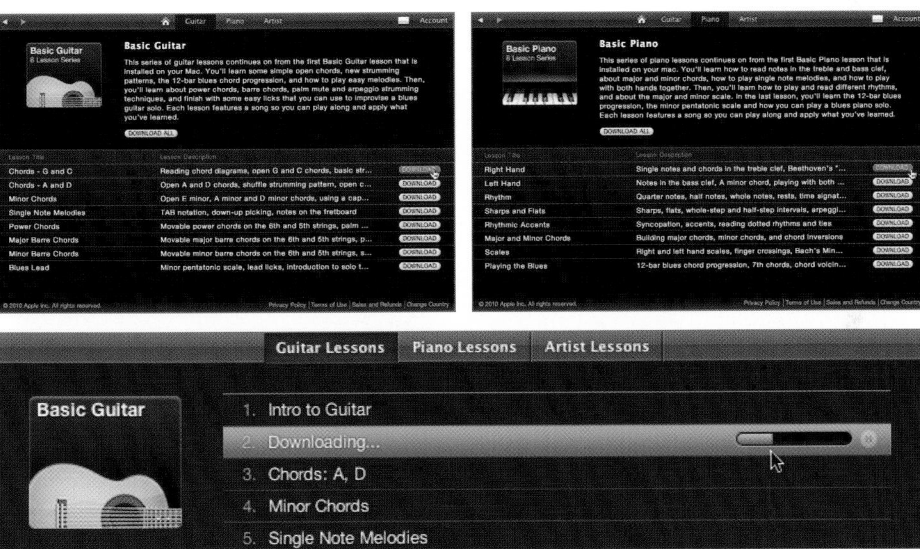

A blue bar appears in the Learn to Play lessons list to show the download progress.

Now one or more new lessons have been downloaded to your Mac, and corresponding icons for each lesson appear in the Learn to Play lessons list in your project window.

Taking an Artist Lesson

If your piano and guitar skills have grown beyond the basic lessons, you're ready to learn from the pros. Artist Lessons use the same interface as the basic Learn to Play lessons with the advantage that your instructor is the actual recording artist who made the music a hit. Want to learn "Roxanne" from Sting, "Spirit of Radio" from Rush, "Thinking About You" from Norah Jones, or "Proud Mary" from John Fogerty? You can do it in GarageBand. The Artist Lessons also include personal stories told by the artists about their songs.

These more advanced lessons are available for purchase from the Lesson Store.

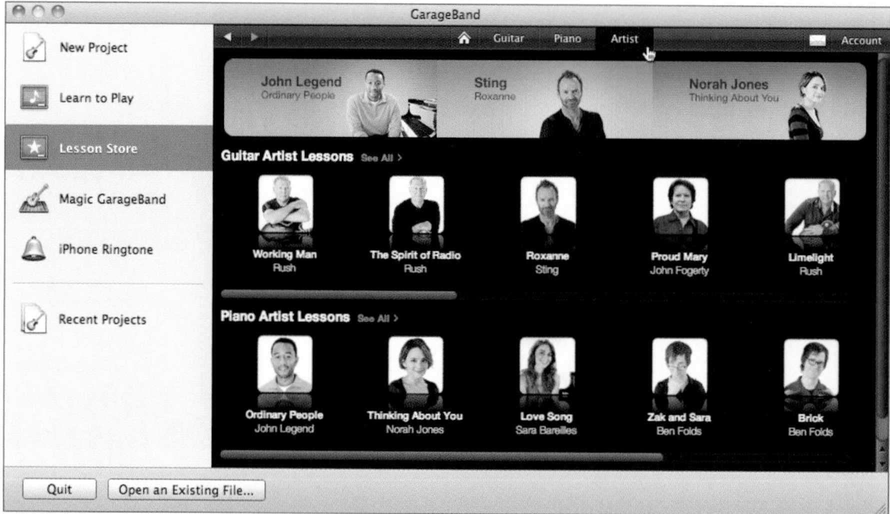

To purchase an Artist Lesson, click the Lesson Store button in the New Project dialog, then click the Artist Lessons button to see the list. You can view the choices and click Add to Cart for the lessons you want to buy; then follow the instructions to purchase and download the lesson.

Lesson Review

1. Which instruments have Learn to Play lessons included with GarageBand?
2. How do you download additional lessons?
3. Do you have to have an instrument connected to the computer to take a Learn to Play lesson?
4. What two chapters come with every Learn to Play lesson?

Answers

1. GarageBand includes Learn to Play lessons for piano and guitar.
2. In the GarageBand project window, choose Lesson Store, then choose the lessons that you want to download.
3. You can take a Learn to Play lesson with or without an instrument; however, having a guitar or keyboard connected to your Mac allows you to tune a guitar and play along with the instructor during the lesson.
4. Every Learn to Play lesson comes with the Learn and Play chapters.

16

Lesson Files ATS iLife11 Book Files > Lesson 16 > Magic Rock Song

Time This lesson takes approximately 40 minutes to complete.

Goals

Choose a Magic GarageBand Jam genre

Audition and select instrument parts

Work with the Mixer during an audition

Select and customize your instrument part

Record a keyboard part using musical typing

Open and save a finished song

Lesson **16**

Jamming and Creating Music with GarageBand

One of the greatest pleasures of being a musician is performing with a band on stage in front of a huge crowd of screaming fans. That might not be a reality for everyone, but playing along with virtual musicians in GarageBand is a great way to practice, create music quickly, play and record original riffs, or just jam along and enjoy the process (screaming fans optional). Magic GarageBand Jam puts you at center stage as the leader of a virtual band.

Whether you're a professional musician, or have just finished your Learn to Play lessons, Magic GarageBand Jam offers a flexible performance experience to take your musical skills to the next level.

The following series of exercises will lead you through a hands-on tour of Magic GarageBand Jam. Along the way you'll choose a genre, audition musicians, select your own instrument, record a simple part, and finally open and save the finished song in GarageBand.

Selecting a Musical Genre

Magic GarageBand Jam offers nine musical genres to choose from including Blues, Rock, Jazz, Country, Reggae, Funk, Latin, Roots Rock, and Slow Blues. You can preview these genres in the GarageBand project window.

1 Open GarageBand. If a GarageBand project is already open, choose File > New. Only one project can be open at a time so you may be prompted to save and close the current project—if there is one—before the GarageBand project window opens.

2 In the GarageBand project window, select Magic GarageBand.

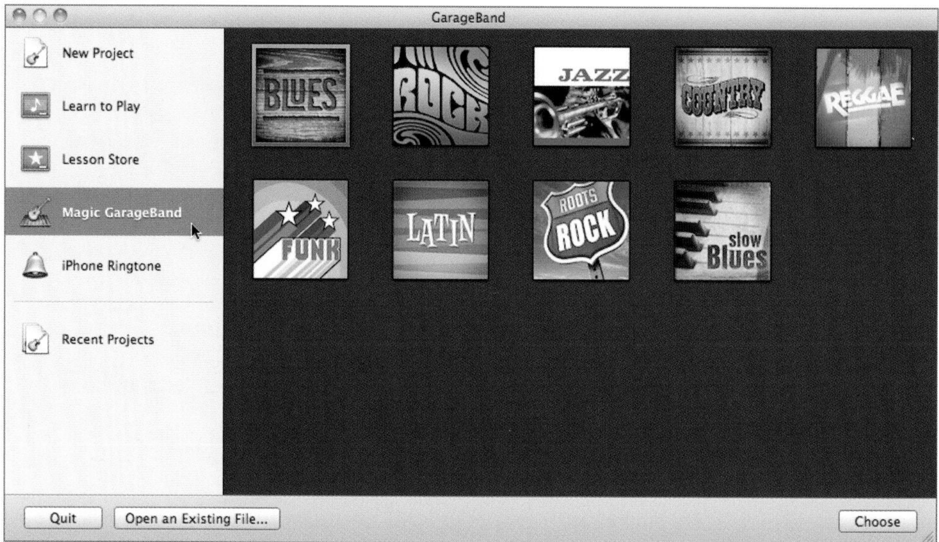

An icon presenting each of the nine genres appears in the project list. To preview a genre, hover your pointer over a genre icon until the preview overlay appears. Then click the small Play Preview button.

3 Hover your pointer over the Blues icon and click the Play Preview button to hear the blues song. Click the button again to stop the preview.

TIP You can use your Mac volume level controls to adjust the preview volume levels.

4 Preview several of the genres to hear the variety of music that you can jam along with in Magic GarageBand Jam. For this lesson, let's choose the Rock genre.

5 Double-click the Rock genre icon to open that project.

After a moment The Magic GarageBand stage appears along with the default instruments used in the Rock genre song.

Navigating and Controlling Playback

Now that you've opened a Magic GarageBand project, you should learn how to navigate around a song and control its playback.

If you already completed the Learn to Play exercises earlier in this section, you'll see some familiar features in the Control bar. If you skipped ahead to this lesson, no problem; you'll get acquainted with the controls soon.

1 Press the Spacebar, or click the Play button in the Control bar to play the song.

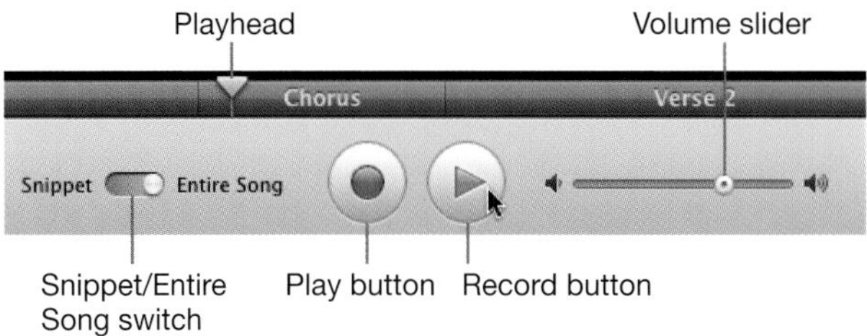

The music plays in its default arrangement. You can drag the Volume slider if you temporarily want to increase the song's volume.

2 Press the Spacebar to stop playback.

3 Press Return to return the playhead to the beginning of the song.

Each Magic GarageBand song includes an Intro, two Verses, a Chorus, and an Ending. You can quickly navigate to the beginning of one of these sections by clicking the corresponding part above the Control bar.

4 Click Verse 1 to select that section of the song. The selected section turns yellow, and the playhead jumps to the beginning of that section.

5 Press the Spacebar or click the Play button to restart playback.

Notice that this time the playback includes only the selected snippet of the song. This feature is handy when you want to practice or play along with just one part of the song.

6 Click the Snippet/Entire Song switch to set it back to Entire Song and pause playback.

The yellow highlighted section of the song disappears, and you can now work with the entire song.

You can also play the project full screen by clicking the View button in the lower-right corner of the stage.

You can click the View button again at any time to return to the window view.

NOTE ▸ If you're using the full-screen view, you can click the close button (X) in the upper-left corner of the screen to close Magic GarageBand at any time.

Auditioning Virtual Musicians and Instrumental Parts

Now that you've opened the song and know how to control playback, you can audition the instrument parts.

Each Magic GarageBand song includes Guitar, Bass, Drums, Keyboard and Melody instruments, and a place for you (My Instrument) at the center of the stage. As the leader of the virtual band, you control which musicians get to play, and with which instruments and playing style.

The good news is that your job is much easier than auditioning musicians in the real world. In Magic GarageBand the virtual musicians are very professional, which means you don't have to deal with egos, tardiness, attitude, or poor playing. Instead, you can focus on choosing the right parts for your version of the song from more than 3,000 possible combinations of sounds for each genre.

1 Roll the pointer over each instrument on the stage. A spotlight illuminates whichever instrument you roll over, and the name of the instrument or part appears.

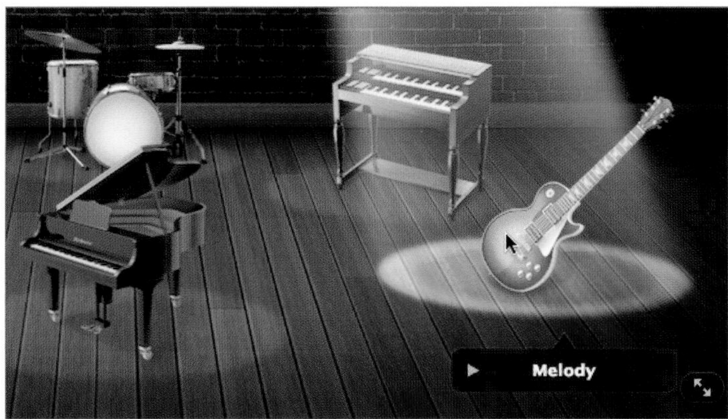

2 Click the Guitar to select that instrumental part.

The instrument list below the stage changes to show the other instrument choices for the song's guitar part. In this case, you have seven guitar styles from which to choose: Jangle, Strumming, Honky Tonk, Punk, Windmills, Big Stack, and Glam.

The No Instrument choice to the far right of the instrument list is also available if you want to exclude that instrument from your arrangement.

If you aren't familiar with these guitar styles, don't worry. You can change them while the song is playing to hear how they modify the feel and sound of the song and then choose your favorite.

TIP It's a good idea to audition instruments against the same section (snippet) of the song, such as the Verse or Chorus, so that you hear all of the choices in the same context.

3 Play the song, and click Verse 1 to loop playback of that section (snippet) of the song.

4 Click each of the guitar styles in the list to audition them with the first verse of the song.

When you change instrument styles, the new instrument (virtual musician) needs to wait until the next measure to jump in—so be sure to give each guitar a chance to play before moving to the next one.

You should notice a clear difference in the sound of the guitars.

NOTE ▶ GarageBand comes with an awesome set of guitar amps and stompbox effects to create these sounds—and more—with your own guitar recordings. You'll learn more about using these guitar effects in the next lesson.

5 Choose your favorite guitar style.

If you're having trouble deciding, try the Big Stack for a nice, over-the-top, heavy electric guitar with plenty of effects. I like this one because it reminds me of the "check out my big amp and effects" sound of the guitars in every band I played keyboards for in high school and college (way back in the '80s, long before GarageBand, though we did practice and record music in the garage).

6 Stop playback.

Mixing Instruments in Magic GarageBand

Auditioning instruments while listening to the other parts works well to get a feel for the way a part fits into the overall sound. However, sometimes you may want to solo or mute a particular instrument before you make your final decision.

Each instrumental part includes a mixer that allows you to control the volume of that instrument in the mix, as well as solo and mute controls.

In this exercise, you'll use the mixer to audition the bass part.

1 Click the Bass to select it.

2 Click the disclosure triangle to the left of the Bass overlay to open the Mixer.

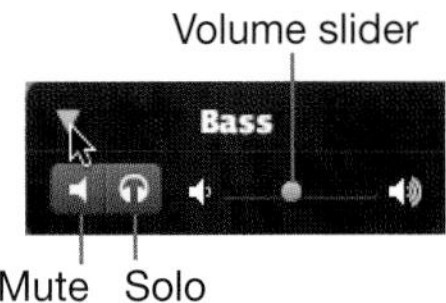

3 Start playback. Feel free to choose a different part of the song for the bass audition.

4 Click the Solo button to isolate the sound of the bass.

You should hear only the sound of the bass instrument. This is a great way to hear the part clearly.

TIP If you want to learn a specific instrumental part so that you can jam with the Magic GarageBand songs, start by soloing that part. When you can play along with the virtual musician, you'll be ready to unsolo the part and join in with the rest of the band.

5 Choose a different bass instrument style from the instrument list and listen to it.

6 Click the Solo button again to unsolo the new part.

7 Toggle the Solo button on and off as needed while you audition the remaining bass instrument styles. Select different parts of the song to hear the bass in the Intro, Chorus, Verses, and Ending. Stop playback when you're happy with your bass selection.

If you can't decide on a bass part, try the Driving bass. It has a nice presence without overshadowing the Guitar. The good news is that there is no right or wrong choice. All of the parts sound great; that is part of the "magic" of Magic GarageBand Jam.

TIP A fast way to find a new combination of instrument parts is to click an empty part of the stage, then click the Shuffle Instruments button. Voila! Now the song has a fresh sound with a new set of instruments. You can also click Start Over to reset the song to the original instruments.

Project Practice

Take a few minutes to practice what you've learned so far, and select new instruments for the Drums, Keyboard, and Melody parts. For a unique sound, try the Sitar for the melody instrument. Now there is something you don't see or hear on stage every day. If you like the way the song sounds as is, you can leave the default instruments and move on to the next section.

> **NOTE ▶** Magic GarageBand Jam automatically saves your changes to the song as you go. If you want to close the project and come back to it later, double-click the Rock genre icon in the Magic GarageBand Jam genre list and it will open exactly the way you left it.

Setting Up Your Instrument

Now that you've selected your musicians and instruments, you should choose the instrument that you'll play. After you've set up your own instrument, you can play along and even record your part.

1 At the center of the stage, click the Grand Piano labeled My Instrument. The default instrument for the Rock genre is a Grand Piano.

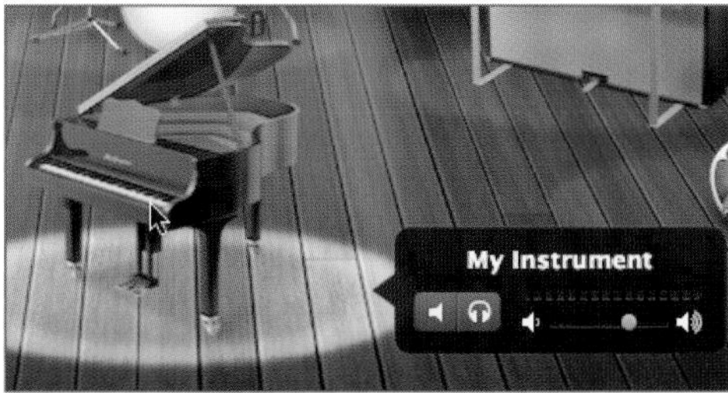

2 Click the My Instrument menu to see the instruments that you can connect to the computer.

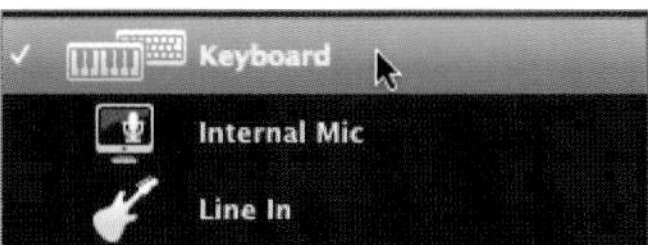

Your choices are:

▶ **Keyboard** is for a MIDI instrument such as a piano or organ. If you don't have an external MIDI instrument, you can also play along using your computer's keyboard.

▶ **Internal Mic** allows you to record your voice or another instrument using the computer's built-in mic.

▶ **Line In** is for an instrument such as a guitar or bass that is connected through the audio-in port or another approved audio interface. This could also include a microphone that you use to record vocals or other acoustic instruments.

For this exercise let's choose the Keyboard setting and play a part using the computer keyboard.

3 If you have a MIDI keyboard connected to the computer, disconnect it now. When the dialog warns you that your device has been disconnected, click Use Built-In Audio.

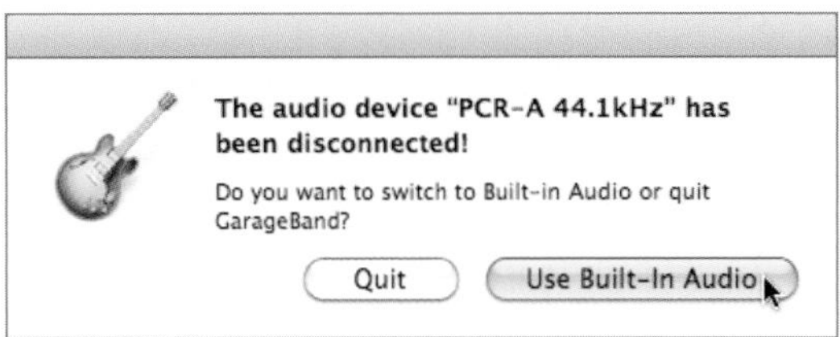

4 From the My Instrument pop-up menu, choose Keyboard, if it isn't already chosen.

Magic GarageBand Jam includes three default keyboard style choices: Grand Piano, Electric Piano, and Arena Run.

5 Choose the Electric Piano instrument. To play this instrument using your computer keyboard, you need to turn on Musical Typing.

6 Click the Tuner button to turn on Musical Typing.

The Musical Typing keyboard appears below the stage. You can click the keys on the Musical Typing keyboard to play them, or type the corresponding keys on your computer keyboard. Notice that the Tab key works as a sustain pedal, and the Z and X keys will shift the notes up or down an octave.

7 Start playback and play a few notes on your computer keyboard to hear how they sound. Don't worry if they aren't the right notes. This is just to illustrate how it works. When you're finished, stop playback.

Adding a Custom Instrument

Unlike the instrument choices specified for other parts of the song, an advantage of the My Instrument part is that you can choose from any sound available in GarageBand. In this exercise, you'll customize the choice and add a new sound that you can play on your computer keyboard, or with an external MIDI keyboard.

1 Click the Tuner button to open the My Instrument keyboard instrument list.

2 Click Customize to show all of the available Pianos and Keyboards in the Instrument menu.

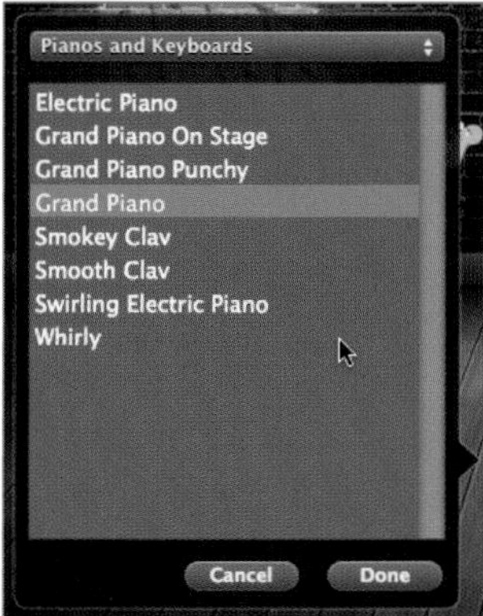

For this exercise, let's choose an interesting Synth Pad to add some electronic '80s texture to this rock song.

3 Click the Pianos and Keyboards pop-up menu to see a full list of Software Instrument categories.

4 From the Instrument menu, choose Synth Pads.

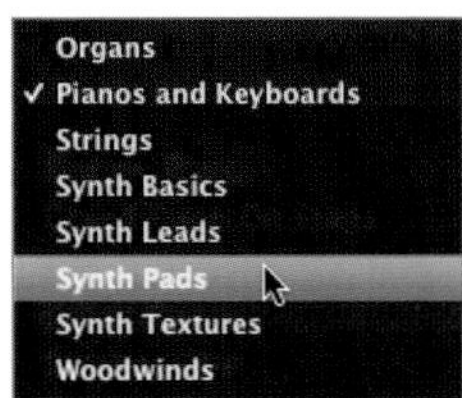

5 From the Synth Pads instrument list, choose Falling Star. Then click Done to close the Instrument menu.

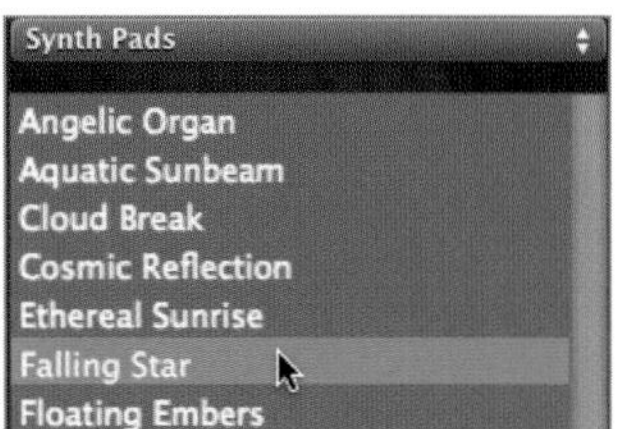

The Customize button is replaced in this list by the Falling Star instrument.

NOTE ▸ You can click the information button (i) in the upper-right corner of the Falling Star icon to open the Instrument menu and choose a different customized instrument.

6 Click the Tuner button to turn on Musical Typing and play a few notes along with the song. When you're finished, stop playback.

The Falling Star sound is easy to work with—even if you aren't a musician. Sure, it isn't a very good choice for showing off your finger work or composing a keyboard solo, but it's perfect for adding a little excitement to the Intro and Ending of the song.

TIP Clicking the Tuner button opens a digital guitar tuner that you can use whenever you have a guitar connected to the computer and the Line In setting selected in the My Instrument window. If you have a MIDI keyboard connected to the keyboard, the Musical Typing area will appear blank.

Recording a Part

You are now two clicks way from recording a part. First you'll need to change the playback to Entire Song, then click the Record button and let the magic begin.

When you record a part in Magic GarageBand it's important to set the playhead position first. The recording will always start at the current playhead position.

Also, if a section of the song is selected, you can record multiple takes of that snippet over and over as the section loops, then choose the take that you like best. You'll work more with multiple-take recordings in the next lesson. For this exercise, a single take should do the trick.

1 Change the playback setting to Entire Song, if necessary.

2 Press Return to move the playhead to the beginning of the song.

3 Play the song once from the beginning and practice playing the Falling Star part wherever you think it will sound good.

   If you aren't sure when to play, remember that for a sound like this, less is more. Try playing once during the intro after the other instruments have started. Play a note again at the end of the first verse or beginning of the chorus, then another at the ending as the other instruments are playing their final notes.

   Too much of this Falling Star sound will make it more of an annoyance than a musical surprise. When in doubt, keep the audience guessing, or wanting more.

4 Click the Record button to start recording. A red recording region appears above the Control bar.

TIP When you play single notes, the name of the note and octave appears next to the Musical Typing interface. When you play multiple notes, the name of the chord appears instead.

5 Click the Play button to stop recording. A green Software Instrument region appears above the Control bar. The horizontal lines within the region represent the MIDI note events.

If you're really unhappy with your recording and want to do it again, choose File > Undo, and repeat steps 4 and 5.

NOTE ▶ Guitar, Vocals, or other Real Instrument recordings appear as purple regions. You'll learn more about the different types of GarageBand regions in the next lesson.

Congratulations! You've recorded an original keyboard part. Next, let's open the song in GarageBand to hear the finished rock song.

Opening and Saving the Song in GarageBand

Now that your Magic GarageBand song is finished, you can open it in GarageBand to see the finished project, edit the arrangement, add additional tracks, save the project, or share it with iTunes.

In this exercise, you'll open the song in GarageBand and save the finished project.

1 In the lower-right corner of the window, click the "Open in GarageBand" button.

The song opens in the GarageBand window.

NOTE ▶ The song in GarageBand is assigned the name "02. Rock." This naming convention is based on the way Magic GarageBand saves your work behind the scenes. 02 and Rock represent the genre. The next Rock Magic GarageBand Jam session you open and change will be named "02. Rock 2" to indicate that this is the second version and so on. Magic GarageBand projects are saved to User > Library > Application Support > GarageBand > Working Copies.

You'll see a timeline with a separate track for each instrument part, and the track names corresponding to the Magic GarageBand instruments that you selected earlier.

The Arrangement track at the top of the window shows each of the sections of the song (Intro, Verse 1, Chorus, Verse 2, and Ending), and can be edited to rearrange or extend the song length.

The short blue regions represent the pre-recorded Magic GarageBand parts. The long green region represents the Software Instrument part that you recorded.

In the next lesson you'll learn how to record and arrange music in GarageBand. For now, let's save this project as is. Later you can re-open this project and edit, arrange, and mix this song on your own.

For this exercise, you'll perform a basic save. In the later lessons, you'll learn about other GarageBand save features.

2 Choose File > Save As to open the Save As dialog.

3 In the Name field, type *Magic Rock Song*.

NOTE ▶ To expand the Save As dialog, click the downward-pointing arrow at the right side of the Save As field.

4 Click the Desktop icon in the Sidebar (left side) of the Save As window to select the desktop as the location to save your project.

5 In the lower-left corner of the window, click the New Folder button. A New Folder dialog opens.

6 In the "Name of new folder" field, type *My GarageBand Projects*. Click Create.

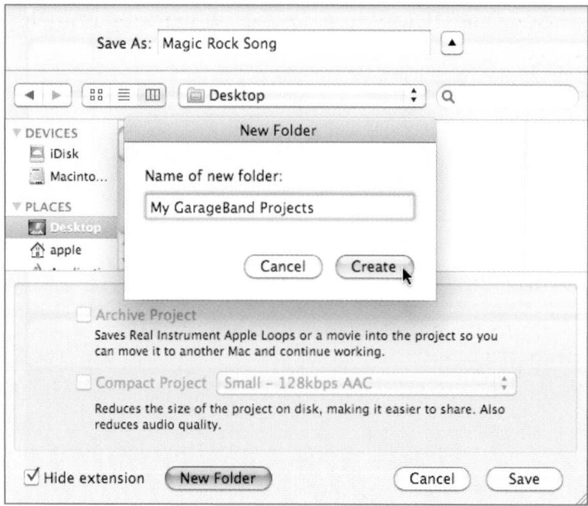

The new folder appears on your desktop.

7 In the Save As window, click Save.

8 Press Command-W, or choose File > Close Project.

An alert dialog appears asking if you'd like to save your project with an iLife preview.

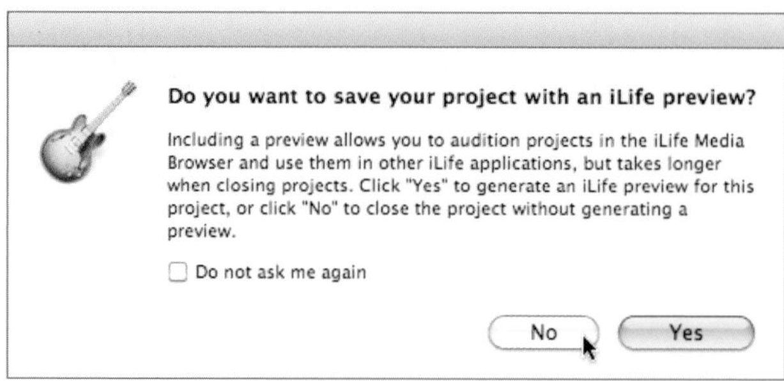

9 Click No to save and close the project without generating an iLife preview.

Your project is successfully saved to the folder you created on your desktop and then closed.

NOTE ▶ iLife preview is a saving method that is great for finished projects, but takes longer to save and isn't necessary until you're ready to share the project with other iLife applications. You also need to be careful about saving recording projects with an iLife preview because it will delete unused recordings that you may have wanted to archive. You'll save files with an iLife preview in Lesson 19.

That's it! You've created and saved a rock song. And you have a good working knowledge of the Magic GarageBand Jam interface.

Lesson Review

1. How do you select an instrument in Magic GarageBand Jam?
2. Can you change or add a Magic GarageBand instrument?
3. How do you isolate the sound of an instrument in Magic GarageBand?
4. Can Magic GarageBand automatically change all of the instruments?

Answers

1. You can select an instrument in Magic GarageBand Jam by clicking the instrument.
2. You can change any Magic GarageBand instrument by selecting the instrument and choosing another instrument in the menu. To add an instrument in the My Instrument category, click the Customize button then choose an instrument from the list.
3. To isolate the sound of an instrument in Magic GarageBand, you can turn on the Solo button in the instrument's mixer.
4. Magic GarageBand can automatically change all of the instruments to a different combination. Click an empty space on the stage, then click the Shuffle Instruments button when it appears.

17

Lesson Files

ATS iLife11 Book Files > Lesson 17 > Magic Rock Song 01, Magic Rock Song 02, Magic Rock Song 03, Magic Rock Song 04, Magic Rock Song 05

Time

This lesson takes approximately 60 minutes to complete.

Goals

Open a GarageBand project

Create and set up an electric guitar track

Work with single-take and multiple-take recordings

Adjust guitar amps and stompbox effects

Experiment with acoustic guitar effects

Duplicate a track and double a guitar part

Record a Software Instrument part using the onscreen keyboard

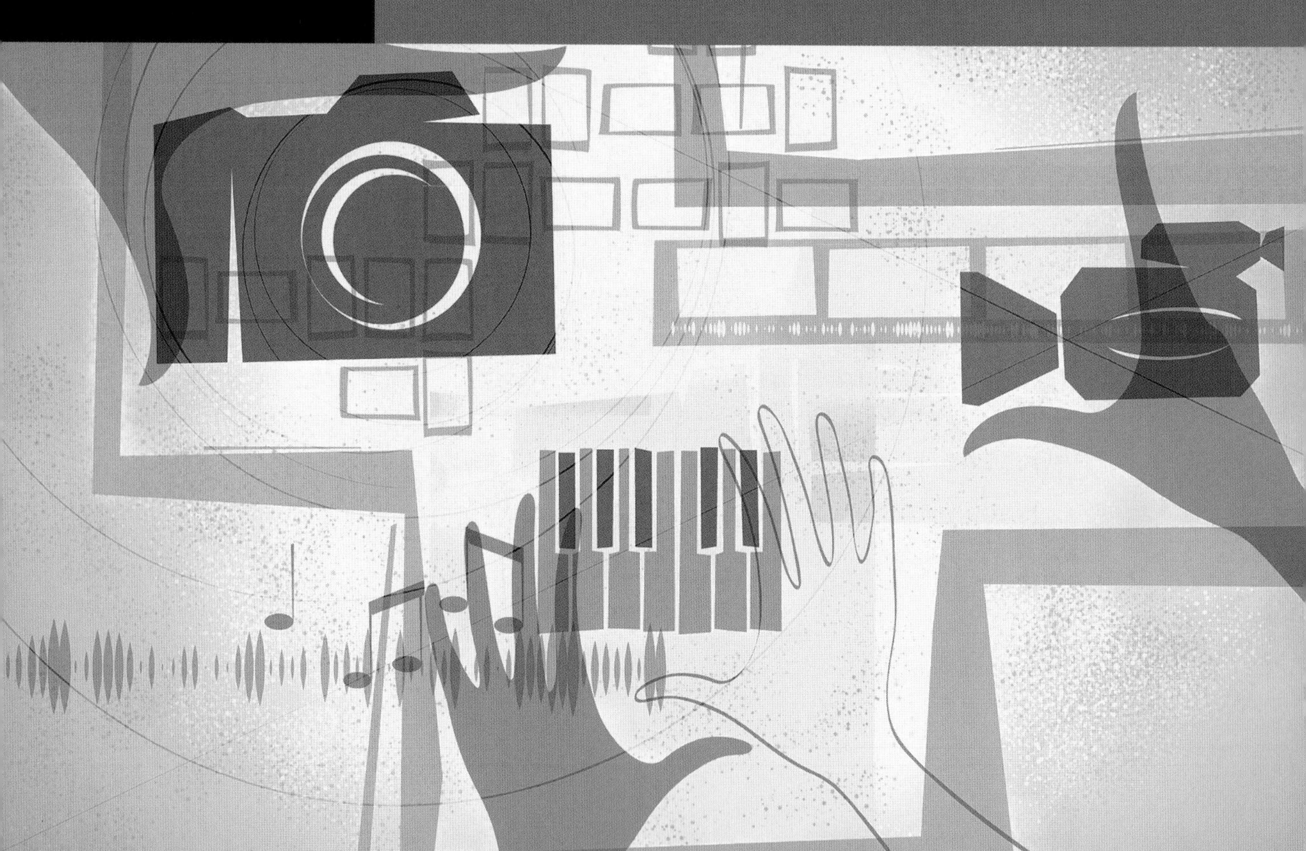

Lesson **17**

Recording Music in GarageBand

GarageBand '11 has evolved into a full-function musician's workshop powerful enough to record and mix a professional-sounding music demo, podcast, or video score, yet simple enough that anyone can use it right out of the box. In fact, you don't have to be a computer science major or audio engineer to record music. You don't even have to be a musician. If you can click a mouse, you can turn your Mac into a basic recording studio—it's really that easy.

This lesson will take you to a recording session where you'll add Real Instrument guitar tracks, and a Software Instrument percussion track to an existing song. To enhance the song, you'll also apply amp effects and stompboxes, adjust input settings, and change instrument sounds.

Recording Music Tracks in GarageBand

This lesson is designed to walk you step-by-step through a GarageBand recording session. In the next several exercises, you'll follow along with a pre-recorded session; however, you'll also be invited to play along or record your own tracks. If you don't have an instrument connected to the computer, you needn't worry. You will still be able to do everything except tune an instrument and record optional guitar parts.

Opening a GarageBand Project

For this recording lesson, you will be working with a version of the Magic GarageBand Rock song that you explored in Lesson 16. Before you can begin, you'll need to open the **Magic Rock Song 01** project and save it to your projects folder.

1 Open GarageBand, if necessary. Close the welcome screen if it is showing. The New Project dialog appears.

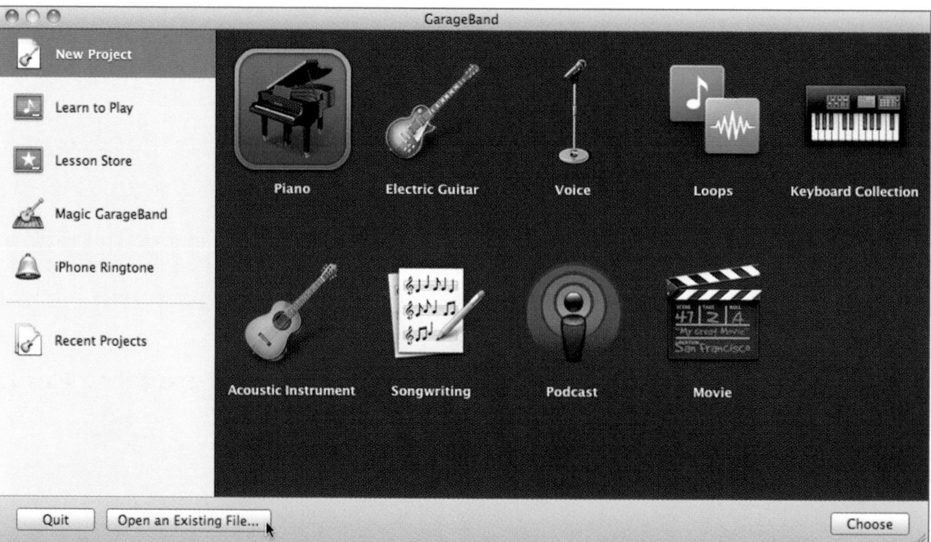

2 Choose File > Open, or click Open an Existing File.

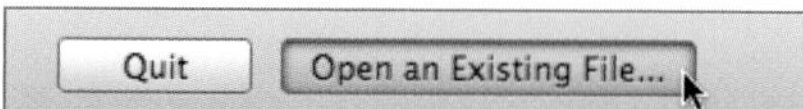

3 In the Open dialog, choose Lesson 17 > **Magic Rock Song 01**, then click Open.

4 Choose File > Save As, and save the project to your desktop in the My GarageBand Projects folder, and click Save.

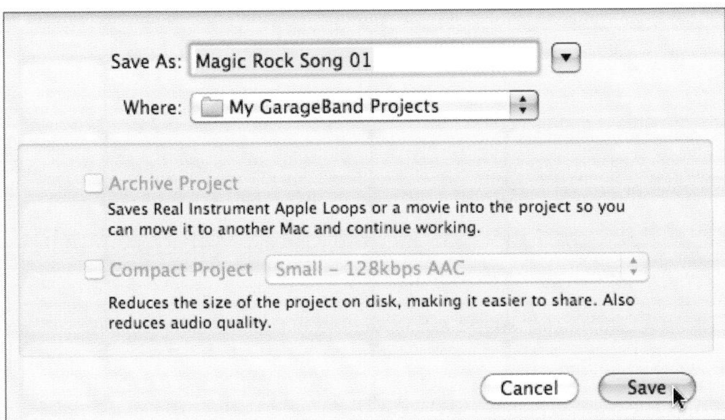
Save As: Magic Rock Song 01
Where: My GarageBand Projects
Archive Project
Saves Real Instrument Apple Loops or a movie into the project so you can move it to another Mac and continue working.
Compact Project
Small – 128kbps AAC
Reduces the size of the project on disk, making it easier to share. Also reduces audio quality.
Cancel
Save

NOTE ▶ If you did not create a My GarageBand Projects folder in the previous lesson, you can make one at this time. In the Save As dialog, select the desktop for the location, then click New Folder and name it *My GarageBand Projects.*

You saved a copy of the project that you can freely modify throughout the lesson, while retaining the original version in the Lessons folder.

Exploring the GarageBand Window

Among the many advantages of GarageBand is the simplicity of its interface. As with all the iLife applications, GarageBand uses one window as the base of operations. This window is your recording studio.

The elements of the GarageBand window are:

- **Track headers**—Show the instrument icon and name to the left of each instrument track. The track headers also include a Mute button to silence a track, a Solo button to silence all other tracks, a Record Enable button that allows you to record to a specific track, and a Lock button to protect the track and its contents from unintended changes.
- **Track Mixer**—Includes a Volume slider for adjusting the track volume and a Pan wheel to adjust the position of the track in the left-to-right stereo field.

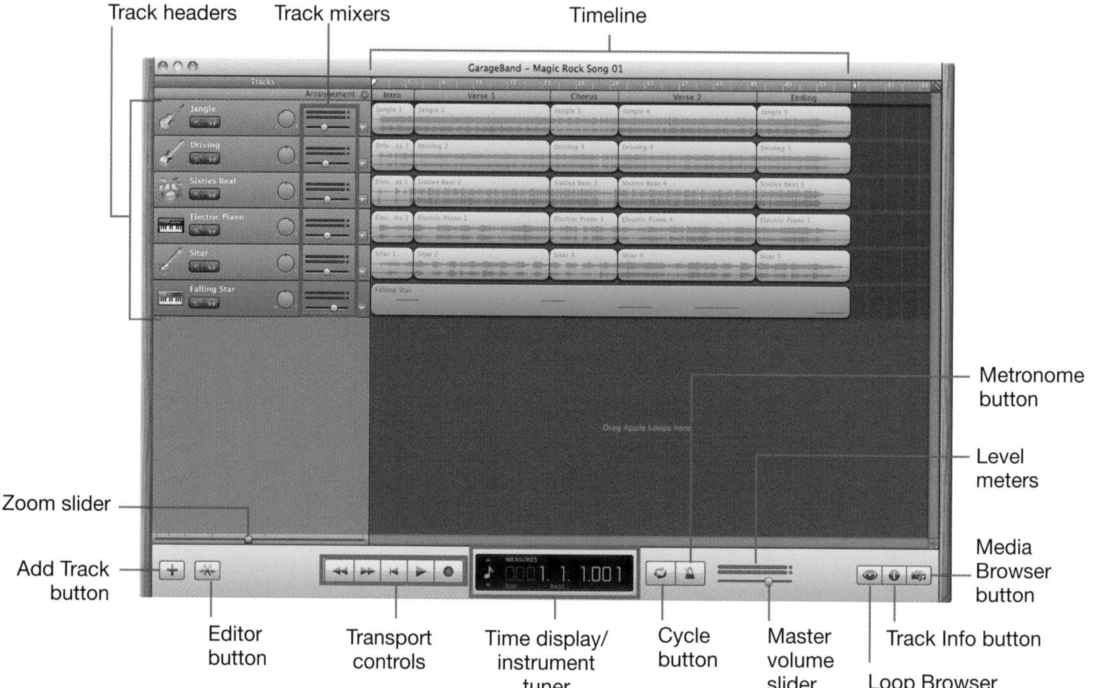

- **Timeline**—Acts as your music recording and arranging workspace. The Timeline consists of a horizontal track for each instrument. The Timeline graphically represents linear time from left to right using a Beat Ruler at the top of the window. The far-left edge of the Timeline represents the beginning of a song.
- **Zoom slider**—Zooms in to or out of the Timeline.
- **Add Track button**—Adds a new track in the Timeline.
- **Loop Browser button**—Opens the Loop Browser.
- **Editor button**—Opens the editor.
- **Transport controls**—Provide the standard recording and playback buttons to navigate in the Timeline—including Record, Go To Beginning, Rewind, Start/Stop Playback, and Fast Forward.
- **Cycle button** – Turns the cycle region on and off for looping playback.
- **Metronome button** – Turns the click track on and off.
- **LCD display**—Shows the song's properties, current playhead position in musical time (measures, beats, ticks), absolute time (hours, minutes, seconds, fractions), or the instrument tuner.

- **Master Volume slider**—Adjusts the output volume level of the project.
- **Level meters**—Indicate the output volume level of a project and include red warning lights if levels are too loud and distorting, or *clipping*.
- **Track Info button**—Opens the Track Info pane.
- **Media Browser button**—Opens the Media Browser.

Identifying Regions and Tracks

Regions and tracks come in a variety of sizes and colors (according to type):

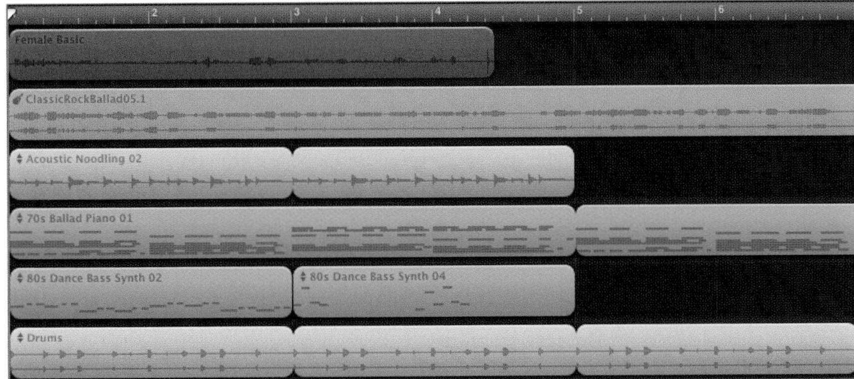

- **Real Instruments**—Appear as purple, blue, and orange regions. You can record Real Instrument parts into GarageBand using a microphone, or a guitar or keyboard that's plugged into the microphone jack on your Mac. You can also record Real Instrument parts through other input devices that you connect to your computer. Imported audio files appear as orange regions.
- **Software Instruments**—Appear as green regions and are recorded using a USB music keyboard, a MIDI synthesizer–type keyboard, the GarageBand onscreen keyboard, or using Musical Typing with the GarageBand software and your computer's keyboard as the MIDI instrument.

This song includes six tracks representing each of the instrument parts selected in the Magic GarageBand song in the previous lesson. Each track, in turn, contains individual musical parts, or regions, as performed by a particular instrument. An instrument track may contain only one region, or it may contain many smaller regions—individual takes and retakes, often called *overdubs*—which, when arranged in a track, are the basic building blocks of an entire instrument's part for a song

A track can include a Real Instrument or a Software Instrument and can be easily identified by the color of the track header when selected, or the regions within the track.

1 Click the Jangle track header, if it is not already selected, to see the color (type of instrument) assigned to that track. The blue track header indicates a Real Instrument track.

2 Double-click the Jangle track header, or press Command-I to show the Track Info pane on the right side of the window. The Track Info pane includes details about the selected track instrument and effects.

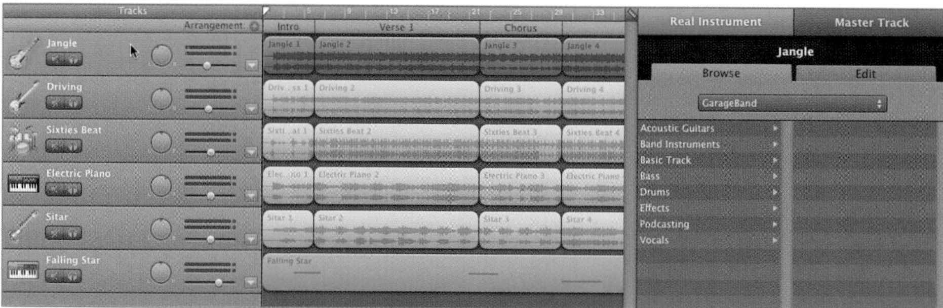

3 In the upper-left corner of the GarageBand window, click the green Zoom (+) so the application fills the entire Mac screen.

With the larger GarageBand window, you'll not only have more room to work, you'll also see a picture detail for each instrument at the top of the Track Info pane.

4 Click the Falling Star track header to see an example of a green Software Instrument track.

Notice that the Track Info pane shows a picture of the instrument and the type of instrument (Software Instrument), and lists the instrument category and specific instrument.

You'll work more with Software Instruments at the end of this lesson. For now, let's move on with the recording session.

Setting Up an Electric Guitar Track

For the guitar tracks in this recording session, you'll be using what GarageBand calls Real Instruments. With GarageBand, you can record a real instrument—such as a guitar, bass, or keyboard—directly into the Timeline. You can also use a microphone to record acoustic instruments that don't have an output jack, such as a trumpet, violin, grand piano, drum kit, acoustic guitar, or even vocals.

To record a Real Instrument into the Timeline, you have to physically perform or play the part in real time. Let's set up an electric guitar track to record a strumming rhythm guitar part. The current project doesn't include an electric guitar track, so let's create one.

1 Choose Track > New Track, or click the New Track (+) button in the lower-left corner of the GarageBand project window.

The New Track dialog appears with three track choices: Software Instrument, Real Instrument, and Electric Guitar. The Electric Guitar option is specifically designed for using built-in GarageBand amps and Stompbox effects.

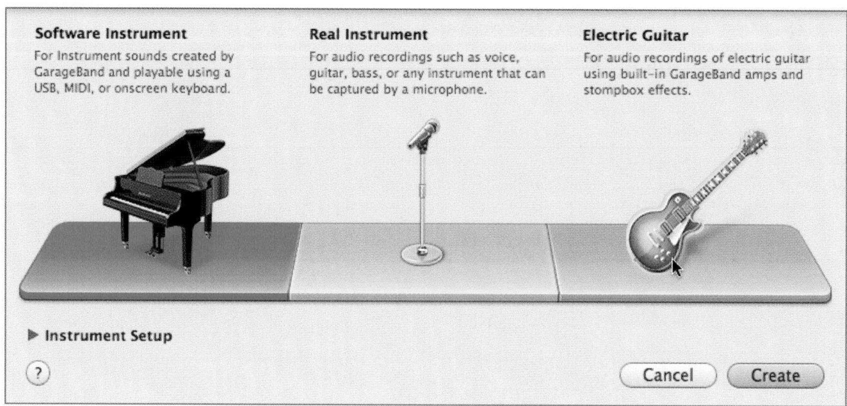

NOTE ▶ The selected instrument glows yellow when highlighted in the New Track dialog. You can also click the Instrument Setup disclosure triangle in the lower-left corner of the dialog to change input settings for connecting your instrument to the computer.

2 In the New Track dialog, click Electric Guitar, and then click Create. A new Real Instrument electric guitar track named Clean Combo appears in the Timeline.

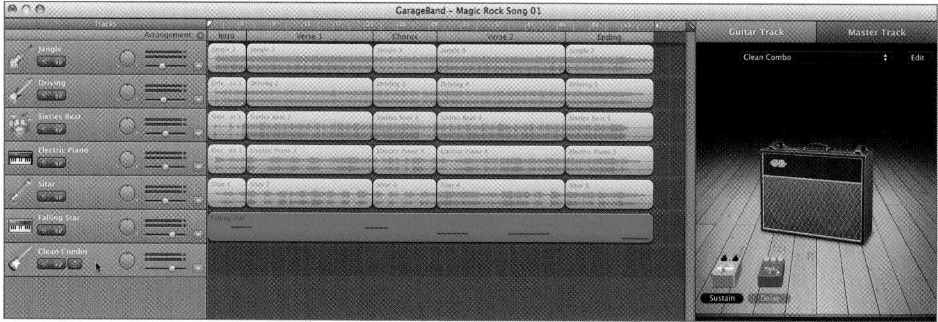

Notice that a tuner appears in the LCD display at the bottom of the window. The instrument tuner can tune any real instrument, even vocals, and is designed to work with one note at a time. It will not work with chords or combined notes.

In tune (blue)

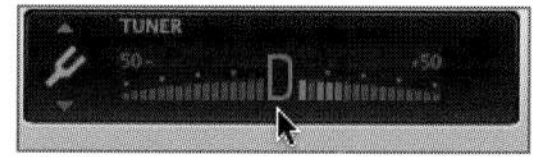

Out of tune (red)

TIP It's a good idea to tune your guitar before recording any tracks. You can access the LCD tuner by selecting a guitar track header, then changing the LCD display to the tuner. You can also press Command-F to show the tuner in the LCD display. The tuner is a fabulous way to see which notes were played in a Real Instrument region so that you can follow along or improvise using the same notes.

3 On the right side of the window, click the amplifier to see the Amplifier controls.

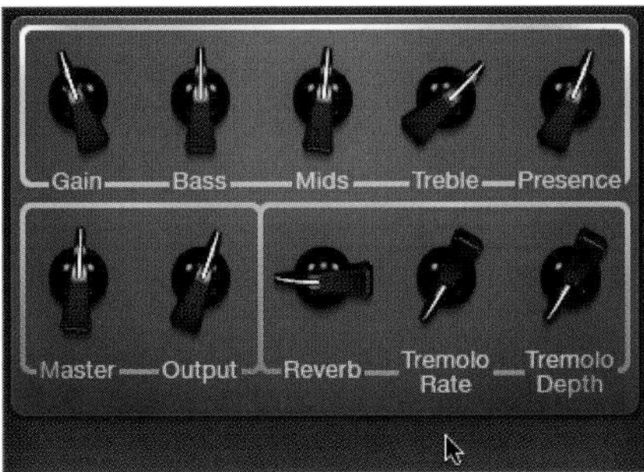

These software controls work exactly like real amplifier controls, so if you play electric guitar you should feel right at home.

You can add additional effects before or after recording. In this case, you'll keep the recording "clean," without effects—and add effects later.

Monitoring Input

Monitoring is a musical term for being able to hear yourself play. Just as you would in a recording studio, you'll probably want to monitor your performance when you record a Real Instrument track in GarageBand. If the Monitor setting is turned off, you won't hear the sound of your instrument going to the computer.

Once any instrument part is recorded into the Timeline, you'll hear it on playback.

1 Select the Clean Combo track, if necessary, and click the Monitor button to turn on monitoring.

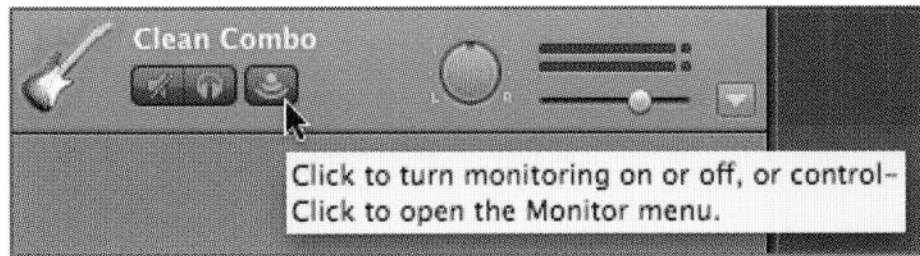

NOTE ▶ If you are working with a Mac with a built-in microphone configured as the current audio input device, you may hear static or yourself when the monitor button is turned on, which could cause feedback. Feel free to turn off the monitor button if necessary.

If GarageBand detects feedback, you'll see an alert dialog with the option to change the current setting. This alert is part of the built-in feedback protection that is the default whenever you monitor recordings.

GarageBand has detected feedback
You have three choices:
Monitor Off
Mutes your speakers while you record to prevent feedback.
Monitor On
Lets you hear your performance while you record. Each time feedback occurs, GarageBand will mute the performance and alert you by showing you this dialog. To avoid feedback, try reducing the playback volume, avoid pointing your microphone towards your speakers, or use headphones to monitor your performance.
No Feedback Protection
Lets you hear your performance while you record. Each time feedback occurs, it will be audible.
Monitor Off
Monitor On
No Feedback Protection

2 Double-click the amplifier to turn it around and see the Input Source and Monitor pop-up menus.

3 From the Monitor pop-up menu, choose Off if you are not planning to record a guitar part at this time.

TIP ▶ You can Control-click (or right-click) the Monitor button in the track header to select a different monitor setting.

While you are looking at the monitor controls, take a moment to set your Input Source and Recording Level.

4 From the Input Source pop-up menu, choose Mono 1 if necessary. This should already be chosen as the default setting.

5 If you have an electric guitar connected to the computer, play a few notes and adjust the Recording Level slider as necessary.

NOTE ▶ If you don't hear your guitar, make sure the volume is turned up on your instrument, and that the input settings on your Mac Sound preferences are set for the correct input.

MORE INFO ▶ To learn more about connecting your guitar to your Mac, see "Connecting Instruments to the Mac" in Lesson15.

Planning Before Recording

You have a few obvious yet essential things to consider before recording. First, make sure that the instruments or microphones you plan to use are connected and working properly. Second, be sure you have enough hard disk space for your recordings. Audio recordings use a fraction of the storage space of video, but they can accumulate over time, especially if you record many takes. The last thing you'd want to do is stop your recording session because you ran out of drive space.

Stereo audio recorded at CD quality (44.1 kHz) uses around 10 MB of disk space per minute. So in a three-minute song, 10 stereo tracks would require around 300 MB.

Recording a Single Take

Now that you've completed all of the instrument connections, monitor settings, and input settings, you're finally ready to record.

In this exercise, you'll walk through a single-take recording. A single-take recording begins on a selected track at the playhead position and continues until you stop recording.

This is an excellent recording method when you're practicing or just want to record a musical riff, melody, or idea so you don't forget it. Before you start, it's a good idea to set a Count In so that the metronome will click for one full bar (four clicks in this case) before the actual recording begins. In essence the count in gives you a "one-two-three-go" so that you don't have to start playing the instant you click Record.

If you don't have a guitar to play and record, feel free to jump ahead to step 9 to open a version of the song with the guitar part already recorded.

1 Choose Control > Count In to turn on the Count In feature. GarageBand will now count in the first bar (four beats in this song) before recording begins.

2 Click the Metronome button, or press Command-U to turn on the metronome click track while you record. Feel free to turn this on and off at will throughout this lesson.

NOTE ▸ The metronome's click track is a standard recording tool to help you play in time with the music. If you find the click track distracting, you can turn it off at any time and use the drum track as a rhythmic guide instead. The Songwriting template in the New Project dialog includes a drum track to use as a guide while you record your other tracks.

3 Select the Clean Combo track to make it active, if it is not already selected.

4 Click the ruler above the Timeline to move the playhead to the part of the song you'd like to record, or press Return to move the playhead to the beginning of the song.

TIP ▸ The keyboard shortcut to start recording is the R key. Pressing this key is often easier than clicking the Record button, especially if you're holding a guitar or another instrument.

5 Press R, or click Record to record your musical riff. A red region appears in the track as it records.

6 When you're finished, press the Spacebar to stop recording. Play your recording from the beginning to hear how it sounds.

7 In the Clean Combo track header, click the Monitor button to turn it off.

8 If you recorded a guitar part, choose File > Save As. Select the Archive Project checkbox, then click Save.

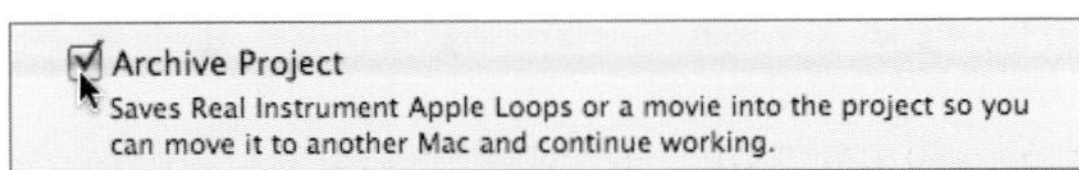

Archive Project
Saves Real Instrument Apple Loops or a movie into the project so you can move it to another Mac and continue working.

NOTE ▶ Archiving the project on save will include any Real Instrument regions—such as recordings with the project file. This preserves your recordings so that the project can be backed up to another storage device with those files included.

Now let's open a project that has the guitar single-take part already recorded in the Timeline.

9 Choose File > Open, and open ATS iLife11 Book Files > Lesson 17 > **Magic Rock Song 02**.

The project opens with a "Clean Single Take" guitar region on the lowest track of the Timeline. Notice that the name of the recorded region is the same as the track header.

10 Play Verse 1 from the beginning to listen to the Clean Single Take track in the song.

NOTE ▶ A new recording will always be assigned the name of the track in which it is recorded. You can change the name later in the Track Editor. In this case, I changed the name of the track to Clean Single Take before recording so that it would more obviously be seen as an example for this exercise. It's actually a supporting rhythm guitar part, and will be named accordingly later.

The guitar parts for this lesson were played by Brian O'Maille. This performance turned out great, and Brian had obviously practiced it prior to the session. However, it turns out that he had several variations that he wanted to try. Rather than try each of them as single-take recordings on a different track, the logical choice was to create a multi-take recording.

You may also have noticed that this guitar recording is so "clean" (effects-free) that it is nearly inaudible against the other instrument parts. Before the next recording, let's add some effects to the track.

Using Guitar Amps and Stompboxes

In this exercise, you'll experiment with the GarageBand guitar amps and stompboxes to modify the sound of the Clean Single Take guitar track to bring it to life in the mix.

These guitar amps and stompboxes were designed to look and respond just like the real hardware, so musicians will immediately feel comfortable in their GarageBand recording studio. In fact, the guitarist, Brian, was so blown away by these effects that we had to stop and tweak the guitar effects before recording the multiple takes—and he did it with no previous GarageBand experience! Let's apply those same adjustments to add sustain, delay, and distortion to the track.

1 Open and save the project **Magic Rock Song 02**, if it is not already open.

  Because the recorded part is only for the first verse, turn on the cycle region to loop playback for that section of the song.

2 Click the Cycle button, or press C to turn on the cycle region.

  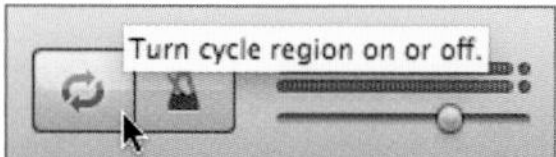

  A yellow bar—the cycle region—appears below the beats and measures ruler at the top of the window. The yellow cycle region includes only the first verse (labeled Verse 1 on the arrangement track above the timeline).

  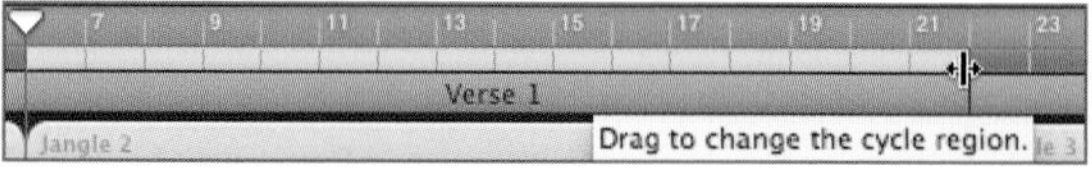

  NOTE ▶ Prior to saving, the cycle region for this exercise was resized to fit the Verse 1 section of the song. If the yellow cycle region in your project is a different length or in a different location, drag the left and right edges of the yellow region to the desired position.

3 Double-click the Clean Single Take track header to show the Track Info pane for that track.

4 In the Track Info pane, hover the pointer over the picture of the amplifier to see a description of that amplifier and hear its signature sound.

While you hover over an amplifier, you'll also see two arrow overlays on either side of the amp. You can click the arrows to change amplifiers. The best way to hear the differences in amplifiers is to compare them while the guitar track is playing. GarageBand '11 includes 12 amplifiers.

5 Play the song and click the arrows to the right or left of the amplifier to change amps during playback. Since the cycle region has been turned on, the song will automatically repeat as you sample the amplifiers.

6 Press S to solo the selected track and listen to only the sound of the lead guitar part while you audition the amplifiers. Press S again to unsolo the track once you've listened to all of the amplifiers.

7 Click the arrows until you return to the black Vintage Stack amplifier. It has a good tone for this type of song. You can feel free to choose a different amplifier later.

Let's raise the reverb sound of the amplifier to help the lead guitar stand out a bit more.

8 Click the amplifier to display its controls. The Reverb dial is in the center of the bottom row of dials.

9 Solo the Guitar track and start playback. Click the center of the Reverb dial, and then drag up to raise the level to around 7 or 8.

NOTE ► Dragging up or down on a control knob will raise or lower its level. Because all of the amps have the same controls, any adjustments you make to a control will be retained even if you change to a different amplifier. The amplifier settings will reset if you change instrument sounds using the menu at the top of the Track Info pane.

Great. The reverb is set. Now all that's left is to check the sustain level and turn on the delay. For that, you'll use the stompboxes.

10 Continue playback and click the Sustain stompbox.

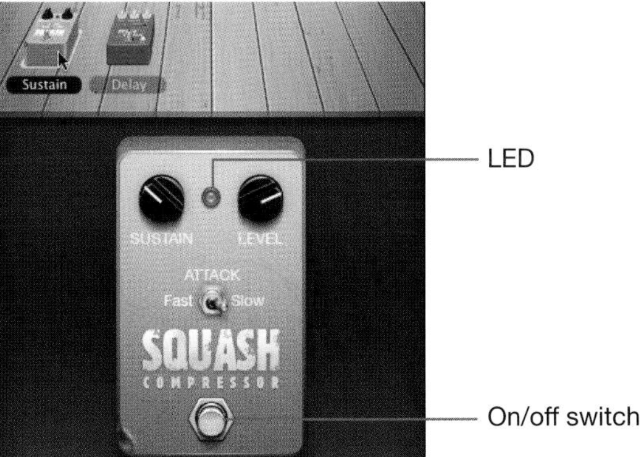

Stompboxes are so named because they're placed on the floor within reach of the musicians, so that they can quite literally stomp on them to turn them on or off as needed. A light tap of the toe also works, but is much less dramatic on stage. In this example, the Sustain stompbox looks exactly like the real thing (dent included).

The button to stomp on or off is located near the bottom where it would be easy to reach with a foot in the real world, or a pointer in GarageBand. If a stompbox is turned off, the name will be dimmed on the stage, as with the Delay stompbox in this project.

NOTE ▶ The sustain is turned on by default for all of the guitar amplifiers. That's a good thing because in almost every musical scenario, instruments (and vocals) sound better with a little sustain or reverb.

11 Click the On/Off switch for the Squash Compressor (sustain) stompbox to hear the track with and without the effect.

The red LED lights up when the stompbox is turned on. When you're finished comparing sounds, leave it turned on.

12 Click the Delay stompbox and turn it on. Then drag the Mix knob upward to about 35.50%. When you're finished, unsolo the track to hear the modified guitar sound in the track.

13 Double-click either stompbox on the stage below the amplifier to see all 15 stompboxes.

You can add stompboxes by dragging them up to the yellow spaces below the amplifier. To remove a stompbox, drag it from the floor.

14 Drag the Hi Drive distortion stompbox (the first stompbox on the bottom row) to the stage.

That guitar sound has come a long way since the original "clean" sound.

15 Stop playback.

Saving Effects Settings

After you've adjusted the amplifier and stompbox effects to your liking, you can save those settings so that you'll be able to use them again on another project.

1 At the bottom of the Track Info pane, click the Save Setting button.

2 In the "Save as" field, type *O'Maille Rock Rhythm,* or your own last name plus "Rock Rhythm ," then click Save.

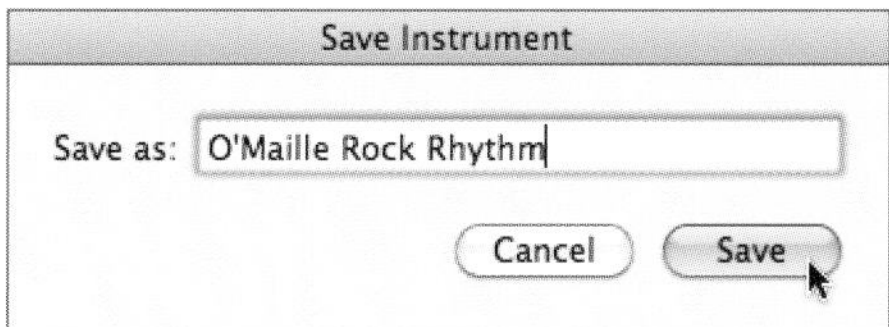

The track name changes to match the selected effect, and the saved effect appears in the Track Info effects menu.

NOTE ▶ If you do not see the saved preset name or the My Settings section in the Guitar Preset pop-up menu, click a Real Instrument track header (such as Jangles) and in the Track Info, set the Presets View pop-up menu to Show All. This will display all GarageBand and My Settings presets. The saved settings will now appear in the presets. You may need to save the effects settings again (as in step 2) to insure that they will appear in the list. If the My Settings section still doesn't appear in the list, save and close the project. When you reopen the project, the My Settings should be visible.

TIP You can save as many customized effects as you'd like. You can also delete any of your custom settings if you no longer need them by clicking the Delete Setting button.

3 At the top at the Track Info pane, click the Guitar Preset pop-up menu to see a list of the available Electric Guitar sounds. GarageBand includes over 50 guitar effects presets.

4 Choose a sound from the list and listen to it during playback. The amplifier and stompboxes change automatically to match the preset.

5 Try as many different presets as you'd like. When you are finished experimenting, from the My Settings area at the top of the presets menu, choose O'Maille Rock Rhythm (or the name you saved) to restore the customized settings for this track.

Multiple Takes Recording

Multiple Takes recordings offer several advantages over single-take recordings. For one, you can record a part as many times as you'd like without stopping. This gives musicians an opportunity to try variations on their performances, as well as correcting any mistakes or missed notes. Another advantage is that you can choose your favorite take, or split the region and assemble a performance from sections of several takes.

Let's set up another track for a multiple-takes recording, then listen to the finished version.

To record multiple takes, you first need a cycle region for the duration you want to record. In this case, the cycle region has been created for you. Because this part of the song—Verse 1—is only 15 bars (measures) in length, the entire part can be recorded at once. It's easier to record full songs in separate sections—such as the intro, verse, and chorus separately—rather than try to record the entire song start to finish.

1 Press C to show the cycle region, if it is not already showing.

   Next you'll want to create a guitar track for the multiple-takes recording. Rather than make a new track and adjust all of the settings, you can simply duplicate the existing track.

2 Select the O'Maille Rock Rhythm track, if it isn't already selected. Then choose Track > Duplicate, or press Command-D.

   A duplicate O'Maille Rock Rhythm track appears below the original. Now all you have to do is change the name of the track and you're ready to record.

3 Click the name of the new track, and then type *Multiple Takes* in the field. When you're finished typing, click anywhere else on the track to close the field.

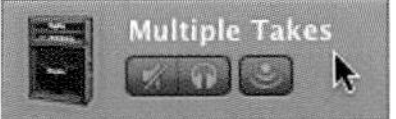

That's it. You're ready to record a multiple-takes guitar part. If you have a guitar handy and want to record along with this song, feel free to do so. If not, you can jump to step 6 to save this version of the project and open the next.

4 Make sure that the Multiple Takes track is selected, turn on the monitor button—if necessary for your setup—and click Record, or press R. Record three or four full takes of the song without interruption.

5 When you're finished, press the Spacebar to stop recording.

The purple multi-take region includes a yellow numbered Take menu in the upper-left corner that displays the current take number and allows you to switch between takes.

6 Save your project (with Archive Project if you recorded a track), then open the Lesson 17 > **Magic Rock Song 03** project to hear a finished recording.

The **Magic Rock Song 03** project includes the cycle region, the O'Maille Rock Rhythm track with the mute button active, and a multiple-takes recording in the lowest track of the Timeline.

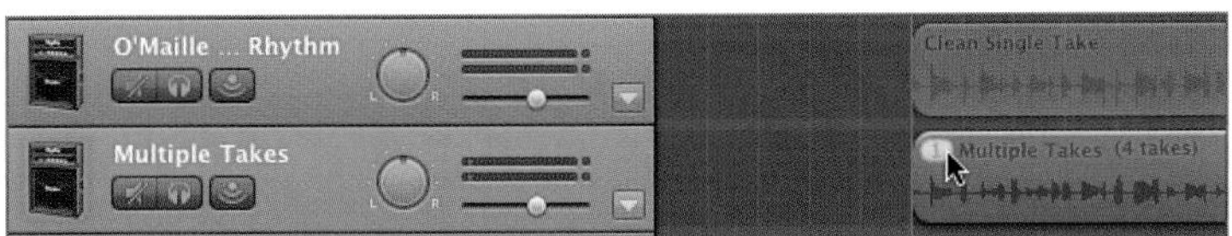

The circled number in the upper-left corner of the region shows the current take number in the track. The number of takes that were recorded is added to the name of the region. In this case, it reads,"(4 takes)". There were actually three full takes. The fourth take included only a few notes that Brian played after the third and final full take.

NOTE ▶ It's common to record an extra take at the end of a multi-takes recording because another take usually starts before you can stop recording. You can always disregard that mis-take (pun intended) when you select the best performance.

7 Play the song to hear the first take with the other tracks. Feel free to unmute the O'Maille Rock Rhythm track to hear both guitar tracks at the same time.

Notice that the region within O'Maille Rock Rhythm track is dimmed when the track is muted to indicate that it is not audible during playback.

8 Stop playback when you have evaluated the first take in the multiple-takes track.

This performance of the guitar part sounds pretty good with the rest of the instruments.

Selecting and Splitting Takes

After you've recorded a multiple-takes region, you can use the Takes menu in the upper-left corner of the region to change to a different take. You can even split regions so that you can use the best portions of each recorded take to create the finished musical part.

1 In the upper-left corner of the Multiple Takes region, click the circled number (1) to see the Takes pop-up menu.

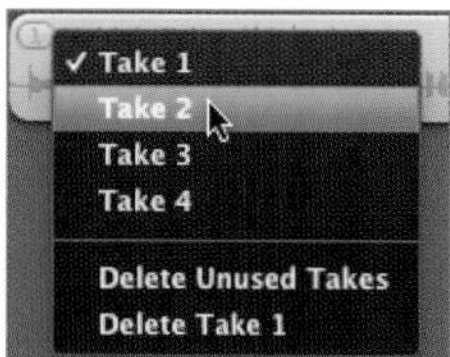

The Takes menu lists each take, plus an option to delete unused takes or delete the current take.

2 From the Takes menu, choose Take 2 and listen to it with the rest of the song. When you're finished, switch to Take 3 and listen to that performance. When you are finished, return to the region Take 2.

What if you like the beginning of one take and the end of another? In that case, you can split the take in a clean place and change the second region to the new desired take.

For this example, you will change the entire region to Take 2, and then split the region on the second beat of the 14th measure. The last step will be to change the new region to the third take.

TIP Before splitting a track, it's a good idea to zoom in on the Timeline so that you can move the playhead more precisely along the Timeline. Also, if you like using keyboard shortcuts to navigate, the more you zoom in, the finer increments of movement you can achieve when pressing the Left and Right Arrow keys.

3 Drag the Timeline Zoom slider near its middle to zoom in on the Timeline. When the Beats and Measures ruler shows each numbered measure, you are zoomed in enough for this exercise.

NOTE ▶ Because the project time signature is 4/4, you have four beats per measure. The tick marks on the ruler represent beats, and the first beat of each measure starts at the beginning of the numbered measure.

The LCD currently shows the Measures view. Your goal is to move the playhead to the second beat of the 14th measure (14.2.1.001 on the LCD).

4 Press Return to move the playhead to the beginning of the cycle region. Then press the Right Arrow key until the LCD shows 14.1.1.001.

NOTE ▶ If you zoomed in farther than the book example, and you are able to navigate through the beats as well as measures to 14.2.1.001, then you can skip the next step.

5 On the LCD, click the number 1 (just after the 14), representing beats, and drag upward to change it to 2.

The playhead is now in a perfect position to split the track. In the visible waveform within the region, notice that the playhead is neatly placed between musical notes.

6 In the multiple-takes track, select the Multiple Takes region, if necessary.

7 Press Command-T, or choose Edit > Split to split the selected track at the playhead position.

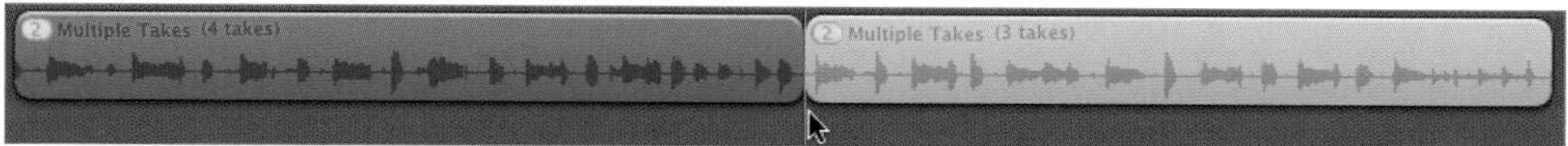

8 Change the second region to Take 3 and save the project as *Magic Rock Song 04a* in the My GarageBand Projects folder.

NOTE ▶ The second part of the newly-split region includes only the three full takes. The fourth partial take was deleted automatically.

There you have it. Now you can split your multiple-takes regions so that you can use your favorite combination of performances within the same track.

Working with an Acoustic Guitar Track

The last guitar part to lay down is the acoustic guitar. In the GarageBand interface, recording an acoustic guitar is almost the same as recording an electric guitar. The difference is that acoustic guitars don't use amplifiers or stompboxes for effects, and the input and monitoring controls appear at the bottom of the Track Info pane.

Let's create an acoustic guitar track.

1 If you didn't complete all of the previous exercises in this lesson, open the project Lesson 17 > **Magic Rock Song 04** and save it to the My GarageBand projects folder.

2 Choose Track > New Track, or click the New Track button.

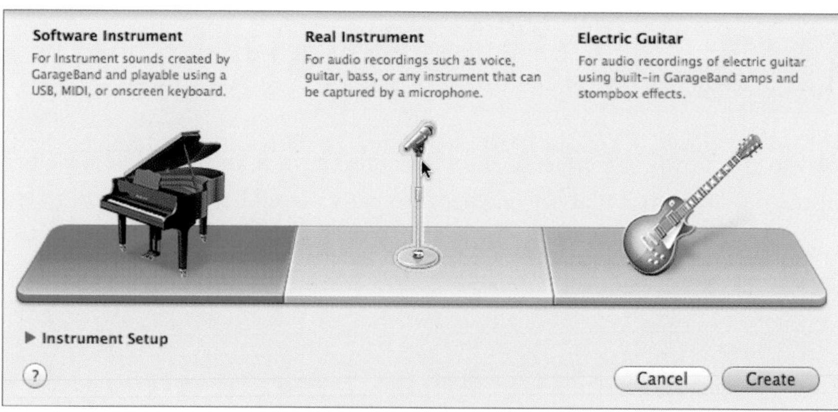

3 Double-click the picture of the microphone on the New Track dialog to create a Real Instrument track.

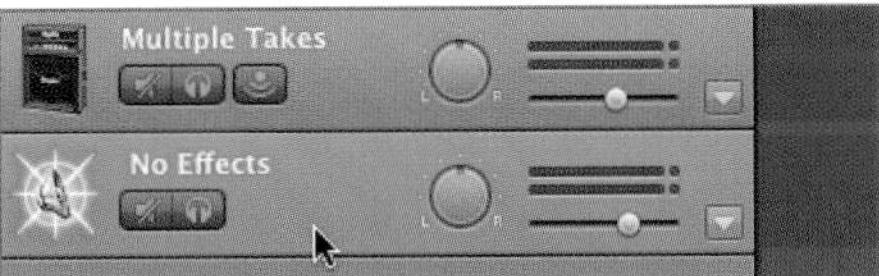

A new Real Instrument track named No Effects appears in the timeline. This track can be set up to record any type of real instrument that is recorded via a microphone connected to the Mac, including a Mac's built-in microphone. You can designate the type of instrumental sound that you will be recording on the Track Info pane.

4 Select the No Effects track, if necessary.

5 In the track Info pane, choose Acoustic Guitars. Choose Large Reverb from the Acoustic Guitars effects list.

The track header updates to match the name of the effects preset applied to that track. Rather than record an entirely new region with an acoustic guitar, let's duplicate the "Clean single take" region and place it in the acoustic track. Doubling two versions of the same part is a great way to *fatten* the sound of the part.

6 Select the O'Maille Rock Rhythm track, and press M to unmute the track.

7 Mute the multiple-takes track so that it does not compete with the duplicate rhythm tracks.

8 Option-drag the "Clean single take" region and drop the duplicate in the Large Reverb track, directly below the original region in the Multiple Takes track.

NOTE ▶ To Option-drag, hold down the Option key while dragging to duplicate a region.

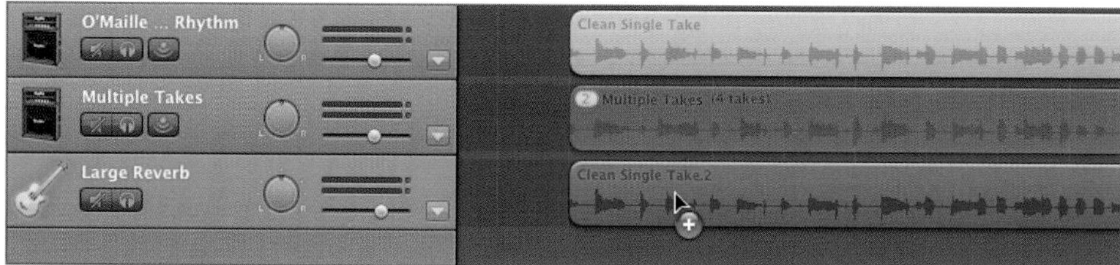

NOTE ▶ Make sure that the duplicate region is precisely aligned with the region that you copied or you will hear an echo as they play slightly out of sync. For some songs, however, moving the doubled parts out of sync to create an echo effect is intentional. It just depends on the song and the part.

9 Solo the O'Maille Rock Rhythm and Large Reverb tracks to listen to them together without the other tracks. Start playback.

Feel free to unsolo the tracks (press S) at will to hear them playing with the remaining tracks. Listen to the song with the doubled guitar regions.

10 While the track is playing, try selecting various acoustic guitar effects in the Track Info pane.

NOTE ▶ Don't worry if the guitar parts seem loud in the mix. You'll adjust individual track levels and panning in the next lesson. For now, you can drag the volume level slider on each of the three new guitars to a comfortable level.

11 When you are finished experimenting with effects presets, stop playback and save your progress.

You created an acoustic guitar part without recording a new one. You could do the same thing in reverse and drag an acoustic guitar part into an electric guitar track to double the tracks and give the impression of two types of guitars playing the same part. Plus, you have the skills now to add stompbox and amp effects to the acoustic part if you like.

NOTE ▶ The Input Source, Monitor, and Recording Level controls for an acoustic guitar (Real Instrument) track are located at the bottom of the Track Info pane.

Recording a New Software Instrument Part

Now that the additional guitar tracks are recorded, it's time to lay down (add) one last track to this part, a cowbell. One thing about rock songs, there's almost always room for cowbell. Sure, you could add any kind of instrument track to the song, but a cowbell track will be a simple percussion enhancement to the music and you don't need to be a musician to try it.

In this exercise, you'll record a short cowbell part for the beginning of the first verse of the song.

You have three ways to play a Software Instrument in GarageBand:

- Connect a MIDI or USB MIDI keyboard to the computer and play the keys on a musical keyboard. (You can find instructions for connecting a keyboard in Lesson 15.)
- Use Musical Typing to turn your computer's keyboard into a musical instrument.
- Use the onscreen music keyboard in GarageBand to click the keyboard keys with your mouse.

Playing the Onscreen Music Keyboard

One option when playing music with GarageBand is to use the onscreen music keyboard to both play and record Software Instruments. First, create a new Software Instrument track that you'll use to record your part.

1 You can continue working with your project from the previous exercise, or open Lesson 17 > **Magic Rock Song 05**.

2 Choose Track > New Track, then from the New Track dialog, choose Software Instrument (Piano picture). Click Create.

   A new Grand Piano track appears below the other tracks in the Timeline. Grand Piano is the default Software Instrument; however, you can change it at any time to a different Software Instrument.

3 To show the onscreen music keyboard, choose Window > Keyboard. The onscreen music keyboard appears, ready for you to play the selected Grand Piano track.

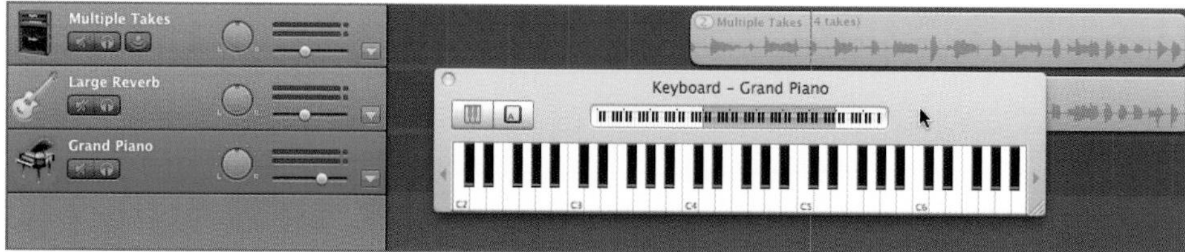

NOTE ▶ The onscreen music keyboard works only for Software Instrument tracks.

4 Drag the lower-right corner of the keyboard down and to the right to resize it and create larger keys that are easier to click.

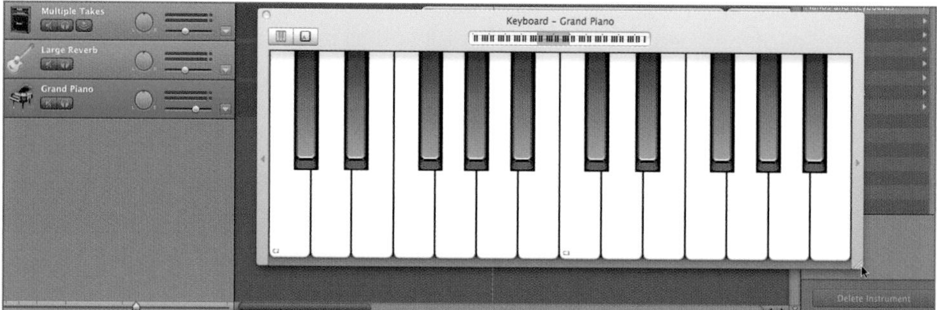

TIP The onscreen music keyboard is touch sensitive. Click the top of the keys near the top of the keyboard to play with a lighter velocity and get a quieter sound. Click the bottom of the keys near the bottom of the keyboard to play with a harder velocity and get a louder sound. You can always change the velocities (volume levels) of Software Instrument notes in the editor after they've been recorded.

5 Play the onscreen keyboard by clicking the notes on the keyboard.

Although you can play music this way, it's not the easiest way to create a complex music arrangement. However, it will work perfectly for this cowbell performance.

Let's change the track instrument to a percussion sound that works better for this project.

6 In the Track Info pane, choose Drum Kits as the instrument category (left column) and choose Rock Kit as the instrument.

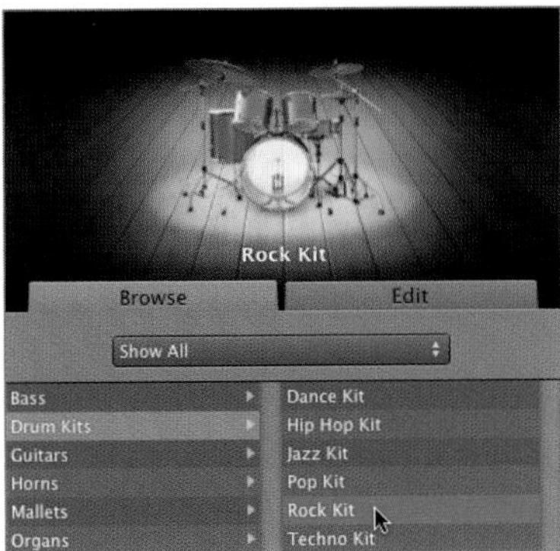

7 Click a few notes to hear the percussion instruments assigned to each note.

NOTE ▶ Standard MIDI keyboards have numbered octaves to keep track of key assignments for MIDI events. Each octave includes 12 notes represented by white and black keys. The lowest octave available on the onscreen keyboard is –2 (two octaves lower than the 0 octave on standard MIDI keyboards). The GarageBand onscreen keyboard includes a label on every C key with its corresponding octave number. You can drag the blue region on the mini-keyboard at the top of the onscreen keyboard window to change the visible octaves showing onscreen.

There are actually three cowbell sounds from which to choose. G#2, G3, and G#3.

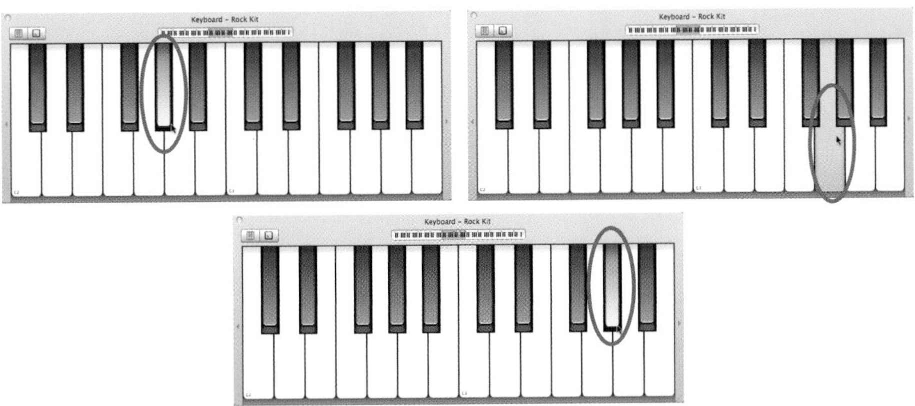

G#2 G3 G#3

8 Practice clicking each of the notes (G#2, G3, and G#3) to play its corresponding cowbell sound. Try again while the song is playing.

9 Press C to turn off the cycle region. Press Return to move the playhead to the beginning of the song. Mute the three guitar tracks at the bottom of the Timeline so that it will be easier to hear your cowbell part as you play along.

The part that you'll record will be incredibly simple. As you listen to the song, click one of the keys on the keyboard that triggers the cowbell in time with the music. Keep in mind, less is more. Feel free to record a percussion sound, other than the cowbell if you prefer. If you aren't sure when to play, try starting at the beginning of the first verse.

10 Press R to start recording, and play a simple part. When you're finished, press the Spacebar to stop recording.

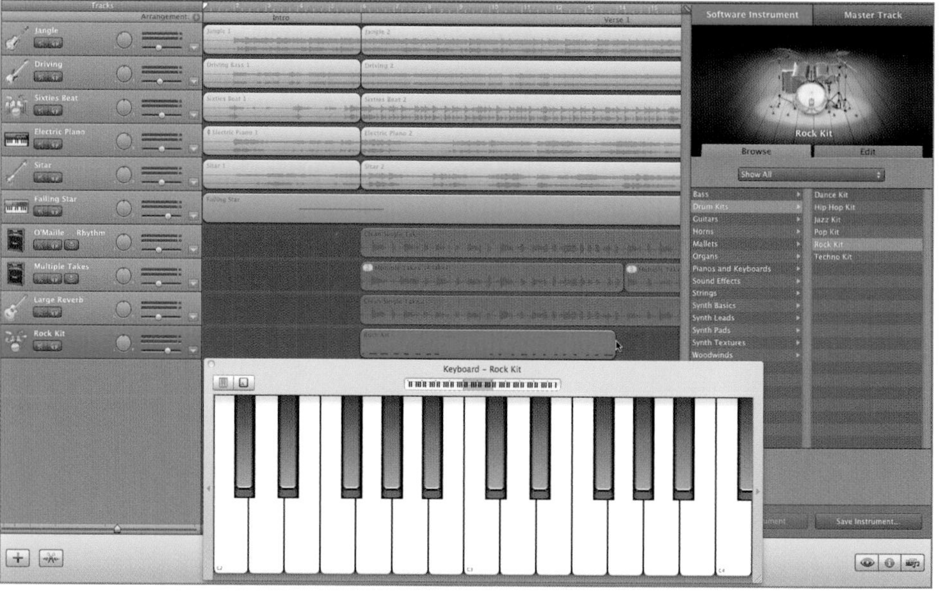

11 Play your recording. If you're happy, continue to the next step. If not, press Command-Z to Undo and try again.

12 Press Command-S to save your project.

Nice work. You've completed the recording lesson. Whatever you played will sound fine in this composition.

Lesson Review

1. Where is the tuner located in GarageBand?
2. Identify the two most common ways to keep musical time as you record a part in GarageBand.
3. When can you change the sound of a guitar track?
4. What types of effects are unique to Real Instrument electric guitar tracks in GarageBand?
5. Where do you change the instrument for a track?

Answers

1. The tuner is located in the LCD at the bottom of the GarageBand window.
2. Turn on the Metronome or use a drum track to help you keep musical time as you record.
3. You can change a guitar track's sound before or after recording.
4. GarageBand includes amps and stompbox effects that can be used with electric guitar Real Instrument tracks.
5. You can change a track's instrument in the Track Info pane.

18

Lesson Files

ATS iLife11 Book Files > Lesson18 > 01 Fix Timing, 02 Trim and Loop, 03 Groove Track, 04 Flex Time, 05 Name and Icon, 06 Notation Scales, 07 Tempo Scales, 08 Apple Loops, 09 Double Track

Time

This lesson takes approximately 90 minutes to complete. This includes a few extra minutes to download additional Apple Loops, Software Instruments, and effects.

Goals

Fix timing in a Software Instrument region

Edit notes in a Software Instrument region

Fix timing in a Real Instrument region

Explore Groove Matching and Flex Time

Change project tempo

Work with Apple Loops

Pan tracks

Transpose regions

Lesson **18**

Fixing, Arranging, and Mixing Music in GarageBand

Anyone can make great-sounding music with GarageBand '11. Really! GarageBand '11 is packed with powerful performance-enhancing features that can help you effortlessly fix timing issues and improve your recordings.

This lesson is an in-depth tour that walks you through fixing, arranging, and mixing techniques as they are applied to three songs. Along the way, you'll get hands-on experience fixing songs, tracks, and even individual notes. Your eyes—and ears—will witness miraculous transformations of clunky performances into tracks that perfectly fit a groove. You'll explore the editor for refined changes in both Software Instrument and Real Instrument recordings. You'll also take a trip to the Loop Browser to explore Apple Loops.

Recognizing Timing Issues

In the next section, you will fix the timing of the Cowbell recording from the previous lesson. However, first it is a good idea to listen to the region in question, and evaluate it against the click track and drums to identify the timing issues. Being able to hear and locate the cause of problem performances is the first step toward fixing them and making them sound great.

In this exercise, you'll open a version of the Magic Rock song that you worked on in the previous lesson and listen to the timing of the notes—or the lack of timing in this case.

1 From the Lesson 18 folder, open the project **01 Fix Timing** and save it to your My GarageBand Projects folder. If asked to save with iLife preview, click No.

 NOTE ▶ If you did not create a My GarageBand Projects folder earlier, you can make one now. In the Save As dialog, select the desktop for the location, then click New Folder and name it *My GarageBand Projects.*

 This variation of the Magic Rock song includes five blue Real Instrument tracks, and a green Software Instrument Cowbell track similar to the one that you recorded in the previous lesson.

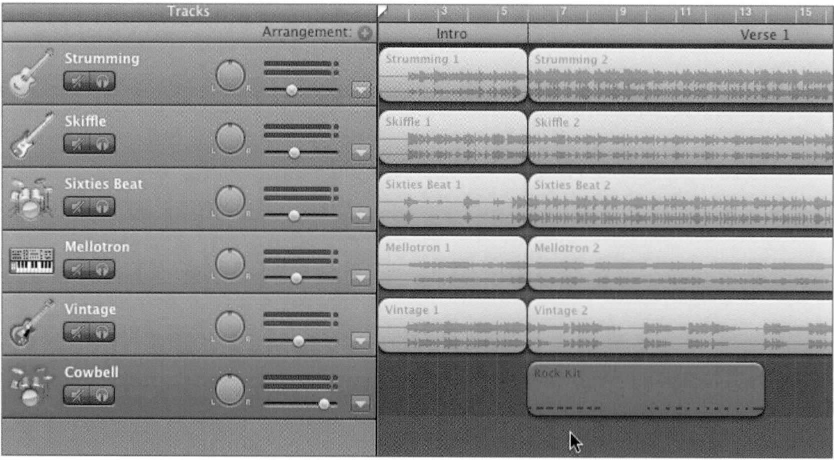

2 Play the song from the beginning and listen to the Rock Kit region in the Cowbell track. Stop playback after you've heard the cowbell part.

You probably noticed that the volume level of the cowbell seemed a little loud, and the notes seemed out of sync with the drums and other rhythm instruments. The volume level was raised intentionally to make it easier to hear for this exercise. The poor performance? Well, that was just what it sounds like.

3 Press C to show the cycle region above the first verse.

4 Drag the right side of the yellow cycle region to the 14th measure so that it matches the length of the green Rock Kit region in the Cowbell track.

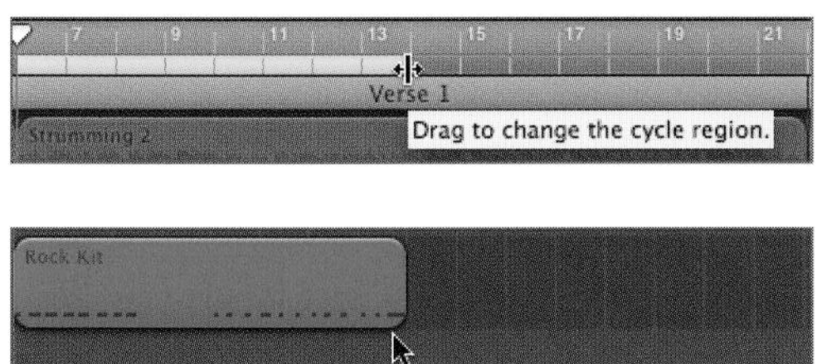

5 Press S, or click the Solo button on the Cowbell track to solo the track. Start playback.

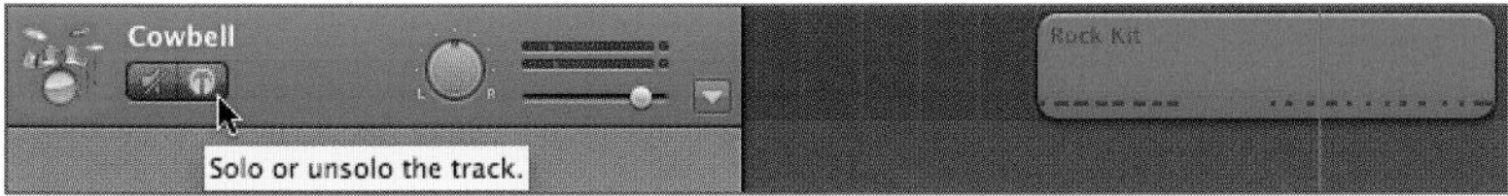

It's hard to tell how bad the timing is when it plays by itself. Let's hear it with the click track and drums.

6 Click the Metronome button, or press Command-U to turn on the click track.

Yikes, the tracks aren't even close.

7 Solo the Sixties Beat track (drums) to hear it along with the click and cowbell. Stop playback, and press Return to move the playhead to the beginning of the cycle region.

Okay, that's just embarrassing. It's time to quantize this region and fix the performance timing.

Quantizing a Software Instrument Region

Though *quantize* sounds like a term you might hear in a science fiction movie, it actually means to divide something into tiny increments according to the rules of quantum mechanics, or in this case, according to fractions of a beat in musical time. Fortunately, when quantizing music, GarageBand calculates the math for you as the application analyzes and fixes the timing of MIDI note events. Sound complicated? It's not. In fact, GarageBand '11 makes it so easy that you can fix an entire Software Instrument region with a single click.

Now that you've listened to and winced at the dreadful cowbell performance, it's time to unclench your teeth and quantize (fix) the note timing so that this part plays "in time" with the rest of the song.

To do that, you'll need to open the editor.

1 Click the View Editor button, or in the Timeline, double-click the Rock Kit region.

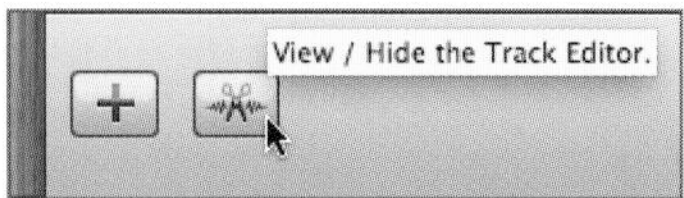

The editor opens at the bottom of the GarageBand window.

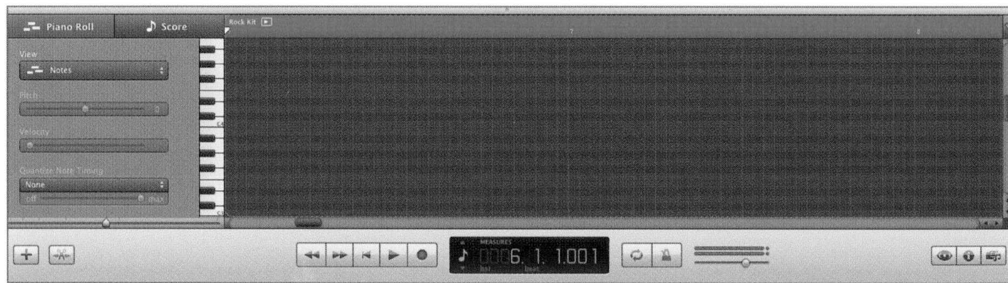

The editor can show a Software Instrument region in Piano Roll or Score (notation) view. For this exercise, you'll work in Piano Roll view.

If you don't see any notes (dashes), that is because the current view shows a different octave range than the recorded notes in this region.

NOTE ▶ MIDI note events appear as dashes on a grid in the Piano Roll view. Each horizontal line of the grid represents a white or black note on the corresponding keyboard. In this example the notes are all G#2.

2 On the right side of the editor, drag the vertical scroll bar until notes appear in the editor.

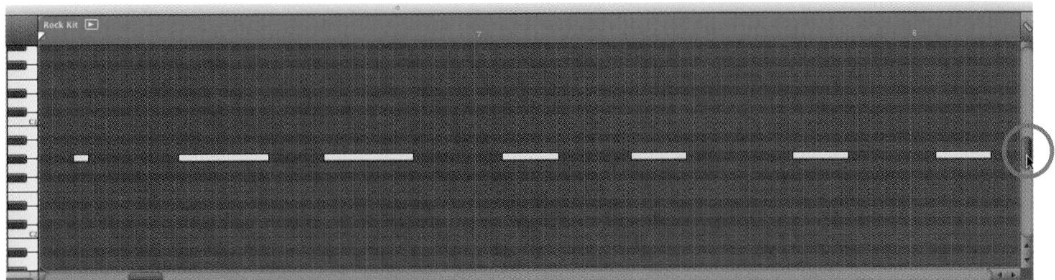

3 Click and hold down the mouse button over the first note (dash) to hear it and to display a tooltip with the specific note and octave.

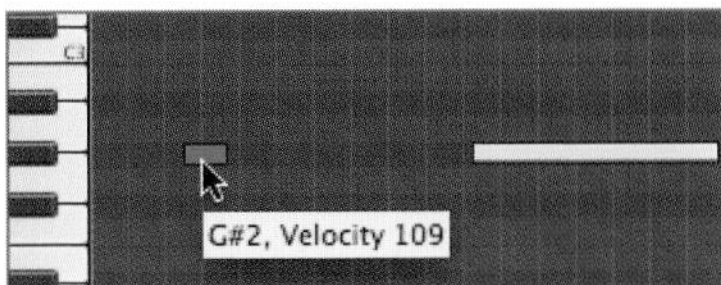

At the top of the editor, notice the numbered measures and the tick marks that indicate the increments of musical time. This song is in 4/4 meter, or 4 beats per measure with 8 tick marks per beat and 32 marks per measure.

4 Look at the grid in the editor to see if any of the dashes (notes) actually start on a grid line. A few do, but most aren't even close.

These are clearly out of time (visually and audibly). Notes don't have to start on a beat, but they should at least line up with the fractions of a beat.

You could manually fix each dash, which would be tedious, or simply quantize the note timing. For this exercise you'll take the easy, quantize route.

5 In the Timeline, select the Rock Kit region if it is not already selected.

6 Click any note to select it. Press Command-A, or choose Edit > Select All.

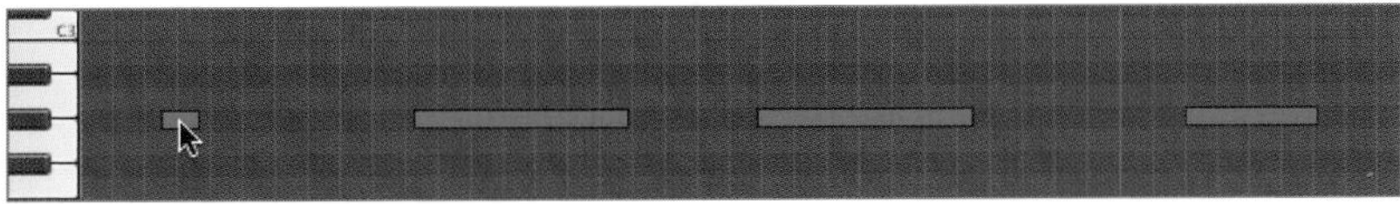

All of the notes in the region appear green to indicate that they have been selected.

7 Near the bottom of the editor controls, locate the Quantize Note Timing pop-up menu. The current setting is None.

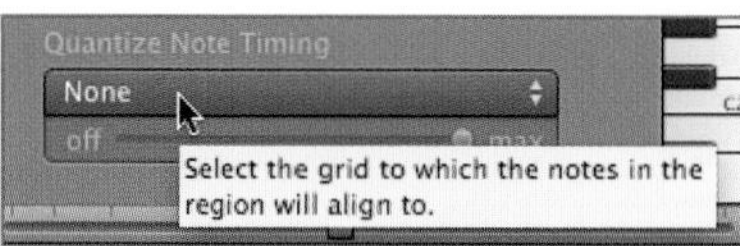

8 From the Quantize Note Timing pop-up menu, choose "1/64 Note."

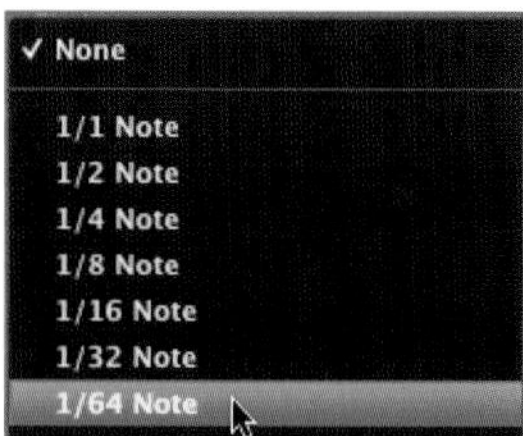

The beginning of each selected note moves to the nearest gridline or exactly between gridlines (because the current zoom level shows tick marks at 1/32).

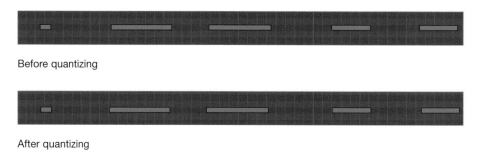

Before quantizing

After quantizing

Let's change the zoom level in the editor and increase the grid to an even higher level.

9 Drag the editor Zoom slider slightly toward the right until you see a grid line at the beginning of each note.

As you can see, the notes were indeed quantized to 1/64 of a measure.

TIP Quantizing notes to smaller fractions of a beat such as 1/32 or 1/64 will move them the least and keep them close to their original performance positions. Quantizing to larger fractions of a beat such as 1/1 (a full measure) to 1/4 (a single beat in 4/4) moves notes farther apart to reach the nearest measure or beat mark. In most cases, quantizing to these large increments will make your performance sound completely different from the original performance. If you accidentally quantize your notes too far, simply press Command-Z to undo and try again at a higher fractional number.

10 To hide the editor, press Command-E, or click the View/Hide Editor button (scissors), or double-click the Rock Kit region in the Timeline.

11 Play the region to hear it with the drums and/or click track. Unsolo the Cowbell and Sixties Beat tracks to hear the cowbell played with the other tracks. When you are finished, stop playback.

Much better. The cowbell works. In fact, what this song needs now is more cowbell!

TIP In the editor, you can change the velocity (how hard/fast a note is played) of Software Instrument notes by selecting them and dragging the velocity slider right to make them louder, and left to make them quieter.

Trimming and Looping a Region

Now that the cowbell is in time with the music, it can be trimmed and looped (repeated) for the entire verse. The trick to trimming a region to turn it into a loop is to make sure that it starts and ends precisely on a measure, or a beat within a measure. Otherwise, as you loop it over and over, it will fall out of time with the other parts.

This entire process can be done in the Timeline. First, you'll need to zoom into the Timeline for a more detailed view of both the region and the Beats and Measures ruler.

1 If you did not complete the previous exercises, open the project **02 Trim and Loop** and save it to your folder on the desktop.

2 Drag the Timeline Zoom slider toward the right until you see three tick marks for each numbered measure in the Beats and Measures ruler.

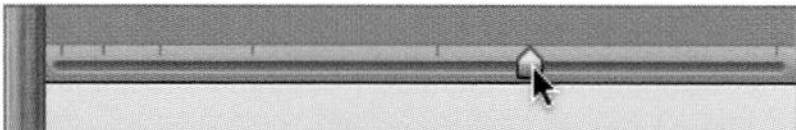

For this exercise, your goal is to make this region two beats in length. To do so, you will need to trim the right edge of the region.

3 Move the playhead to the beginning of the eighth measure in the Timeline. The playhead will be your guide for trimming the end of the region.

4 Hover the pointer over the upper-right corner of the Rock Kit (the cowbell region in the Timeline.) Then watch the pointer as you move it down to the lower-right corner of the region.

The pointer changes from a Loop tool (circular arrow) to a Resize/Trim tool (left-right pointing arrows).

5 Drag the lower-right corner of the region to the playhead position (at the beginning of the eighth measure).

The Rock Kit (cowbell) region is now exactly two measures (eight beats) in length.

6 Drag the Timeline Zoom slider toward the left until you can see the entire Verse 1 (ends at 22.1.1001).

7 Drag the upper-right corner of the Rock Kit region to the beginning of the 22nd measure (22.1.1001). The entire region should loop (repeat) eight times.

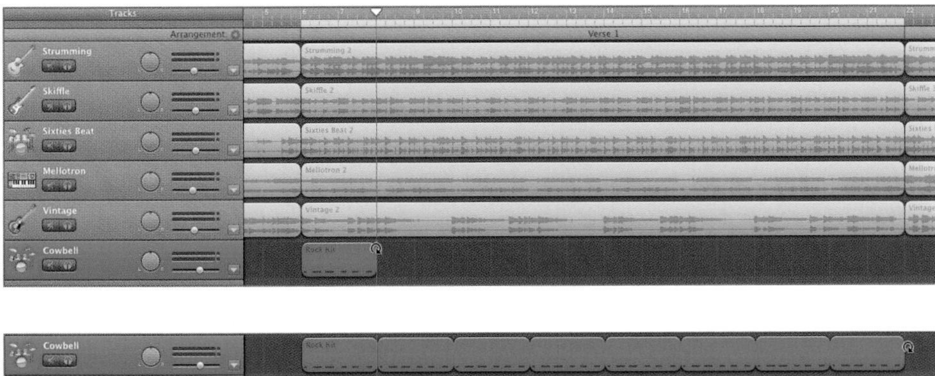

8 Play the cycle region to hear the loop throughout Verse 1.

9 Solo the Cowbell and Sixties Beat tracks to hear them together for the entire verse. Stop playback and save your progress.

Does it sound like the Cowbell loop isn't working well with the song anymore toward the middle and end of the verse? How can that be?

Quantizing fixed the original region, but it didn't take into account the *groove*, or *feel*, of the song. As it is, the cowbell has a predictable rhythm, as if precisely performed by a computer. The other musical parts were performed by actual musicians and have a looser rhythmic feel that the loop doesn't have or fit—yet.

Working with Groove Matching

Prepare yourself for a very cool exercise. This feature goes way beyond what you might expect from GarageBand. Truth is, the powerful Flex-Time analysis used to make Groove Matching possible came from Logic Studio, Apple's professional music recording software. The good news for GarageBand '11 users is that all of the work is done for you.

What is Groove Matching? Well, it's a more advanced form of quantizing the music that considers the groove (meter, pacing, and feel) of a selected Groove Track and matches the other tracks to it. Best of all, it works with both Software Instrument and Real Instrument recordings. In this exercise, you'll fix the Cowbell track and two guitar tracks that might otherwise be unusable.

1 Open the project **03 Groove Track**, and save it to the My GarageBand Projects folder.

The project that you were working on in the previous exercise opens, with the addition of two guitar tracks, Out of Pocket 1 and 2. Also, the volume levels of the original Magic Rock Song tracks have been reduced to make it easier to hear the new tracks.

2 Play the cycle region (Verse 1) to hear the Cowbell track along with the two Out of Pocket guitar tracks.

NOTE ▶ "Out of Pocket," "Out of the Pocket," or "Not in the Pocket" are polite ways for a musician or music producer to say that a track or performance does not quite fit the groove of the song. In this case, the tracks are so far out of whack they sound like an acoustic train wreck.

In the old days, you might as well have rubbed a lamp and hoped for a genie to salvage those guitar tracks. Otherwise, you had no choice but to re-record them. Fortunately, the new Groove Tracks in GarageBand can perform its own magic—without the genie.

Before you turn on Groove Tracks, it's a good idea to decide which track best represents the feel of your song. Drum tracks are usually a safe bet, but you might also choose the track that could stand alone. Do you have a track that a vocalist could sing along to "unplugged?" In that case, the rhythm guitar or a lead piano part would work. For this song, the Strumming guitar track includes all of the chord changes and rhythm of the song. If the Cowbell and Out of Pocket tracks followed the Strumming guitar track's lead, they just might work.

3 Move the pointer over the left edge of the Strumming track header.

An open star overlay appears. Clicking the star turns on Groove Tracks and makes that track the "star" from which the groove will be applied to other tracks.

4 Click the star on the Strumming track. Then in the dialog, click Continue to analyze the audio for Groove Tracks.

Analyzing audio for Groove Tracks
To use Groove Tracks, GarageBand needs to analyze the audio material in your project. This may take a few moments. To begin analyzing your project, click Continue, or click Cancel.
Don't show again
Cancel
Continue

You now see a gold star in front of the Strumming track, and selected checkboxes next to all of the other tracks to indicate they will be matching the groove of the Strumming track.

NOTE ▶ You can deselect the checkbox in front of any track to play it without applying Groove Matching. This may be necessary for vocal performances, or instrument parts such as chimes, that are intended to come in at a very specific time regardless of the rhythm tracks.

5 Play the cycle region again to hear the tracks with Groove Tracks applied. While the cycle region plays, solo the Strumming, Out of Pocket, and Cowbell tracks to hear how they sound together. Feel free to lower the volume levels on the bottom three tracks to better match the level of the Strumming track.

6 Continue playback. Select and deselect the Groove Tracks checkboxes to compare the before-and-after results. When you are finished, make sure that all of the tracks are selected and unsoloed. Save your progress.

Can you hear the difference? Sure, the guitar recordings aren't perfect, but they have certainly been improved and finally work with the other tracks in the song. The tracks now sound like musicians jamming together and having a good time.

TIP You can drag the gold star from one track to another to reassign the Groove Track.

Exploring Flex Time in the Editor

Quantizing and Groove Tracks work wonders on entire tracks or regions of tracks. However, occasionally you may have individual notes that need manual tweaking. For a Software Instrument region, that's easily done with the editor, but how do you manipulate notes in a Real Instrument recording? Once again, the answer lies in the editor. GarageBand '11 includes Flex Time technology that analyzes every note, including Real Instrument waveforms. Seeing (or hearing) is believing, so let's venture to the editor to adjust the timing of a note near the end of the Out of Pocket 2 region.

1 Continue working with the current project, or feel free to open the project **04 Flex Time**, and save it to the My GarageBand Projects folder.

2 Press C to turn off the cycle region, if necessary. Then solo the Out of Pocket 2 track.

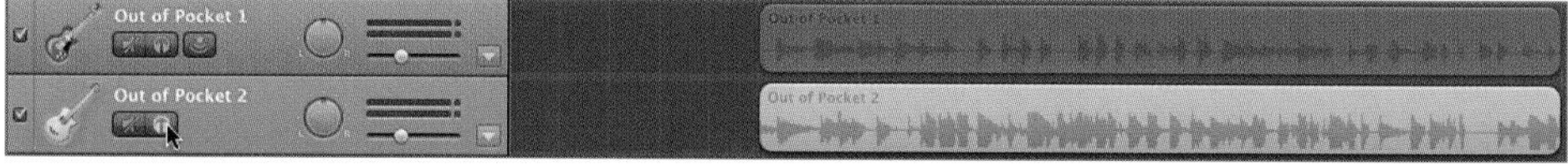

3 Drag the Timeline Zoom slider toward the right until you can clearly see three tick marks between each of the numbered measures in the Beats and Measures ruler.

4 Move the playhead to the second beat (the first tick mark) of the 20th measure (20.2.1.001 in the LCD).

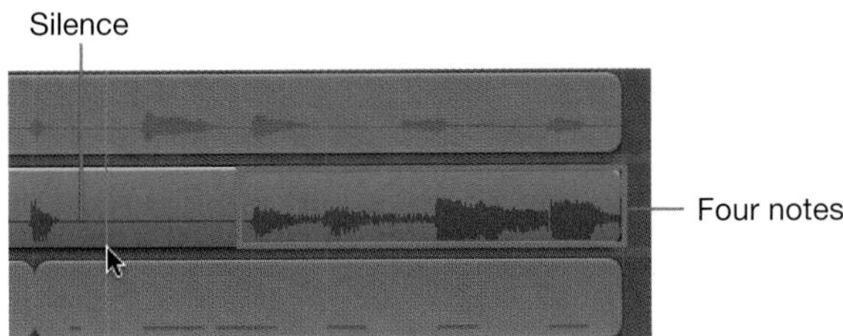

If you look at the audio waveform inside the Out of Pocket 2 track, the playhead should now be over an area with a flat line. A flat line in an audio waveform indicates that no sound is played at that point. Notice the four bumps in the waveform following the flat line that represent four individual notes.

Let's refer to those four notes as the four notes at the end of the region. Your goal is to move the beginning of the first note so that it starts earlier and in time with the notes in the neighboring tracks.

5 Double-click the Out of Pocket 2 region at the playhead to show it in the editor. Unlike the dashes in the Software Instrument editor, the Real Instrument editor shows the audio waveform of the recorded region.

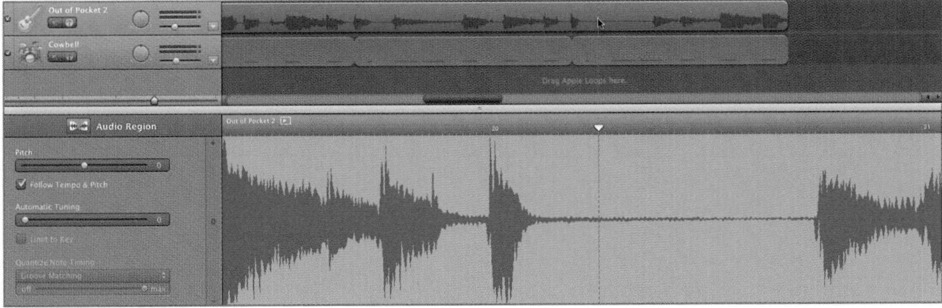

6 In the editor, drag the head (triangle top) of the playhead toward the right until the LCD reads 20.2.3.001.

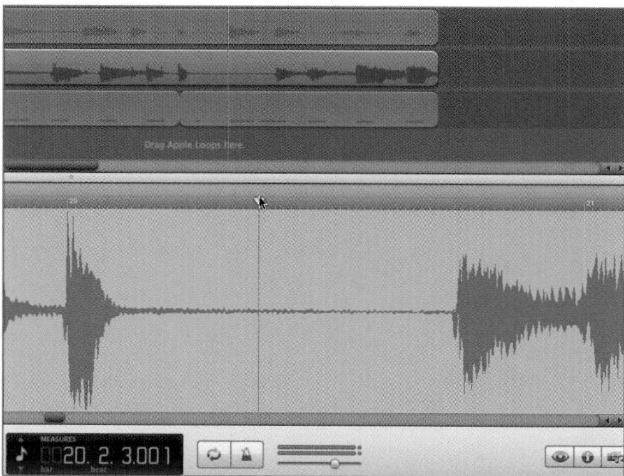

If you look at the playhead in the Timeline, you'll see that this position is precisely when a note also begins on four of the other tracks, including the Out of Pocket 1 and Cowbell tracks.

NOTE ▶ Be careful where you drag in the Real Instrument editor. Clicking or dragging the waveform can select, move, or change Flex Time depending where you click. For now, just drag the head of the playhead. If you accidentally move or change something, press Command-Z to undo the error.

7 In the editor, move the pointer to the red part of the playhead until the pointer changes to a Flex pointer. (The Flex pointer looks like two arrows pointing inward toward the playhead, indicating that exact position.)

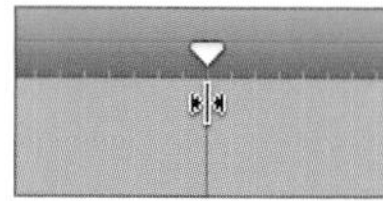

8 Click the Flex pointer at the playhead position to add a Flex marker.

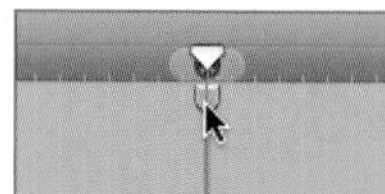

Flex markers can be moved to manipulate music or to act as barriers so that changes don't ripple down the line and affect earlier notes by mistake. Setting this initial marker means that as you drag the next note (by means of a Flex marker) the change will affect only the music between the Flex markers.

NOTE ▶ The Flex marker that you created will be visible only when you hover the Flex pointer over it. Also, the Flex pointer is only available in the top half of the Real Instrument editor. The lower half of the editor changes the pointer to a Crop pointer (crosshairs) for selecting portions of a region to copy or delete.

9 Move the Flex pointer to the beginning of the first note (just where the waveform grows significantly). Make sure that the pointer is in the upper half of the editor with the Flex pointer showing. Click to add a Flex marker at the beginning of the note.

10 Drag the second Flex marker (at the beginning of the note) to the playhead position marker.

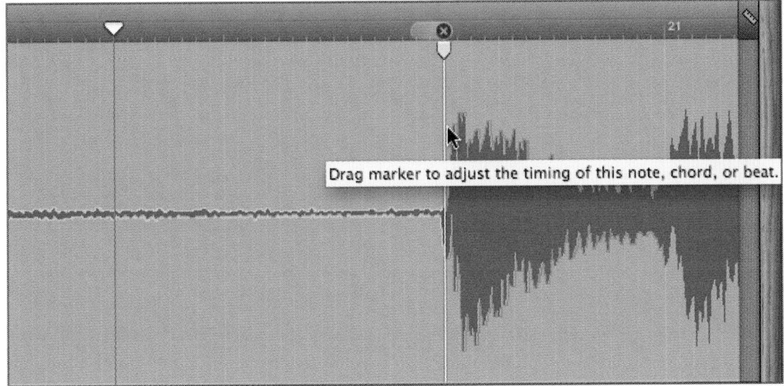

The note stretches until it starts at the first marker.

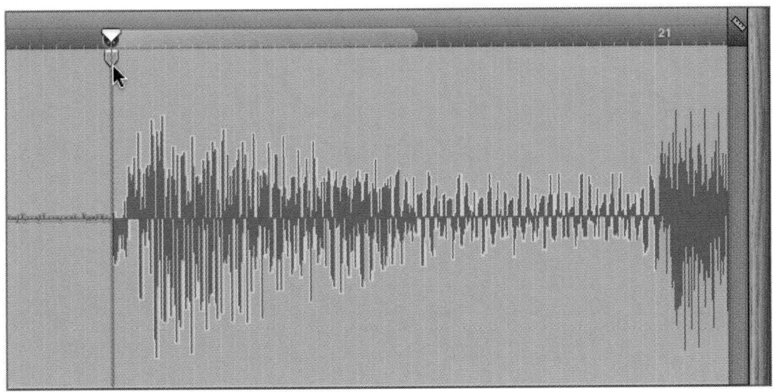

NOTE ▶ Stretching or moving a note using Flex editing does not change the note's pitch. The more you work with Flex Time editing, the easier it will be to use. Feel free to experiment with these tracks after the lesson. Also, to undo a Flex edit, click the (x) at the top of the Flex marker.

11 Press Command-E to close the editor, and play the end of the soloed track to hear the fixed note. When you are finished, unsolo the track, and save your progress.

Voila! Not only did you just complete a bit of musical magic, but you also have a basic understanding of how to use Flex Time to fix individual notes in the Real Instrument editor.

Naming Regions and Changing Track Icons

You'll perform two last housekeeping details for the Rock Kit (cowbell) region and Cowbell track before closing this project. First, let's change the name of the region to Cowbell. Second, you will change the icon for the Cowbell track to look like a cowbell. Though these changes don't affect the sound of the music, you'll find them helpful in organizing your projects.

1. If you didn't complete the previous exercises, open the project **05 Name and Icon**.
2. In the Cowbell track, double-click the Rock Kit region to open it in the Software Instrument editor.
3. Double-click the name of the region (Rock Kit) at the top of the editor to access the Name field. Type *Cowbell* in the Name field, and press Enter.

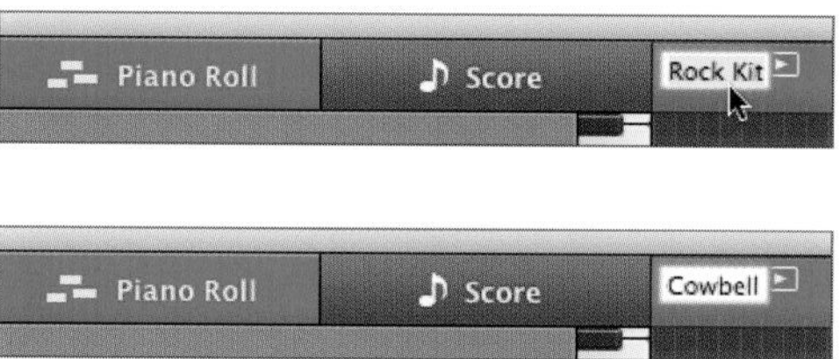

   The region name changes to Cowbell in the Timeline.

4. Hide the editor.
5. Double-click the Cowbell track header to show the Track Info pane for that track.

6 At the bottom of the Track Info pane, from the Track Icon menu (Drums icon), choose the Cowbell.

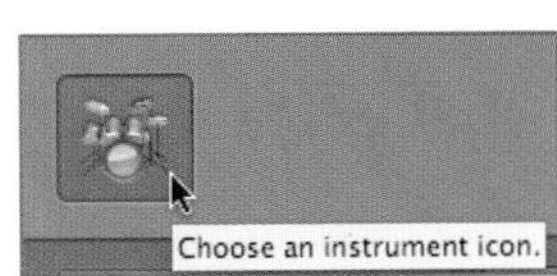

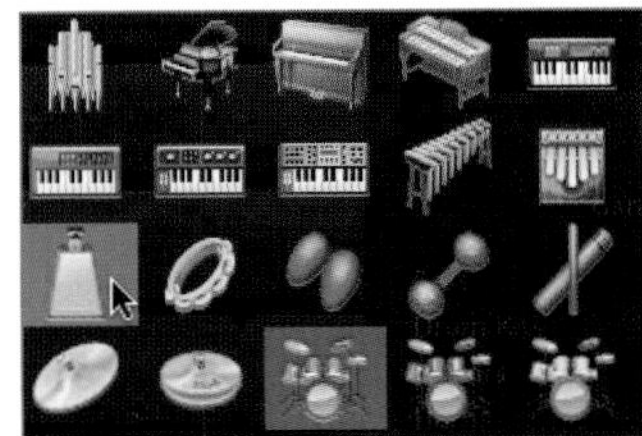

The Cowbell track icon now matches the track instrument, and the region within the track.

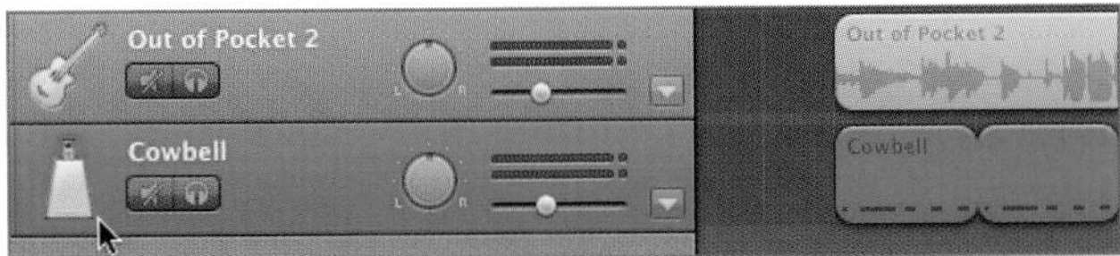

7 Press Command-I to hide the Track Info pane. Press C to hide the cycle region (if it is still showing). Save and close the project.

Project Practice

Now it's your turn to quantize and edit the cowbell recording that you performed in the previous lesson. Open the project **Magic Rock Song 05** (or whatever name you gave it at the end of Lesson 16). Quantize, trim, and loop your cowbell recording so that it repeats (in time) for the entire Verse 1. If you wish, try using the Groove Tracks to further enhance your cowbell region. When you are finished, change the name of the region in the editor, and change the track icon in the Track Info pane. Don't forget to save your finished project.

Working with Musical Notation

Traditionally, musicians rely on sheet music for writing and playing music. Whether you read musical notation or you are just learning, GarageBand includes a musical notation view for all of your Software Instrument tracks—and you can print them too!

In this exercise, you'll open a routine scales exercise that was partially orchestrated to demonstrate the simplicity of the orchestration process in GarageBand. Nearly every music student has at one time or another (perhaps daily) had to practice fingering by playing major scales (regardless of the instrument). Let's open the project and use the Score (musical notation) view in the editor to find and fix a missed note.

1 Open the project **06 Notation Scales** and save it to the My GarageBand Projects folder on your desktop. Keep the first two tracks soloed for now. You'll listen to them and the rest of the tracks shortly.

  The scales project opens with two soloed Grand Piano tracks. The remaining tracks have been temporarily muted for the beginning of this exercise. The overall project includes seven Software Instrument tracks, and one Real Instrument Horns track. The Kits track comprises Apple Loops from the GarageBand Loops library. The other tracks were recorded.

2 Double-click the first Grand Piano region in the Grand Piano 1 track to open it in the Software Instrument editor.

  The editor opens in Piano Roll view. Notice that the played notes (dashes) follow a very methodical pattern, as would be expected in a scales exercise.

  NOTE ▸ The term Piano Roll refers to a roll of paper containing punch hole data once used by player pianos.

3 Play the first few measures to hear the scales, and follow the playhead along the Piano Roll view in the editor. Pause playback, and press Return to return the playhead to the beginning of the song.

4 In the editor, click the Score button to change to Score (musical notation) view.

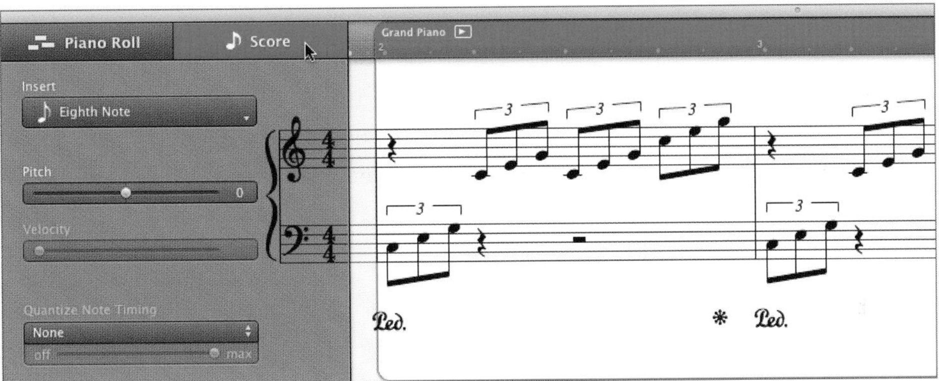

NOTE ► To print the sheet music (musical score) for a Software Instrument track, select the track, open the Score view in the editor, then choose File > Print.

5 Play through the 14th measure and then stop playback. Use the playhead or LCD as a guide.

Did you notice the *clam* (the missed note) in the 14th measure? If not, play the 14th measure again. It's hard to miss.

6 In the editor, play the 14th measure and pause playback when you hear the missed note (14.3.1.001). Hint: It's right in the middle of the measure and looks like two notes stuck together.

One of the two notes belongs in the middle of the 14th measure, the other does not. Because these are scales, it's easy to figure out which one doesn't belong because you won't see it played in the repeated scale notes to the left or right of the missed note in the musical notation.

7 Click each of the two notes to hear them. The first of the two notes (G) is the mistake.

8 Select the first note at 14.3.1.001, then press Delete to remove it.

9 Play the 14th measure again to hear the new, improved version. When you are finished, hide the editor and save your progress.

Now that you've learned how to view and edit notes in Score view, let's move on to adjusting the pace of the entire song.

TIP Not only can you select and delete notes in the Software Instrument editor, you can move a note up or down to change its pitch. In Score view, you can also Control-click (or right-click) a note to change the length of the note (quarter note, half note, and so on).

Adjusting Project Tempo

Tempo is pacing—the pulse or speed of the song—and it affects how the song sounds and feels. Software Instruments and Apple Loops automatically change tempo to match your project.

You may have noticed that the piano scales you worked with in the previous exercise played at an easy-going, medium pace. There's nothing wrong with that, especially if you are playing scales to warm up your fingers. However, those scales would be a lot more exciting if played at a faster tempo.

In this exercise, you'll listen to the orchestrated tracks with the slower version of the scales song, then speed up the tempo in the LCD and listen to the overall change.

1 Continue working with the Notation Scales project, or if you didn't complete the previous exercise, open **07 Tempo Scales** from the Lesson 18 folder.

2 Press C to show the cycle region. Unsolo both of the Grand Piano tracks, if necessary. Start playback and listen to the beginning of the project. Feel free to stop playback at any time.

NOTE ▶ The Horns track should remain muted for now. The horns are Real Instrument recordings and were recorded at a faster tempo. Real Instrument recordings may sound stretched or distorted when played at a tempo other than the originally recorded tempo.

Did you notice the slow, laid-back feel of the song? It sounds okay, but not dramatic. Time to give the musicians a shot of espresso and pick up the pace.

3 On the LCD, locate the LCD View menu (the Note icon). From the LCD View menu, choose Project.

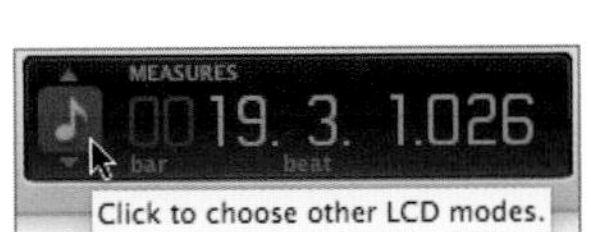

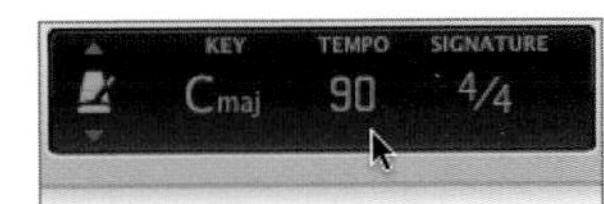

Stepping up the tempo of the piece is so easy. As you can see in the LCD, the current tempo is 90 beats per minute (bpm). You've already established that the current tempo feels a bit slow. A tempo of 120 bpm will be significantly faster and give the entire piece a more lively feel.

4 In the LCD, click the current tempo (90) and drag the Tempo slider up to 120.

5 Play the cycle region again at the new tempo. Unmute the Horns track to hear it played with the other tracks. When you are finished, save your progress.

Much better. Too bad you can't actually change the tempo of a live performance that easily. As far as the partial orchestration goes, I played a variation of the chord notes for each chord change on the Software Instrument strings to draw attention away from the piano scales. That way the scales became a rhythm part, rather than the lead. The point of the song was merely to demonstrate that if you can make a scales exercise sound dramatic, then you can use GarageBand to make *any* musical idea into a song.

TIP If you are planning to record a Software Instrument part that is difficult to play, or needs to be played faster than you can physically play it, record the part at a slower tempo, then speed up the project's tempo after you're done recording.

Showing the Project Notepad

A musician's workshop/studio would not be complete without a notepad to jot down ideas and notes to yourself—or others—as you create. GarageBand '11 includes a handy onscreen Notepad for each project.

1 Choose Window > Notepad, or press Command-Option-P to open the Notepad.

The Notepad appears as a floating window, and looks just like a standard yellow pad. If you don't like yellow, you can change the color or font using the controls at the top.

NOTE ▸ For this project, I used the Notepad to keep a breakdown of which chords/notes are played during which measures (bars). This type of guide is handy for orchestrating a piece. Feel free to use these notes to finish the project. You can play a MIDI keyboard, enable the Onscreen Keyboard, or use Musical Typing to record parts for the rest of the song. Have fun!

2 In the upper-left corner, click the Close button (the red X) to hide the Notepad.

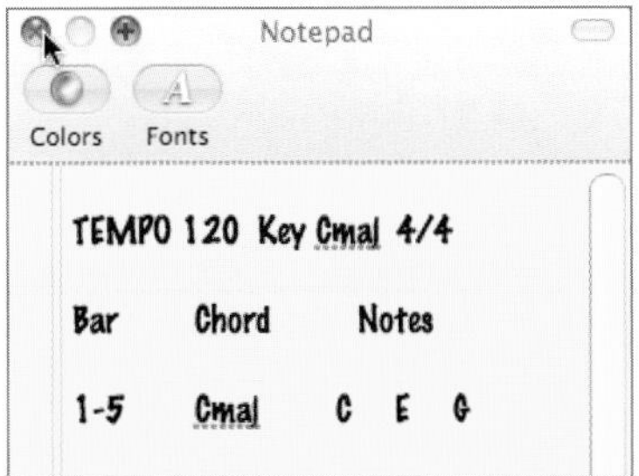

3 Save and close the project.

Working with Apple Loops

Using musical parts that can be looped over and over to build a song plays a major role in the foundation of GarageBand. In fact, GarageBand '11 includes over 1000 professional-quality Apple Loops.

Apple Loops are prerecorded music files that can be used to add drum beats, rhythm elements, and other repeating musical parts to a project. Loops contain musical patterns that can be repeated seamlessly and combined into new musical arrangements. You can extend a loop to fill any length of time in a project.

These loops are stored in the Loop Library. In the next series of exercises, you'll work with a song made almost entirely from Apple Loops. Along the way, you'll find and add a loop from the library, change a track's instrument, and transpose (change the key of) a loop to enhance the song.

NOTE ▸ If this is the first time that you have used the Loop browser in GarageBand, you will be prompted to download the additional Apple Loops and instruments. This may take a few minutes. If you would like to skip the download, you can move ahead to the next lesson. Otherwise, follow the download prompt when it appears.

1 Open the project **08 Apple Loops** from the Lesson 18 folder and save it—without iLife preview—to the My GarageBand Projects folder on your desktop.

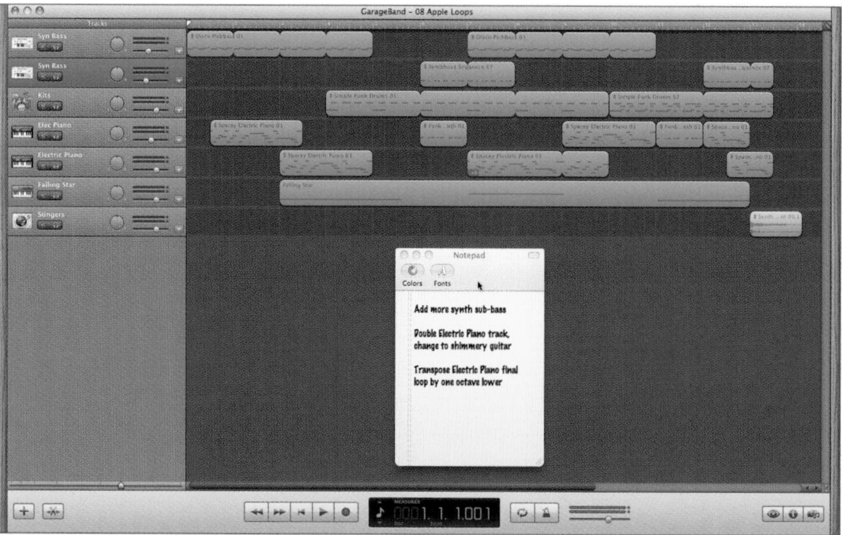

The song opens with seven tracks assembled with Apple Loops. The only recording is the Falling Star track, which is similar to the track that you recorded in Lesson 16. Notice that the Notepad is showing a list of three things that need to be done to finish arranging this song.

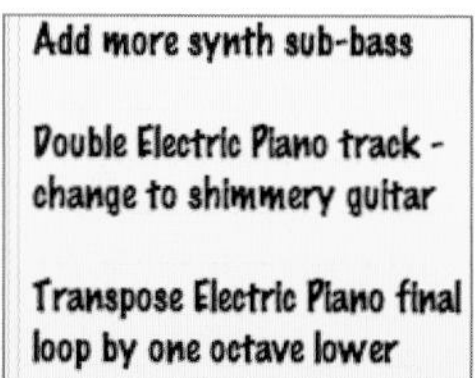

2 Move the Notepad to the lower-left corner of the window to move it out of the way, but keep it in view as you work.

3 Click anywhere in the GarageBand window to make it active and listen to the song.

What did you think? Perhaps you noticed that it sounds okay, but unfinished. You may have also noticed a gap in the music around the fifth measure. No problem, you're about to find the perfect loop to fill that musical void.

Browsing and Adding Loops to the Project

Now that you've heard the work in progress, let's get to work improving it. The first order of business is to add a low pulsing beat (sub-bass) to fill that musical gap around the fifth measure. Technically, you could try any type of instrument loop to hear how it fits; however, a sub-bass part would work nicely with this song.

To start, create a cycle region from the third to the seventh measures to make it easier to find a loop that works with that section of the song.

1 Press C to show the current cycle region.

   The yellow cycle region is the correct length (four measures) for this exercise, but in the wrong position.

2 Drag the middle of the cycle region to the right until it begins on the third measure (bar 3) and ends on the seventh (bar 7).

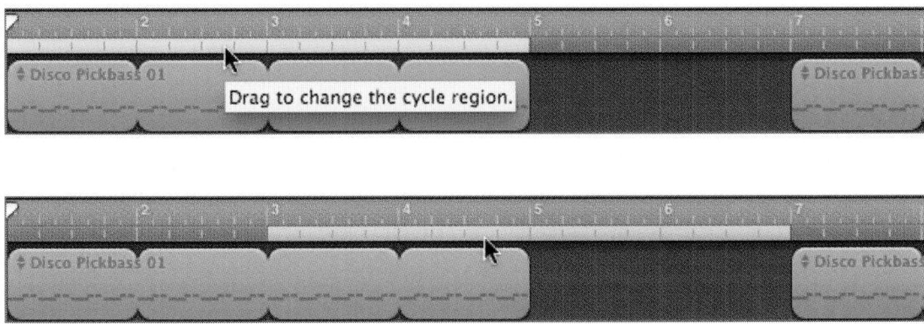

3 Play the cycle to hear the section of the song that needs another musical part. Your goal is to add a loop that has the same electronic energy as the rest of the song.

4 Press Command-L, or click the Loop Browser button (the eye icon) to open the Loop Browser.

5 At the top of the Loop Browser, click the Musical Buttons View button (the eighth-note icon) if it isn't already in that view. Click the Bass button to confine the search to bass parts.

These buttons help narrow the search of over 1000 loops to just those parts that match the selected button or buttons. In this case, the search has been narrowed to 183 items, as indicated at the bottom of the browser.

6 Press the Spacebar to start playback, then click one of the bass loops in the list to audition it with the video. Try auditioning several loops.

NOTE ▶ There are two types of Apple Loops: Real Instrument loops and Software Instrument loops. The color of a loop's icon indicates which type of loop it is. Real Instrument loops (which are recordings of actual instruments) have a blue icon with an audio waveform. Software Instrument loops have a green icon with a musical note. The beats column shows the length of the loop.

It's funny how so many loops seem to fit the song. That's because Apple Loops have been programmed in perfect musical time. Plus, they automatically change key and tempo to match the current song. However, let's dig a little deeper to find the synth-bass sound to complete the section.

7 Scroll down to **Synthbass Sequence 01** and audition the loop with the music. Stop playback when you are finished.

This loop will sound great, and it's 16 beats (4 measures) in length. Perfect! Of course, if a loop isn't long enough, you can always extend (loop) it to make it as long as necessary.

To add a loop to the project, you can drag a loop to an existing track or to the empty space below the tracks. By dragging the loop below the existing track, you'll automatically create a new track named after the loop instrument. Let's try it.

8 Drag the **Synthbass Sequence 01** loop from the Loop Browser to the empty space below the Stingers track in the Timeline. Place the loop so that it starts at the beginning of the cycle region (bar 3).

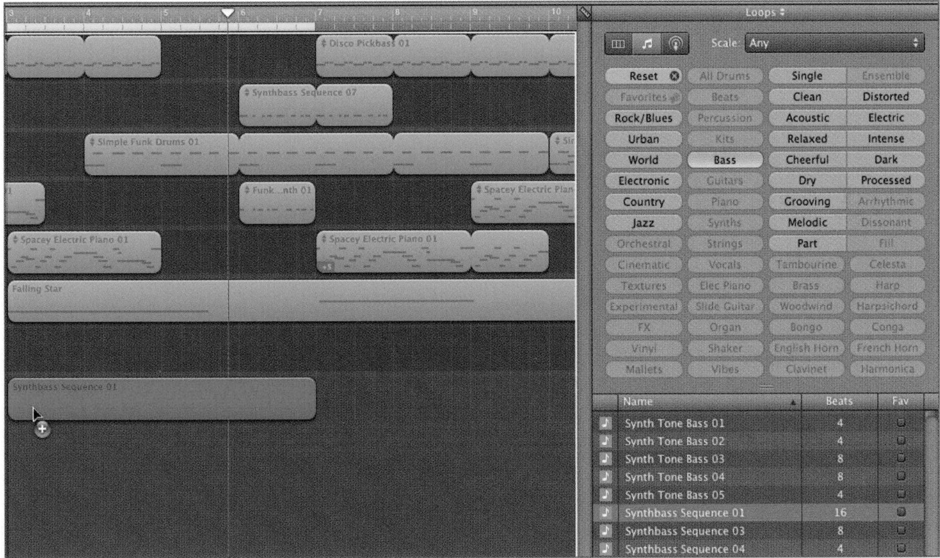

TIP Use the alignment guide (the dark vertical line that appears when you add a loop to the timeline) to align the loop to the desired position.

The loop is added to the Timeline and lasts for four measures.

9 Press C to hide the cycle region, and play the song from the beginning to hear the new synth bass part.

What do you think? It's cool, but too loud.

10 Drag the Volume slider on the new Syn Bass track header to lower the volume. A value of around –8.0 dB ought to do the trick for now. You can later finesse the levels of all the tracks.

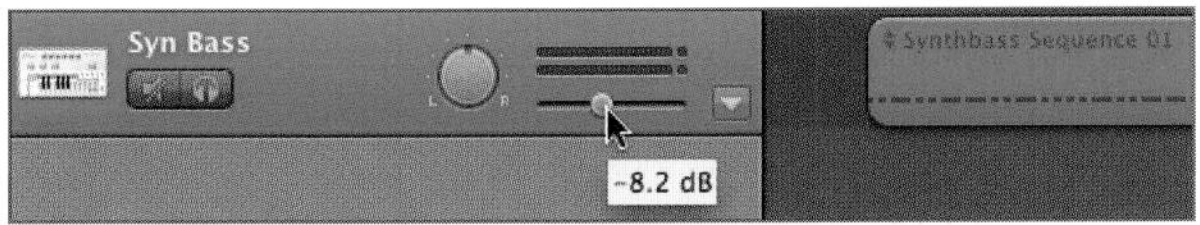

11 Play the beginning of the song again to hear how it sounds with the adjusted volume. Press Command-L to hide the Loop Browser and save your progress.

Excellent! The new synth bass part works so well you should use it again later in the song.

TIP You can save your edited recordings as loops in the Loop Library by selecting the region and choosing Edit > Add to Loop Library. You will also be prompted to tag the loop with search metadata such as the type of instrument, style, or genre that will group it with other similar loops in the library.

Arranging Loops and Tracks in the Timeline

You can copy, paste, and delete regions in the Timeline as easily as editing text in a word processor. As a matter of fact, GarageBand uses the same shortcut keys for those editing features as most other applications. In this exercise, you'll copy the Synthbass Sequence 01 region and paste it in the same track so that it starts at the ninth measure (bar 9). Then you'll move the entire track up in the track list so that it starts below the other two Syn Bass tracks.

1 Click the **Synthbass Sequence 01** region at the bottom of the Timeline to select it, if necessary.

2 Choose Edit > Copy, or press Command-C.

3 Move the playhead to the beginning of the ninth measure (bar 9).

4 Click the lowest Syn Bass track header, at the bottom of the Timeline, to make sure that it is selected. The selected track header appears colored green or blue depending on the type of track instrument, while the deselected tracks remain gray.

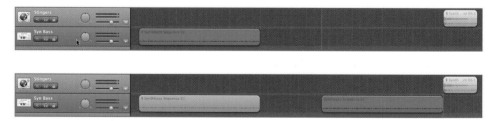

5 Choose Edit > Paste, or press Command-V to paste the loop at the beginning of the ninth measure in the Syn Bass track.

NOTE ▶ Copy and paste always applies to the selected regions and selected tracks. If you accidentally paste the region into the wrong track, press Command-Z to undo the error, and try again.

6 Play the project to see and hear the results.

Sounds great. Now let's move the track up in the list to keep the synth bass parts together.

7 Drag the new Syn Bass track header upward and release it below the other two Syn Bass tracks.

Now that the new part is finished, it's time to move to the next item on the Notepad list.

Duplicating Tracks

One of the most exciting things about Software Instruments parts is that they will change to any Software Instrument that you assign to the track. For this exercise, you'll duplicate the second Electric Piano track, drag copies of the parts to the duplicate track, and change the track instrument to a guitar. Doubling tracks like this is a sure way to "fatten" the sound and make a particular musical line stand out.

1 If you didn't complete the previous exercises, open the project **09 Double Track** and save it to your folder. Close the Notepad if it is still showing.

2 Select the second Electric Piano track header (the third track from the bottom).

TIP When you select a track, the regions within that track are also selected. You can press the Up and Down Arrow keys to change which track is selected (Up Arrow selects the previous higher track, and Down Arrow selects the next lower track).

3 Choose Edit > Duplicate, or press Command-D to duplicate the selected track.

A new duplicate Electric Piano track appears. Now you'll duplicate the regions and drag them to the new track.

4 Select the original (middle) Electric Piano track to automatically select all of the regions within that track.

5 Option-drag the selected regions down to the same position on the new Electric Piano track.

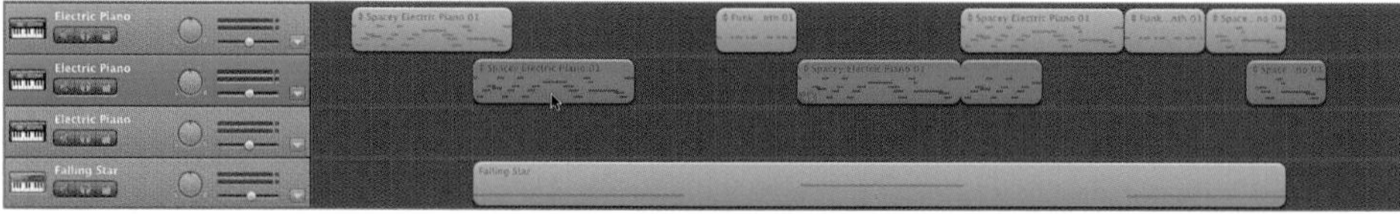

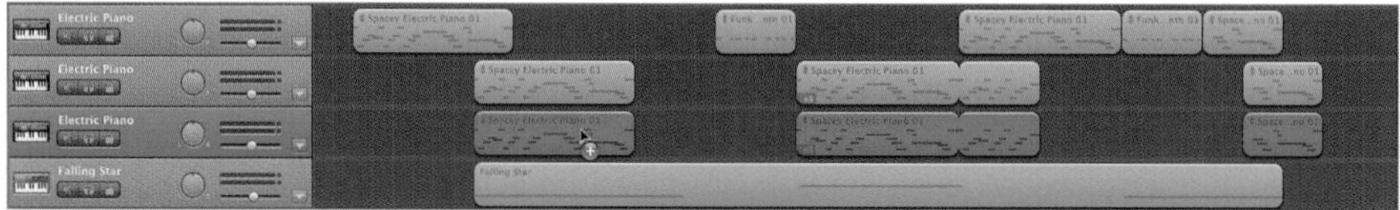

Now that you've duplicated the track and regions, let's change the track instrument.

6 Double-click the new (lowest) Electric Piano track header to show the Track Info pane for that track.

7 In the Track Info pane, select Guitars as the instrument category (left column) and Nylon Shimmer as the specific instrument sound (right column).

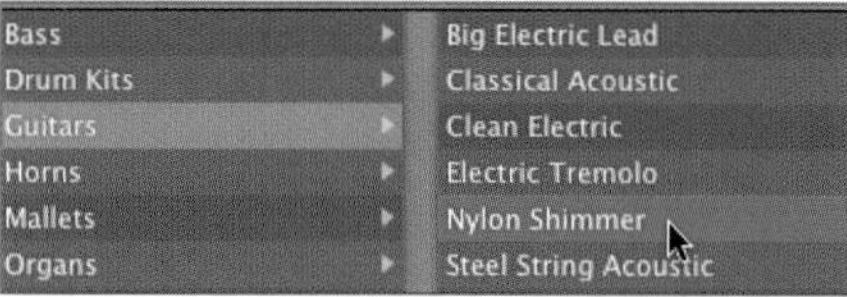

NOTE ▶ You may see a dialog to warn you that you're changing the track instrument. If so, click Continue.

8 Notice that the track header changes to Nylon Shimmer. Play the song and listen to the newly doubled tracks.

   The part is really working, but could stand to be a little louder in the mix.

9 Drag the Volume sliders on the lowest Electric Piano and Nylon Shimmer tracks to zero (0.0 dB). Setting the tracks to 0.0 dB plays the loops at the default level (loudness). Feel free to adjust the levels of the other tracks to taste.

You have successfully doubled the part, which sounds great in the song. Now all the tracks need is a little finessing.

Panning Tracks

Not only is it important to adjust the volume of a track, you also need to consider the position in the stereo field that the track is perceived in the listener's ear.

The Pan Wheel controls the left-to-right placement of a track within the stereo field. The *Pan* in Pan Wheel stands for *panoramic*. A panoramic photograph is an image that includes everything you can see without turning your head. A stereo field is everything you can hear from the far left to the far right, without turning your head.

Imagine a panoramic photograph of the Rocky Mountains with a train cutting through the far-left side of the image. Visually, you place the train on the left side of your field of view. You would also place the sound of the train on the far-left side of the stereo field.

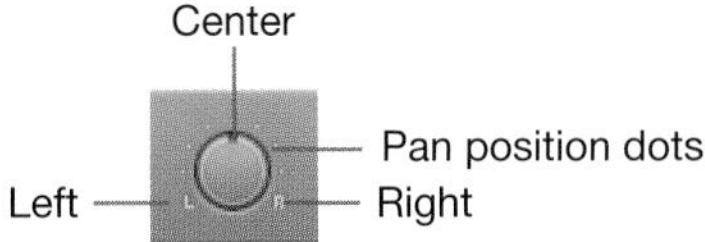

By default, all of the tracks in GarageBand start with the pan position set to the center (0). When at center pan position, a sound is heard equally out of both speakers as though it's directly in front of you in the middle of the audio space.

Your goal is to adjust the pan position of the doubled tracks so that they are separated acoustically.

This exercise works best if you're listening through headphones, so take a minute and put on your headset before you start. Make sure your headphones have the right speaker (R) on the right ear and the left speaker (L) on the left ear.

1 Solo the Electric Piano and Nylon Shimmer tracks that you doubled earlier.

2 On the Electric Piano track, click the second dot to the left of center, –32 degrees (the 10 o'clock position) on the Pan Wheel.

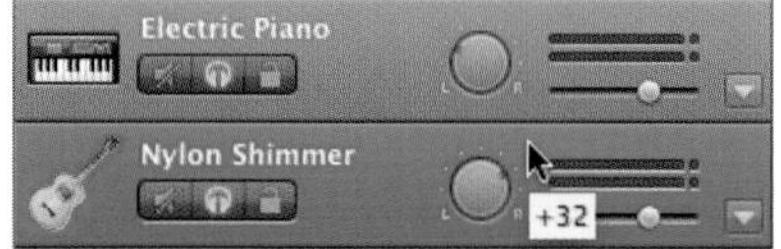

3 Pan the Nylon Shimmer track in the opposite position, the second dot to the right of center, +32 degrees (the 2 o'clock position).

TIP You can set specific increments on the Pan Wheel by dragging up or down accordingly. To quickly reset the volume and pan controls to their default settings, Option-click the controls. The default volume level is 0 dB, and the default pan position is Center.

4 Play the soloed tracks to hear them in the stereo field. They should each sound like they are coming from different positions on stage. Unsolo the tracks to hear them in the mix with the other tracks. Save your progress.

Now that you have adjusted the volume, and panned the tracks, you're ready for the last order of business on the Notepad.

Transposing a Region in the Editor

Transposing music means to change the key and pitch. This is often done to more closely match a song to a vocalist's range, or with a lead instrument. In this case, you'll simply change the pitch of a region so that it plays the same notes, just an octave lower.

Up to this point you have fixed the timing of regions in the editor, but you haven't actually changed their pitch. Now is your chance. As the Notepad suggested, your goal is to lower the last region in the doubled part by one full octave. Let's start with the Nylon Shimmer track.

1 Double-click the last region in the Nylon Shimmer track to show it in the editor.

2 Select the bass region in the last region in the Nylon Shimmer track to show it in the editor. The Software Instrument region appears in the Score view, in the editor.

NOTE ▶ A common scale has twelve notes, including sharps and flats, before a note repeats an octave higher or lower. To play the same note one octave higher, you simply change the pitch to 12. To play it one octave lower, you would change the pitch to –12. Changing the pitch of a musical part is called *transposing*.

3 In the editor, drag the Pitch slider to the left until it reads –12.

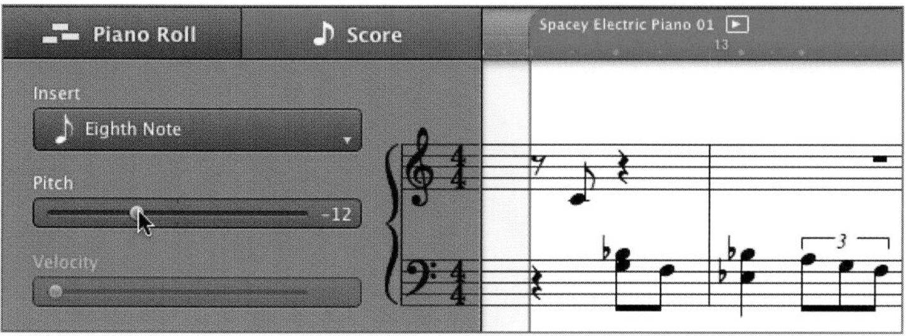

The musical notation adjusts accordingly, and a small –12 appears in the lower-left corner of the region that you transposed. Notice the small –5 in the previous region on the doubled tracks. That part was transposed to make it sound less repetitive.

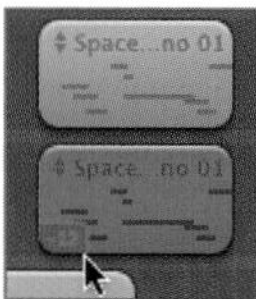

4 Repeat the process to transpose the same part in the Electric Piano track to –12.

5 Press Command-E to hide the editor. Unsolo the tracks and play the song to hear the finished piece. When you're finished, save your progress.

Congratulations. You now have hands-on experience working with many of the powerful and exciting editing, fixing, arranging, and mixing features in GarageBand '11. Have fun applying what you have learned to your own projects.

Lesson Review

1. Where do you find the pan and volume controls for a track?
2. What methods are available in GarageBand '11 for fixing timing issues in recorded regions?
3. How can you view the musical notation for a Software Instrument region?
4. Where can you change the musical icon for a track?
5. Can you adjust the tempo of a song *after* recording musical parts?
6. How do you transpose (change the key of) a region?

Answers

1. The pan and volume controls for each track are located in the Track Mixer.
2. GarageBand '11 includes quantizing, Groove Tracks, and Flex Time editing for fixing timing of regions or individual notes.
3. Double-click the region to show it in the Software Instrument editor, and change the view to Score to see the musical notation. Piano Roll view shows the notes as dashes.

4. You can change a track's musical icon in the Track Info pane.
5. Yes, you can adjust the project tempo in the Tempo menu on the LCD. Software Instrument recordings and Apple Loops follow project tempo changes without changing the key or quality of the sound.
6. To transpose a region, open it in the editor, then drag the Pitch slider in the editor controls.

19

Lesson Files
ATS iLife11 Book Files > Lesson 19 > 01 RootsRockArrange, 02 RootsRockEffects, 03 RootsRockCurves, 04 RootsRockFinal, 05 PodcastTheme, 06 Podcast, 07 PodcastArt, 08 PodcastFinal, 09 TouchPetsScore

Time
This lesson takes approximately 60 minutes to complete.

Goals
Work with the arrange track

Add effects and automation to a song

Prepare a project for iTunes

Evaluate a song's output

Share a finished song with iTunes

Finish a podcast

Edit podcast artwork and add a URL link

Export a movie project to disk

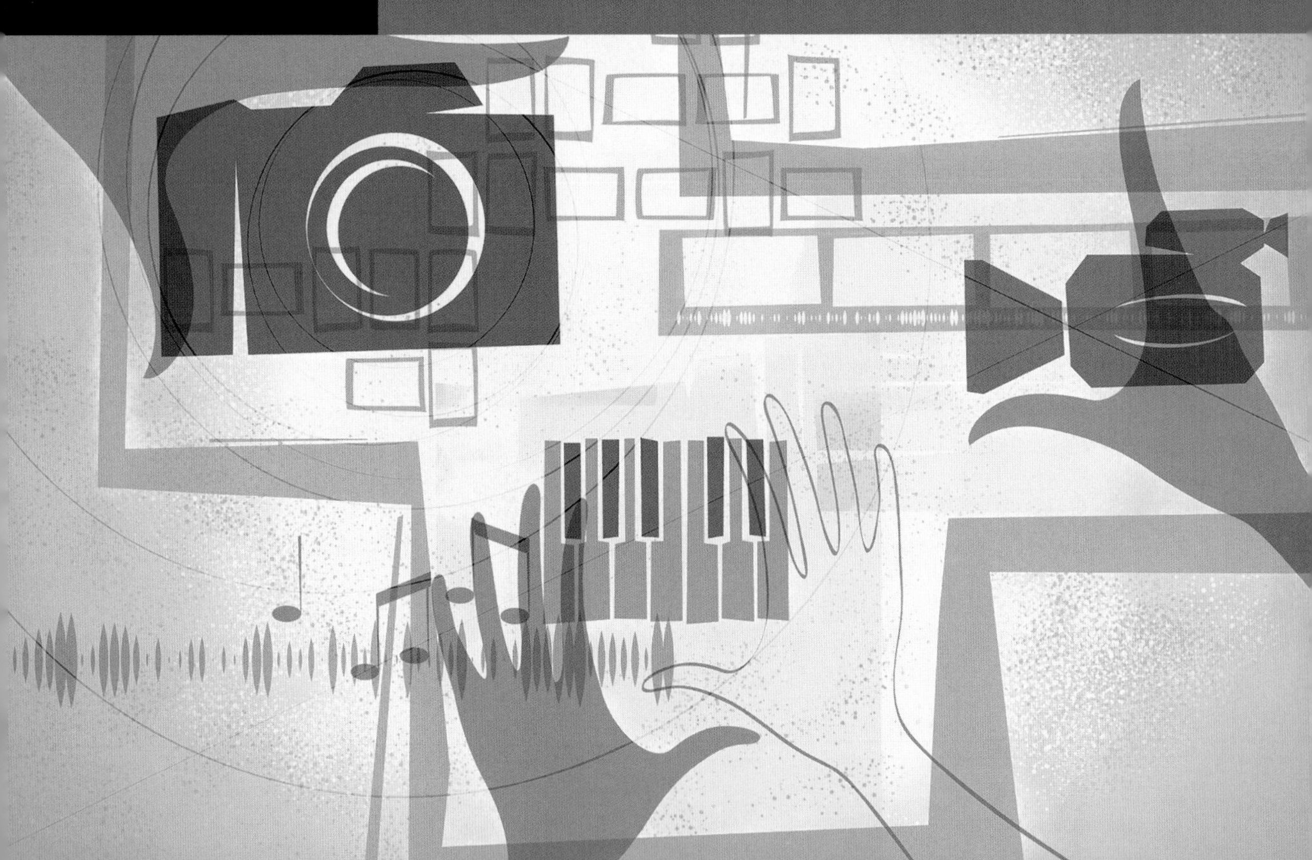

Lesson **19**

Finishing and Sharing Projects

Now that you know the basics of recording, arranging, and mixing your projects in GarageBand, you're ready to learn some finishing techniques. When your projects are finished, you can share them with other iLife applications and export them to iTunes, where they can be downloaded to your iPod or burned to a CD.

All the iLife '11 applications are designed to work together seamlessly. You can write music in GarageBand and export your songs to iTunes; score your iMovie video and export it as a QuickTime movie or send it to iDVD; send your finished podcast to iWeb to publish on the Internet; or create a whole playlist of original songs to be shared with any of your applications.

The focus of this lesson is learning how to finish and prepare your GarageBand projects to share with other iLife applications.

Finishing a Song

Even after you've mixed and refined your tracks, you may have to answer several more questions to finish a song. First, does the song need to be lengthened or shortened? Would the song benefit from some added effects to the tracks, or to the overall song? Finally, does it need some automation—adjustment to levels within the tracks? The Roots Rock song that you will be working with in the upcoming exercises actually needs all three of these finishing touches before you share it with iTunes. As you follow along, you'll not only see how easy it is to apply these advanced techniques, but you'll also hear the difference in the final song.

Let's get started.

1 Open the project Lesson 19 > **01 RootsRockArrange** and save it—without iLife preview—to the My GarageBand Projects folder on your desktop.

2 Play the project once to hear the song as it is, and then stop playback.

Chances are you won't hear anything obviously *wrong* with the song. The trick to making great-sounding music is to recognize what *is* working, and know how to improve what isn't. In this case, the song needs to be a little longer to fit the title sequence of a video project. Also, a few of the instruments could use some effects to help them stand out in the mix.

Using the Arrangement Track

Most songs are arranged in distinct sections such as introduction, verse, and chorus. The Arrangement track—which appears below the time ruler—makes it easier to see these parts of your song and to move, duplicate, or delete those sections at any time.

In this exercise, you'll use the Arrangement track to duplicate the chorus section of the song and extend the overall length of the piece.

1 Click the Chorus arrangement region located at the top of the GarageBand window. The Chorus arrangement region brightens to show that it's been selected.

NOTE ▶ If the Arrangement track isn't visible, choose Track > Show Arrange Track.

2 Option-drag toward the right to create a cloned version of the section. Place the Chorus copy region between Verse 2 and the Outro section.

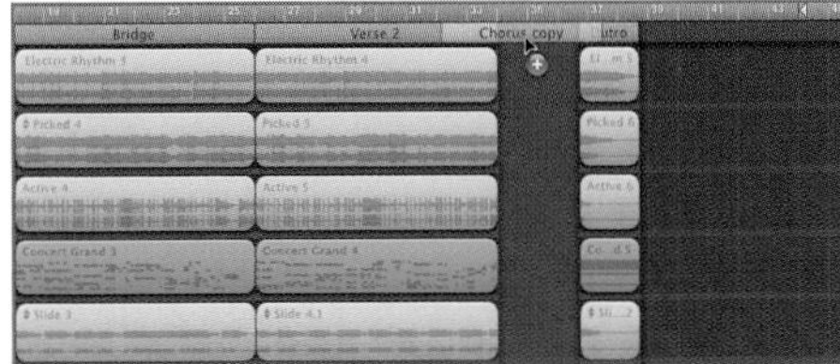

NOTE ▶ If you moved the original chorus section rather than a duplicate, press Command-Z to undo your work, and then try again. Be sure to hold down the Option key before dragging the Chorus section to duplicate as you drag.

Because the song's chorus is the same part, you can change the name to remove the word "copy" from the second chorus.

3 Double-click the Chorus Copy arrangement region's title. Change the title for the region to *Chorus*.

4 Play the last half of the song to hear the modified ending.

Well, it's almost there. The song is indeed longer, but the lead guitar in the Slide track cuts off abruptly as the song progresses from Verse 2 to the Chorus. Fortunately, there is an easy fix. You can simply duplicate the piece of slide guitar in the Outro region and place it at the beginning of the second chorus.

5 Option-drag the Slide section in the Outro region and place the duplicate copy at the beginning of the second Chorus section.

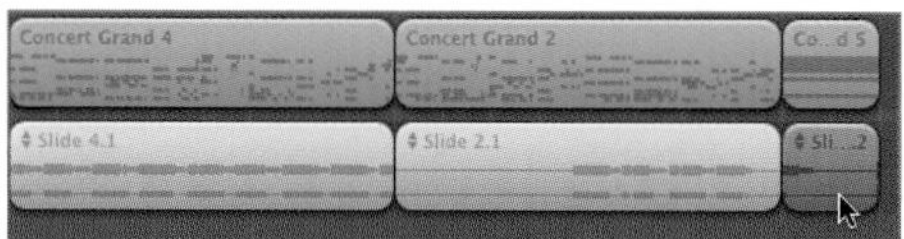

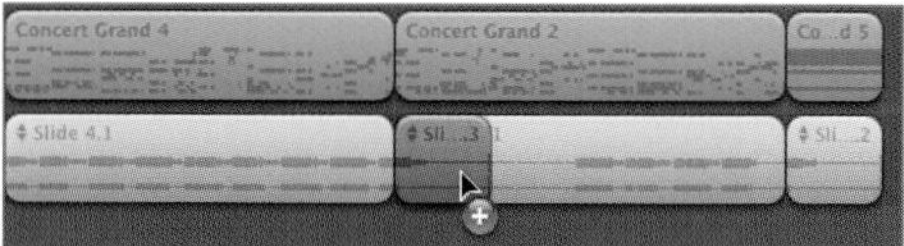

Make sure that you place the duplicate over the silence at the beginning of the chorus and do not overlap the end of the Verse 2 region. If you make a mistake, choose Edit > Undo and try again.

6 Play that section again to hear the finished arrangement. When you are done, press Command-S to save your progress.

TIP To add a new region, click the plus sign in the Mixer area of the Arrange track.

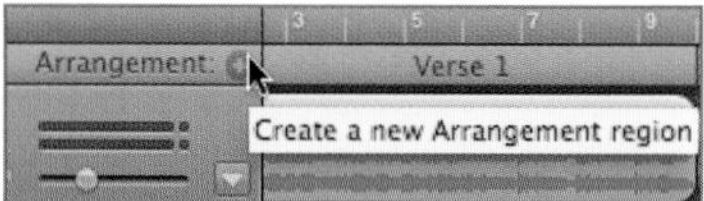

Adding Effects to a Track

Effects are the secret to perfecting your sound. GarageBand is fully loaded with professional-quality effects. You can choose from the effects presets included with each Real Instrument and Software Instrument, or customize the effects and save your own preset.

Let's add some effects to bring out the Slide track and bring the Grand Piano forward in the mix. You'll start by soloing the track you're working with and creating a cycle region to hear how the track sounds before and after you adjust the effects.

1 If you didn't finish the previous exercises, open Lesson 19 > **02 RootsRockEffects** to catch up.

2 Select the Slide track and press S to solo the track. Then, press C to open the cycle region.

3 Create a cycle region over the Verse 2 region if the cycle region isn't positioned over that section of the song.

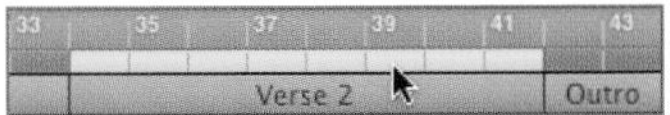

4 Press Command-I or double-click the Slide track header to open the Track Info pane.

5 If the Track Info pane is hiding at the end of the song, drag the horizontal scroll bar at the bottom of the Timeline toward the right until you can see the Verse 2 section.

6 In the Track Info pane, click the Edit tab to display the track's effects.

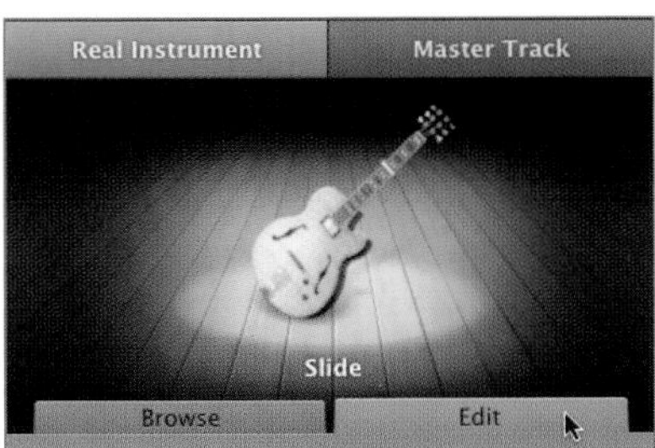

Each track includes Noise Gate, Compressor, and Visual EQ effects, along with four empty effects slots.

NOTE ▶ If you'd like to add more effects to a track, you can click an empty slot and choose another effect.

The two Sends sliders near the bottom of the Track Info pane control the amount of the track's output that is sent to the master Echo and Reverb effects. Notice that the blue LEDs on the Echo and Reverb sends indicate those effects are active. For this exercise, you'll use the Compressor, which can modify the instruments' frequencies to improve the sound in the mix.

7 Click the LED on the Compressor to make it active (blue).

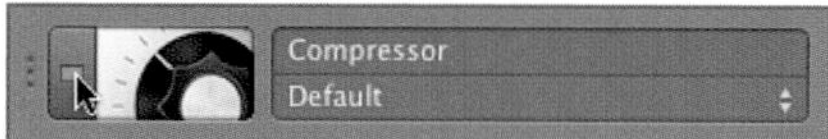

8 Click the Presets menu, currently set to Default, to see the Compressor presets, and choose Electric Guitar Smoothen.

A dialog warns you that you're changing the track's instrument setting.

9 Click Continue and start playback to hear the sound of the Slide guitar with the new Compressor setting. Press S to unsolo the track and hear it with the other tracks. Click the Compressor LED to turn off the effect and hear the guitar without it. Click the LED again to turn it back on.

What a difference a little compression can make! The guitar sound really feels like a lead instrument now. In fact, it sounds so good that you may want to turn it down a bit in the mix. It isn't uncommon to need to tweak volume levels after effects are applied.

10 Lower the volume of the Slide track to around -4.8, and then pause playback.

11 Select the Grand Piano track. Press S to solo the track. Then turn on the Compressor effect for the Grand Piano track in the Track Info pane.

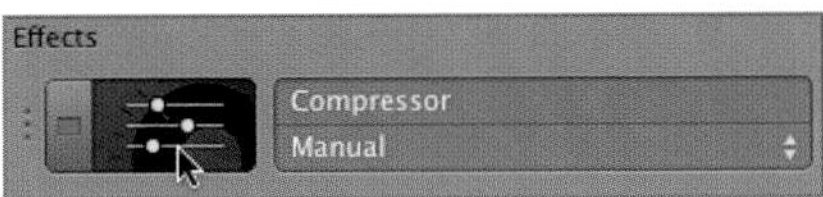

12 Click the rectangle next to the LED to open the manual controls for the current effect.

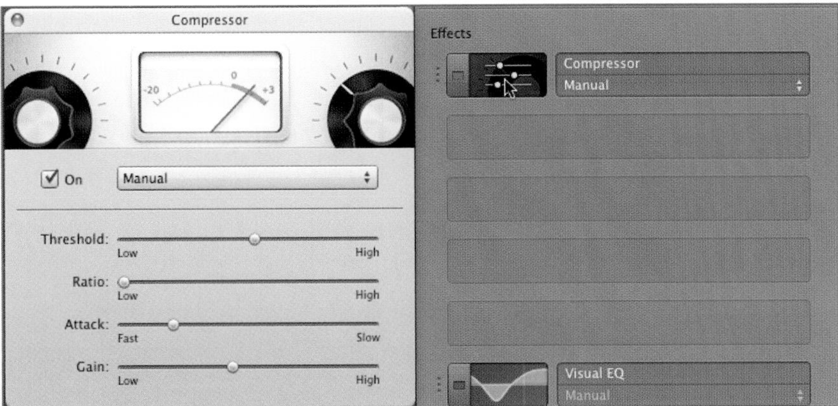

The Compressor controls window appears. You could manually adjust the parameters here, or add a preset. Feel free to experiment with the controls before choosing the preset in the next step.

13 In the Compressor controls window, from the Preset menu, choose Piano Upfront. Click Continue in the warning dialog, and then listen to the Grand Piano track with the Compressor.

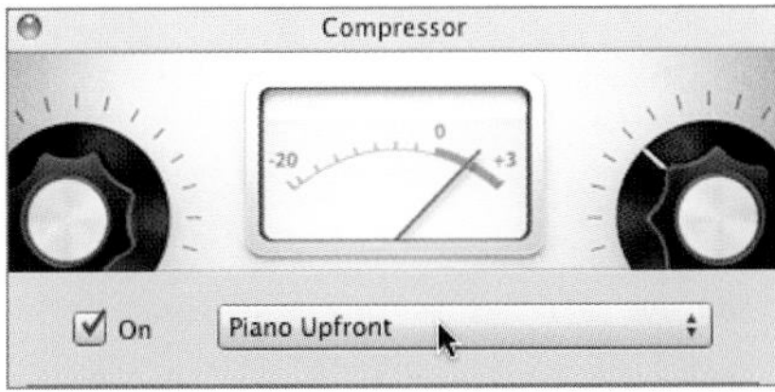

14 Unsolo the Grand Piano track and listen to it with the song. When you're finished, hide the cycle region, pause playback, and close the Compressor controls window.

Once again, the results are quite extraordinary. For the first time, you can really hear the piano in the song and it doesn't step all over the lead guitar. As you can plainly hear, effects such as the Compressor presets can really make your music sound better.

NOTE ▶ If you manually adjust an effect, you'll see a dialog asking if you want to save the instrument settings. If you think you'll use those settings again, go ahead and save.

Adding Effects to the Overall Song

To add an effect to a specific track, you used the Track Info pane for that track. The Track Info pane for the Master track shows the effects settings for the overall project.

Let's open the Master Track Info pane and add an effects preset to the entire song.

1 Press Command-I, or click the Track Info button, if it isn't already visible.

2 In the upper-right corner of the Track Info pane, select Master Track to show the Master Track effects.

You can add and modify effects in the Edit pane of the Master track just as you work with effects for an individual track. You can also click the Browse tab to choose a preset that fits the song.

3 In the Track Info pane for the Master track, click the Browse tab.

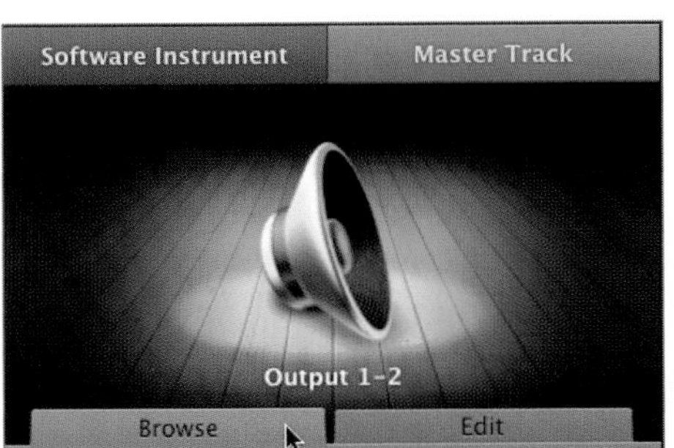

4 Choose Rock as the Master category, and then choose Rock Basic as the specific master preset. If a dialog appears, click Continue to apply the preset.

5 Start playback. While the song is playing, press the Down Arrow to hear other Rock preset effects applied to the song. Stop playback when you've selected an effect.

Did you find a favorite preset? They all sound good, but the Classic Rock and LA Rock presets stand out. You can select whichever preset you like best.

NOTE ▶ The master presets are combinations of EQ and Compressor effects. You can turn the effects on and off, or modify them under the Edit tab of the Track Info pane, just like the effects applied to a track.

6 Press Command-I to hide the Master Track Info pane. Now that you've finished your mix and added effects, it's a good idea to update the name of the project.

7 Choose File > Save As and change the name of the project to *RootsRockFX*. Close the project.

Your mix sounds great. The last step is to adjust the volume of the tracks dynamically so that they raise or lower at different points of the song.

Working with Volume Curves

So far, you have adjusted the volume and pan levels for individual tracks using the controls in the track mixer. This method is great for setting one volume or pan level for an entire track. But what if you want the level to change during the song? Dynamically changing pan, volume, or effect levels over time is called *automation*.

In the next exercise, you'll change volume within a track by using control points along the volume automation curve.

First, let's check out a version of the song that already has a prominent set of automation curves.

1 Open the project Lesson 19 > **03 RootsRockCurves** and save it to the My GarageBand Projects folder without iLife preview. The project opens with the volume curves visible on both guitar tracks.

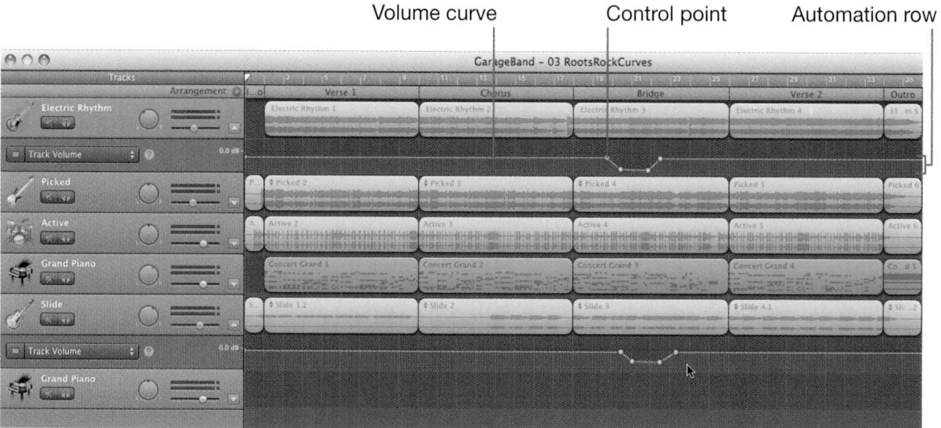

The volume curve appears as a line below a track in the automation row. By default, the volume curve isn't actually a curve. It's a straight line that represents the steady volume of the track. By adding control points, you can bend the curve to fade levels up or down.

2 Press C to show the cycle region, and play the Bridge section of the song. As it plays, watch the playhead travel along the volume curve/line below the Electric Rhythm and Slide tracks. As the levels in the curve dip down, so does the volume of those tracks.

When the control points on the guitar tracks were at their lowest level, you may have noticed that the Grand Piano became the lead instrument. Then the guitar parts faded back in and joined the piano to finish the bridge.

NOTE ▶ Carefully fading tracks up and down to shift the acoustic focus is a music producer's trick for enhancing and finishing a song mix.

Now that you've seen and heard volume curves in action, it's time to try them for yourself. First, you need to show the volume curve.

Showing Volume Curves

You have two ways to show the volume curve for a track:

- Press A to show the volume automation curve for the selected track.
- In the track header, click the triangle in the lower-right corner.
- Let's show the Volume curve for the Grand Piano track.

1 On the Grand Piano track header, click the triangle in the lower-right corner.

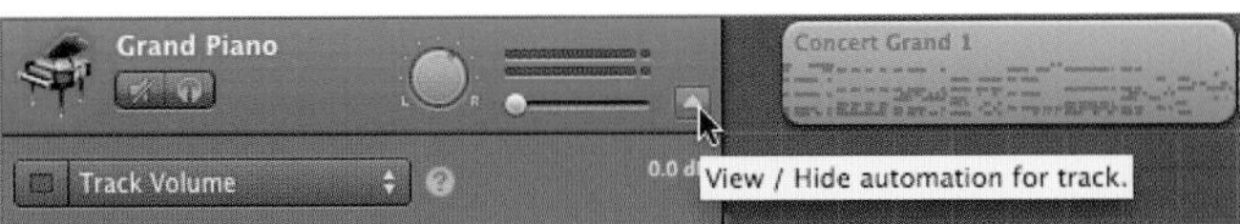

The volume curve appears as a green line in the automation row below the Grand Piano track. Curves are color coordinated with the track instrument: Real Instrument (blue) or Software Instrument (green).

2 Drag the Grand Piano track volume slider all the way to the left and watch the volume curve move.

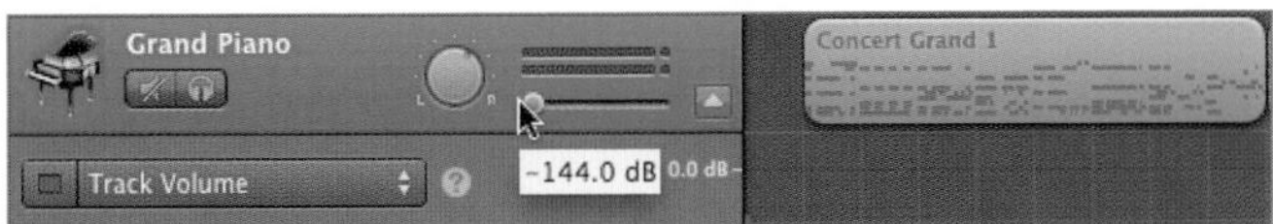

As you can see, the volume slider alters the volume curve. However, once you turn on the volume curve (automation), the volume slider will become inactive and merely show/hide the track curve.

3 Option-click the Grand Piano track volume slider to reset the slider to the default position.

NOTE ▶ If the volume curve does not move to the default position, click the Grand Piano track volume slider to apply the new position to the volume curve.

4 On the Grand Piano track header, click the LED on the Track curve menu to turn on the track curves.

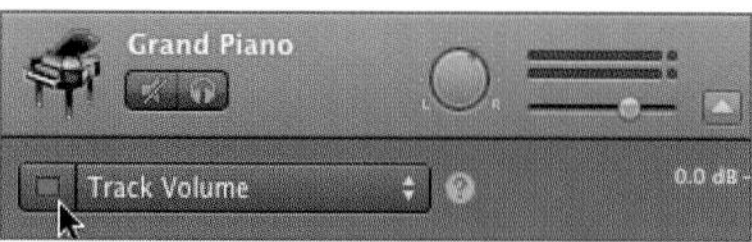

Adding and Adjusting Control Points

Now that you can see the volume curve, you can adjust it using control points. Control points set a fixed volume level on the volume curve at a specific point along the Timeline. Changing a control point's position allows you to bend the volume curve, which raises or lowers the volume between the control points.

Control points are often used to fade music in or out. Slowly increasing the song volume from silence is *fading in* the music; slowly reducing the song volume to silence is *fading out* the music.

Dynamic volume change between control points

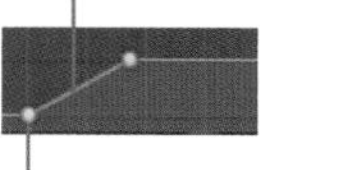

Control point at lowest volume level

Your goal for this song is to duck (lower) the volume level of the Grand Piano at the beginning of the Bridge section so the guitar parts become more prominent. Then, fade in the piano part again toward the middle of the Bridge while the guitar parts are ducked (lowered). Acoustically, this technique will change which instrument parts stand out during the bridge—first the guitars, then the piano, then all three parts play together equally to finish the Bridge.

You need two control points to change the volume dynamically. The first control point sets the starting volume level. The second control point sets the new volume level. You can add a control point by clicking the volume curve, and you can move it by dragging the point.

Let's add some control points to duck the Grand Piano track at the beginning of the Bridge.

1 On the Grand Piano track, click the volume curve to set a point at the beginning of the Bridge section (18.1.1.001).

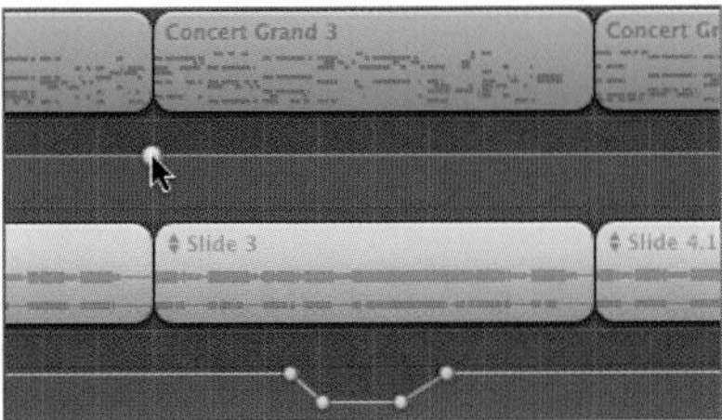

2 Add another control point at the beginning of the 21st measure (21.1.1.001).

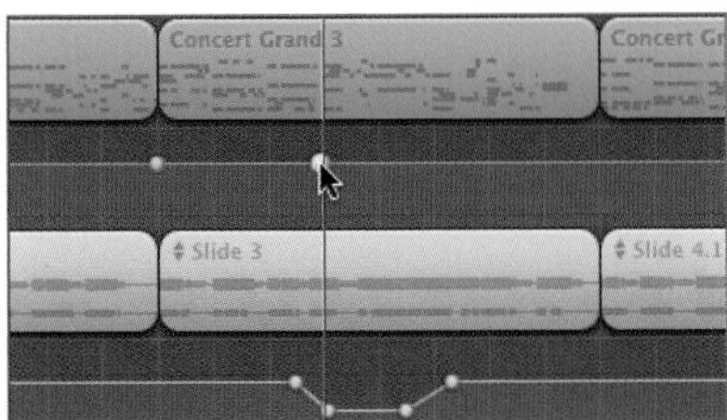

TIP If you are trying to add or move control points at specific places, use the playhead and the LCD as guides. Otherwise, you can simply guess and use the ruler to place points in the general positions.

The first control point that you set marks the beginning of the ducked piano section, while the second control point marks the end of the ducked section. Notice that the second control point is placed when the Slide guitar volume curve is at its lowest level. Remember, these parts are taking turns in the spotlight, so as one is lowered, the other should be raised.

3 Add another control point at the beginning of the 20th measure (20.1.1.001). Once you've added the point, drag it down to around -40 dB.

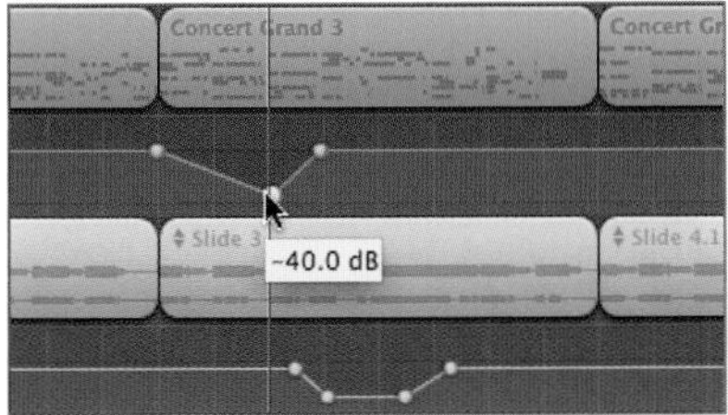

There's no need to silence the track by lowering it all the way to -144 dB. Ducking means to lower the level to change the acoustic focus to a different track, or to give another track priority.

NOTE ▶ GarageBand includes automatic controls for ducking entire tracks. You will see them in action shortly in the "Finishing a Podcast" section.

4 Add a final control point just to the right of the first one, and lower it to -40 dB.

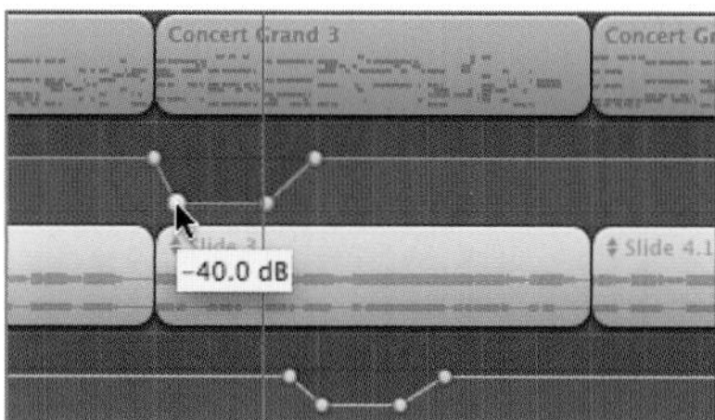

5 Play the Bridge of the song to hear the piano part duck in the beginning, and the guitar parts duck near the middle.

6 Press C to turn off the cycle region. Select the Grand Piano track, and press A to hide the automation for that track. Hide the automation for the guitar tracks. Save and close the project.

Excellent work! The parts each take turns, and you've successfully added another professional music finishing technique to the song.

NOTE ▸ You can use the Track Curve menu to show curves for volume, pan, or effects applied to a track.

Sharing with Other iLife Applications

If you haven't experienced the ease of working across multiple iLife applications, you will do so shortly as you explore the various ways to share GarageBand projects. The key to iLife integration is the Media Browser, which is accessible from both iLife and iWork (as well as many other applications).

The Share menu includes six choices that you will explore in the next series of exercises. Along the way, you'll also add a few finishing touches to a podcast, and place a marker into a movie score.

When you're ready to share your project, click the Share menu and then choose one of the following menu commands:

- Send Song to iTunes—Place a mixed copy of the track into your iTunes library. You'll explore this option fully in the next section.
- Send Ringtone to iTunes—Create a cycle region to determine the Ringtone loop, then share.
- Send Podcast to iWeb—Open your project in iWeb where you can choose compression settings, select a template, and publish it to the internet.
- Send Movie to iDVD—Open your project in iDVD where you can choose compression settings, select an iDVD template, and burn it to a DVD. If you don't have a video track, this option is dimmed.
- Export Song to Disk—Save an MP3 or AAC file to a hard disk.
- Burn Song to CD—Burn a finished song directly to an audio CD.

Sharing Projects with iTunes

Exporting to iTunes is as simple as choosing Share > Send Song to iTunes. Before you begin exporting, however, you'll need to do a few things to prepare your songs. You'll set your GarageBand preferences to create a playlist in iTunes. Then you will evaluate a song to make sure that you're exporting the whole song, and check the output level for clipping. Finally, you'll export your song to a new playlist in iTunes.

Setting Preferences for iTunes

To prepare a song for export to iTunes, set your song and playlist information in the Export pane of GarageBand preferences. For these exercises, you'll continue to use the RootsRock song.

1 Open the project Lesson 19 > **04 RootsRockFinal**.

2 Choose GarageBand > Preferences to open the Preferences window.

3 Click the My Info button to open the My Info pane, if it's not already showing.

Next, you will name the iTunes playlist, composer, and album. By default, GarageBand names the playlist and album after the registered user of the computer.

4 In the iTunes Playlist field, type *GarageBand '11*. In the Artist Name and Composer fields, type your name. In the Album Name field, type *iLife '11 Book Album*.

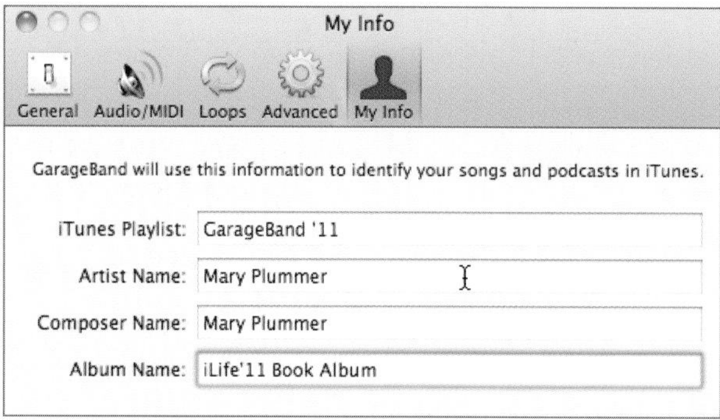

5 Click the Advanced button and make sure that the Auto Normalize checkbox is selected.

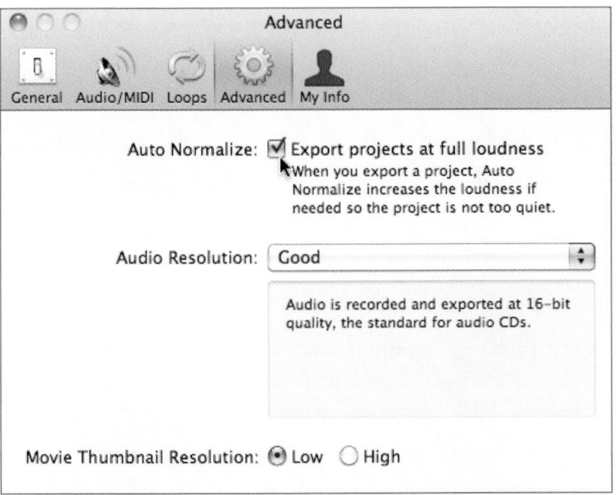

The Auto Normalize feature is great for exporting songs to iTunes because it automatically adjusts the volume level to make sure that the song will be loud enough to match the maximum volume levels of professional CD's.

6 Set the Audio Resolution to Good, if necessary. The Audio Resolution menu offers three choices:

- Good—Audio is recorded and exported at 16-bit quality, the standard for audio CDs.
- Better—Audio is recorded at 24-bit quality for higher fidelity and exported at 16-bit quality. Choosing this option will take approximately 50 percent more disk space than Good for recording.
- Best—Audio is both recorded and exported at 24-bit quality for the highest audio fidelity. Choosing Best will also take approximately 50 percent more disk space than Good for both recording and exporting.

TIP Leave the Audio Resolution setting to Good whenever you are just experimenting or you're recording simple projects or podcasts that will be compressed for CD or web distribution. The Better and Best settings use a lot of disk space. If you're laying down tracks as masters for music publishing or other high-end recording, change the setting when you start the project.

7 Close the Preferences window.

Now that you've set up the export information, iTunes will automatically create a playlist titled GarageBand '11 and include the other information in the playlist. Technically, this composition was crafted by Magic GarageBand Jam, but the settings on your computer will be ready for the next song that you create in GarageBand.

Evaluating a Song's Output Level

It's time to check the output level for the song to make sure it isn't clipping. Remember, the master volume level meter is located in the lower-right corner of the GarageBand window. You can drag the master volume slider to raise or lower the output level as needed.

Let's play the song and check its output level. If the level is too high, you'll need to lower the output. If the level is too low, you'll need to raise the output.

1 Press Return, and then press Spacebar to begin playback. As the song plays, watch the master volume level meter for signs of clipping.

   NOTE ▶ If you don't see the master level meter along the bottom of the GarageBand window, increase the size of the window. You may need to change the resolution of your monitor to make more room. You can also hide the Track Info pane if it's visible.

   If you see any clipping (red) in the meter, stop playback. If you aren't sure if you saw red, the handy clipping indicators (red dots) at the end of the meter light up to let you know that clipping did indeed happen. You'll discover red indicators and some clipping throughout the song.

   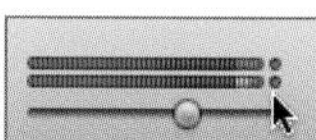

2 Drag the master volume slider to -3.8 dB to lower the output volume and avoid clipping. Click the red clipping indicators to reset them.

   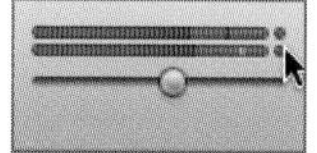

3 Play the song again from the beginning and check the new output level in the meter.

   Be careful not to set your level too low. Ideally, your level should peak between the highest green and yellow portions of the meter. Fortunately, you selected Auto

Normalize in the GarageBand preferences, so the level should still output with plenty of volume for iTunes.

TIP If a song sounds as though it ends abruptly, you can choose Track > Fade Out to add a fade to the master track's volume.

4 Choose File > Save As, and save the project to the My GarageBand Projects folder. If you already have a version of the song saved at that location, feel free to overwrite it with this version, which has a corrected master volume level.

Sending a Song to iTunes

When you export a song to iTunes, the entire song is exported, from the beginning of the first measure to the end of the last region. (If a cycle region is active, only the portion of the Timeline included in the region is exported.) But, remember, if you mute or solo tracks, only those tracks set to play are exported. Let's export the current song to iTunes.

1 Choose Share > Send Song to iTunes to export the song.

2 The Share dialog opens. Here you can choose to modify the playlist information. You can also select the Compress checkbox, and then choose compression settings from the Compress Using and Audio Settings pop-up menus. If you don't select Compress, GarageBand will create a CD-quality AIFF file.

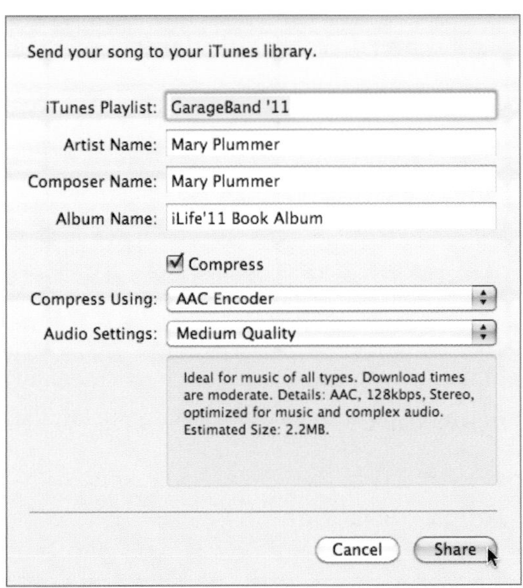

NOTE ► By default, GarageBand projects are sent to iTunes as AIFF (Audio Interchange File Format) files at 44.1 kHz (kilohertz). This is a CD-ready format so that your songs can be burned to an audio CD. You can also change the file type from within iTunes so that the file can be downloaded to an iPod, or converted to another format, such as MP3.

3 Click Share. GarageBand begins to mix down your song.

During the mixdown process, all of the tracks are mixed (at their current levels) into one stereo pair (left and right) for iTunes. A progress indicator shows the mixdown progress. You can cancel the export process during mixdown by clicking Cancel.

When the mixdown is complete, iTunes opens with your song in the new playlist, and plays it automatically.

4 Press the Spacebar to stop playing the song, and then press Command-Q to close iTunes.

After your song has been sent to iTunes, you can access it from any of the iLife applications through the Media Browser.

5 Select the GarageBand window to make it active, if necessary, and press Command-R to open the Media Browser. Select the Audio pane, if necessary.

The GarageBand '11 playlist appears in the iTunes library of the Media Browser. Your song can now be used in any of the iLife applications, including GarageBand and iMovie.

6 Save your project. When asked if you'd like to save with iLife preview, click Yes. Then close the project.

NOTE ► Any tracks that are muted at the time you export will not be included in the song. This can work to your advantage if you want to make a practice version that excludes certain instruments.

Saving a Project with iLife Preview

In this exercise, you'll open the project **05 PodcastTheme** and save it with iLife preview so it can be used later in a podcast project. If you've been following the exercises in the book, you've frequently been instructed not to save projects with iLife preview because it takes longer to save projects and the feature is useful only for the projects you want to share with other iLife applications—or GarageBand itself. This is the first time you've needed that feature.

1 Choose File > Open and choose ATS iLife11 Book Files > Lesson 19 > **05 PodcastTheme.**

2 If you completed all of the exercises in Lesson 18, play the project once for nostalgia's sake. If not, this is an example of a project created in GarageBand primarily using Apple Loops.

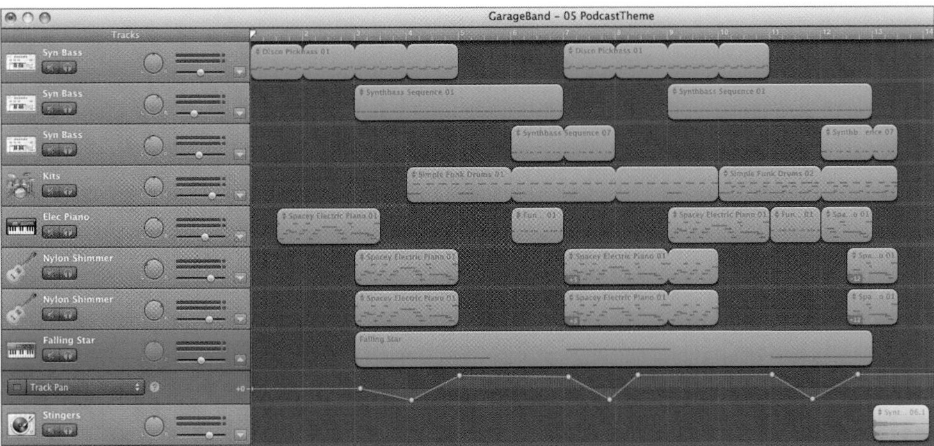

Notice the Pan curve showing below the Falling Star track. This automation was created to dynamically pan the sound of the Falling Star track between the left and right speakers throughout the song.

3 Choose GarageBand > Preferences. In the Preferences window, click the General button.

4 At the bottom of the General preferences, select the Audio Preview checkbox, if it is not already selected.

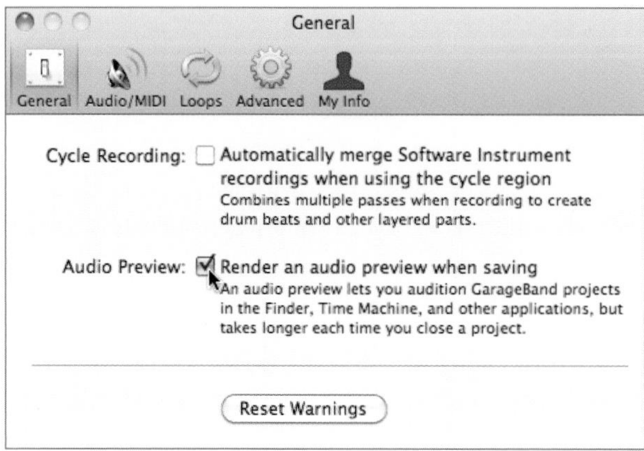

NOTE ▶ When you turn on this feature, an alert about saving with iLife preview will appear when you save other GarageBand projects until the feature is turned off. When the feature is on, saving each project will take longer.

5 Close the Preferences window.

Because you want to make this project available in the Media Browser, let's change the location while saving with iLife preview.

6 Choose File > Save As. In the Save As field, type *PodcastTheme*. Select the Music folder, and then click the GarageBand folder. Choose Save.

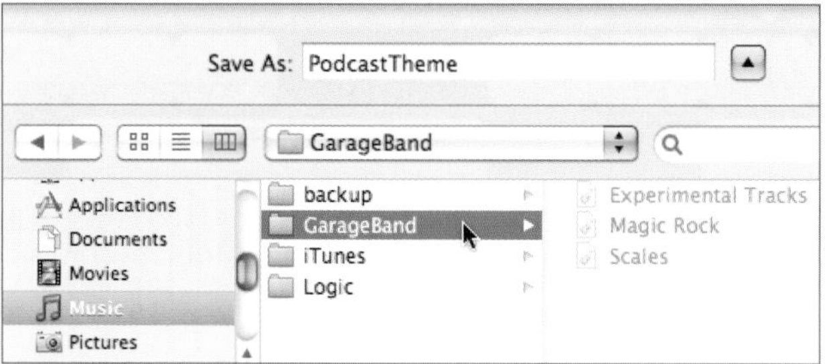

TIP The /Music/GarageBand/ folder is the default location for saving GarageBand projects. If you want to make all of your projects easier to locate and use them in other applications, make a practice of saving to the default location.

7 Choose File > Close. When prompted to save with iLife preview, choose Yes.

This project now includes a rendered preview of the project so you can preview it in other iLife applications. In fact, you'll next use that song as the title theme for a podcast.

Finishing a Podcast

Podcasts are like radio or TV shows that can be downloaded over the Internet, and they are one of the fastest-growing forms of multimedia. With GarageBand, you can create podcast episodes and then upload them to the Internet using iWeb or another application.

There are four primary types of podcasts: audio podcasts; enhanced audio podcasts with markers, artwork, and URLs; video podcasts containing a movie; and enhanced video podcasts containing a movie, markers, artwork, and URLs.

In these exercises, you'll add the finishing touches to a podcast and prepare it for sharing with iWeb. You'll add theme music, edit the artwork, and add a URL link. Then, you will check the podcast info to see if it needs updating before sharing. Let's get started.

> **NOTE** ▶ A project can include either a podcast track or a movie track, but not both. If you try to show the video track for a project that contains a podcast track, a dialog appears asking if you want to replace the podcast track with a video track, and vice versa.

1 Open the project Lesson 19 > **06 Podcast** and save it to your My GarageBand Projects folder. The project contains a lot of media files and is fairly large, so it may take a few minutes to save.

Podcast Track artwork

2 On the right side of the Podcast Track header, click the Preview button to show the Preview window.

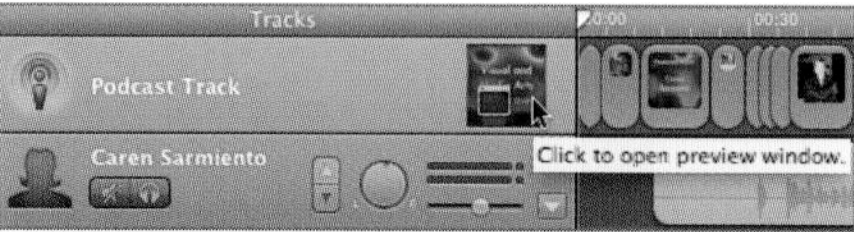

3 After the Preview window opens, drag the lower-right corner of the window to make it larger to suit yourself.

4 Play the first few seconds of the podcast to see how the podcast artwork is displayed in the preview window during playback. Stop playback. You probably noticed the lack of music during the introduction at the beginning of the episode. No problem, you'll fix that in the next exercise.

This podcast project is an interview with visual artist Caren Sarmiento about her career as an art teacher, innovative professional painter, and sculptor. The podcast is an episode of an ongoing series, Visual and Media Arts Showcase, that features visual artists and musicians as well as professionals and industry leaders in film, television, and multimedia production.

The podcast episode that you will be working with includes two recorded Real Instrument voice tracks, and two Jingles tracks containing royalty-free jingles installed with the GarageBand Apple Loops. The podcast track is showing above the audio tracks, and includes artwork to be displayed as the podcast plays.

Importing a GarageBand Project

If you have listened to the beginning of the podcast, you'll notice that it's pretty darn boring without any music. Let's add the official podcast jingle to the beginning and end of the project. In the loop browser, you could choose one of the many professional jingles included with GarageBand. However, because this is a real podcast series, you'll be using the official podcast theme created in GarageBand.

When you create a piece of music in GarageBand, you could mix and export the finished song, and then import it into the podcast project; or you could simply import the GarageBand project. That's right! You can import one iLife project into another project. If you save a project with iLife preview, you can preview and use it in any of the other iLife applications, including GarageBand.

Adding a GarageBand Project from the Media Browser

To use a GarageBand project in another project, you need to place it in the Media Browser. Earlier, you saved the PodcastTheme project to the /Music/GarageBand folder, so it should be ready add to your project. Saving the project with iLife preview means that you can add it to your GarageBand Timeline. By default, the Media Browser gives you access to your iTunes library in the Audio pane of the Media Browser. You can also add other folders containing audio files, including GarageBand projects.

1 Press Command-R to open the Media Browser. Click the Audio button to show the Audio pane within the browser. Your iTunes folder and default GarageBand folder are automatically displayed in the Audio pane.

2 In the Media Browser, select the GarageBand folder, and then double-click the project **PodcastTheme** to preview it.

NOTE ▶ Normal GarageBand project file icons look like a paper document with a guitar printed on it. GarageBand project files saved with an iLife preview show only a guitar icon.

3 Drag **PodcastTheme** from the Media Browser to the beginning of the lowest Jingles track in the Timeline.

The project file appears in the Timeline as an orange (imported) Real Instrument region. The small guitar icon in the upper-left corner of the region shows that it is a GarageBand project instead of a standard audio file.

4 In the Timeline, move the PodcastTheme region so that it starts at the beginning of the project.

5 Play the first part of the podcast to hear the PodcastTheme project as the intro music.

The volume levels on the Jingles track are low to keep them in the background, rather than step over the vocal tracks. Notice the ducking controls in front of the pan controls on the track headers. In this project, these controls are automatically ducking (lowering) the volume level of the Jingles tracks to give volume priority to the narration.

NOTE ▸ Ducking controls can be turned on in the Media Browser or the Controls menu. They include two arrows pointing up to indicate that a track is a priority, and an arrow pointing down to indicate that the track will be ducked (lowered) any time audio is present in the priority tracks. If no arrow is selected, ducking will be ignored on that track.

6 Press Command-S to save your progress.

Why Use a GarageBand Project Instead of an Audio File?

- You've successfully added a GarageBand project to the Timeline of another project. So what's the big deal? You could also export a finished mix of a song and add the mixed audio file to a project instead.
- But, wait, what if you change your mind? More importantly, what if your clients change their minds? It happens more often than not, depending on the client. What if someone wants you to make changes to the song in the Timeline? If you added an audio file, you'd have to find the original project or

Continues on next page

Why Use a GarageBand Project Instead of an Audio File? *(continued)*

re-create it, make the changes, and export the file again. Oh yeah, then you'd still have to add the exported mix to the project. On the other hand, if you have a project in the Timeline, you can simply open the project in the editor, and click the Open Original project button.

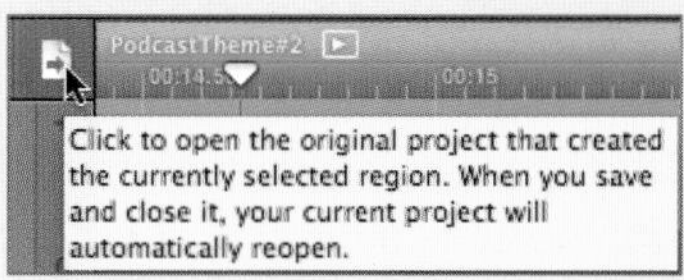

- Voila! You're working on the original song again. Best of all, when you save the changes, the project automatically updates in the Timeline.

Working with Artwork and Markers

When you add artwork to a podcast, the artwork appears as you play the podcast episode in iTunes and work with it in iWeb.

Artwork added to the Podcast track creates a marker region the same length as the artwork in the Podcast track. Marker regions are used in podcasts to literally *mark* a specific region in the Timeline to include artwork, a chapter title, or a URL. When you publish your podcast, iWeb or other software will use these marker regions to include the designated information for that region in the project.

You can edit, move, and resize marker regions anytime while creating your podcast project. You can also add and edit chapter title markers and URL markers to the podcast track. In addition to the artwork used as marker regions in the podcast track, you can also designate the episode artwork in the editor. The episode artwork appears in the Podcast Preview window whenever no artwork is present in the current marker region.

NOTE ▶ If you didn't complete all of the previous exercises, feel free to open the project **07 PodcastArt** to catch up.

Using the Artwork Editor

The artwork for this podcast was added to the Podcast track by dragging it from a folder on the desktop. In this example, the podcast artwork has been mostly completed. However, on closer inspection at least one picture needs a little cropping and repositioning.

Fortunately, GarageBand includes a handy Artwork Editor you can use to resize and crop your artwork. To access the Artwork Editor, double-click the Artwork box in the Artwork column of the editor.

First, you'll want to open the podcast editor and locate the Artwork column.

1 Select the podcast track header, and press Command-E to open the editor, if necessary.

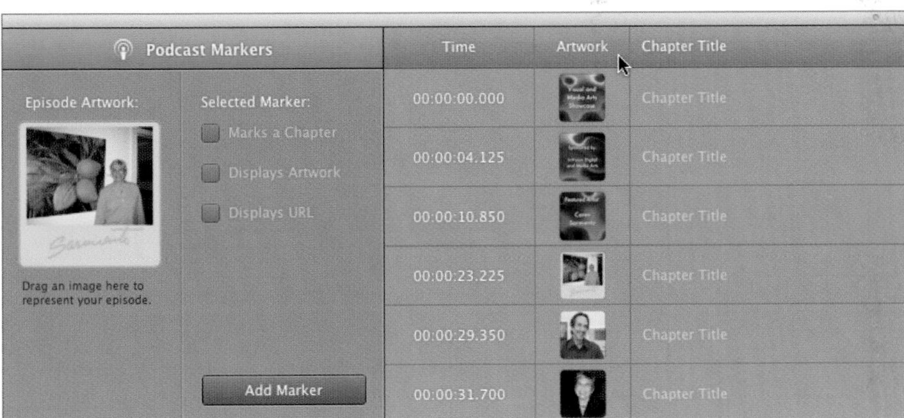

The podcast editor displays information about each marker and has an Add Marker button to create new markers. The Artwork column shows a thumbnail picture of each marker's artwork in order from top to bottom. The Time column indicates the time in the LCD when the marker starts.

2 Scroll down through the marker list until you find the marker starting at 00.00.57.000. Double-click anywhere in the empty space between the number in the Time column, and the thumbnail in the Artwork column to move the playhead to that marker position. As you can see in the preview window, the picture of Caren is not framed very well. Part of her arm is cut off, and she is too far to the left in the frame.

3 In the Artwork column, double-click the thumbnail for the selected marker. The Artwork Editor opens with the artwork. The square frame represents what will be displayed in your podcast.

4 Drag the image to the right to center Caren's face. Feel free to drag the zoom slider left or right to scale the image if you'd like.

5 Click the Set button to save the image changes. Close the Artwork Editor.

The artwork updates based on the changes you made in the Artwork Editor. As for the amount of artwork that you use in your podcast, that is left to personal preference. Some podcasts contain only the episode artwork. Others, like this example, include supporting photographs and examples of the artist's work, in addition to photographs of the artists that are displayed during the interview.

TIP ▶ If you have only a few photos for your podcast artwork, modifying them in the Artwork Editor can help add variety and keep the episode visually interesting.

Viewing Additional Marker Information

In addition to the Time and Artwork columns, the podcast editor also includes chapter title, URL title, and URL for each marker.

1 In the Timeline, click the podcast track header to select the podcast track. Notice that all of the marker regions appear white (selected) in the Timeline, and all of the markers are also selected in the podcast editor.

2 Click any empty space in the Timeline below the podcast track to deselect all of the markers. The podcast track remains selected until you select another track header or a region in the Timeline.

NOTE ▶ You can use the Track menu to show/hide the podcast track.

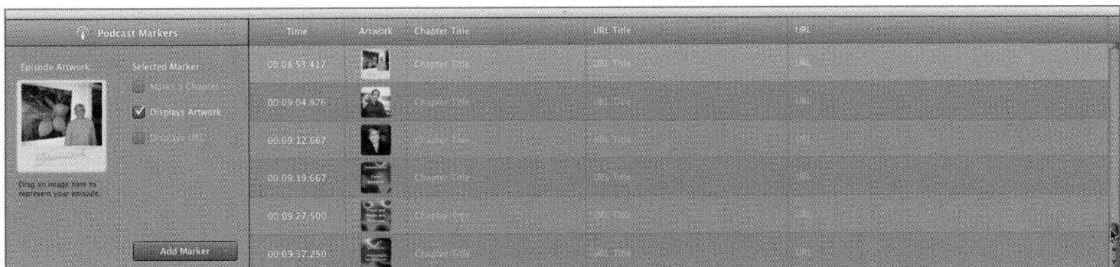

In the podcast editor, the marker regions are listed in chronological order from the beginning of the project. Notice the columns from left to right: Time, Artwork, Chapter Title, URL Title, and URL for each marker. You may have to scroll right to see all of the columns.

3 Drag the vertical scroller to look at all of the project's markers.

As you can see, a title sequence at the end of the project is similar to the one at the beginning. You'll add URL information for Caren Sarmiento's website in the next exercise.

The checkboxes in the editor show how the marker will be designated. Adding artwork to a marker region automatically selects the Displays Artwork checkbox for that marker.

Adding a URL to a Marker

You can add a website address (URL) to a marker region in a podcast or a marker in a movie and view the URL when you play the movie or podcast in iTunes. Not only will viewers see the URL when they play the finished project, they can also click the URL onscreen to open the webpage in their browsers.

If you add a URL title, the title appears in the Album Artwork window of iTunes (in a published podcast). Clicking it opens the webpage for that URL. An example of a URL title might be "For More Information," or "Check out our website."

Let's add a URL title and link to the end of the project where the guest says the web address. You'll add the URL to an existing marker region. To get there, you can navigate in the Timeline or simply double-click the marker in the editor.

1 In the editor, scroll to the end of the marker list, and locate the marker that begins at 00:8:53:000. Then double-click any blank area in the marker's row in the marker list to jump the playhead to the marker's location in the Timeline.

You can now see the selected marker's artwork in the Podcast Preview window. The selected marker region is also selected (and colored white) in the podcast track.

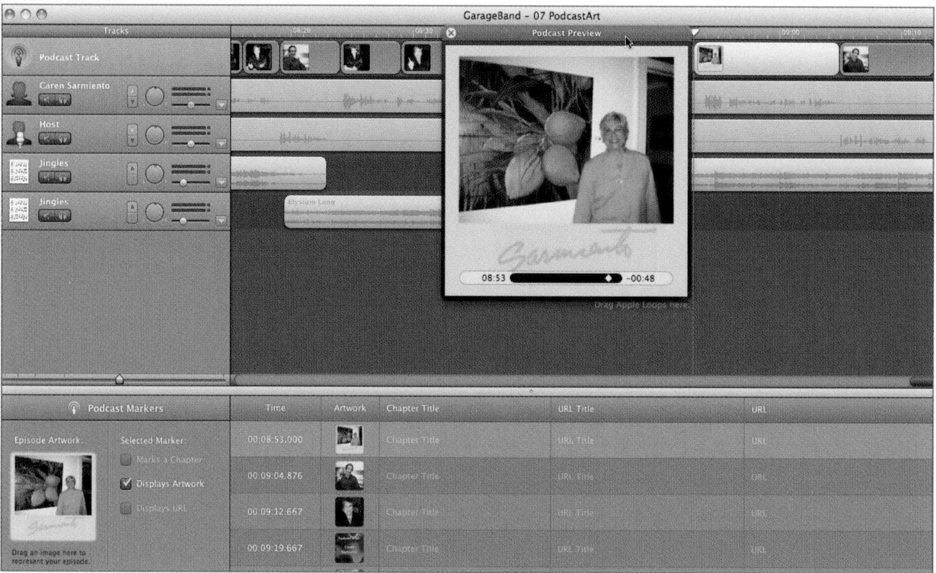

2 Press the Spacebar to play the project from the playhead position and listen to the dialogue that goes with the selected marker.

You can clearly hear the guest, Caren Sarmiento, giving her website address. This is a prime opportunity to add a URL title and link.

3 For the selected marker in the editor, in the URL Title field, type *Click here to visit CarenSarmiento.com* and press Return.

This message will appear below the podcast artwork when the podcast is published or played in iTunes.

4 For the selected marker, in the URL field, type *CarenSarmiento.com* and press Return. GarageBand will automatically add the *http://* to the address.

Notice that Displays URL is selected after you add a URL to the marker.

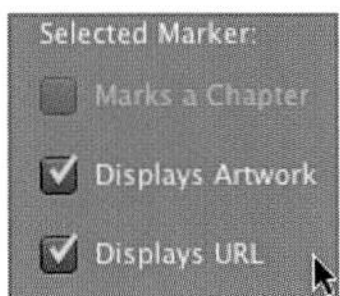

When you add a URL, the URL title for that marker appears over the marker artwork in the Podcast Preview window to show that the marker includes a URL. Don't worry if it looks like the URL title is in the middle of the artwork. In the exported podcast, it will actually show up below the artwork.

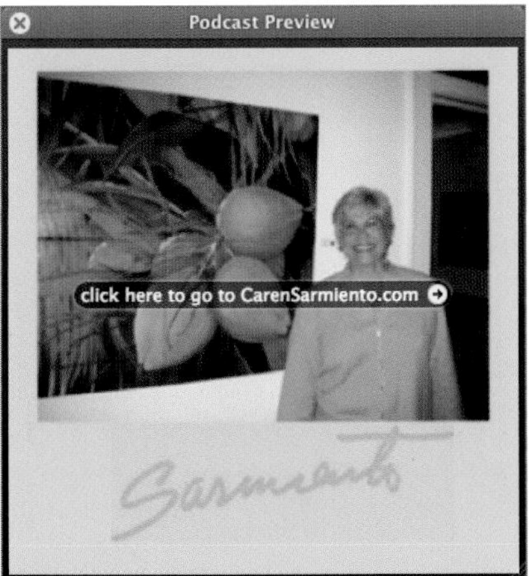

5 Play the marker to see the URL title appear in the Podcast Preview window.

Feel free to click the URL title in the Podcast Preview window to open the webpage. If your computer is not currently connected to the Internet, your browser will try to open the page and then tell you that you're not connected.

Adding Podcast Episode Info

The last step to finish your podcast episode is to add the episode information, which includes the title, artist information, a description of the episode, and a parental advisory. The episode information is available when you work on the podcast in iWeb and when you view the podcast in iTunes.

1 Press Command-I or double-click the podcast track header in the Timeline. The podcast track appears in the Track Info pane.

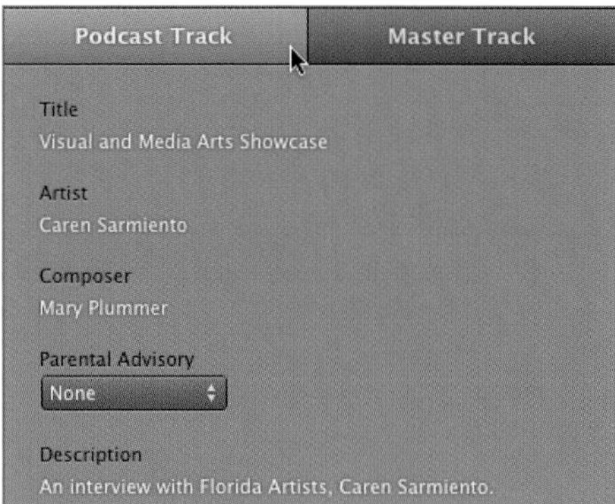

For this exercise, leave the default information in the Artist and Composer fields as designated in GarageBand preferences. These fields could be modified to reflect the name of the company producing the podcast, or whatever is appropriate for this specific podcast.

2 From the Parental Advisory pop-up menu, choose Clean.

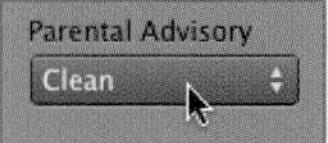

3 Choose File > Save As and save the finished podcast as *PodcastFinal* to the My GarageBand Projects folder.

4 Play the podcast from start to finish to see the completed project.

NOTE ▸ If you didn't complete all of the steps in this lesson and would like to see the finished version of the podcast, open the project Lesson 19 > **08 PodcastFinal**.

Sending a Podcast to iWeb

When you finish your podcast project in GarageBand, you can either send it to iWeb for publishing on the Internet, or you can export it to disk so it can be finished using another application. Compression settings for podcast episodes are available if you choose to export the podcast to disk.

Unlike music projects, turning on the cycle region has no effect on the length of an exported GarageBand project. When you export a project containing a podcast track, the entire project from the beginning to the end of the last region is exported.

Exporting a Project as a QuickTime Movie

GarageBand projects that contain a movie file can be exported as QuickTime movies. A QuickTime movie exported from a GarageBand project includes both the video and the soundtrack that you created. The Movie Sound track that came with the original movie file is also included in the soundtrack unless the track is muted when you export the movie. Let's export a project called **TouchPetsScore** as a QuickTime movie.

1 Open the project **09 TouchPetsScore** from the Lesson 19 folder.

2 On the right side of the video track header, click the Preview button to open the Movie Preview window, if necessary.

3 When the Movie Preview window opens, drag the lower-right corner of the window to make it larger.

Because you aren't currently working on the soundtrack, you might as well make the Movie Preview window larger so you can get a good look at the show. This larger preview will also come in handy in the next section when you add markers to the video track before sending it to iDVD.

4 Play the project once through to familiarize yourself with the movie and the score.

What you're watching is a trailer for the TouchPets Dogs game by ngmoco:). This game is available exclusively for the iPhone/iPod Touch and iPad, and needs a score that captures the fun, energy, and personality of the virtual puppies. This type of project is a composer's dream, not only because it sparks the imagination to infinite musical opportunities, but also because it could be scored with nearly any music genre. Feel free to try composing your own score after this lesson.

Now that you've seen and heard the project, let's export it to disk.

5 Choose Share > Export Movie to Disk.

The Export dialog appears at the top of the screen, with a pop-up menu for changing the video settings. You may need to move or resize the Movie Preview window to see the Export dialog.

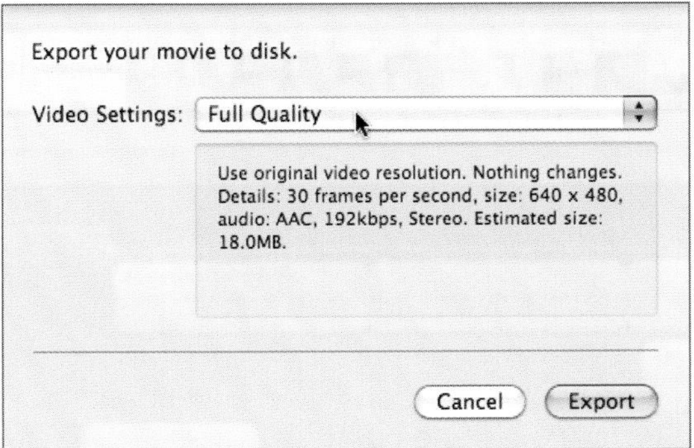

Export your movie to disk.
Video Settings: Full Quality
Use original video resolution. Nothing changes. Details: 30 frames per second, size: 640 x 480, audio: AAC, 192kbps, Stereo. Estimated size: 18.0MB.
Cancel
Export

6 From the Video Settings pop-up menu, choose Full Quality. This setting will maintain the original video resolution and settings. The file size will be only 18 MB. Feel free to experiment with the other export settings after you finish this lesson.

The other settings include Email, Web, Web Streaming, iPod, and AppleTV.

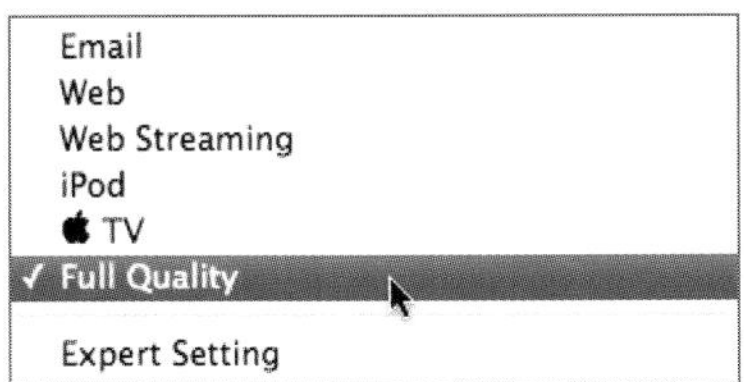

7 Click Export. The Export to Disk dialog opens to allow you to choose a destination for the file.

8 Save the project to your desktop.

You'll see a series of three progress indicators for creating a mixdown (mixing all of the audio tracks down to a stereo pair), converting the file to the specified format, and compressing the movie.

As you can see, it's incredibly easy to export a scoring project from GarageBand as a QuickTime movie.

Congratulations! You have completed the sharing lesson and are ready to share, send, or export your own projects.

Lesson Review

1. What should you do to a music project before exporting it to iTunes?
2. Where is the Arrange track in the Timeline?
3. What determines the length of the song file exported to iTunes?
4. Where do you set the information for exporting songs to iTunes?
5. What are the two ways that you can export or send a podcast project so that it can be published in iWeb or another application?
6. How do you open the Artwork Editor in a podcast project?

Answers

1. Check the master volume level to make sure the song is at a good level and not too low or too loud (no clipping).
2. The Arrange track is above the instrument tracks.
3. The length of a song exported from GarageBand is its duration from the beginning of the first measure in the Timeline to the end of the last region in the Timeline. If you use a cycle region, only the portion of the Timeline included in the region is exported
4. You can set song and playlist information for iTunes in the GarageBand preferences window.
5. You can either send a podcast to iWeb, or save the project to disk, if you want to export it so that it can be published in iWeb or another application.
6. You can open the Artwork Editor by double-clicking a marker thumbnail in the Artwork column of the podcast editor.

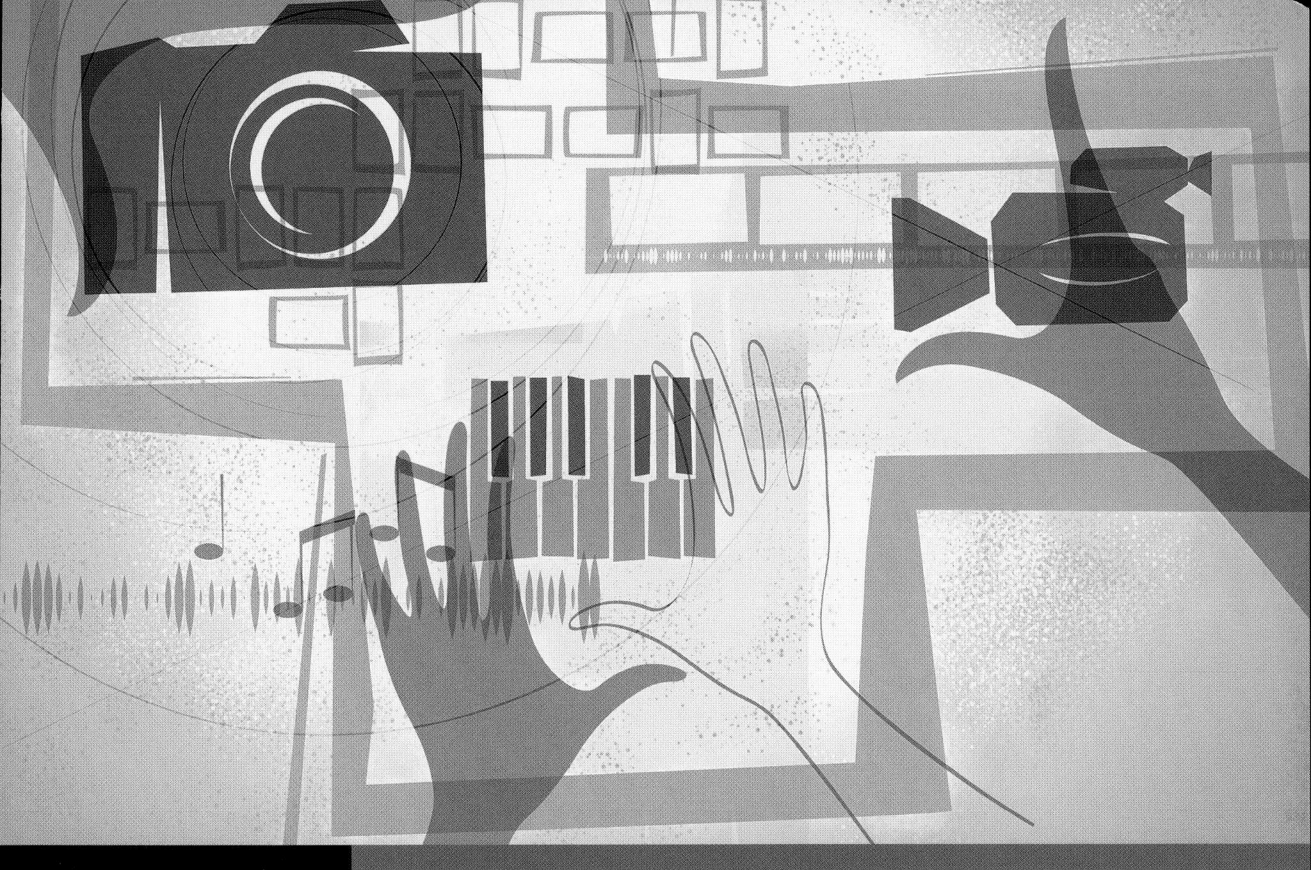

iDVD and iWeb: Sharing and Publishing with iLife

20

Lesson Files

Desktop > ATS iLife11 Book Files > Lesson 20 > ATS All My Movies

Desktop > ATS iLife11 Book Files > Lesson 20 > Pendulum.caf

Time

This lesson takes approximately 75 minutes to complete.

Goals

Switch projects in the Library

Use a theme

Create sports-oriented video effects

Make a highlights DVD

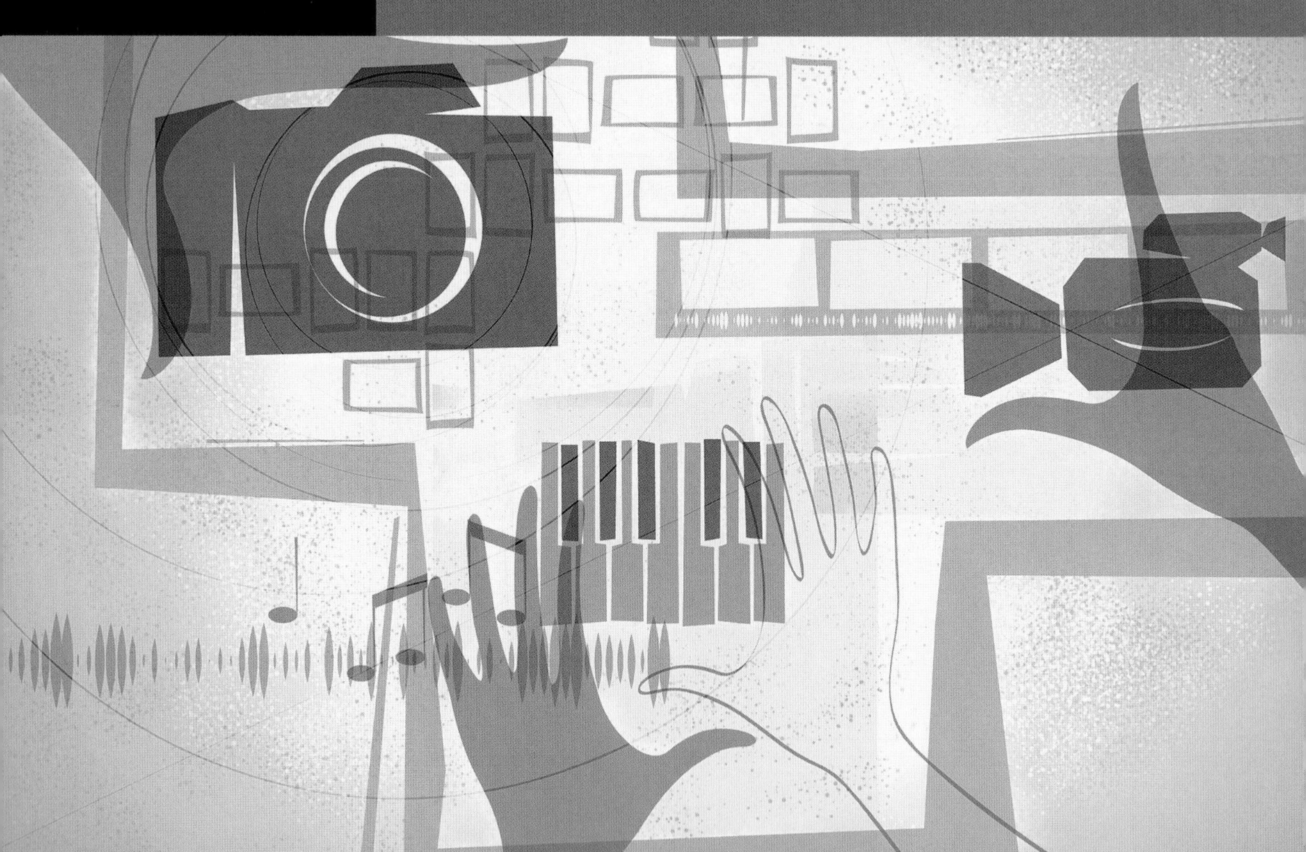

Lesson **20**

Creating a DVD with iDVD

One way to ensure your movie can be played by almost everyone is to burn a DVD. When someone trips over a wire and pulls the plug on the Internet, or your Mac is in use by another family member, you can still pop your video and photo masterpieces into a DVD player and curl up on the sofa with a bowl of popcorn and a remote control.

Using iDVD, you can create very simple DVDs that start to play as soon as you insert them into a DVD player, and move up to more sophisticated DVDs with menus, movies, and slideshows.

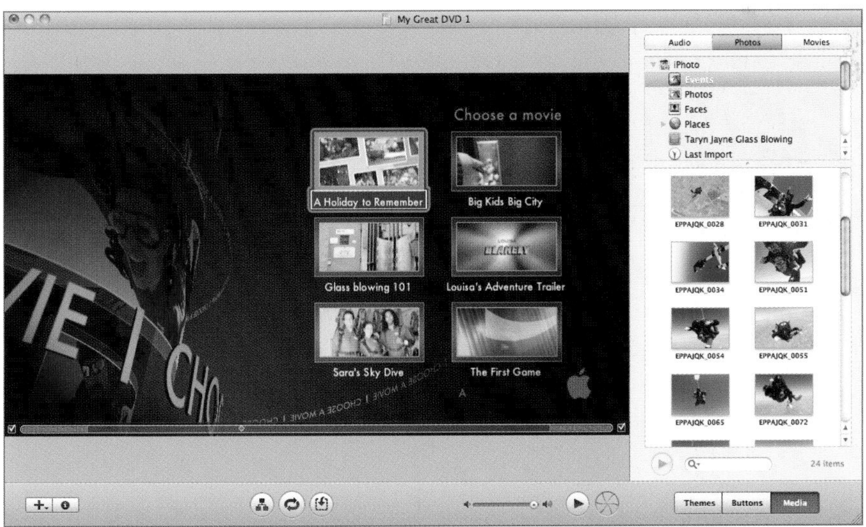

Preparing a Movie for iDVD

It's easy and convenient to put your iMovie projects on DVD. DVD players are everywhere. iDVD is the iLife application that you use to make DVDs of your other iLife creations. The popcorn is optional.

Creating Chapter Markers in iMovie

One important step for creating a DVD must be performed with iMovie. You add chapter markers to your project so viewers can use their remote controls to jump directly to key parts of your program. iDVD converts these chapter markers into chapters menus just like the ones you see on the commercial DVDs you buy or rent.

1. Open iMovie, and open the The First Game project.

2. If advanced tools aren't already enabled from earlier iMovie lessons, choose iMovie > Preferences and select the Show Advanced Tools checkbox. Then close Preferences.

   You'll use advanced tools in this lesson to access chapter markers. Two buttons appear in the upper-right corner of the project browser: Comments Marker and Chapter Marker.

   Adding comment markers to your project is a great way to add notes to yourself. Chapter markers are specifically used on DVDs to jump from one scene of a movie to another using the DVD's remote control.

   NOTE ▶ Comment markers are not visible outside of iMovie, but chapter markers are visible when a movie is opened in another application that supports them, such as QuickTime Player and GarageBand.

3. Drag an orange chapter marker icon with the arrow from the upper-right corner of your project to just before the "Player Stats" title you added in Lesson 10.

   The marker is added as an orange flag above the video track. By default, the markers are numbered, but you can type any label you want.

4 Triple-click the marker to highlight its text, then type *Damian's big play*.

5 Click the pop-up menu to the right of the marker buttons in the upper-right corner of the project window.

This menu lists all the markers and titles in your project. Choosing an item will take you to that spot in the project.

Your chapter marker is in, and you are ready to create a DVD version of the movie.

Sharing a Movie to iDVD

Sharing to iDVD from iMovie is even easier than sharing to Facebook or YouTube because you do not have to log in or choose a movie size. iMovie handles everything for you.

1 In iMovie, choose Share > iDVD. iMovie immediately begins to make your movie. When the movie is complete, iDVD opens.

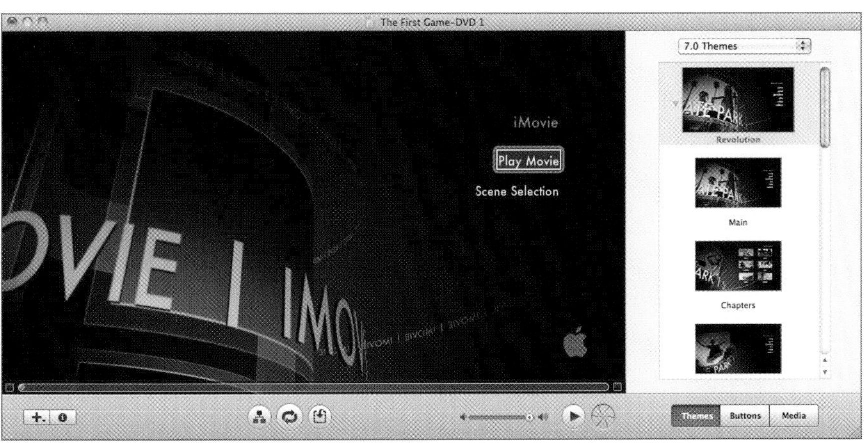

You can burn your DVD as soon as iDVD opens by choosing File > Burn DVD. Once you have a burned disc, you can insert it into a DVD player and the movie will begin playing automatically with no menus to navigate. It's the easiest way to create a DVD.

2 Quit iMovie.

3 In the upper-left corner of the iDVD window, click the red close button, and then click Don't Save. After some time, the iDVD window closes and the iDVD Start screen appears.

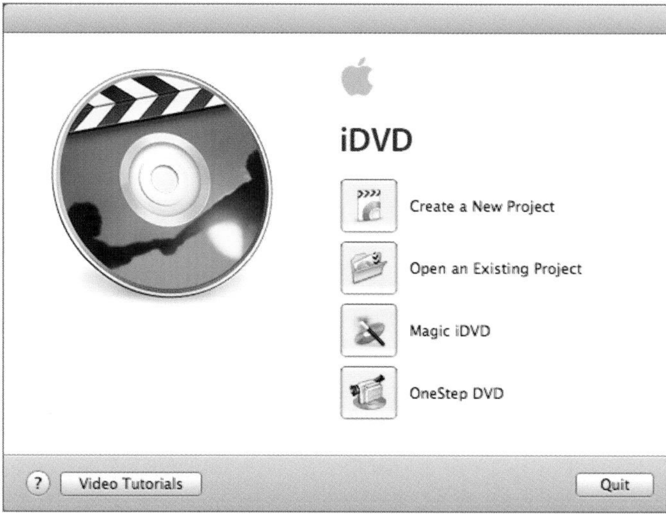

The Start screen also appears if you open iDVD from the Applications folder. It is the starting point for creating a more sophisticated DVD in iDVD. Four buttons on the Start screen allow you to start a new project or open an existing project.

Starting Your iDVD Project

Sharing from iMovie works fine if you have only one movie to place on a DVD, but what happens when you want to include multiple movies on a single disc? Magic iDVD is a quick way to create a DVD containing multiple movies and photo slideshows. You simply drag movies and sets of photos into the main iDVD screen, choose a theme, and click a button—at which point you're ready to burn a DVD or further customize your disc.

The iDVD project you're about to build uses completed versions of all the movies you created in iMovie from Lessons 8 through 13. If you skipped those lessons, don't worry about it. We've included finished movies on the DVD packaged with this book.

1 In the iDVD Start screen, click Magic iDVD. The Magic iDVD window appears.

2 At the top of the window, replace the DVD title with *All My Movies*, because this will be a collection of the movies you've made in iMovie.

At the right, above the "Choose a Theme" thumbnails, you can choose to view the themes included with different versions of iDVD. By default, this menu is set to show you the most recent themes provided with iDVD 7.0.

3 From the "Choose a Theme" thumbnails, click Modern.

4 On your Desktop, open the ATS iLife11 Book Files folder > Lesson 20. Drag the ATS All My Movies folder to the Drop Movies Here area in the Magic iDVD window.

This folder contains six movies similar to those you created in the iMovie lessons. When you drop the folder onto the strip, all six movies are placed in the strip as thumbnails.

Instead of burning the DVD now, which you could do, let's customize it further.

5 At the lower right of the window, click Create Project.

A progress dialog appears as iDVD creates the project. The Magic iDVD window changes to display the project's main DVD menu using the Modern theme.

NOTE ▸ If you don't plan on making a movie in iMovie, the simplest way to use iDVD is to connect your video camera to your Mac, open iDVD, and click the OneStep DVD button. iDVD then imports the video directly from your camera and creates a DVD.

On the window's right side, you'll see a list of available themes. These are similar to the themes that you used for iPhoto books or iMovie. On the window's left is the main area where you build your DVD menu.

NOTE ▸ DVD menus do not look or act like the menus you use in Mac applications. A DVD menu refers to an entire interactive screen that you see when you view a DVD.

6 Click the Motion Menu button to stop playing the menu.

A number of iDVD themes incorporate animation, just like the DVDs you buy. Menus that include animation are known as *motion menus*.

Notice that the main menu screen already has a Movies text box. This text is a DVD button that points to the movies you dragged into the Magic iDVD window. Before you explore those movies though, you need to change the Movies text to something more informative.

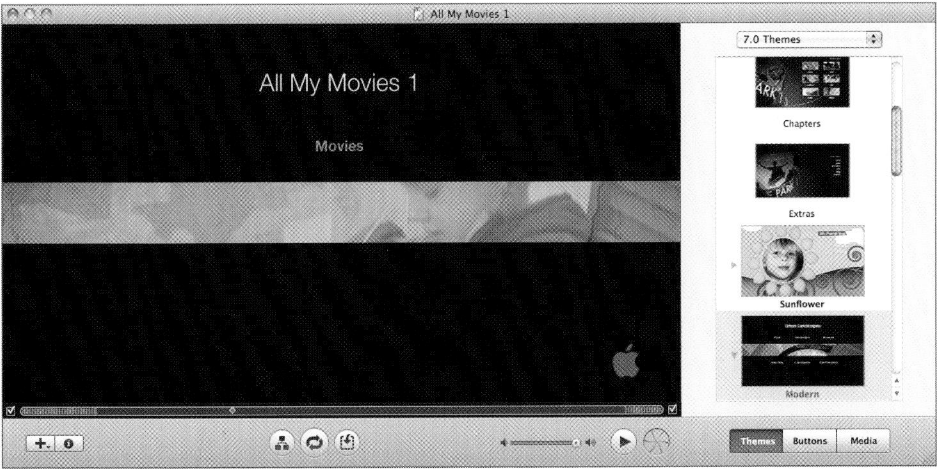

7 In the iDVD window, click the Movies text to select it, and then click the text inside the menu button to highlight the text for editing.

The text inside the menu button is selected and a formatting panel appears. In the formatting panel, you can change the typeface, style, and size of the menu button's text.

NOTE ► Don't double-click a menu button to edit its label. Instead, click once to select the button, pause for a second or two, and then click a second time. Double-clicking a menu button causes iDVD to perform the action associated with that menu button. For example, double-clicking the Movies button causes iDVD to show the submenu to which the button links. If you've already double-clicked the menu button, click the left pointing arrow at the bottom of the chapter selection menu (below the list of movies) to return to the previous menu.

8 Change the button text to *Choose a movie*, then click in the black area of the menu to deselect the text.

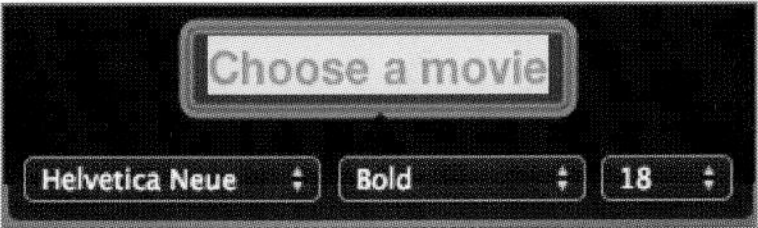

When typing a button's text, try to choose a short name that best describes where the button's action will lead the viewer.

Navigating Your Project with the Map

Now that you have the main menu's button label set, you should look to see where the menu button currently leads.

1 At the bottom of the iDVD window, click the Map View button.

iDVD displays a navigation map of your project. In the map, the main menu, each submenu, and the movies they lead to are displayed as boxes with connecting lines so that you can see all the links. For example, the All My Movies menu (marked with a folder icon next to its title) links to the Movies 1-6 submenu, which is linked to individual movies, marked with a clapboard icon. The Movies 1-6 menu is a chapters submenu.

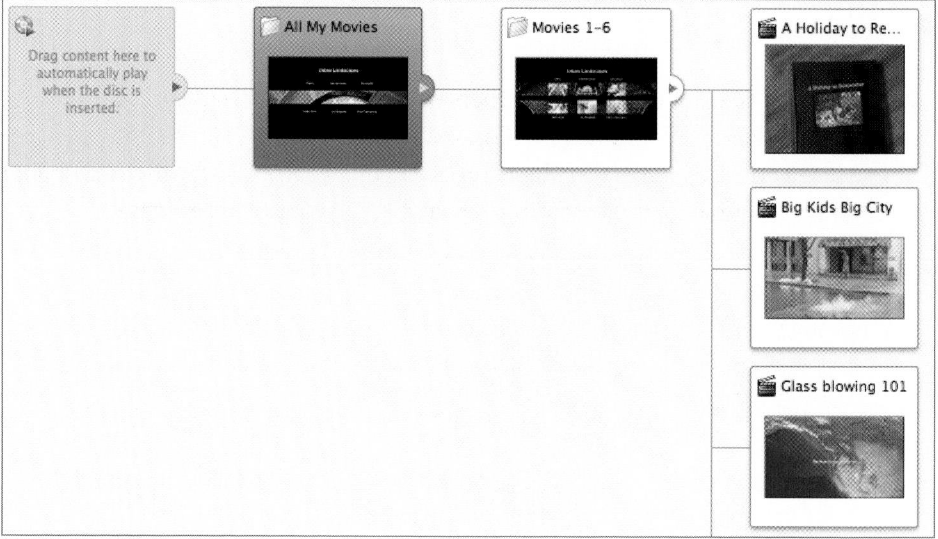

2 On the toolbar below the map, drag the slider until you can see the entire map. The map changes size so you can see more of the items without scrolling.

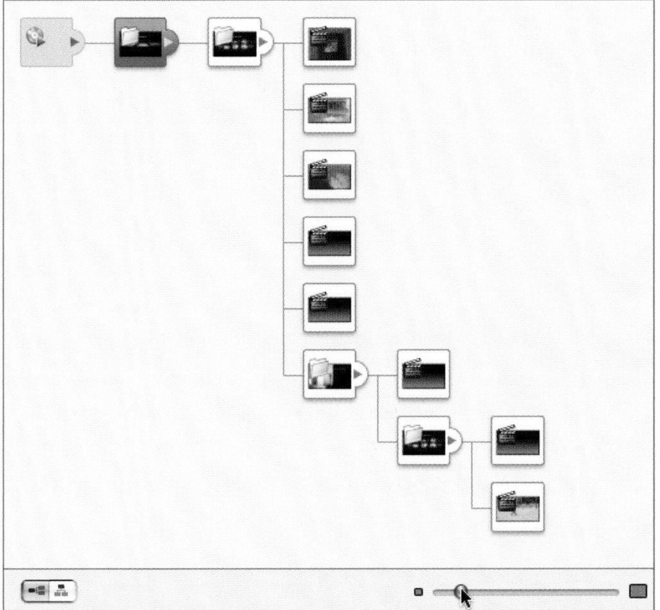

Earlier in this lesson, you added a chapter marker to The First Game movie in iMovie. Because of that, The First Game movie is slightly different from the other movies on the DVD. The First Game thumbnail appears last in the list. It has a folder icon because it is a menu that is linked to a Play Movie item and a Scenes 1-2 menu.

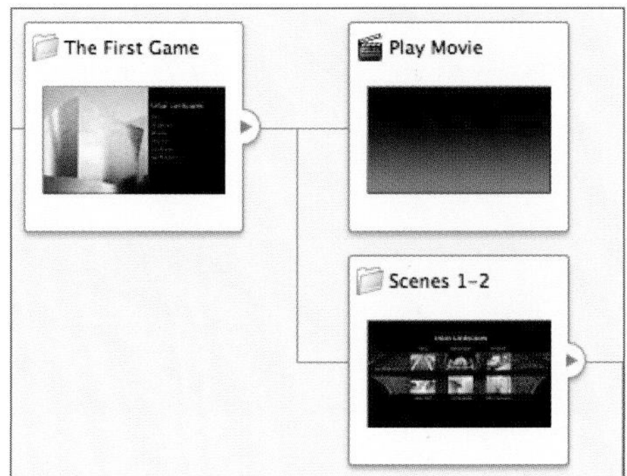

TIP You may have to scroll down the Map window to view the items below the thumbnail for The First Game.

The Play Movie Item is marked with a clapboard icon to indicate that it's a movie. The Scenes 1-2 menu is a chapters submenu, which links to two movies based on the chapter markers given in iMovie.

Now you can use the map to navigate your iDVD project.

3 Double-click the Movies 1-6 submenu.

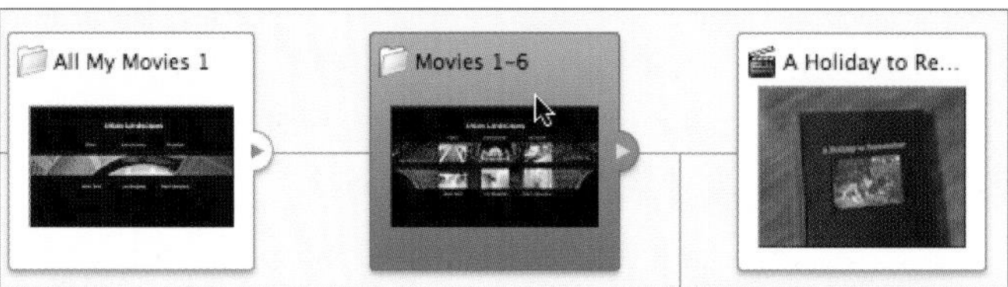

The Movies 1-6 submenu appears in the iDVD window. When you double-click an item in the navigation menu, iDVD displays that item in its window.

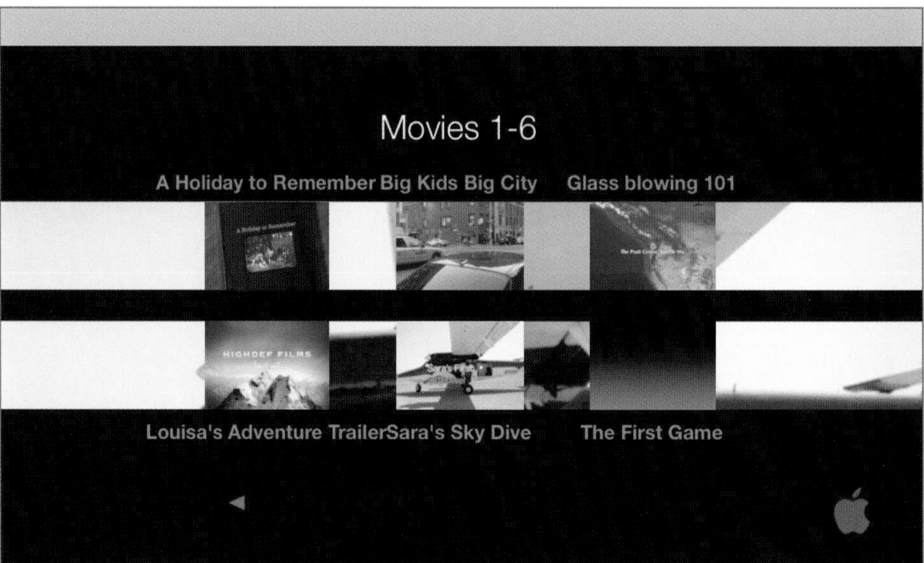

"Movies 1-6" may mean something to you as the author of this DVD, but it won't mean much to a viewer. Let's change the title label at the top of the menu to something a little more enlightening.

4 At the top of the submenu, double-click the large "Movies 1-6" text label and then type *Choose a movie*. Because this is a text label and not a button, you can double-click the text to edit it.

5 Change the label font size to 48.

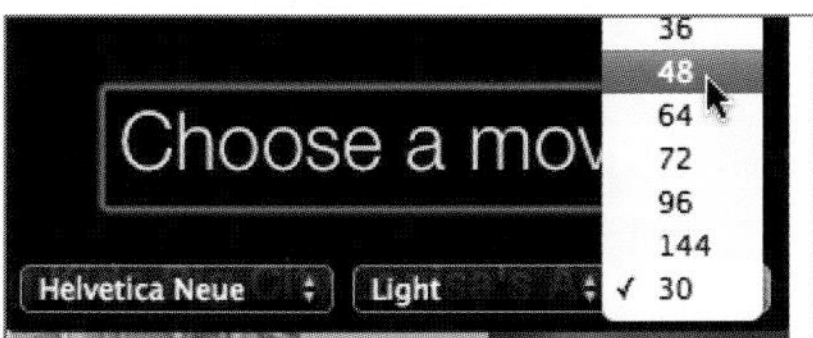

You could also change the text size for each movie because the text appears too large. Because these are buttons, you will need to select the button once, pause, and then select the text to edit it.

6 Click the "A Holiday to Remember" button, pause, then click the text to highlight it.

NOTE ▶ If you accidently double-click the movie linked to the button, text will start playing. Use the DVD remote that appears to exit the movie and return to the menu.

7 Change the font size of the label to 14, then change the font size of the remaining five movie labels.

8 Save your work.

You should always save your project before and after you make major changes to it. In fact, you should develop the habit of saving your iDVD projects regularly.

Switching Themes

When you created your project with Magic iDVD, you chose the DVD theme. But you aren't stuck with that theme if you decide you don't like it. In this exercise, you'll see how easy it is to change.

1 If the Theme collection isn't visible in the right pane of the iDVD window, click the Themes button in the lower right of the iDVD window.

2 Scroll up, and click Revolution.

A dialog appears telling you what happens when you switch a project's theme. The theme for the main menu and all submenus in the project will change. If you'd like, you can click the disclosure triangle at the sheet's lower left to read addition information.

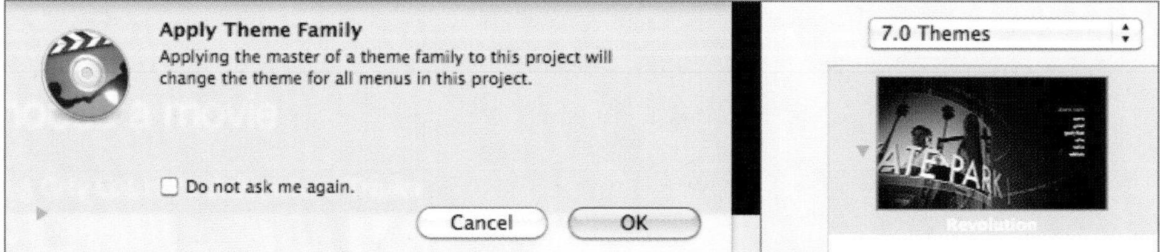

Apply Theme Family
Applying the master of a theme family to this project will change the theme for all menus in this project.
Do not ask me again.
Cancel
OK
7.0 Themes

NOTE ▶ Many of the themes in iDVD are provided in two sizes: the 4:3 aspect ratio used by standard definition televisions sets, and the 16:9 widescreen aspect ratio used by HDTVs. You choose the aspect ratio for your project when you create it, though you can change it at any time. iDVD also chooses the appropriate aspect ratio for your project when you create it by sending a movie to iDVD from iMovie.

3 Click OK.

iDVD changes the theme of the submenu shown in the window; it also changes the theme of the main menu in the project. As a result, the menu buttons and text labels move and change, but the text remains the same.

Editing Drop Zones and Menus

Magic iDVD automatically filled areas in your theme with videos when it created the project. These areas are called *drop zones.* They are built in to add visual interest. Drop zones can contain a photo, slideshow, or movie.

In this exercise, you'll change the contents of a single drop zone that appears on this "Choose a movie" submenu.

1 At the bottom of the iDVD window, click the Drop Zone button.

The Drop Zone editor appears in the main pane of the iDVD window, listing the drop zones on the current submenu. (In this case, only one drop zone is present but you may find more on other menus.)

The pane at the right of the iDVD window now displays the iLife Media Browser. iDVD shows the Media pane automatically when you edit a drop zone, because you usually fill a drop zone with media from iMovie or the iPhoto library.

2 At the top of the iDVD window's right pane, click Photos, then click Events in the list below.

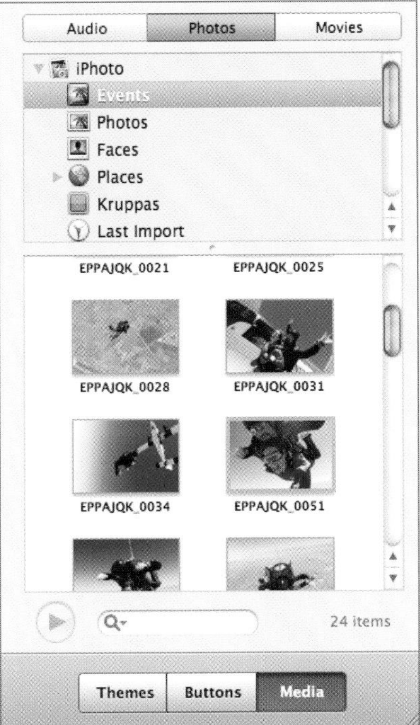

3 Double-click the Sky Diving Event to view the sky diving pictures.

4 Drag any action-packed sky diving picture from the Media Browser into the first (and only) drop zone showing in the iDVD Drop Zone editor.

The drop zone in the editor shows a small version of the picture. The submenu displayed above it shows a larger version in the menu's drop zone.

5 At the bottom of the iDVD window, click the Drop Zone button again to hide the Drop Zone editor.

6 Click the Motion menu button to preview the submenu in action, and then click it again to stop.

You've just modified one aspect of the submenu for your DVD. Normally, you would go back and fix the main menu at this point, but you can still change a few more things.

Editing a Menu

As you may have noticed, this theme plays a hoppin' tune when you click the Motion Menu button. You'll change this and make a few other adjustments.

1 With nothing highlighted in the submenu, click the Inspector button.

The inspector appears showing the Menu Info inspector. The inspector will vary depending on the item selected in the current menu. When nothing is selected, the inspector provides options for modifying characteristics of the entire menu—in this case, the project's "Choose a movie" submenu.

The Loop Duration slider in the inspector's background defaults to 30 seconds, so the background motion menu will play for 30 seconds and then loop and start over again. The maximum loop duration is set by the length of the longest media in the menu, whether in a drop zone, background audio, or movie. Depending on the length of your music, you can set the maximum duration of the menu or loop the audio as a longer menu continues to play. Let's change the music and reset the loop duration.

2 On your Desktop, open the ATS iLife11 Book Files >Lesson 20 folder.

3 Drag the **Pendulum.caf** file to the Audio well in the iDVD inspector.

The music is 30 seconds long. Let's set the motion menu background to last for 60 seconds so the music will play twice before the background menu loops.

4 Drag the Loop Duration slider to the left to the 1:00 minute mark.

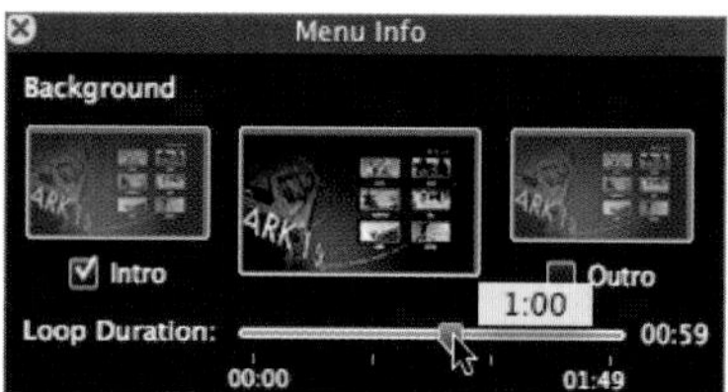

As you drag, a tooltip above the slider shows the current time setting.

You can choose to showcase the audio by raising the volume, or blend the audio in to the background by lowering the volume. A lower level is more suitable for short sound loops like this one.

5 In the inspector, slide the Menu Volume slider to the left until it's above the first tick mark. This will reduce the audio volume.

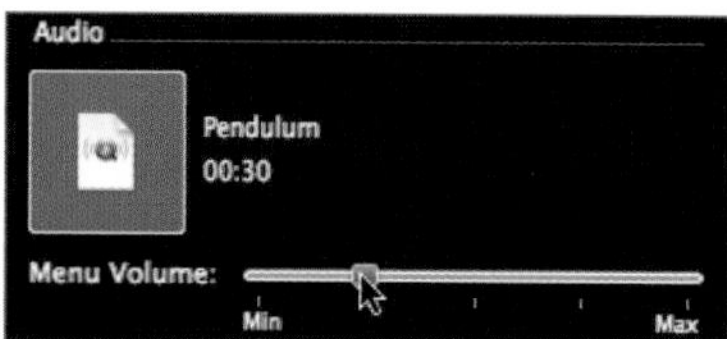

6 At the bottom of the iDVD window, click the Motion Menu button, listen to the music, and then click the Motion Menu button again to stop playback.

NOTE ▶ In a motion menu, the shaded areas that may appear at the left and right of the scrubber bar indicate the presence of animation intros and outros. These are sequences of animation that play when the menu first appears onscreen and when the menu leaves the screen, respectively.

The next item to customize is the button highlight color. This color is a way to indicate which menu button is selected when you view the DVD. You can change the default highlight color to one that best suits your DVD.

7 In the button section of the inspector, click the Highlights swatch. A color picker appears.

8 Select another menu button highlight color, such as a bright yellow.

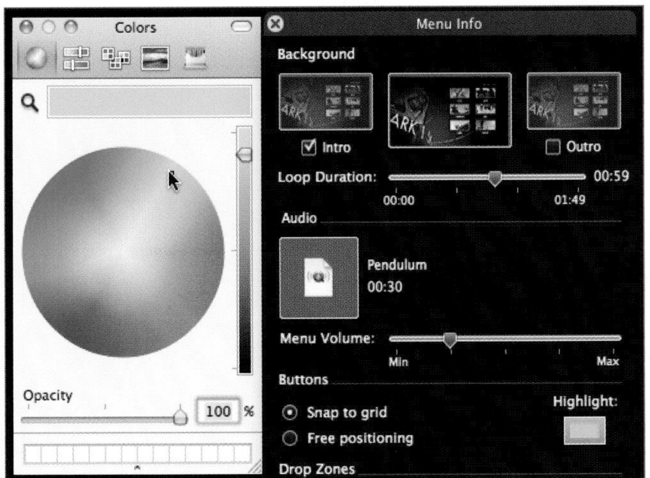

As you view the DVD, the individual movie buttons on the submenu will use the new highlight color when you select any of them.

9 Choose File > Save (Command-S) to save your project.

10 Close the inspector and the colors window.

So far you've made a number of changes to the submenu, but you can update the main menu and its content as well. You can add additional movies or photos to create a slideshow.

Creating a Photo Slideshow in iDVD

DVDs are not for videos only. You also use a DVD to show off your photo slideshows. You won't have access to the great-looking themes that are available within iPhoto, but you'll still have a convenient, though basic, way to view your photos on DVD.

Making a Slideshow Submenu

To begin making a slideshow in iDVD, you need to build a button to access the slideshow. In this exercise, you'll make a few slideshows using the Events you have in iPhoto. Instead of creating just one slideshow button, you'll build an entire submenu of multiple buttons to access each of your slideshows.

1 Click the Back button built into the "Choose a movie" submenu to return to the main menu.

In the main menu, you'll add a button for a submenu to contain the slideshow buttons.

2 Click the Add (+) button, and choose Add Submenu.

A My Submenu button is added to the main menu under the "Choose a movie" button. Let's change the text to match the movies button.

3 Click the My Submenu button to select it, pause, then click it again to select the text. Type *Choose a slideshow.*

TIP To exit text entry mode, you can click the black background when you've finished typing instead of pressing return.

Now you'll add the photos for each slideshow to the "Choose a slideshow" submenu.

4 Double-click the "Choose a slideshow" button to open that submenu.

The new slideshow submenu appears. It includes a title for the submenu based on the theme you selected earlier. You'll now change the submenu title to match the button you previously clicked to get here.

5 Double-click the Revolution Extras text to select it, and then type *Choose a slideshow.* You now have a blank submenu ready for all your photos.

Adding Slideshow Photos

Your new submenu is ready to receive the multiple buttons that will link to each slideshow. To add a slideshow button, you will use the Add button just as you did to create the submenu.

1 In the lower left of the of the iDVD window, click the Add button (+), and from the pop-up menu, choose Add Slideshow.

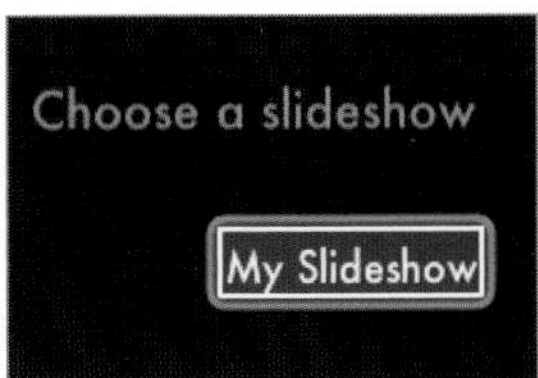

A slideshow button is added to the submenu under the submenu title. The slideshow button does not yet link to a slideshow, and it doesn't have a helpful name either. So you'll rename the button and add some photos.

2 Click the My Slideshow button text.

3 Type *Travel*, then click in the black background to deselect the button text.

4 At the bottom right of the iDVD window, click the Media button. In the Media Browser, click the Events tab and drag the San Francisco Event to the Travel button.

Dropping photos on the slideshow button creates a slideshow. You can add as many photos to a button as you like.

5 In the Media Browser, drag the Taj Mahal Event on top of the Travel button to add those photos to the slideshow.

When you are making a slideshow of just a single album or Event, you can drag it directly onto the submenu from the Media Browser.

6 Drag the Glass Blowing Event from the Media Browser to the submenu under the Travel button.

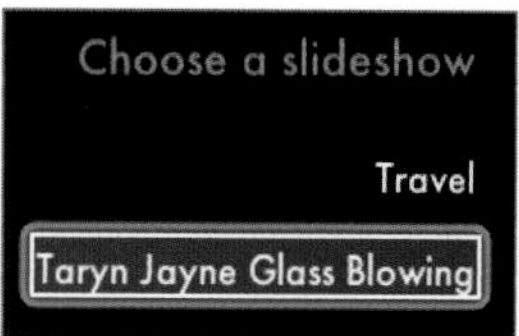

7 Drag the Sky Diving Event from the Media Browser to the submenu under the Glass Blowing button.

   As you drop the Events onto the menu, new buttons are created and linked to the Event's photos in a slideshow.

8 Double-click the "Sara goes sky diving" button to open the Slideshow editor.

If you want a basic, no-frills slideshow you now have it. You needn't add music and transitions, or customize the settings in any way. But if you are slightly more adventurous, you can do all those things. Somehow, you look like the adventurous type.

Using the iDVD Slideshow Editor

The Slideshow editor has all the settings required to customize a DVD slideshow. In this exercise, you'll preview the no-frills slideshow and you'll customize the default settings to improve the slideshow experience.

1 At the bottom of the Slideshow editor, click the Preview button. The Play button turns the iDVD window into a preview window, and opens the iDVD remote control window so you simulate using the DVD in a dedicated DVD player.

2 After you've watched enough of the simple slideshow, click the Exit button on the iDVD remote control window.

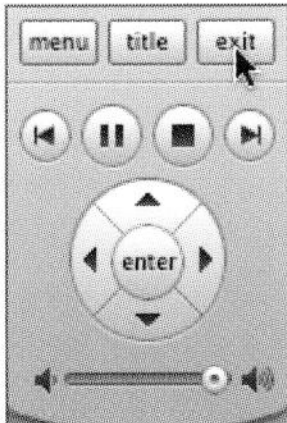

You return to the Slideshow editor where you'll add some music and transitions.

3 On your desktop, open the ATS iLife11 Book Files > Lesson 20 folder.

4 Drag the **Pendulum.caf** file to the Audio well in the Slideshow editor.

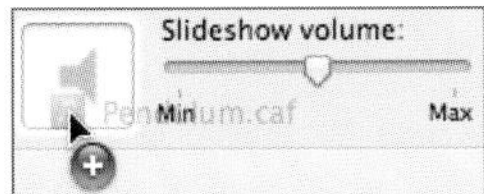

Although you could have used the Audio tab in the Media Browser to access your iTunes library and choose a song there, you added the same song from the main menu.

From the Transition pop-up menu, choose Dissolve. All the photos will now dissolve from one to the other. Now you can set the length that each slide will remain onscreen.

5 From the Slide Duration pop-up menu, choose Fit to Audio, if it's not already chosen. iDVD automatically determines how long each slide should remain onscreen based on the length of the music file.

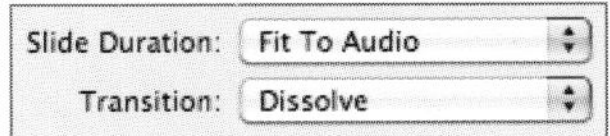

6 Click the Preview button to play the customized slideshow.

The iDVD window turns into the preview window with the iDVD remote control window.

7 After you've watched enough of the customized slideshow, click the Exit button in the iDVD remote control window.

8 Click the Return button to view the submenu.

You now have a great-looking DVD complete with movies and slideshows. It's time to preview the entire DVD and its menus, then burn it to disc.

Previewing and Burning Your DVD

You glimpsed the iDVD Preview feature in the slideshow, but in the preview window you can fully simulate how the entire DVD will work by clicking buttons, moving through menus, and watching movies.

1 Click the Map View button and double-click the All My Movies main menu to return to the main menu in the iDVD window.

2 At the bottom of the iDVD window, click the Play button. The preview window opens along with the iDVD remote control window. The main menu plays the motion menu with the two buttons.

You can use the iDVD remote control to simulate a remote control provided with a DVD player. The "Choose a movie" button is highlighted and ready to be selected.

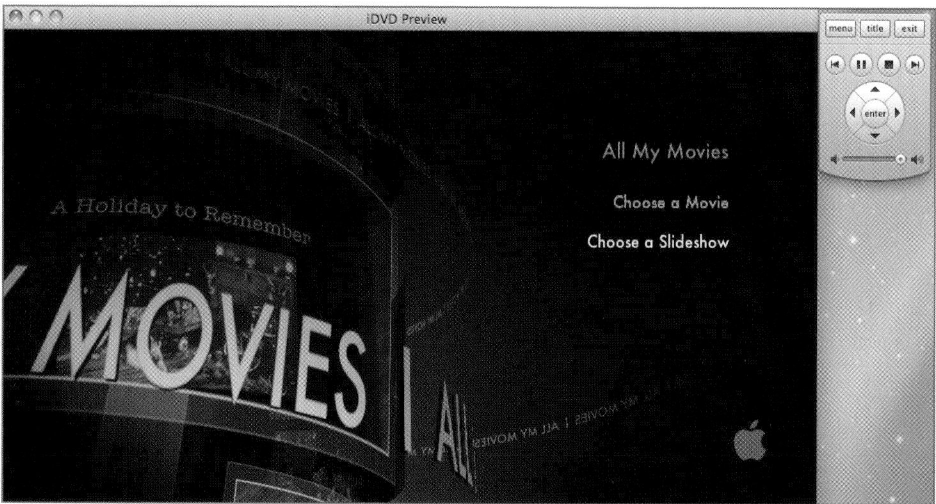

3 Click the Enter button to go to the "Choose a movie" submenu.

You can click the arrows around the Enter button to highlight each movie. This submenu plays the music you added and uses the yellow highlight you chose.

4 Click the arrow buttons on the remote control to highlight The First Game movie.

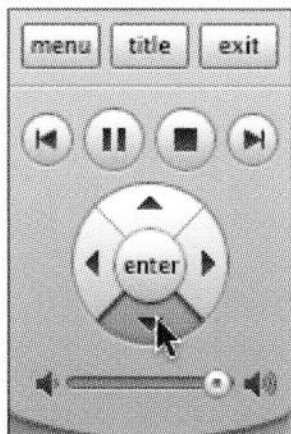

5 On the remote control, click Enter to open that submenu.

The preview window now shows The First Game submenu. Because this movie has the chapter marker you added earlier, you can play the movie, or select a "scene" that refers to the chapter markers you set.

6 Click the remote control's Down Arrow button to highlight the Scene Selection button, then click Enter.

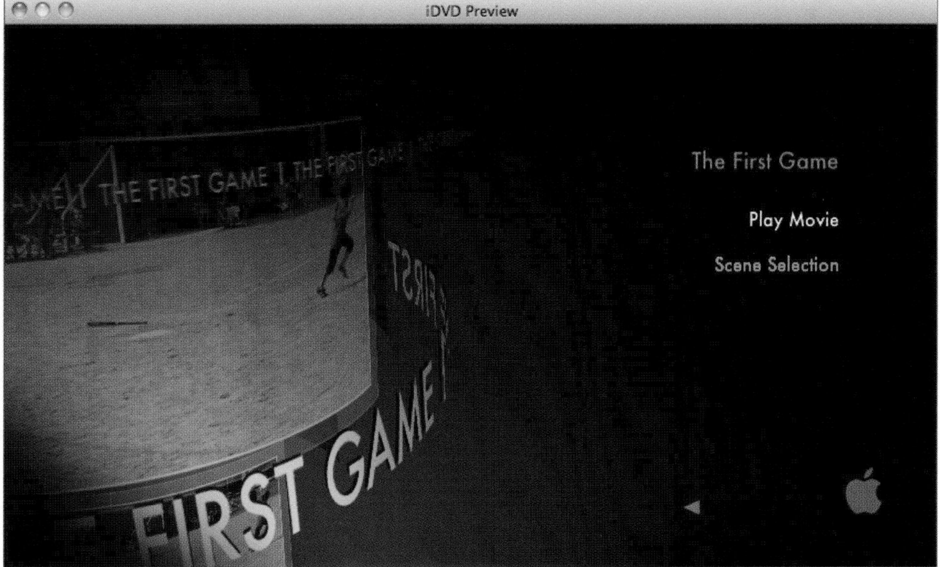

7 Click the remote control's Right Arrow button to highlight the "Damian's big play" button, then click Enter.

The movie starts playing at the point where the chapter marker was placed in iMovie.

TIP When you preview a DVD, take written notes to list all the things that you may want to change later.

8 On the remote control, click Menu to return to the Scene Selection menu in the preview window.

9 On the remote control, click Title.

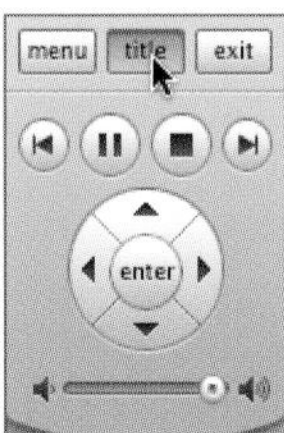

The DVD's main menu appears in the preview window.

10 On the remote control, click the Down Arrow to highlight the "Choose a slideshow" button.

11 Click the Enter button to open that submenu. The "Choose a slideshow" submenu appears.

12 On the remote control, click the Down Arrow twice to highlight the "Sara goes sky diving" button.

13 Click the Enter button to play that slideshow.

TIP You can also use your mouse to click the menu buttons directly in the preview window. However, using the control gives you a better sense of how users will experience the DVD.

The preview window now shows the "Sara goes sky diving" slideshow.

14 On the remote control, click Exit.

The remote control closes and the iDVD window replaces the preview window. If this were a real DVD project, you would now go on and change the remaining menus to match the main menu's music and highlight color or burn the DVD.

Burning a DVD

When your iDVD project looks the way you want, you can burn a DVD using the optical drive on your Mac. But before you actually burn your disc, you should perform a few final checks.

NOTE ▸ If your Mac doesn't have a DVD burner or if you don't happen to have a recordable DVD available, you can just read through this section.

1 Click the Map View button at the bottom of the iDVD window.

Before you burn a DVD, it's always a good idea to take one last look at the map to find any warning icons that you may need to address. If iDVD spots a potential problem with a menu, a yellow caution icon appears in the map. When you place your pointer over the caution icon, a help tag appears that describes the problem. In most cases, the icon indicates that one or more of the drop zones is empty. That's an easy fix. Just drop a movie, photo, or group of photos into the empty drop zone and you are done.

2 At the bottom right of the navigation map, click Return, and then choose Project > Project Info.

The Project Info window appears and, boy, is it an eyeful! But it's not really as bad as it may first look. This window has a lot of useful information. The Capacity bar near the top of the window shows you how much space on the DVD your project will require, along with the amount of space occupied by each type of media in your project.

In the Media area at the bottom of this window, you can see which files iDVD will use when it creates the DVD and check whether they're all available. If a checkmark doesn't appear in the Status column for a particular file, iDVD couldn't locate the file.

This can happen if a file has been moved or changed after you added it to your project. To fix this, move the file back to its previous location, or replace it in your project with a different file.

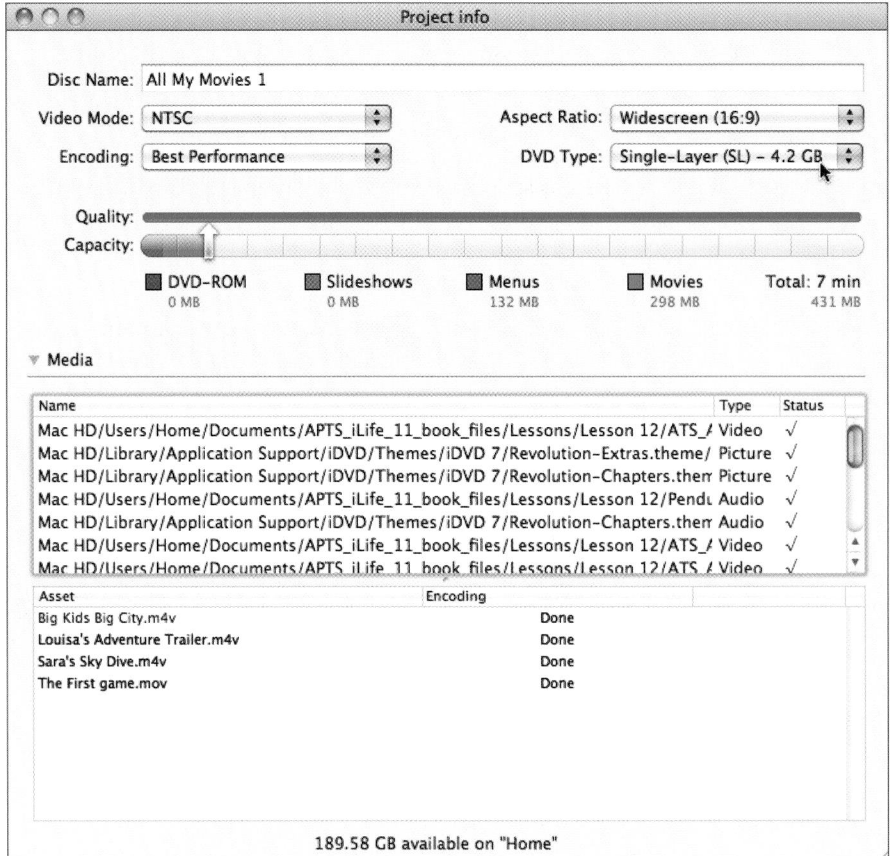

NOTE ▸ If you don't see the Media area, click the disclosure triangle at the bottom of the window.

Most importantly, in the Project Info window, you can change the encoding method for the DVD.

NOTE ▶ The encoding methods are Best Performance, High Quality, and Professional Quality. Best Performance is the fastest, but it requires more space on your DVD. If you have the time and want the highest-quality image, Professional Quality is the optimal choice.

In the Project Info window, you can also specify whether your television system is NTSC (for North and Central America, Japan, and half of South America) or PAL (for Europe, Africa, Australia, Russia, and most of Asia).

Finally, you can set the project's aspect ratio, and whether the DVD is to be burned to a single-layer or dual-layer DVD.

NOTE ▶ Double-layer recording allows DVDs to store almost twice the amount of media on a single disc. However, dual-layer DVDs can cause problems for some DVD players.

3 Set the Disc Name field to *My 2010 Movies*, then close the Project Info window.

When you create a project with Magic iDVD, iDVD automatically chooses a name for the disc that's the same as the name of your project. When you change the disc name, the name you specify is converted to uppercase as the disc is created. You can use only letters, numbers, and spaces in disc names. (Spaces are converted to underscores.)

NOTE ▶ If you need to move your project to another Mac to burn it or to continue working on it, choose File > Archive Project. This places all the media needed by the project into an archived project file that can be copied to any other Mac.

4 Ready a recordable DVD disc, and click Burn to create your DVD.

The button opens up to show the standard Mac disc-burning icon, and iDVD prompts you to insert a blank disc.

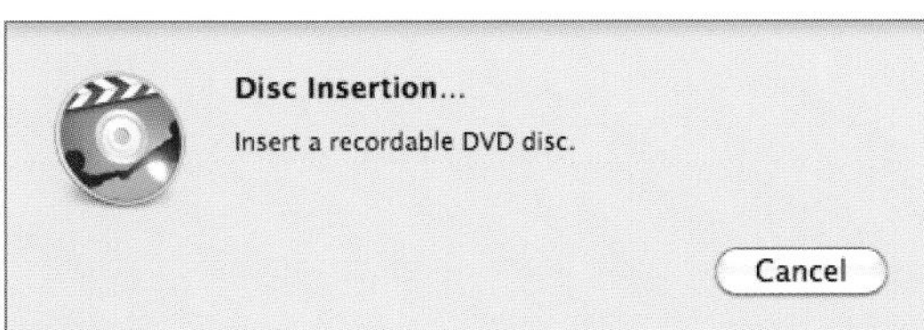

5 Insert the blank disc into your DVD drive.

After a few seconds, iDVD detects the disc and begins the disc-burning process, which can take from a few minutes to several hours depending on the amount of video content you've included in the project and the encoding method you've chosen. A dialog appears to keep you informed of the current stage of the disc burning process, along with an estimate of how long it will take to burn. You can cancel the process at any time, but canceling renders the recordable disc useless.

NOTE ▶ When iDVD finishes burning the DVD, it ejects the disc and gives you the opportunity to burn another copy. Subsequent copies may take less time to burn because iDVD doesn't have to reencode the content.

When the DVD is burned, you can close iDVD, put the disc back into your Mac, and play it with DVD player application. Or even better, you can pop some popcorn, turn off your iPhone, and enjoy a personalized night at the movies.

Lesson Review

1. What is a OneStep DVD?
2. What is a DVD menu?
3. What is a drop zone?
4. Describe the function of the navigation map.

Answers

1. A OneStep DVD is a DVD created by connecting a video camera to your Mac. iDVD imports the video recorded on the camera and burns it to a DVD in a single step.
2. A DVD menu is an interface screen that includes buttons you can select, using your DVD player's remote control, to perform actions such as playing a movie or opening another menu.

3. Drop zones are areas on a DVD motion menu that present images, slideshows, or short video clips to provide visual interest; they have no other function.
4. The navigation map shows where each menu leads in your iDVD project. It shows which media files are accessed from each menu, so you can see the path that a user must follow to get to a particular section of the DVD. The map also displays icons that alert you to potential problems, such as menu buttons that don't lead anywhere or empty drop zones.

Bonus **Lesson**

Designing a Website with iWeb

Sharing your photos and videos on popular sharing sites is a convenient way to show friends and family what you've been up to. However, they fall a little flat when you want to personalize their appearance or present a more professional façade. If you want just a bit more flexibility over the look and layout of your web presence, iWeb is the answer. iWeb can give you a polished website in minutes that looks like it was done by a professional designer. To learn how, read the bonus chapter available on this book's companion DVD.

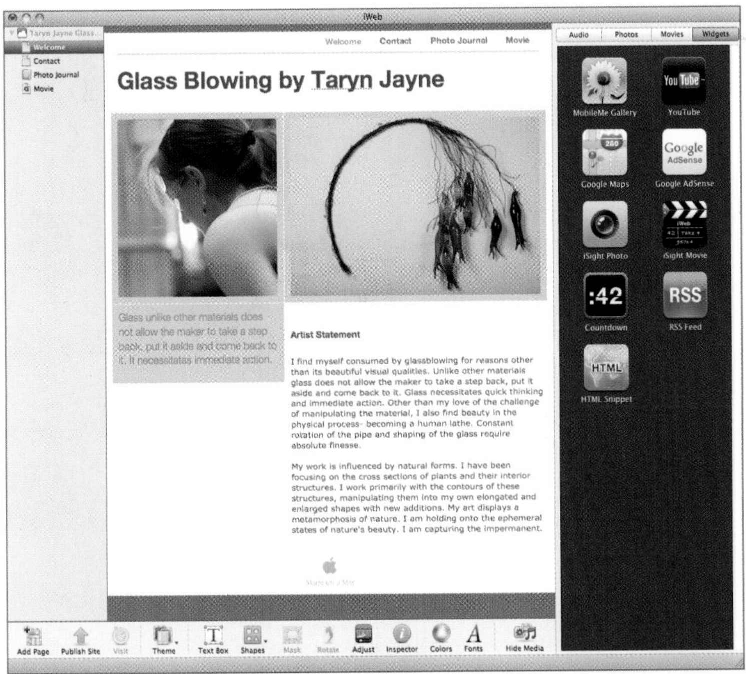

Index

E

J

K

N

O

P